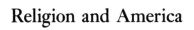

Religion and America

Religion and America

Spiritual Life in a Secular Age

Mary Douglas
Steven Tipton
editors

Introduction by Robert N. Bellah

BEACON PRESS   BOSTON

With the exception of the Introduction by Robert N. Bellah, "From the Crisis of Religion to the Crisis of Secularity" by Peter L. Berger, "The Future of Religion" by Wolfgang Schluchter, "Preachers of Paradox: The Religious New Right in Historical Perspective" by George M. Marsden, "*Did* the Fundamentalists Win?" by Edwin Scott Gaustad, "The Voice of Theology in Contemporary Culture" by Jeffrey Stout, and "The Religious Center of the Jews: An Essay in Historical Theology" by Arthur A. Cohen, which are published here for the first time, the essays in this book appeared in the Winter 1982 issue of *Daedalus*, the Journal of the American Academy of Arts and Sciences.

Copyright © 1982, 1983 by the American Academy of Arts and Sciences

Beacon Press books are published under the auspices
of the Unitarian Universalist Association of Congregations
in North America, 25 Beacon Street, Boston, Massachusetts 02108

Published simultaneously in Canada by
Fitzhenry & Whiteside Limited, Toronto

Printed in the United States of America

(hardcover) 9 8 7 6 5 4 3 2 1
(paperback) 9 8 7 6 5 4 3 2 1

Library of Congress Cataloging in Publication Data

Main entry under title:

Religion and America.

A collection of papers based on the winter 1982 issue of Daedalus.
Includes bibliographical references.
1. United States—Religion—Addresses, essays, lectures. 2. Religion—Addresses, essays, lectures. 1. Douglas, Mary Tew. II. Tipton, Steven M.
BL2530.U6R39   1983   200'.973   82-72500
ISBN   0-8070-1106-1
ISBN   0-8070-1107-x (pbk.)

Foreword

TO THINK ABOUT RELIGION in America under the rubric of spiritual life in a secular age poses a problem in itself. Does the idea of secularity enable us to grasp the quicksilver soul of modernity, or does it mystify the enduring truths of culture? In the light of varied answers to this question we look at the religious moment in American society and history, ranging from the fundamentalist through the mainline churches to alternative religious movements. We ask what recent religious changes mean for the moral order of public life and for the ongoing conversation of theology with tradition, with science, and, not least, with God.

At the beginning and end of these essays we reflect on their diversity of viewpoint. What limits as well as breadth of vision are implied by our location in (or outside) particular churches, academic disciplines, social classes, and historical generations? For university-trained intellectuals no less than church-bred believers, awareness of the angle of our vision deepens both the criticality and the faith needed to carry on the cultural conversation that religion inspires.

This volume is based on the Winter 1982 issue of *Daedalus*, the last of three issues funded by the Andrew W. Mellon Foundation treating the basic institutions of society—family, state, and religion. For making this issue possible we are grateful to the Mellon Foundation and to the editor of *Daedalus*, Stephen R. Graubard, whose sustained efforts have made our task as light as it has been rewarding.

M.D.
S.T.

Contents

Foreword   v

Introduction   ROBERT N. BELLAH   ix

I. SACRED, SECULAR, AND MODERN

Spiritual Life in a Secular Age   LOUIS DUPRÉ   3

From the Crisis of Religion to the   PETER L. BERGER   14
Crisis of Secularity

The Effects of Modernization on   MARY DOUGLAS   25
Religious Change

Israel and the Enlightenment   FRANK E. MANUEL   44

The Future of Religion   WOLFGANG SCHLUCHTER   64

The Moral Logic of Alternative   STEVEN M. TIPTON   79
Religions

II. WEIGHING THE RELIGIOUS MOMENT

Revived Dogma and New Cult   DAVID MARTIN   111

America's Voluntary Establishment: WADE CLARK ROOF   130
Mainline Religion in Transition

Preachers of Paradox: GEORGE M. MARSDEN   150
The Religious New Right in
Historical Perspective

Did the Fundamentalists Win?   EDWIN SCOTT GAUSTAD   169

Roman Catholicism: RICHARD P. MCBRIEN   179
E Pluribus Unum

The Popes and Politics: PETER HEBBLETHWAITE   190
Shifting Patterns in "Catholic
Social Doctrine"

III. THE ONGOING CONVERSATION

Faith, Freedom, and   GEORGE ARMSTRONG   207
Disenchantment: KELLY
Politics and the American
Religious Consciousness

Spiritual Innovation and the Crisis   DICK ANTHONY AND   229
of American Civil Religion   THOMAS ROBBINS

The Voice of Theology in   JEFFREY STOUT   249
Contemporary Culture

The Religious Center of the Jews: ARTHUR A. COHEN   262
An Essay in Historical Theology

Religion in America since   MARTIN E. MARTY   273
Mid-century

List of Contributors   288

ROBERT N. BELLAH

Introduction

THIS IS A COLLECTION of extraordinarily lively, vigorous, and interesting essays. It is also a collection of extraordinary diversity. Some of the papers are polemic; others are, in the nonpejorative sense, apologetic. But they do not, on the whole, seem to be addressed to one another. They speak in quite different languages to quite different audiences. This is partly but not entirely because their writers belong to different disciplines within the university. While they all concern something called "religion," there is no consensus on theory, method, or subject matter and so, clearly, no consensus on what "religion" might be. All this might suggest that religion is an unclear and problematic element in contemporary society. That is probably true, but one should perhaps also draw another conclusion: that the place of religion in the life of the contemporary university and contemporary intellectuals is unclear and problematic.

The creation of the modern research university involved the deliberate abandonment of the idea that higher education was concerned with the formation of Christian character, an idea that lingers today only in small denominational colleges but until nearly the end of the nineteenth century was widely accepted. Religion could be either abandoned altogether, as in the state universities, or relegated to "professional" schools involved in training for the ministry. The ethos of the modern university was dominated by an Enlightenment tradition that viewed religion as a negative influence on human culture and one destined to be replaced by science. Even today university professors are among the least religious people in American society, although, ironically, natural scientists are somewhat more apt to be religious than their humanist and social scientist colleagues. Religion could not, of course, be eliminated from the modern university, because religion empirically cried out for and received the serious study of many scholars. Still, religion as a separate discipline was slow to crystallize, is still far from crystallized. Religious studies do not dominate the study of religion the way departments of literature dominate the study of literature or economics dominates the study of the economy. As an indication of that fact, consider how few of the contributors to this volume teach in departments of religious studies. Mary Douglas chooses as her exemplars of religious studies two sociologists.

One of the reasons religious studies is so uncertainly institutionalized has to do with the cultural politics of the university. In my experience with religious studies at Harvard and Berkeley I observed opposition to the creation of such a department on the grounds that it might "proselytize" the students (neither school to this day has a department of religious studies, although both now have undergraduate majors in the field). But besides the lingering Enlightenment suspicion of religion there are also doubts as to whether it is a genuine field or discipline. Mary Douglas poses a fundamental issue in asking, if I may rephrase it, whether religion is optional, something some individuals and some cultures do and others don't, or compulsory, something like politics or economics that some individuals and some cultures are more interested in than others but that none can avoid. This is a serious question (whether religion is a "good thing" seems to me a red herring; no serious student of religion fails to observe that religion is often associated with the worst behavior of which humans are capable) and the fact that it is still open suggests how far we are in this field from the most elementary consensus. In any case, not only are there no paradigms, there is no body of common knowledge that students of religion are assumed to share, coming from diverse disciplines, studying different parts of the globe, and asking different questions as they do.

All the papers in this volume deal with religion in modern Western society, most of them with religion in modern America. This common focus does not produce consensus but accentuates the tension between the writers. Mary Douglas's view that modern people are no different from anyone else, and so modern religion is no different either, could hardly contrast more strongly with George Kelly's somber view of the fate of religion (and politics) under conditions of modernity. Peter Berger is relatively sanguine about a pluralism that includes religion and secularity but is concerned about our growing "moral pluralism." For reasons quite different from Mary Douglas's, Martin Marty asserts that religion is alive and well in modern America, whereas Jeffrey Stout suggests that Protestant theology has reached the end of the road. Wolfgang Schluchter, like George Kelly heavily influenced by Max Weber, nonetheless reminds us that Weber did not believe that the "mechanized petrification" of the rationalization process was absolutely inevitable. Weber held out the possibility of "new prophets" or "a great rebirth of old ideas and ideals," and Schluchter, in the light of the same somber realities observed by Kelly, hopes wistfully that these possibilities might materialize. If this be nostalgia, then even the master realist, Weber, was nostalgic.

It is not only civil religion that the man in the street, as Kelly quotes Marty as saying, would be surprised to learn of. Much of what is said in this volume would come equally as a surprise. This points up again the problem of disentangling the analysis of religion from the analysis of the problems intellectuals have with religion. Jeffrey Stout suggests that because theologians are intellectuals their function as "organic intellectuals" (to borrow a term from Gramsci) for religious communities is imperiled. At least he argues that James Gustafson, his type case, can derive very little that is specifically Christian to say about ethics. Regardless of whether this argument about Gustafson is right, the article by Richard McBrien in this volume shows a contemporary Catholic theologian calmly confident that his tradition has much to say to our present situation. Arther Cohen calls for a Jewish theology grounded in historical reflection, and Frank Manuel gives a splendid example of such historical reflection. In any case, as Martin Marty and others point out, however the intellectuals interpret it, religious practice on a rather massive scale survives in America. The intellectuals themselves did not predict this, although, contra Mary Douglas, I think many scholars in religious studies did know that traditional religion had plenty of potential for vigorous revival. George Marsden suggests that religious conservatism and fundamentalism are vigorously alive, and Wade Roof and Edwin Gaustad argue that it would be imprudent to hold funeral rites for liberal religion, as the patient is far from dead.

Yet the question of meaning is not merely an internal squabble among the intellectuals. Kelly's description of American religion as increasingly privatized, secularized, and nostalgic may be accurate, even if those described would not put it that way. Schluchter points out that a massive shift in the place of religion in the West since the eighteenth century has resulted in the privatization and depoliticization of religion. This shift is as characteristic of America as elsewhere. In seventeenth-century New England the church was established, the minister the most important and longest-tenured public officer, and religion and culture were almost synonymous. Today religion is both plural and private and controls only a small corner of the cacophony that is culture. Turning from external institutional conditions to inner meaning, we can certainly say that religion has become more inner and individualistic, a fact that Louis Dupré rather unnostalgically celebrates. Kelly quotes Kant as saying, "At the very outset, we must carefully distinguish the church from religion, which is an inner attitude of mind." This particular view had certainly reached the American masses by 1978 when George Gallup reported that 80 percent of Americans agreed with the statement "An individual should arrive at his or her own religious beliefs independent of any churches or synagogues." As Dupré points out, this situation is not the exclusive product of modernity, for it conforms to the mystical strand that has been part of the biblical tradition from the beginning.

But George Marsden, Steven Tipton, and Anthony and Robbins all suggest that individualistic mysticism is not the whole story. Sectarian movements that generate strong commitment and exert firm discipline have been part of the American religious scene from colonial days and are very much alive today. Sectarian movements, as several of these writers as well as George Kelly suggest, may pull religion away from the public sphere and undermine the possibility of any religious consensus, however vague. But sectarian movements may also be the experimental staging ground for new ideas and new social forms that may subsequently influence the cultural and social focus of society as a whole. In any case, the capacity of a society to allow a degree of sectarian experimentation does not necessarily indicate the collapse of the center that several of these writers predict.

If we see mysticism and sects alive and well in America, do we see the third type of institutionalization so brilliantly analyzed by Ernst Troeltsch, namely, the church? The church according to Troeltsch is neither individualistic nor withdrawn but seeks to influence the whole of society and to understand and transform secular culture rather than reject it. The Catholic Church and the mainline Protestant denominations have been effective representatives of the church type in America, even though they are permeated by the atmosphere of religious individualism and sectarianism that has long influenced all religious tendencies here. The question is whether they can continue their traditional role or whether they have been too decisively displaced from the social and cultural center. None of the writers in this volume is very optimistic about the prospects but some are more optimistic than others. Peter Hebblethwaite indicates that the Catholic Church since Vatican II has moved away from its sectarian rejection of the world toward a much more active engagement with the world and its culture. Certainly the Catholic Church in America has become both more ecumenical and more socially engaged, as demonstrated by its current efforts for a nuclear freeze. David Martin suggests that the movement toward social relevance by Catholics and Protestants may end in evacuating the tradition of any coherence and so leave the field to the secularists and sectarians. This is not a new problem for the churches. Precisely because the church takes the world so seriously, it tends to oscillate between embracing the world too uncritically and then pulling away too sharply in an effort to reassert its identity. But we should not assume because of any particular oscillation that the church type has lost its vigor and left the field entirely to others.

The Troeltschian church must be concerned with secular culture in a way that mysticism and the sects are not. Mystical religion, being concerned with pure innerness, can coexist with almost any form of secular culture. Sectarian religion ignores the world in order to create a world of meaning of its own. Schluchter, Kelly, and Stout have the most misgivings about the church's task of relating to secular culture. And yet all of them recognize (Stout more in *The Flight from Authority* than here) that, as Louis Dumont put it, the modern paradigm is itself in crisis. It is itself more and more evidently incapable of giving the alternative system of meaning that the Enlightenment thought it would. Kelly even speaks paradoxically of the "secularization" of politics and science when it becomes clear that they cannot provide a substitute for religion. Berger too notes that a "crisis of secularity" has followed the "crisis of religion." Such a situation would seem to give an opportunity to the "great rebirth of old ideas and ideals" that Weber saw as a future possibility, but it does not guarantee it. And yet there are some signs that the theological enterprise is regaining confidence after the chaos that followed the end of the era of Barth, Tillich, and the Niebuhrs.

This is not the place to reassess the rather gloomy prognosis of Jeffrey Stout about theology's ability to rejoin the serious cultural conversation of our day. Only a few possibilities might be mentioned. The criticism of foundationalism in the work of such philosophers as Taylor, Rorty, and MacIntyre and the consequent emphasis on practice as the context of theory open up a space for theology as a form of reflection on religious practice that does not require, in the older sense still enunciated by Schluchter, "the sacrifice of the intellect." Perhaps David Tracy is not just "clearing his throat" when he speaks of the importance of religious classics in defining a living religious tradition. Nor can Paul Ricoeur's elucidation of the implications of religious language be dismissed simply as late Lutheran theology that does not fit the data. The present sophistication of biblical studies gives extraordinary resources to theologians concerned with developing theology as a form of rational reflection on living practice. If the theologian has become too isolated from the layperson who recites the Nicene Creed and takes communion each Sunday, the present situation offers opportunities for the bridges to be rebuilt.

If there are at least modest hopes that in a period when secular culture has lost confidence in itself theology might rejoin the conversation, it is even more clear that religion continues to speak to central issues of political order, however far privatization, secularization, and nostalgia have progressed. Lest we too quickly assume that religion has become totally marginalized in America, we might remember the extraordinary role of Martin Luther King, Jr., in articulating a language that was authentically biblical and American and in leading a movement that transformed the relations between the races in America. The churches were effective in opposition to the Vietnam War, are effective today in the nuclear freeze movement, and, although they have not yet found the right voice for it, may yet be effective in mobilizing the moral basis for a new social contract that might make it possible for American society to overcome its severe economic problems. In none of these tasks have the churches been alone. They require the cooperation of a republican tradition, which in turn must not be so privatized, secularized, and nostalgic that it is ineffective. Perhaps these remarks are simply nostalgic, but in view of the stakes involved, the greater danger may be a self-fulfilling prophecy of despair.

I suppose I have, in this introduction, attempted to play the role of mediator and translator so that the conversation that seems only implicit when one reads the papers as they stand might more explicitly be joined. The papers have the great virtue of pointing out most of the major problems and calling to mind many of the salient empirical facts. May we continue to converse.

I. Sacred, Secular, and Modern

LOUIS DUPRÉ

Spiritual Life in a Secular Age

IN THE EIGHTEENTH CENTURY, the idea of God ceased to be a vital concern for our intellectual culture. Almost without transition, deism merged into a practical atheism. In the nineteenth century, this secularized consciousness, no longer satisfied with a *de facto* absence of any meaningful transcendence, attempted to convert its attitude into a *de jure*, justified one. Thus originated the virulent antitheisms of scientific positivism, of sociological structuralism, and of axiological humanism. These antitheist trends have survived into our own day, yet they no longer dominate the religious situation of the present. Today's atheism by and large considers its position sufficiently secure to feel no need for defining itself through a negative relation to faith, nor does it exclude the range of religious experience. Indeed, it has extended its territory to include the significant, yet previously neglected, area of spiritual phenomena. It certainly has abandoned the nineteenth century dream of a purely scientific humanism. As a rule, it no longer expects an integral world view from science, and it is even beginning to abandon the previous identification of science with human progress. In short, contemporary humanism is less polemical, more comprehensive, but also more thoroughly immanent than that of the recent past.

Strangely enough, this humanism beyond atheism was prepared by the three men we most commonly associate with modern atheism, Freud, Marx, and Nietzsche. These "prophets of suspicion," though leaving no doubt about their personal atheism, nevertheless felt that the future would move beyond this polemical attitude. Freud conceded that the neurotic character of faith, which he was satisfied to have scientifically established, did not *per se* preclude the possibility of an objective truth; but to search the foundations of such a negative possibility, after an exhaustive positive interpretation had already been given of all religion's features, did not appear to him to be a very useful enterprise. As he tolerantly informs the reader: "Just as no one can be forced to believe, so no one can be forced to disbelieve. But do not let us be satisfied with deceiving ourselves that arguments like these take us along the road of correct thinking. If ever there was a case of a lame excuse we have it here. Ignorance is ignorance; no right to believe anything can be derived from it."[1]

What can be more polemically atheistic than Marxism, both in its actual policies and in the very words of Marx upon which these policies are founded? Yet even a superficial acquaintance with Marx's mature theory suffices to convince one of the humanist trend of his thought. To be sure, Marx set out as a

3

belligerent antitheist. With Feuerbach, he saw religion as man's projection of his own nature into an ideal sphere that alienated him of his own positive attributes. But Marx, detecting in this projection a more fundamental estrangement between the individual and his social-terrestrial world, felt less and less induced to fight the enchanting shadow image instead of the harsh reality that caused it.

> Atheism as a denial of this unreality [of God] is no longer meaningful, for atheism is a *negation of God* and seeks to assert by this negation the *existence of man*. Socialism no longer requires such a roundabout method; it begins from the theoretical and practical sense perception of man and nature as essential beings. It is positive human self-consciousness; no longer a self-consciousness attained through the negation of religion.[2]

Atheism is itself no more than an ideology, an idle and ill-directed theoretical attitude that only drains much needed energy away from the battle for a true humanization. The communist position rejects both theism and atheism. "Communism begins where atheism begins, but atheism is at the outset still far from being *communism;* indeed it is still for the most part an abstraction. The philanthropy of atheism is at first only a philosophical philanthropy, whereas that of communism is at once real and oriented action."[3]

Axiological humanism has basically followed the same evolutionary path since Nietzsche so boldly declared genuine freedom to be incompatible with the idea of a value-creating God. I know that Nietzsche and most of his followers as late as Sartre formulated this thesis in antitheistic polemical phrases. But they advocated a totally self-sufficient humanism, which goes well beyond these polemics. Maurice Merleau-Ponty articulated the new attitude when he refused to be called an atheist, because atheism is still "an inverted act of faith."[4] The humanist must start not with the denial of God, but with the affirmation of man, the sole source of meaning.

In sum, scientific, Marxist, and axiological humanisms all have abandoned their antireligious stand for an attitude of all-comprehensive openness that, instead of fighting the values traditionally represented by religion, attempts to incorporate them into more accommodating syntheses. To the extent that these attempts have succeeded, they have changed the perspective of our culture and have replaced religion in what used to be its unique function of integrating all of life. For many of our contemporaries, religion has been reduced to an experience, one among others, occasionally powerful, but not sufficiently so to draw the rest of their existence into its orbit.

Of course, the distinction between the sacred areas of existence and the more profane ones occurred very early in our culture, nor do I doubt that the increasing complexity of our lives will make such a distinction ever more necessary. Yet nowhere before have profane matters become secular—that is, entirely independent of what once was their transcendent life source. In our own age, science, social structures, and morality, having developed into full, albeit purely immanent, forms of humanism, have lost virtually all need for the public support of religion. Our contemporaries, particularly the young and the educated, the ones most susceptible to cultural change, have to a large extent resigned themselves to a fragmented world view. The old battles between science and faith marked the final attempts to find a unified vision in which either the religious or the secular had to prevail. Most of us now regard the old controversies as dated; believers, as well as unbelievers, have moderated their claims. Far from "explaining" everything, believers now admit, faith may not even be able to reconcile all its claims with other, partial "world" views by which they live. Today the famed earthquake of Lisbon would cause hardly a ripple among the faithful—not because it creates no problems, but because they have given up looking for theological solutions in all domains of life.

Highly visible and audible fundamentalist movements are attempting to turn this tide of secularization. Deliberately closing themselves to the beliefs and values of their age, their followers hope to reestablish the lost objective certainty by simple denial of historical change. Their presence is felt in the violently antimodernist revolutions that shake the world of Islam and in the aggressive regressiveness of fundamentalist power lobbies. But this same separatism also inspires groups and individuals who appear perfectly attuned to the rhythms of modern life and feel no desire of turning the clock back. By leading lives of "hidden interiority," they manage to disconnect their deeper existence from the prevailing culture. Yet their schizoid attitude is bound to become untenable before long. This desperate attempt to isolate the secular reveals an inability to incorporate it in some manner into the relation to the transcendent. Such inability is itself an entirely new phenomenon among Western attitudes. In the past, the dynamic opposition between the sacred and the profane always secured some measure of integration with transcendent ultimacy to *all* facets of human existence. Today "the sacred," wherever it is still experienced, has lost the power to integrate directly the rest of life. We are now witnessing the unprecedented phenomenon of a religion that is rapidly becoming desacralized. The "experience of the sacred," with which phenomenologists since Rudolph Otto have readily identified religion, can no longer be considered normative of the religion of our time. Few of our contemporaries connect their faith with the kind of private or communal sacred experience described by Otto, Van der Leeuw, or Eliade. To be sure, intensive religious experiences continue to exist, but they have become the exception rather than the rule, and happen mostly to those who have already, and on different grounds, actively committed themselves to transcendent reality. Generally speaking, this new relation is marked more by personal reflection and deliberate choice than by direct experience.

Of course, everyone who settles on a religious life-style does so on the basis of *some* experience. Faith—as we understand that word (an understanding that, I suspect, is strongly colored by a Christian outlook)—has at all times consisted of both experience *and* decision. What uniquely distinguishes our present situation is the nature of the experience. Direct and self-interpretative in the past, it is now ambiguous and open to a multiplicity of interpretations. In our time, the religious interpretation comes as a result of further reflection, and only rarely with the experience itself. Since the interpretation remains separate from the experience, the doubt about its correctness can be resolved only by a subsequent, full commitment to it. Hence, the experience receives its definitive meaning only in this final, voluntary act of assent. When Newman detached the assent of faith from its preceding premises, he anticipated a condition that today is no longer restricted to the logical sequence from inconclusive premises to a firm conclusion. The void between an immanent awareness and the affirmation of a transcendent reality also affected past experience. Yet that experience was sufficiently determined by the surrounding culture to carry the believer across the void by his or her participation in an objective communion of faith. Experience, interpretation, and decision occurred in one continuous act. That connection today is broken. An identical experience justifies the believer's faith as well as the unbeliever's unbelief.

Let me illustrate this by a typical experience, the awareness of radical contingency. This awareness, almost universal in a world whose awesome complexity and unimaginable vastness modern science has revealed, invites some to an unquestioning acceptance of the given. To them, the unpromising quest for *ultimate* intelligibility merely detracts from the urgent and immediate task of exercising rational control over their lives. For others, the mystery of inexplicable gratuitousness points to a transcendent horizon. Clearly, the interpretation here colors the experience. What makes some people favor one interpretation and others the opposite? Social tradition? But this is precisely the factor that has lost much of its original impact in a society that is itself pluralistic, and where even the ties with the immediate family have ceased to function as ideological bonds. The orthodox are right in referring to "grace," a choice for which no clear logical, social, or psychological reasons are available. But, of course, the student of religion is not allowed to invoke one unknown factor in order to explain all others.

Religious men and women will continue to attribute a "sacred" quality to persons, objects, and events closely connected with their relation to the transcendent. But they will do so because they *hold* them sacred, not because they *perceive* them as sacred. Even today they rarely find the source of sacralization in the symbolic reality itself, but in a free subjectivity that determines what is to function as a symbol of transcendence. "The religious person embraces only those doctrines which cast light upon his inner awareness, joins only those groups to which he or she feels moved from within, and performs only those acts which express his self-transcendence."[5] The external and institutional elements of religion seem to have been reduced to an instrumental role. I do not mean to predict that religion will ever be without communally established symbols, but rather that those who opted for a religious dimension in their lives will use institutions and symbols to the extent of their *personal* needs. This undoubtedly gives religion a somewhat eclectic and—for those who judged it by past objective standards—arbitrary appearance. In an unexpected way, the religious impulse has now started to incorporate the religious pluralism that, to a considerable degree, triggered the secularist crisis of the modern age. The existence of such phenomena as Christian Zen, Jews for Jesus, and Calvinist monasteries signals a wholly new way of coming to grips with religious "otherness." But first the center of gravity had to shift from the objective institution to the subjective individual.

In the modern world, religion no longer exercises its integrating function—so essential to its survival—primarily by means of ecclestical power or discipline, or even by means of doctrinal authority. Rather, it does this by means of a personal decision to *adopt* a traditional doctrine and to *use* it for guidance and integration of the various aspects of social and private conduct. It is not that doctrine has been replaced by an arbitrarily eclectic *choice* of symbols. The existing devaluation of signs of ultimate meaning to objects of transitory and superficial interest merely marks the extreme form of secularization itself, not a genuine confrontation of religion with it. Genuine religion in the present (and, presumably, in the future) differs from the past in that it integrates from *within* rather than from without, but it continues to uphold the commitment to a particular doctrine and cult. Their authority, however, becomes operative only *after and to the extent* that they have been previously accepted and interiorized. Spiritual men and women of the modern age are, and will be in the foreseeable future, recognizable as Christians, Jews, or Muslims, even though they may be less exclusive in their doctrinal allegiances.

Nor does the preliminary requirement of a personal decision stamp modern religion into a purely individualist affair. To be sure, today's believers must first decide which, if any, faith they accept, and to what degree they are able to embrace its principles and norms. But having once opted for a particular faith (most likely a variety of the one in which they were raised), they readily join their efforts with those of fellow believers in implementing its religious ideals. How broadly or narrowly they interpret that faith will not likely affect their common effort and worship in the future any more than at present.

It is precisely the private and reflective origin of religion in a secularized culture that explains its inward trend, as well as the high interest in mystical literature. The latter may appear especially paradoxical at a time when authentic religious experience is perhaps less available than ever before. But what attracts the modern believer to the masters of spiritual life is, I think, less affinity of disposition than that in an atheist culture, there is nowhere to turn *but* inwardly. The mystics start their spiritual journey from within, and that is the only place where the believer *must* begin, whether he wants to or not. But a major obstacle arises at once, for what the believer encounters in himself is the same absence that surrounds him. His own heart remains as silent as the world of which the creatures have ceased to speak in sacred tongues. Yet it is precisely in this deliberate confrontation with this inner silence of absence that I detect the true significance of the believer's current urge toward a spiritual life. For only after having confronted his atheism can the believer hope to restore the vitality of his religion. The masters of spiritual life—and they alone—have been able to convey a positive meaning to what Simone Weil so aptly called that sacred "sense of absence." If fully lived through, the emptiness of one's own heart may turn into a powerful cry for the One who is not there. It is the contradiction of a simultaneous presence and absence. "I am quite sure that there is a God, in the sense that I am quite sure my love is not illusory. I am quite sure that there is not a God, in the sense that I am quite sure nothing real can be anything like what I am able to conceive when I pronounce this word." Here, the very godlessness of the world is invested with religious meaning, and another dimension opens up in this negative encounter with a world that has lost its divine presence. Thus the believer learns that God is entirely beyond his reach, that He is not an object but an absolute demand, that to accept Him is not to accept a "given," but a Giving. As in the night of St. John of the Cross, the night of absence, intensely experienced and accepted, becomes the meeting

place between the soul and divine transcendence. Yet it is a transcendence not
sensed as the source of all beings removed from their space and time yet
permanently present in the heart of man, but the transcendence of a God who
has "emptied himself into the world, transformed his substance in the blind
mechanism of the world, a God who dies in the inconsolable pits of human
affliction."[6]

Religion as consciousness of absence has roots in more spiritual traditions.
The intensive encounter with God has always summoned man to take leave of
the familiar words and concepts to venture out into a desert of unlimited and
unexplored horizons. The oldest and purest Buddhist doctrine proposed no
other ideal than the attainment of total emptiness. Of "God" there is no
question; emptiness itself becomes the space of transcendence. The monk must
remain silent, yet silently he thanks the nameless source. Nor does the Samkhya
Hindu feel the need for an idea of God to carry his awareness of what can have
no name. Christianity, the religion of the Word, of God's manifestation, has no
room for an a-theist piety as such. (The atheism of some recent theologians is
intrinsically bound to remain a heterodox, marginal phenomenon.) But even in
the religion of manifestation, those who engage upon a serious spiritual journey
invariably begin their pilgrimage by leaving the creatures behind.

Though religious mysticism always entails an intensive awareness of God's
presence in creation, Christian mystics invariably commence their journey by
emphasizing the difference (and hence the absence) between God and the
creature. Their negative attitude must not be attributed only to practical
wisdom but, first and foremost, to an immediate awareness that the creature as
such is totally unlike God. For years Newman attempted to explain how,
through the phenomena of the visible world, we gain "an image of God." But
more and more he became convinced that only a previous awareness of God's
inner presence—in conscience—would enable man to detect a divine presence in
the world at all. In contrast to this "definite" presence in conscience, "the
phenomena are as if pictures, but at the same time they give us no exact measure
or character of the unknown things beyond them." Man lacks the power to
derive an image of God from the cause and system of the world. "What strikes
the mind so forcibly and so painfully, is His absence (if I may so speak) from
His own world. It is a silence that speaks. It is as if others had got possession of
His work. Why does not He, our Maker and Ruler, give us some immediate
knowledge of Himself?"[7] In the moving sermon "Waiting for Christ," this
alienation appears even more strongly.

> When he came in the flesh "He was in the world, and the world was made by
> Him, and the world knew Him not." Nor did He strive nor cry, nor lift up His
> voice in the streets. So it is now. He still is here; He still whispers to us, He still
> makes signs to us. But His voice is too low, and the world's din is so loud, and His
> signs are so covert, and the world is so restless, that it is difficult to determine
> when He addresses us, and what He says. Religious men cannot but feel, in
> various ways, that His providence is guiding them and blessing them personally
> on the whole; yet when they attempt to put their finger upon the times and places,
> the traces of His presence disappear.[8]

Once again the inner presence must mediate the visible world with its Creator.
Whatever divine clarity radiates from the creature is reflected back from the

mind's internal light. In this light, "things which come before our eyes, in such wise take the form of types and omens of things moral or future, that the spirit within us cannot but reach forward and presage what it is not told from what it sees."9 The ambiguous signs of the visible world must await the interpretation of the inner voice. God remains "hidden" in a world that does not allow Him "to display His glory openly."10 Like Pascal, Newman concludes that without the "eyes of faith," the mind is unable to recognize God in His creation. Nor is this inner light derived from the mind's reflective powers. Even the voice of conscience becomes the voice of God only to him who knows how to listen to it as to a message originating beyond the self. We are reminded of Augustine's entreaty to move beyond memory and beyond the self.

The more the awareness of God's presence increases, the more the idea of a similarity between God and the creature recedes. The spiritual soul does not look for "God-resembling" creatures. It embraces all beings with equal fervor— the high and the lowly, the good and the bad—for none are more "like" God than others.

Since the third century, the mystical tradition of Christianity has recognized a theology in which all language is reduced to silence. In his *Mystical Theology*, Pseudo-Dionysius, the sixth century Syrian monk, teaches that all striving for spiritual perfection must abandon all experience, all concepts, and all objects, to be united with what lies beyond all cognition. "Into this Dark beyond all light, we pray to come and, unseeing and unknowing to see and to know Him that is beyond seeing and beyond knowing precisely by not seeing, by not knowing."11 This mysticism of negation culminated in fourteenth century Rhineland. Thus Eckhart writes about the place where the soul meets with God:

> When I existed in the core, the soil, the river, the source of the Godhead, no one asked me where I was going or what I was doing. There was no one there to ask me, but the moment I emerged, the world of creatures began to shout: 'God.' . . . Thus creatures speak of god—but why do they not mention the Godhead? Because there is only unity in the Godhead and there is nothing to talk about.12

Clearly, a negation such as Eckhart's or that of the *Cloud of Unknowing* did not emerge from a weakened religious consciousness. Quite the opposite, it emerged from a more intensive awareness of a transcendent presence—precisely what is missing in our contemporaries. Yet my point is not to compare two entirely different mentalities. Rather, it is to show that if the believer, who shares in fact, if not in principle, the practical atheism of his entire culture, is left no choice but to vitalize this negative experience and to confront his feeling of God's absence, he may find himself on the very road walked by spiritual pilgrims in more propitious times. What was once the arduous route traveled only by a religious elite is now, in many instances, the only one still open to him. To be sure, not all believers of our age are spiritual men or women, nor need they be, but to those who *are*, religion will continue to be an integrating power of life. The desert of modern atheism provides the only space in which most of them are forced to encounter the transcendent. It is a desert that in prayerful attention may be converted into the solitude of contemplation—a solitude that Thomas Merton wrote of as not something outside us, not an absence of men or of sound, but an abyss opening up in the center of the soul, an abyss created by a hunger and thirst and sorrow and poverty and desire.[13] Our age has created an emptiness that for the serious God-seeker attains a religious significance. The mysticism of negation provides him with an ideal model. The affirmation of God is rarely still the center of his search for transcendence.

Yet, unless the modern believer in some manner overcomes the pure negation, he or she has not fully surpassed the secular atheism of the age. Even a religion of silence, such as Buddhism, moves beyond absence, however strongly it may refuse to name the transcendent. Nirvana is a purely negative concept only to the outsider. To those who live it, it is, in the words of one monk, "unspeakable bliss." Much less can traditions that so strongly emphasize the intrinsic value of the finite, as do Christianity and Judaism, tolerate their spiritual theology to remain purely negative. Christian mystics have commonly admitted some kind of theological negation, but somehow they have all succeeded in moving beyond it. The dialectic seems to have developed somewhat in the following way. Having first found the finite incommensurate with the infinite, they felt compelled to abandon their own finite negation, by which they had separated the finite from the infinite, and to consider their union in the divine creative act. In this perspective, transcendence, rather than constituting the opposition between finite and infinite, reveals the divine essence of the finite and, with it, the emanationist quality of God's Being. The final word, then, about God is not "otherness," but "identity." God is the ultimate dimension of the real. Thus Ignatius of Loyola, at the end of his Spiritual Exercises, invites the exercitant who has previously renounced the creaturely world to consider now "how God dwells in all creatures." Similarly, John of the Cross, after having first denied any proportion between God and the creatures, reasserts their equality. Even Eckhart's negation of an analogy between God and the creatures results in a new analogy, based not on similarity, but on partial identity.

At present we are merely concerned with how this complex movement of reaffirmation can still be achieved in an age that has lost the very idea of God. Clearly, to answer that, it does not suffice to embrace the finite as if it were infinite. Abolishing the distinction between one and the other can merely result in an aesthetic pantheism incompatible with the transcendence so essential to all genuine religion. What actually happens appears to be this. The spiritual person comes to view the world in a different perspective. Underneath ordinary reality he or she recognizes another dimension. At the very core of each creature, the contemplative finds an otherness that compels him to allow it to be itself and to abstain from the conquering, objectifying attitude that we commonly adopt. This does not reveal a new idea of God; rather, it allows reality to reveal itself. But that is a decisive break with the approach to reality, in terms of power, that lies at the root of our present loss of genuine transcendence. Transcendence is more than a concept that can be made and unmade at random. It expresses a fundamental attitude. Once it disintegrates, it cannot be replaced by a readily available equivalent, as we do when replacing an inadequate concept by a more adequate one. It has to be rebuilt from the bottom up. The first task here is not one of creating a more viable system (if that were sufficient, theology would have solved our problems long ago), but of a different outlook on the real. A description of what does not exist is bound to be inadequate. But I can think of no better characterization than the one contained in the Roman *pietas*, an obedient attention to possible messages, or as Simone Weil has appropriately defined it, a waiting in expectation.

At first blush, this may not appear to differ much from the open-minded, considerate attitude of any civilized person of our age. Yet far beyond ordinary open-mindedness, the spiritual man of the present must be willing to suspend even apparently unquestionable assumptions. His respect for others consists not in benign tolerance, but in an active search for the well-being of others, and in a submission to it on *their* terms. Even with respect to nature, it is not sufficient to move beyond scientific control and practical utilization; we also have to avoid turning nature into a narcissistic mirror of subjective feelings. As John Fowles observes, "We shall never fully understand nature (or ourselves) and certainly never respect it, until we dissociate the wild from the notion of usability—however innocent and harmless the use."[14] In adopting this selfless approach, we merely remove the principal obstacle to the perception of the transcendent dimension of the real. We must not expect to come up with a new name for the emerging transcendent, but only to acquire a new perceptiveness for detecting it. Hence, we overcome the negative theology only in this limited sense, that we once again turn toward the finite for a revelation of the infinite. We no longer know the infinite itself, nor do we know the nature of its revelation. We can hardly distinguish a specifically religious realm of experience, as the "sacred" was in the past. In direct experience, hardly any "object" appears more sacred than any other. The worldliness of contemporary experience tends to erase the traditional distinction between the sacred and the profane.

But if the distinction largely vanishes, does not traditional religion likewise disappear? What happens to the "positive" elements of faith, to revelation, sacraments, Church? In advocating a new attitude, are we, in fact, not proposing a new religion? Is any room left for those specific elements that make a particular faith Christian or Jewish? Or must we admit that these declining faiths are in fact doomed to total extinction, even among spiritual men and women? The objections are to be considered seriously, all the more so since there seems to be no alternative to what I would call the inevitably "worldly" character of spiritual life in this age. Yet they do not appear to be peremptory. For the attitude here described is the very one proposed by the religious models of the tradition. Exemplifying this in the case of Christianity—the religion that has been exposed most widely to the erosion of modern secularism—the obedience to a higher calling, the submission to a law that surpasses the person, and the search for the transcendent core of all selfhood are the very essence of the Christ ideal. Nor is that ideal here taken as a mere moral model, remembered from the past only for its exemplary features. To the modern Christian it remains a living presence that reveals the fullness of the obedient attitude and at the same time provides the very means for establishing it.

Here, one might object that to accept this model as unique, and the sacramental link with it as efficacious, one must already be a "believer," and how can anyone be a religious believer without a preliminary commitment to a distinctly perceived, transcendent reality. Yes, to be a Christian one must be a believer, but at least the modern believer must first *discover* the model as a viable one in his own world before he can accept it as transcendent. It has become quite futile to establish the divine authority of Christ before the potential believer admits the significance of His message, for that authority itself is most under question. The existential significance must at least in some measure be established before dogmatic concepts become acceptable. I am not claiming, as was occasionally done in nineteenth century apologetics, that Christ's significance proved His divinity, and hence legitimated the entire Christian faith. Apart from its obvious logical flaw, that argument begs the most crucial issue in the modern problematic—whether the idea of God has any meaning left. Faith will, more than ever, remain what it always was: a leap beyond experience. But, contrary to what the theologians of the leap of faith usually claim, that leap was never blind. It always led from partial insight to total acceptance. The same structure is maintained today when the "believer," dissatisfied with the shallowness of a closed, secular world, abandons the conquering, grasping attitude for a more receptive one.

It would be incorrect to assume that the community loses its role in the highly personal spiritual religion of the present, for as soon as the believer adopts a model such as Christ (and the entire culture that has been shaped by it induces him to prefer this model over others), he joins a community, becomes a member of a group of like-minded individuals in the present. In this link, however loose, with a mystical body, the believer becomes united with his model, which ceases to be a mere ideal, because the community makes it into a *present* reality. By providing him with sacraments, scriptures, and a whole system of representations, the religious community enables the individual to incorporate his attitude into a living union with his model.

Since much of the traditional nomenclature is preserved in the new attitude, one might well wonder whether the current changes, decisive as they appear to us, are in fact no more than a theological adjustment to different circumstances. I think not. Theology articulates a particular vision of the transcendent. Although the articulation may be challenged, the vision is not. But in the present situation, the very reality of the transcendent is at stake, not a specific conceptualization of it. It is the possibility itself of a relation to the transcendent in the modern world that is under fire. Theology assumes some experience of the sacred. This assumption can no longer be taken for granted. Those who do not have it will start their reflection from a presumption of atheism that refuses to reserve an irreducible area of human experience to the sacred. The religious attitude, then, has largely become what it never was before, a matter of existential choice. The choice is usually not made on the basis of a relatively clear experience, but of an accumulation of experiences inviting reflection and confronting man with possibilities, one of which his decision—his choice—must convert into existential certainty. Thence the joining of a religious community, the reception of sacraments, even the acceptance of an established doctrine, mean something essentially different from what they meant for our ancestors, for symbolic gestures and doctrinal representations, accepted by deliberate decision rather than conveyed by direct experience, turn into empty shells, unless they are constantly replenished by a rather intensive and deliberate spiritual awareness.

The search for a deeper spiritual life is, in fact, more than a passing phenomenon on today's religious scene; it is a movement for religious survival. For without the support of a sustained personal decision, a religion that remains unassisted by the surrounding culture and is constantly under attack in the believer's own heart is doomed to die. It is a mistake, however, and one frequently made by those who undertake this spiritual journey, to believe that the solutions to all our problems lie buried in old masters and ancient monasteries. The doctrines, life-styles, and methods of a previous age were conceived within the reach of a direct experience of the sacred. This has for the most part ceased to exist. The language of past mystics, of the eighteenth as well as the fourteenth century, unlike that of the classics of philosophy and literature, strikes the modern reader as antiquated, because the experience therein articulated is no longer even minimally present. A confrontation with the past may be necessary, but the shape of spiritual life in the future will be entirely our own.

Instead of the traditional distinction between sacred objects, persons, and events, and profane ones, spiritual men and women in the future will regard existence increasingly as an indivisible unity, wholly worldly and self-sufficient, yet at the same time of a depth that invites further exploration. They will tend to take the representational content of their spiritual life straight out of their daily secular experience, yet they will be reluctant to attribute precise meanings and clearly defined intentions to this worldly structure of symbols. They will start, mostly, from the negative experience of life lived in a secular environment, lacking in universal signs of transcendence, yet less than ever, I suspect, will they remain satisfied with a mysticism of negation. Theirs will rather be a spirituality of world-affirmation, a mystique of creation that discovers a transcendent dimension in a fundamental engagement to a world and a human community at once totally autonomous and totally dependent.

REFERENCES

[1]Sigmund Freud, *The Future of an Illusion*, in the *Complete Psychological Works*, translated under the direction of James Strachey, volume 21 (London: Hogarth Press, 1961), p. 32.

[2]Karl Marx, *Economic and Philosophic Manuscripts of 1888*, in Marx-Engels *Collected Works* (New York: International Publishers, 1975), volume 3, p. 306 (slightly changed).

[3]Ibid., p. 297.

[4]Maurice Merleau-Ponty, *Eloge de la philosophie* (Paris: 1953), p. 59.

[5]Louis Dupré, *Transcendent Selfhood* (New York: Seabury Press, 1976), pp. 29-30. See also Peter Berger, *The Heretical Imperative* (New York: Doubleday, 1979) pp. 32 ff.

[6]Susan A. Taubes, "The Absent God," in *Toward a New Christianity*, Thomas J. J. Altizer (ed.) (New York: Harcourt, Brace and World, 1967), p. 116.

[7]John Henry Newman, *A Grammar of Assent* (New York: Doubleday, 1955) pp. 109, 39.

[8]John Henry Newman, *Parochial and Plain Sermons* (London: Longmans, 1900-02) VI, p. 248.

[9]Ibid, p. 249.

[10]John Henry Newman, "The Omnipotence of God, the Reason for Faith and Hope," *Parochial and Plain Sermons*.

[11]P. G. Migne, 3, p. 1925; in *Varieties of Mystical Experience*, translated by Elmer O'Brien (New York: Holt, Rinehart, Winston, 1964) p. 84.

[12]*Nolite Timere*, in *Meister Eckhart: A Modern Translation*, by Raymond B. Blakney (New York: Harper and Brothers, 1957) p. 225.

[13]Thomas Merton, *Seeds of Contemplation* (New York: Dell, 1958) pp. 51-52.

[14]John Fowles, *The Tree* (Boston: Little, Brown, 1980).

PETER L. BERGER

From the Crisis of Religion to the Crisis
of Secularity

A THEORY ABOUT the relationship between religion and modern secular society
that has been prevalent since the Enlightenment is the focus for current debate
about the place of religion in modern society. This theory, now known as
"secularization theory," contends that modernity is intrinsically and irrevers-
ibly antagonistic to religion. As a society becomes increasingly modernized it
inevitably becomes less religious. The original Enlightenment version of the
theory was highly ideological. It did not simply state that the antireligious
animus of the modern age was an empirical fact, but that it was to be welcomed
and furthered. The decline of traditional Judaeo-Christian religion was part of
the "progress" Enlightened minds were striving for. Others, while less committed to this "progress," acknowledged the decline of religion. And those who
were committed to religious traditions bemoaned this decline as a deplorable
development.

In recent decades historians, social scientists, and others have debated the
validity of secularization theory. While it cannot be fully discussed here, the
import of this debate is clear: Modernity may not be as antagonistic to religion
as had previously been asserted.[1] Some critics have argued that secularization
was never a reality and that religion is as important in the modern world as it
was in earlier times. But very few would go this far in repudiating the theory. A
more common criticism is that secularization is neither as pervasive nor as
irreversible as had been argued. Both the extent and the inexorability of secularization may have been exaggerated by earlier analysts.

A closer look at modern society reveals a curious twist to the discussion of
religion and secularity. For while there has been a crisis of religion in the
modern world, there now appears to be a crisis of secularity as well. Secularity
as a world view, along with Enlightenment thinking as a whole, has been
severely shaken in recent times. This inevitably affects the status and prospects
of religion in this society.

Enlightenment thought was the ideology of the bourgeoisie, as a rising and
eventually revolutionary class, a fact Marx understood clearly. It follows, then,
that Enlightenment ideas, including the "myth" of progress and belief in secularity, enjoyed their greatest popularity in the era of secure bourgeois dominance, the nineteenth century, which remained intact as a sociocultural reality
until World War I. It is not surprising that some of the greatest intellectual
challenges to Enlightenment thought came into their own only after the war,

14

which in many ways can be seen as an act of collective suicide for European, if not Western, civilization. Kierkegaard, Nietzsche, and Dostoyevsky are some prime examples of this criticism. It may be argued that since 1918 the sociocultural world created by the triumphant bourgeoisie has experienced a deepening crisis. The economic and political dimensions of this crisis are evident. But it is equally important to see the cultural and even psychological dimensions of it, such as the loss of plausibility for the myth of progress and its concomitant ideas, values, and consolations.

An additional comment on consolations may be useful. As Max Weber showed, every human society requires a "theodicy," an interpretation of the suffering and injustice endemic to the human condition. This, of course, has always been one of the social and psychological functions of religion. Modern secularity has had a problem consoling individuals for *private* suffering and injustice. An individual facing bereavement, physical pain, or even an intolerable marriage is unlikely to be consoled by any of the great ideals of the myth of progress—the eventual triumph of natural science, the attainment of national independence, or the success of revolutionary struggles. But the *public* woes of life could be consolingly explained by such ideals, and it is conceivable that some individuals even found their private woes more tolerable in a world perceived to be progressing. As the ideals themselves lost plausibility, Enlightenment secularity lost whatever potential it had for theodicy, and the consoling capacities of religion gained new credibility as a result.

In recent history, first in Europe and then globally, secularity has been closely linked to the overall phenomenon of modernity. Secularization and modernization have been seen as interconnected processes. This view is important because it points to several peculiar features of contemporary secularity. One of these features is the linkage of secularity and pluralism, the latter meaning the peaceful coexistence of a variety of world views and value systems within one society. Examples of secularity and pluralism existing independently of one another may be found in earlier periods of history. Confucianism has been described as highly secular, yet traditional Chinese society did not have the dynamic pluralism characteristic of the modern world. An obverse example is premodern, or more accurately pre-Muslim, India. This society was marked by a very high degree of religious pluralism, but the secularizing potential of the pluralism was "contained" by the segregating structures of caste. In modern society, by contrast, secularity and pluralism are mutually reinforcing phenomena. Secularization fosters the civic arrangements under which pluralism thrives, while the plurality of world views undermines the plausibility of each one and thus contributes to the secularizing tendency.

Because secularity and pluralism today are perceived as parts of modernity, they are subject to many of the attitudes and reactions toward modernity. While modernization brings promises and tangible benefits, it also produces tensions and discontents both institutionally and psychologically. In addition to the external institutional dislocations resulting from changes in the economic and political structures, there is massive alienation as a result of the loss of community and the turbulent upheavals caused by social mobility, urbanization, and the technological transformations of everyday life. For these reasons, there has always been resistance to modernity, in the form of countermodernizing movements and ideologies. Precisely to the extent that secularity and pluralism are phenomena of modernity, they are also the targets of miscellaneous countersecular and counterpluralistic "resistance movements." Such reactions have occurred in Europe for a long time (the Fronde, for example) and in other parts of the world undergoing modernization. It is arguable, however, that manifestations of countersecularity in recent decades have been particularly vigorous, and it is these manifestations that have provoked questions about the viability of secularization theory.

The most massive manifestation is the upsurge of religious movements in the Third World. Iran alone raises questions about the inexorable nexus between modernization and secularization. There are special circumstances in the Iranian case, both in the sociopolitical context of modernization under the Shah's regime and in the peculiar features of Persian Islam, but Iran is not the only country in the Muslim world to have experienced violent reaffirmations of religion and tradition that can aptly be described as both countersecular and countermodern. Islamic revivalism is a potent force from Indonesia to the Maghreb, and it is likely to remain so for a long time. While this Islamic resurgence is probably unique in its forcefulness, comparable phenomena have occurred in the non-Muslim world—forms of neo-Buddhist activism, the militant movement of Hindu traditionalism, the astounding growth of indigenous African religious movements (most of them uneasily syncretistic to Christianity), and the proliferation of various Christian sects in Latin America. It is very difficult to look at the Third World today and conclude that modernization leads inevitably to a diminished role for religion. In many Third World countries even the two most distinctively modern phenomena—nationalism and socialism—have strong religious overtones.

Another manifestation of countersecularity, less massive and more difficult to assess, is the revival of religion in the Soviet Union. Its extent is hard to gauge, partly because of the obvious difficulties of obtaining reliable data but also because political dissidence apparently takes on a religious coloration for some individuals who would otherwise be unlikely to be drawn to religion. Still, we know enough to be able to say that a remarkable revival of religious faith has taken place in the Soviet Union, despite more than a half-century of determined antireligious policies by its totalitarian regime. The revival is all the more remarkable in that one of its foci seems to be the elite of the regime—the children of the commissars. These observations refer to recent developments in Russian Orthodoxy. If one adds to these the signs of religious survival among Soviet Jews, Protestant sectarians (especially Baptists), and the Muslims of Soviet Central Asia, one raises serious questions about secularization theory in the country in which, more than any other, one would expect it to be confirmed. In other words, the contribution of the Soviet case to the general critique of secularization theory takes the form of an *a fortiori* argument: If the theory breaks down in the Soviet case, where the practice of religion is actively discouraged, then it will be discredited all the more where the political circumstances for religion are more favorable.

For American social analysts, of course, developments within the United States have been most significant in raising questions about secularization theory. Since the 1960s there have been two developments, quite different from each other in many respects yet both clear manifestations of countersecularity. The more celebrated development has been the so-called counterculture. Some analysts, such as Paul Goodman, consider the entire phenomenon as religious in character. This view may be somewhat distorted. Clearly, however, the counterculture has brought to the fore definite religious impulses, some of which may be termed "superstition" by unfriendly observers. These impulses include the remarkable growth of astrology and spiritual healing, the religiously tinged elements of the ecology and health movements (which may be broadly characterized as the cults of salvation through natural manure), and the personal growth and encounter movements (including the amazing reincarnation of archaic sacred sexuality). Religious elements are evident also in some sectors of the American drug culture. And, probably most important, the counterculture has provided a hospitable milieu for the importation of miscellaneous oriental cults, especially those fostering meditation and other spiritual exercises. The counterculture is now very likely a past phenomenon, but one reason for this may be that many of its impulses have been firmly established in the wider culture, especially in the upper-middle-class strata. Again, it is interesting to note that it is precisely in these strata and age groups that secularization made its greatest strides.

The other significant American development has been the resurgence of Evangelical Protestantism, a sharp contrast to the anemic condition of mainline Protestantism and the troubles of Roman Catholicism since Vatican II. It is not fanciful to say that American churches flourish today in negative correlation to their degree of *aggiornamento*. The churches that flourish are those that have compromised the least with the spirit of modern secularity. This fact challenges not only secularization theory but also those liberal theologians and churchmen who have argued that Christianity must be adapted to the "irresistible" cognitive demands of "modern man." The Evangelical revival differs from the counterculture in important ways: its class and regional location, its capacity to form durable institutions, and its social and political attitudes. Both movements, however, share the important quality of being countersecular, and both therefore are very relevant to a critique of secularization theory.

Clearly, the relative positions of religion and secularity vary greatly from country to country. It is arguable, for instance, that modern secularity continues in unbroken dominance in the Scandinavian countries, most notably in Sweden, a society that, more than any other, appears to the outsider as a frozen tableau of Enlightenment utopianism. In other countries, modern secularity is in trouble. In the United States this is related to the condition of the "civil religion," as Robert Bellah named it, a distinctively American blend of Enlightenment faith in progress with bits and pieces of Judaeo-Christian morality. That "religion" has certainly been in trouble, though some revival movements are evident here as well. There is no need to reiterate the well-known shocks this American ideology has experienced in the period since the 1960s as a result of surges of countersecularity. In fact, there may be some causal connection between civil religion and the development of countersecular movements.

But another, less noted point to be made about the specifically American crisis of secularity is what may be called the passage from religious pluralism to moral pluralism. America has been very successful in institutionalizing religious pluralism within a vaguely secular civic order, with the coexistence of religious denominationalism (in Richard Niebuhr's sense of the term *denomination*, as referring to a church that has willingly surrendered its claims to monopoly status) and a state constitutionally separated from religion. In light of human history, with its multitude of religious wars and repressions, it is amazing how peacefully American religious groups have coexisted. The American language itself exhibits this religious pluralism. That statements such as "My religious preference is Presbyterian," or "I happen to be Jewish," or even "I'm into Buddhism" do not raise eyebrows in most quarters today testifies to the acceptance of religious pluralism. Even if one agrees that there is a unifying civil religion presiding over this religious "market," it would have to be seen as a guarantor rather than a rival to religious pluralism.

It is also true, however, that until very recently most, if not all, the religious groups coexisting in America have shared a broadly common morality. This has provided a practical basis for social life, even where it has been secularized and deprived of its earlier religious anchorage. It is precisely this common morality that now seems threatened at a number of critical points. Moral pluralism is becoming increasingly prevalent, and it is much harder to institutionalize than religious pluralism. Imagine statements such as "My moral preference is for the use of arson in labor disputes," or "I happen to be a rapist," or "I'm into spying for the Soviet Union." This is not as farfetched as it sounds. It is becoming commonplace for firefighters and medical personnel to go on strike with full knowledge that they may be endangering human lives, an act that would have been morally intolerable in an earlier period. The controversy over abortion stems from two sharply differentiated moral positions, one regarding abortion as an act of murder, the other considering it a matter of individual "choice" (a synonym for the denominational term *preference*). Barely beneath the surface of recent debate over national defense is the question of whether *any* values of the society are worth defending by force of arms. Anyone schooled in Durkheimian ideas about the role of moral consensus in the integration of human societies must ask whether American society can survive long with such fundamental moral divisions. In such a society, moral disputes must be referred to the political process and the courts, self-consciously secular institutions that are ill equipped to function as sources of a binding common morality. The development of moral pluralism in America, unresolved and probably unresolvable in secular terms, thus contributes to the crisis of secularity.

In America, if not also in other Western industrial societies, the crisis of secularity has a specific class location. This is no surprise, since religion is also closely tied to the class system. Even if one is not completely persuaded by Max Weber's thesis on the causal nexus between Protestantism and capitalism in the early modern period, it is clear that Protestantism in America fulfilled important functions within the class system as a vehicle of social mobility and as a class symbol. Sociologists of religion have shown how class affiliation can predict religious affiliation—from the upper-class regions of certain Episcopalian or Unitarian parishes to the broadly bourgeois Methodist or Baptist congregations, and the "upper lower class" (to use Lloyd Warner's slightly dated term) gathered in Pentecostal or Holiness assemblies (though the upwardly mobile impetus of Protestant morality was always very evident in precisely these nether regions of the class system). The progress of secularization has always had class indices as well, making greater inroads in the upper as opposed to the lower classes of the system.

Since World War II an important change has occurred in the American class system—the rise of the so-called knowledge class (often called the "new class" *tout court*). It is not possible to enter in detail into the debate over this phenomenon. Put very briefly, it is argued that the old middle class has split in two, leaving on one side what remains of the old bourgeoisie (also called the "business class," including its managerial and professional affiliates) and congealing on the other side into a new stratum deriving its livelihood from the production and distribution of symbolic knowledge, by no means limited to "intellectuals," but including a much larger population of education, "communications," therapeutic ("caring"), and bureaucratic occupations. It can be argued further that it is in this class (rather than in the upper middle class in general) that secularity has been most firmly established.

If this perception of the changed class system is correct, many social, political, and cultural conflicts of recent American history may be understood in terms of a struggle for power and privilege between these two successors to the old bourgeoisie. As Marx taught, in cases of class struggle cultural symbols become instruments in the struggle. Thus, the current class struggle in America also takes the character of a *Kulturkampf*. The whole range of "social issues," whatever their intrinsic merits or putative consequences, has taken on a symbolic quality; they are emotional issues in part because of the class interests they represent. Abortion, the Equal Rights Amendment, gay rights, as well as the miscellany of environmental and consumer issues are typical of this symbolic struggle. Class is the main predictor of individual positions taken on these issues. The issues have become symbols of knowledge-class ascendancy; opposition to them originates in class resentment as much as in intrinsic moral or political convictions.

The knowledge class has tended to espouse secularity much more than other classes, and in recent years they have done so in a highly politicized way. The efforts of that class have focused mainly on the courts and the imposition of a European-style radical understanding of the separation of church and state, best expressed by the classical French term *laique* (very different from what the Founding Fathers envisaged for the American polity). The Supreme Court prohibition of prayer in the public schools is the major symbolic victory of this newly militant secularity. The current court battles over the rights of Christian schools in the South and elsewhere is another major focus of this *Kulturkampf*. The movement illustrates how the contest between religion and secularity, at least in America, has been drawn into the politics of class conflict. It follows that the outcome of the contest will be strongly influenced by the outcome of the class conflict, though certainly not determined completely by it. If so, the most likely result will not be complete victory for either side, but rather the negotiation of miscellaneous compromises—a position to the right of the American Civil Liberties Union but to the left of the militant Evangelical groups.

Class dynamics aside, compromise is the most likely outcome in view of the overall softening effect of the pluralistic milieu as well. Just as pluralism reinforces secularization during its ascendancy, so, paradoxically, does pluralism soften any form of established or institutionalized secularity. In other words, as pluralism undermines the certainties of religious absolutism, it also weakens any secular forms of dogmatism. So, for example, secularists (and let their probable class position not be forgotten) feel a tension between their strong belief in tolerance and their conviction that their world view is the only correct one. In acute conflict situations, to be sure, stances may harden on both sides. But barring unforeseeable (and presumably catastrophic) changes in American society, a rigid institutionalization of the religious and secularist camps along the lines of, for example, the "two Frances" during the period of the Third Republic does not seem probable.

Pluralism, like modernity in general, produces specific discontents that invariably result in counterformations. The reason for this can be stated succinctly: Pluralism makes any quest for certainty more difficult; it encourages skepticism rather than faith, cognitive and normative openness rather than closure. But human beings have a deeply rooted urge for certainty and faith, and the endless openness of pluralism—especially, as discussed earlier, in moral matters—is difficult to bear. The consequence is a series of hardening reactions alternating with periods of softening—counterformations of militant, sometimes fanatical reiteration of this or that erstwhile certitude. Such counterformations may, in principle, be either religious or secularist. Indeed, the social-psychological profile of the dogmatic secularist is formally very similar to that of the orthodox or neo-orthodox religious believer.

At present, there are strong movements of both counterpluralism and countersecularity. The hunger for religious certainty is merged with a more mundane desire, for a restored community in which the differentiations and alienations of modern society will be overcome. These movements take two general forms. The politically milder form does not aspire to a restored community embracing the society as a whole, but limits itself to constructing smaller social worlds that create a similar sense of community. This may also be called the sectarian or subcultural form, or (without intending this pejoratively) the "ghetto" solution. This form, of course, has a long history in religion. It becomes plausible in a new way in the era of pluralism and secularity as a social construction explicitly designed to shelter individuals from these corroding influences. Both the religious variants of the counterculture and various movements of neotraditionalism frequently take this form, in America as elsewhere. While this option does provide a solution for individuals in quest of certainty and faith, it also faces formidable problems of social engineering. The main problem is the erection and maintenance of barriers strong enough to keep out the forces that undermine certainty—a difficult feat in the context of modern urban life, mobility, and mass communication. The most grandiose effort of this type was made by the Roman Catholic Church prior to Vatican II, in America and elsewhere, when it sought to create a subculture strong enough to withstand the pressures of the engulfing culture. This effort failed, perhaps in part because it tried to include too large and too heterogeneous a population within its "ghetto" walls. Less grandiose efforts, from Zen communes to neo-Chassidic synagogues in affluent suburbs, have better prospects for survival. Most so-called cults also belong in this category.

The other, more ambitious form of counterpluralism/countersecularity seeks the restoration of religious and moral community in the society as a whole, typically by way of a *reconquista* of the society under the banner of traditional beliefs and values. The Iranian revolution is again a Third World prototype of this form, but the phenomenon is not limited to Islam or the Third World. The Falangist revolution in Spain was precisely and explicitly such an undertaking—the reconquest of the society in the name of Christ the King, as its slogan declared. In Western societies today, armed revolution is rarely the means chosen for such a purpose, but the organization of neotraditionalists into political groups participating in a democracy may have exactly the same goal—to reimpose on an entire society the beliefs and values of a religious subculture. Portions of the current Evangelical movement in America are marked by this intent: to restore (with however dubious a historical warrant) a Christian America in which neither pluralism nor secularity would have a place. Paradoxically, this dream of restored community may also be found in movements that consider themselves to be on the "left" politically. Richard Neuhaus has persuasively argued that one of the central motifs in contemporary liberation theology is the reconstruction of an all-embracing religious and moral community—a profoundly countermodern, indeed medieval, aspiration aptly expressed by the phrase "the new Christendom," the title of Juan Luis Segundo's influential treatise.

If the sectarian solution is socially and psychologically totalistic, the dream of *reconquista* is politically totalitarian at least *in nuce*. The reason for this is quite simple: Only by massive political coercion can a new unity be reimposed effectively after a period of pluralism. It is important to note that these two forms of reaction to the discontents of pluralism also appear in secularist variants. Counterpluralistic secular movements of the "right" and the "left" have taken both forms. In the first case, the group forms a sect (like the communities designated "utopian socialism" by Marx) within which the alienations of an allegedly rotten society are kept out. In the second case, the movement organizes itself for revolutionary action to take over the entire society. The history of Marxism provides the most ample illustration of a secular/secularist variant of this progression from sectarian totalism to political totalitarianism, and quite possibly it proves that this progression is nearly inevitable. In the traditional Catholic phrase, "error has no rights." It certainly has none within the confines of a sectarian subculture, and it evidently gains none in a society taken over by a sect that has transformed itself into a successful revolutionary regime.

In America, if not elsewhere, the prospects are better for milder forms of countersecularity, which attempt to reconstitute "sheltering" religious communities that fall short of the rigid structures of sectarianism and do not aspire to impose their norms on the society as a whole. If such efforts are successfully institutionalized, the society will indeed become less secular; and, as indicated earlier, there are signs that this is already occurring. In other words, the symbolic center of the society would move to the right religiously. It has always been an aspect of the American sociopolitical genius that it has been able to undergo such shifts without the turbulent disruptions characteristic of other societies. But it should be clear that arriving at such an outcome from the current *Kulturkampf* would require compromises on both sides.

The various resurgent religious communities would have to pay both an external and an internal price. Externally, in terms of their position in the wider society, they would have to forgo their counterpluralistic animus. In Richard Niebuhr's phrase, they would have to accept the status of being one denomination among many. Or, as John Murray Cuddihy has put it more recently, they would have to undergo the "ordeal of civility" by which American society has repeatedly domesticated ("civilized" in the literal sense) the aggressive bigotries of Europe. But the internal price would be heavy, too. Each religious community would have to accept the fact that its particular world view will not regain its old accepted position in the society. Absolute certainty in the area of religion is no longer attainable; the religious communities would have to live with the modern burdens of doubt. To pay *this* price is harder than to forgo the romantic dream of *reconquista*, because it touches on the innermost impulses of the religious consciousness. For several centuries, the struggle to maintain its accepted position of authority has been the great inner drama of Protestantism, the religious tradition that has borne the brunt of the corroding assault of modernity more than any other. While this must be disturbing to all newcomers into the pluralistic arena, the Protestant example may also be somewhat consoling. After all, Protestantism *has* managed to survive the ordeal, repeatedly showing unexpected signs of vitality, and it seems in no imminent danger of leaving the stage of history.

The reconstitution of these sheltering religious communities would require compromise on the part of the secular community as well, especially by the new knowledge class. The compromise on its part, however, would be much less than that of the religious communities themselves. The secular community would have to abandon its counterpluralistic tendencies and agree to allow all communities of meaning, including the religious ones, to create their own institutions without interference from an ideologically monopolistic state. This freedom must extend to the creation and maintenance of educational institutions, a practical consequence of the right to pass on a meaningful world to their children, a basic human right if there is any. In conceding such freedom to religious communities (which in the American case amounts to no more than returning to the original meaning of the First Amendment), the secular community would *ipso facto* come to understand itself as a denomination within a pluralistic society instead of some sort of state Shinto to which all citizens, including children, owe allegiance. Quite apart from a normative preference one may have for such an understanding, it is sociologically more valid, for secularity is precisely a "denomination" in social form if not in ideational content. If one agrees with Niebuhr's notion that in America not only sects become churches (a universal phenomenon) but churches become denominations, then one may say that it is time secularists recognize this.

Giving up monopolistic conspiracies means entering a market in the realm of ideas as well as economics, and it is by no means a pejorative statement that religion in America finds itself in a market situation. The statement simply brings into view the voluntary and competitive character of this situation. The state coerces no one into this or that religious community, and therefore each such community must inevitably compete with others for the allegiance and support of freely opting individuals. To be sure, such a situation allows all sorts of mediocrities and even charlatans to thrive in religion, as in every other area of culture. In this respect an uncoerced culture shares the disadvantages of an uncoerced polity; democracy too has been charged with fostering mediocrities and charlatans. This is why many who consider themselves noble souls despise both democracy and capitalism and the religious vulgarities both encourage. But if a religious market brings about theologically displeasing standardization and marginal differentiation, it also brings about a situation in which every reflective believer must return to the original motives for his or her beliefs, which cannot be found in an accepted social establishment. And that should be theologically pleasing.

Seen in this light, the contemporary situation of religion in America is full of contestations, some of which may well lead to new theological configurations. It is, of course, not possible to make sociological statements as to which current religious phenomena hold this promise; such statements will have to be made on the basis of individual theological or philosophical convictions and thus cannot be the result of sociological description. There is one statement, however, that can be made with reasonable objectivity: A rather surprising phenomenon in America today is the strong new presence of Asian religiosity, both in organized institutional forms (notably Buddhist and Hindu) and in more diffuse cultural influences (especially evident in California). Given present sociocultural trends, including intensified contact with Asian culture, it is likely that this phenomenon will continue to grow and may possibly have far-reaching repercussions for the future of American Christianity.

Sociology is hardly an exact science, and the foregoing reflections cannot lead to assured predictions. By the nature of the case, they must remain tentative. All the same, some informed guesses about the future are possible. Barring catastrophic developments, international or domestic (such as global war or economic disaster), the outlook for the future of religious pluralism in America is optimistic and somewhat less so for moral pluralism. Neither the crisis of religion nor that of secularity is likely to be resolved easily. It is not reasonable to expect a definitive victory for either secularization or countersecularization in the foreseeable future. Rather, the prospects are for a continuing uneasy coexistence of religion and secularity under the conditions of a pluralistic "market." There will be conflicts but also compromises, depending largely on the class and political dynamics rather than on movements in the realm of ideas. This scenario is neither inspiring nor terrifying, but it does contain a potential for interesting religious possibilities.

In contrast to religious pluralism, the problem of coexisting moral "denominations," though also shaped largely by class and political forces, poses a more serious challenge to the society as a whole. It is difficult to see how a society can survive without a basic moral consensus. Without such a foundation, a society would be constituted by a purely pragmatic "contract" between competing interest groups who could never trust each other to abide by the contractual arrangements, since even such minimal trust presupposes a moral consensus. Such a society could not demand any sacrifices from its members and, therefore, could not withstand any serious threat. It is thus plausible to assume that there are definite limits to the further development of moral pluralism. At some point, a new consensus on at least the basic issues of common social life will have to appear and be institutionalized. The boundaries of this consensus are yet to be determined. Within those boundaries, to be sure, a measure of moral pluralism will continue to be possible on issues consensually defined as private. It is likely that the continuing moral denominations will very largely coincide with the religious ones, since so much of morality is grounded in religion.

REFERENCE

[1] I wish to express my great appreciation for Mary Douglas's contribution to this volume, and her thoughtful and stimulating criticism of my work. She raised several important theoretical and methodological issues I hope to address in the future. To do so here, however, would break the framework of my paper for this volume, and so I have refrained.

MARY DOUGLAS

The Effects of Modernization on Religious Change

EVENTS HAVE TAKEN RELIGIOUS STUDIES BY SURPRISE. This set of university institutions devoted to understanding religion without the constraints of the divinity school has generally included religious change in its subject matter. No one, however, foresaw the recent revivals of traditional religious forms. According to an extensive literature, religious change in modern times happens in only two ways—the falling off of worship in traditional Christian churches, and the appearance of new cults, not expected to endure. No one credited the traditional religions with enough vitality to inspire large-scale political revolt. The main direction of empirical inquiry was concerned with the inception, growth, and decline of small communities and their relations to the outside society,[1] and was matched by an elaborate finesse in distinguishing the terms *sect, cult,* and *movement.* Thus no one foretold the resurgence of Islam. Its well-known expansion in Africa was not expected to presage anything for its strength in modern Arabia—but why not? Habituated as we are to Catholic bishops supporting reactionary forces in South America, who was ready to interpret their radical politics in other parts of that continent? The civil war conducted in Lebanon in the rival names of Catholicism and Islam was not on the syllabus of courses on religious change, any more than was the terrorism always threatening to turn the strife of Irish Catholics and Protestants into civil war. Perhaps these bloody events have been classified as religious continuation rather than change, or perhaps religious studies were too polite to talk about the bad religious things happening abroad. But the explicitly Catholic uprising in Poland, which evokes deep Western admiration, was as unpredicted as the rise of the fundamentalist churches in America.

Religious studies were taken unawares because of the rigid structure of their assumptions. Their eyes were glued to those conditions of modern life identified by Weber as antipathetic to religion. Perhaps, also, their inclinations misled them in ways that apply to the social sciences more generally. If the renewal of right-wing political values in the West surprised all political scientists, it is natural that those who least welcomed it would have been the most surprised. Similarly, certain religious forms might have a natural appeal to intellectuals if they are going to be religious at all. People whose occupations do not require submission to authority or conformity to outward forms, and who are paid to ask searching questions and to take an independent stance, are likely to be more drawn to a personal style of religious worship than to a publicly conforming one. Their own religious preferences could conceivably dim their perception of what other people like.

Such an explanation of a theoretical weakness is pertinent here, since one of the shortcomings of all the social sciences has been the neglect of beliefs and values, and the failure to establish a critical methodology for examining cultural bias. In the sociology of science, it is widely accepted that the choice and framing of problems and the judgment on procedures for inquiry are influenced by social concerns. Some considerable sophistication on the effect of such choices and judgments could be expected in a field such as religious studies, where, after all, ideas and values are the very subject matter. But, alas, the social critique of all ideas, which Louis Dupré in an exemplary essay on culture sees as one of the main tasks of twentieth century sociology,[2] has been applied only spottily to the effects of modernization on religion. A caricature of the modern consciousness has credibility only if the contrasting caricature of premoderns is accepted. The latter are presented as custom-bound: so Malinowski wrote in vain,[3] as having fewer sexual choices and stricter sexual morality; so Mead wrote in vain,[4] as having a comfortable, nonmoralizing, nonconfrontational relation with their gods; so all the social anthropologists wrote in vain. It is tempting to interpret the myopia in sociological studies as a failure of modernization that could have been avoided if certain anthropological methods of inquiry had been adopted.

Three assumptions that dominate contemporary religious studies, and that seem most questionable to me, tend to protect the subject from the probing of sociological criticism and from uncomfortable comparisons. The most fundamental of these assumptions writes into the definition of the subject the notion that religion is good for the human psyche. To assume that religion has integrative functions or is otherwise conducive to the good life makes immediate sense to those who start from the same assumption. However, the usefulness of a definition depends on the use to which it is to be put. Clearly this definition leaves out a lot of religious behavior that is widely regarded as emotionally restrictive, bigoted, fanatical, or psychotic. Thus the first question is why the subject should be so selectively defined.

The second of these assumptions is that moderns are utterly different from everyone else because of modernization. I believe this view to be highly subjective. Every tribe that we study believes in its own uniqueness. No one doubts that our modernity follows from a unique development of technology, science, and bureaucracy. What is more dubious is the general nineteenth century presumption that modernity adversely affects religion by taking the wonder and mystery out of the universe—as if religion depends more on the physical environment than on the quality of social relations. This general demystification is supposed to have reduced the credibility of old, traditional forms of religion that once sacralized social institutions and allowed them to partake of divine mystery. These two assumptions have led scholarship to focus on secularization. Since religion is defined as having integrative value for the personality, our present psychological troubles can then be attributed to the lack of religion, an analysis that leads to the anxious question whether any religious belief is possible for modern man. Fortunately, an alternative form of religious life is available that does not try to sacralize social institutions and is not inhibited by modernization. In the wake of this tradition, distinguished scholars have recommended the cultivation of spiritual awareness in the interior self as the general cure for the ills of modern disbelief. One trouble with this line of argument is that a hidden theological point of view is offered under the guise of independent social analysis, a point I will return to later.

The third assumption is the idea that culture is always capable of being somehow autonomous and is becoming so increasingly in modern times. Again the anthropologist recognizes a tribal style of thinking that claims autonomy for its own world view. Those who write on religious studies believe that a historic schism between moderns and the rest of the world allows moderns to claim immunity from the social influences that help to interpret the shared beliefs of other civilizations: because of our cultural autonomy those sociological analyses do not apply to us. Thus the strong cutting edge of sociological criticism is deflected. These three assumptions taken together seem to absolve the scholars from any duty to promote field studies of the full range and variety of religious experience, and allow them to avoid developing systematic frames of comparison. In general, religious studies start with the conviction that there is no clear, researchable relation between beliefs and social influences. This belief got them off on the wrong foot, and they were caught on the hop.

When bias is hidden to themselves, academics can blithely expound beliefs that are not independent of social influences, even while proclaiming a general disjunction between culture and society. To illustrate this point I take Peter Berger's powerful description of two religious visions, the double historical development they represent, and his recommendation that, one having become impossible, the other be sought. He says that for millennia of human history the cosmos was treated as divine in its own right;[5] man enjoyed a comfortable, nonconfrontational experience of religion in which every point of the compass and every physical, emotional, and social experience was sanctified. The East Asian tradition is developed continuously from this experience, and leads to interior transcendence. The West Asian tradition is represented as a break in this accumulated human experience: in the West, man has had to confront God as a person and take on the enduring moral responsibilities of one person dealing with another. The two prototypes of religious experience have their typical forms of mysticism. In the first, individual personality is lost or irrelevant; in the other, it is affirmed and enhanced. Each tradition is inhospitable, hostile, or contemptuous of the mystical teachings of the other.

In the West Asian tradition, the moralizing encounter with God's grandeur and separateness has more sharply individuated the human person, entailing a rupture between man and cosmos. Berger now calls for a theological contestation between the vision of Jerusalem and that of Benares, where

> the divine does not confront man from the outside but is to be sought within himself as the divine ground of his own being and that of the cosmos. The divine here is metapersonal and beyond all attributes, including those of will and speech. Once the divine ground of being is grasped, both men and cosmos pale into insignificance or even illusiveness. Individuality is not sharpened but absorbed and both history and morality are radically relativized.[6]

While admiring the subtlety and profound insight of this characterization of two metaphysical traditions, one looks around for some way of relating it to Berger's earlier work, especially his insistence that beliefs are held because and insofar as they can be legitimated within a general structure of plausibility for the society that the believers have together constructed.[7] It seems likely, from an anthropological perspective, that the former, the West Asian moralizing, juridical concept of God's relations with man, is plausible wherever people are concerned to pin responsibility on each other, especially for founding families, businesses, and empires, while the second is plausible for defending a social choice of withdrawal. That is, one seems plausible for conquering the world, the other for renouncing it. Being neither a Buddhist nor a Hindu scholar, my questions as to how deeply this particular Eastern vision penetrates the various layers of social and political life, or how much it belongs to the specialized thinking of theologians. must be shelved. I do not see how Berger, who has said so much about compatibility between attitudes (even using the expression "elective affinity"),[8] can recommend to modern Western culture a cosmology that was notoriously uncongenial to scientific inquiry[9]—or at least I can see how he might *wish* to recommend it, but not how he can do it plausibly. The issue here, however, is that the wise men missed what was happening in the West because they were gazing toward the East.

But there is another, cruder contrast of theological perspectives that cuts across Berger's grand historico-geographical divide: to distinguish doctrines of corporate personality—doctrines that consecrate the community and elevate its ideal unity and ritual forms to the status of efficacious sacraments for all members—from doctrines of the transcendental self. The first has the aim of consecrating society; the second encourages the believer to withdraw from society. Robert Bellah puts it vividly: "In India we find perhaps the most radical of all versions of world rejection, culminating in the great image of Buddha, that the world is a burning house and that man's most urgent need is to escape from it."[10] Anyone who believes that modernization has made the consecration of society impossible to achieve may perceive the doctrine of the transcendental self as the residual option. This is evidently Berger's view.

Notice, however, the supporting religious ideas that tend to cluster consistently around each doctrinal choice. The currently less favored mystic incorporation implies more public celebration, more expressive rituals, more emphasis on instituted sacramental channels. It attracts supporting theories of mutual interdependence, and tends to transform the spiritual realm into a model of what the consecrated society would be like. Furthermore, according to this doctrine in its highly developed forms, individuals should not all expect to play the same roles: in an organic system the head and the hands perform different functions. Within this doctrinal form there is often the idea that great sanctity is exceptional. Yet thanks to the mystical incorporation of individuals, the sharing of grace evens up the inequities between people or over time, the spiritually well-endowed providing a welfare fund from which benefits flow to the rest. More honor for public formality allows less pressure on personal sanctity, more tolerance for compromise, and lower levels of spiritual aspiration. By contrast, the doctrines of self-transcendence are more egalitarian, more individualist, and more optimistic about the human potential for sustaining great spiritual achievement. It seems obvious that the latter religious trend, however well it thrives in the East, also matches the favored principles of an achieving society organized in a democracy dedicated to the freedom and equality of individuals.

A modern thinker who recommends the theological choice that replicates his dominant political culture can be suspected of bias: all the more implausible any claim from that quarter for the independence of religious ideas from surrounding social influences. The tradition in religious sociology that I am noting indulges its bias against public religion. It vigorously rejects sociological determinism, but does not enjoy the intellectual freedom that strict rules of comparison would promote.

Uncritical nostalgia for past ages of faith being out of place in religious studies, let us note at once that there is no good evidence that a high level of spirituality has generally been reached by the mass of mankind in past times, and none at all that their emotional and intellectual lives were necessarily well integrated by religion. Some people have been religious in a commercial way, buying and selling occult powers. Sometimes they withdrew into the desert. Sometimes they focused their religious energy on celebration of the social calendar, sometimes on obtaining states of trance. Given all this variety of religious life in our past, when we also recall that charlatanism, skepticism, and forsaken churches are also part of our heritage, we dare to question the whole modernization argument. Our modernity has not yet been analyzed in a way that explains religious decays and renewal.

Not being committed to supposing that people are always better off with religion, anthropology has a wider perspective. Anthropology was founded in a mood of rationalism in which scholars rejoiced in intellectual liberty and freedom from arbitrary ceremonial and moral constraints. Religion as such was not thought necessarily to be good for people, and *supernatural* was no more a good word than was *taboo*. If they were not rationalists, likely as not anthropologists had been bred in a Christian missionary tradition that deplored heathen darkness. Consequently, with no other axe to grind but the need to establish a comparative field, anthropologists tried to start with as unloaded a definition of religion as possible. I am not especially fond of the one based on belief in spiritual beings,[11] but at least it defines a field without begging any questions about the integrative power—moral, intellectual, or social—of religion. Nor does it teach that modern times show a decline from ancient standards of piety. Indeed, reflection shows that the evidence for old-time sanctity comes from suspect sources such as hagiography, panegyrics, and sermons. If we were to read even that biased evidence more critically, we would notice the professionals upbraiding the mass of ordinary people for lack of faith, as if the gift of which, we are told, modernity has deprived us was always rather the exception. Just as fundamental, there can be no evidence that there is more unhappiness and mental disturbance now than in those famous ages of faith. How can anyone possibly say? The evidence is weak, the arguments weaker. In many of the writings of religious sociology we cannot but recognize the sermons of our childhood. The idea that humans are beings who need religion belongs to creation mythology. To say that only religion heals the sick soul is traditional evangelism. The idea that modernization is bad for religion echoes preaching that directly opposes worldliness to salvation. To insist that culture is autonomous is saying that the spirit moveth where it listeth. To have no interest in the social mechanisms by which faith is roused and sustained is to be faithful to the

model of pentecostal inspiration. It is proper to use empirical evidence only as illustrative material when the object of the discourse is spiritual counseling. None of this helps to understand better the relation of beliefs to society, yet this is the very problem at issue for understanding religious change.

The great religious renewals of modern times have not been of the expectedly appropriate kind that strengthens the transcendent sense of the interior self. On the contrary, modernization turns out to be quite compatible with the corporate personality doctrines that sacralize life in external ritual forms of celebration, compatible even with all the narrowness of spirit and intellectual closure thought to be maladaptive in modern life.[12] The old compensatory-psychological models used to assume that if the drive to get worldly satisfactions is checked, it will come out in the form of religion: thus was explained the prevalence of religious belief among the lower classes. But this modern religious behavior cannot be swept under the theoretical carpet again by classing all the new devout as marginal categories or relatively deprived.[13] The hydraulic model of religious expression having lost its plausibility, we can learn to be wary of this new version, which says that if the road to Jerusalem is blocked, religious feeling will take the road to Benares.

The central argument about a crisis of religion due to modernization rests on the chosen definition of religion. A definition laden with good values supports the idea that religion is good for you; since modernization is bad for religion, we are in an unprecedented cultural crisis. The most exalted definition starts with subjective experience of the sacred. This follows a prestigious line of Lutheran theology leading to studies in phenomenology. Naturally, the emphasis on subjectivity rules many empiricist questions out of court. This kind of discourse tends to use examples from the world selectively, illustratively, and often wittily for an interpretative and analytic exercise. The insights gained from this tradition, to which Paul Ricoeur is an outstanding contributor, are most brilliantly displayed in philosophy. It certainly does not fit comfortably to the empirical and systematically descriptive tradition of anthropology.

At this point we need to examine various definitions of religion. Peter Berger starts from phenomenology: "Empirically speaking, what is commonly called religion involves an aggregation of human attitudes, beliefs and actions in the face of two types of experience—the experience of the supernatural and the experience of the sacred."[14] Berger distinguishes the sacred as another kind of reality, one that overlaps with the supernatural and carries redemptive significance. The sacred affirms the individual at the center of his being and integrates him within the order of the cosmos. Dupré, well versed in comparative religion, is able to dismiss this approach briskly, using ethnographic evidence and the well-known epistemological difficulties of the concept of the sacred.[15] Like Berger, he recognizes that a sense of the sacred may or may not be present with a recognition of transcendent reality, but he is more ready to take the rough with the smooth in the concept of transcendence, witchcraft and angels, the fairy ring with the burning bush. His own alternative definition of religion drops out the difficult notion of the sacred and concentrates on "a commitment to the transcendent as to *another* reality."[16] Because it starts from contrasted realities—that is, from evidence that can be observed in behavioral and linguistic activity—transcendence makes a more satisfactory basis for talking about religion comparatively than does a subjective feeling. One can ask about kinds and degrees of transcendence, and map the way it overlaps with ordinary reality in different cultures or between different believers. In itself this definition is less value-laden, but Dupré adds that transcendence entails integration: for him, the integrating synthesis of values is essential to the religious attitude. Thus his definition also prepares the argument for the crisis of an unbelieving world.

Daniel Bell's definition of religion rests on coherence rather than integration. He starts by defining culture as modalities of response to core existential problems, questions about life, death, obligation, and love. Within that category, religion is a set of coherent answers to the universal existential problems of mankind. Its answers may be codified into a creed and celebrated with rites, and these may be established in institutions. The general effect of religion is to create coherence in experience and emotional bonds between those who adhere to the credal form.[17] Bell's emphasis on questions and answers gives this approach to religion an intellectualist bias, one that fits an old tradition in anthropology that has produced interesting comparisons between the entities postulated in scientific theorizing and religious explanations.[18] By emphasizing coherence and answers, however, Bell's definition predicates the special problems of integration faced in a secular culture. Thus this argument is also something of a closed circle.

Whenever religion is defined as integrative and, by implication, as providing something needed by humans, inquiry has cut off from its view the possibility of the integration being overnarrow, unbalanced, distorting, and so on. To stress the integrative function of religion fits the Weberian teaching that modern man suffers from lack of integrating beliefs. The scholars urbanely acknowledge the crowd of exceptions to any particular thesis. Berger admits that "for every Nietzsche or Dostoyevsky there are a thousand more or less well-adjusted agnostics, more or less *Angst*-ridden atheists."[19] But these disclaimers are not intended to change the arguments that proceed as if it were proved that mankind always needs the kind of integration provided by religion. The reports of anthropologists are selectively cited in support. But since there is no attempt at systematic evaluation or classification of these reports, the evidence is worth a mere wave of the hand, a salute to a body of material that supports a thesis too well attested to need further demonstration.

It seems important to challenge the modernization thesis just here by insisting that in many times and places men seem to have got on very well without being integrated by religion, unless that word is being used so broadly as to sap meaning. A theodicy in the strict sense explains the experience of suffering, evil, and death in terms of religious legitimations.[20] Theodicy bestows meaning on life. When I am referred back to Berger's adaptation of Weber's idea of theodicy, I am bound to admit that it is general enough to apply to most people. Following Durkheim's equation of religious feeling with acceptance of society's authority, this extended concept of religion can be found in the most unreligious of explanations, so long as they locate the individual's life in an all-embracing fabric of meanings. Berger would recognize a theodicy whenever the individual is able to transcend himself by accepting and internalizing the requirements of society. The power of social forms achieves for the individual the transcendence that is at the center of all definitions of religion. On this approach, when Berger says religion is good for you, he means commitment to society is good for you, or again that it is good to be integrated.

Berger further recognizes that theodicies differ in the degree of rational coherence and consistency in their explanations.[21] This suggests that a typology based on degrees of rationality would be very interesting. Unfortunately, Berger puts this project aside: "Needless to say, no attempt will be made to elaborate an exhaustive typology."[22] If the attempt were to be made, he would find that we have to change the definition of religion so that it is unable to bear inferences about integrating the personality. To carry on usefully any conversation that makes sense about whether religion is good for you, one set of measures would need to be carefully constructed for judging the rational coherence of a theodicy and another set for locating and assessing the kinds of social relations for which the theodicy is used. If Berger were to argue that the theodicy of modern American society invokes two principles for explaining misfortune, one psychological and one political, anyone would recognize this part of our social environment. But surely it is located only in a very small privileged elite. Were I to counter by contending that a larger part of American society explains fortune and misfortune in terms of someone's lucky number coming up, Berger, if he admitted that it is a widespread form of explanation, would have to get down to minute detail about whether it is rationally coherent enough to count as a theodicy, as well as assessing who actually appeals to it. Anthropologists largely support Weber's idea that explanations of misfortune are the best key to cultural bias.[23] But ultimate explanations (or theodicies) are closely related to the structure of social relations, and given the variety of these, the claim that all theodicies have an integrating effect on the personality will be difficult to prove.

So much for a loaded definition that does not sharpen problems or clarify debate. I now turn to dispute the alleged effects of modernization on religious belief. With different emphases here and there, modernization is generally held to have quenched the sources of religious feeling and undermined religious authority by producing four main effects. The first is the prestige and authority of science, which is supposed to have reduced the explanatory appeal of religion. Even if we did not ourselves know the answers, we moderns have it as an article of faith that somewhere there are, or could be, adequate scientific explanations for anything that puzzles us. This trust in science is held to be antithetical to religious faith. In consequence of the continuing development of technology and the resulting perturbation of social institutions, we moderns are supposed to enjoy more freedom of choice. Thus the second effect is that, since our lives do not unroll according to the dictates of custom, religious regulations are subject to challenge. Third is the effects of bureaucracy. And the fourth is that we are so separated from direct dependence on nature that our experience of it is too artificial to sustain religious inspiration.

Let us start with the effects of science and technology, go on to what bureaucracy does to our social experience, and then consider whether our distance from nature inhibits religious faith, and end with what is meant by saying that moderns enjoy more freedom of individual choice. There is a case for arguing that the various effects of modernization have at this point cancelled each other out, so that we are now actually closer in important respects to the general experience of preindustrial mankind. This may sound farfetched. It is less perverse to argue that these are the wrong modern influences for explaining contemporary religious behavior. It is true that the authority of science has undermined religious authority whenever religion made rash claims for revelation. But all that dust has mostly cleared away, and the demarcation has been clarified. Even in Arkansas, where "scientific creationism" is taught side-by-side with the theory of evolution, it is recognized that religious and scientific explanations mostly apply to very different kinds of problems. The collective solidarity of scientists has weakened since the 1950s, and we observe scientists quarreling more publicly than ever before. Without the debate on religious versus scientific authority, our confidence in esoteric knowledge not personally revealed to ourselves plausibly brings us closer to the civilizations of Africa and New Guinea, not further away. It is not easy to see why their experience of high specialism in knowledge corresponds so little to our lay experience that there is a big gulf between modern consciousness and all others because of science. Substantially, they rely on experts and we rely on experts. It is wrong to assume that the mysteries unveiled to initiates in primitive culture are not so much instructions and statements about the workings of the universe as ethical and spiritual teachings. Their religious bias is often not very pronounced. If we want to base religion on the subjective sense of awe and mystery, we can hardly deny that the more modern science reveals, the more awe-inspiring (and so presumably sympathetic to religion) the universe appears. The argument that modern science is incompatible with religion is a nineteenth century relic that depends on religion being set up as an alternative authority to science. Anyone who wants to define religion as an experience having its source in subjective feeling would be perverse to promote an argument based on defining religion as providing explanations about physical existence. What was true in the nineteenth century, when traditionalism made religion its cause, is not a part of modernism as constituted now.

As to the extraordinary growth of bureaucracy in our day, I find it difficult to accept that it has any negative effect on religious belief. The fact is undeniable that bureaucracy depersonalizes our relations with our fellow human beings. No one would deny that it reduces us to ciphers. But bureaucracy works at many levels. At one extreme it deals with us in our thousands and millions. At this level it is not reducing our intimacy with one another. We never could have known those millions personally, with or without bureaucracy. When we march in columns through the vision of those responsible for our lives as so many statistics, we are not being denied a warm human contact with one another that we might otherwise enjoy. Bureaucracy tries to treat us all the same: it universalizes the rules and applies them impersonally. The other extreme is the interface between the abstract rule and its application. Here it separates us from one another and denies human feeling. Although it is clear that bureaucratization at this level, by restricting the perception of humanity, creates problems of identity, it is not obvious why this should be counterproductive for religion. Crises of identity are at the origin of every saint's biography.[24] Insofar as bureaucracy reduces the range of emotional experience, it makes our lives more like those prescriptive social systems of premodern times where all feelings are institutionally channeled and individual variation controlled. Insofar as bureaucracy reduces the number of people each of us can expect to know as a human being, and increases the number of impersonal forces with which we, with our few human friends, have to contend, it counteracts the effects of scale. The more modern bureaucracy grows, the more we hear it being compared to ancient Byzantium or the Vatican of the fifteenth century. Any good description of bureaucracy brings modern society closer to the stereotype of those small, closely regulated traditional societies that are popularly thought to be so congenial to religious belief. The fact that the bureaucracy is secular is the most important thing about it in this context, not its inherent effects, nor even its extent.

The argument about nature is largely sentimental. It is true that we have little direct experience of it nowadays. The idea that being without fresh air or clear spring water weakens our capacity for religion may stem from the definition of religion as arising in a mystic experience of wonder and awe, but it is a mistake that calls for criticism. First, let us distinguish three ways of thinking about nature. The most concrete is in reference to natural objects—trees, mountains, streams. Slightly more abstract is reference to elemental forces, wind, tides, seasons. Speaking at an altogether more abstract level, nature contrasts with culture; nature is that part of the cosmos that humans do not fabricate, that humans can learn about but cannot change. Only at this more abstract level can there be any sense in saying that moderns have a different experience of nature that might affect their disposition to religious belief. Unless Lévi-Strauss has also written in vain,[25] no one will argue that premoderns do not make this abstract distinction between nature and culture. Nature works by inexorable laws beyond human control. Nature is impersonal. No amount of cajolery or threats can change the conditions of nature. However much technology shifts the locus of control, so that now this or now that gets into culture or counts as nature, the important point is that the boundary itself is an artifact of culture that reflects the limits of human control. When Bell says that in the postindustrial order "men live more and more outside nature," he is thinking of mountains and trees, and it is difficult to see what use he can make of this in an argument about religion in modern times. When he says that "for most of the thousands of years of human existence, life has been a game against nature, . . . to find shelter from the elements, to ride the waters and the wind, to wrest food and sustenance from the soil," he is thinking of the second level of abstraction, elemental forces. It is true, as he says, that "the industrial revolution was, at bottom, an effort to substitute a technical order for the natural order."[26] But I query whether the arrival of a new technical order is fundamental in these particular ways for the creation of modern consciousness. For the contrast between nature and culture always depends on culture and the state of society. Once entered into the order of life, railways and steamships, with their schedules as fixed as the tides, readily transfer to the humanly nonnegotiable side of the boundary. This is especially so for the mass of the population who do not see themselves as getting the scheduling adjusted to suit their convenience. Presumably, the sense of isolation and helplessness before one set of impersonal forces has the same effect as before another set, whether before tides and seasons or before welfare rules and parking regulations. Insofar as the experience of modern bureaucracy is an experience of ponderous regularities and inescapable laws, it qualifies fairly to replace the earlier experience of nature. Its ways are impersonal, it is as impervious of entreaty as the sky, unresponsive to bribes. I would even argue that any sense of being constrained by bureaucracy could take modern man closer to, and not further from, premoderns.

In short, the growth of science and the growth of bureaucracy between them counteract the argument that our distance from nature puts distance between moderns and religious believers of other times. For the sense of wonder in nature is deepened by the discoveries of science, and the sense of a game against nature to wrest a living from impersonal forces is still provided by bureaucracy.

The strangest conceit of all is that modernization has endowed us with greater freedom of choice than our parents. The evidence for greater freedom of individual choice, apart from sexual matters, has to be carefully dissected. The idea is a central liberal axiom upon which important institutional structures rest. Moderns certainly love to tell one another that they have free choice. We tell those who fail exams or miss promotion that they could have chosen to work harder. Thus we assert that in a free country, success and failure are largely self-chosen. Undoubtedly, some of us have more free choice than others. Social constraints limit the choice of a career in the liberal professions. The very attractive plausibility that the idea of wide-open options has for the upper classes in a supposed meritocracy should make it suspect.[27] Psychologists have long liked to believe that we moderns work out our intellectual problems by systematic inference, while primitive thought and behavior run in institutionalized grooves. This draws on an established stereotype of primitive society that should be contested. Apart from being flattering to ourselves, the ascription saves the psychologists the work of thinking out a basis for comparative studies of cultural effects on cognition.

It is difficult to turn the idea of increased choice into anything that can be closely compared. There could be a wider range of trivial choices and a smaller range of weighty ones, or the other way around. If the choices we have are mostly of the bazaar kind, small, similar items purveyed at similar prices—like the choice between numerous highly standardized programs on cable television—the case for our enjoying increased options is not made. Quite the contrary, it has to be reconciled with a daily lament against the dull uniformity of our lives—the same menus, the same clothes, the same sports, and the same homes. Where is free choice? Our Viking ancestors had much more of it, free to spend a few years in Greenland, nip back to Scandinavia to help a political ally, or join a raid on Britain.[28]

The arguments for the unique effects of modernization on consciousness do as little to explain modern secularity as to explain modern religion. It would not be possible to talk so loosely about beliefs and values, and the kinds of influences they respond to, were it not for the idea, so widely accepted, that culture is autonomous. By implication, evidence and argument are not needed to justify opinions that can only be speculations on culture, since culture partakes of the free life of the spirit whose workings are unconstrained and mysterious. When a scholar proclaims that nature has been demystified by modernization, I know that I am going to witness some mystification of culture. The only full sense of cultural autonomy used in anthropology applies when a domain of expressive behavior has been isolated for analysis. Then the changes within a medium of expression—say, myth or dance—are treated in a restricted context that is assumed to be independent of society. In another sense, anthropologists treat culture as autonomous when autonomy means more than independence, when it means initiative to move the society. The interconnection of ideas and values with social relations is not denied. The question is: Wherein lies the initiative for change? This sense of autonomy qualifies the Marxist notion of a dependent, epiphenomenal culture, strictly determined by the economic base. It starts from the potency of ideas for driving the rest of the system.

In a third sense, anthropologists habitually interpret changes in beliefs and values by reference to changes in the social institutions and ecological systems. This is the sense that predominates when a fieldworker is reporting on cultural change. If a reported shift in beliefs and values cannot be linked plausibly to changed institutional structures and to the material base, there will be skepticism and sharp criticism. A large experience of comparative ethnography presses the anthropologist who does not intend to lean toward historical materialism to find a way of describing the interconnection without selling out to total mystification. A simple disciplinary formula that helps to keep the lines straight is to treat cultural categories as the cognitive containers in which social interests are defined and classified, argued, negotiated, and fought out. Following this rule, there is no way in which culture and society can part company, nor any way in which one can be said to dominate the other. This discipline forces discussion of culture to clarify *who* in the society is alleged to hold a particular idea or value, *who* in the society rejects it. From this disciplinary standpoint it becomes impossible to argue that one of the containing categories can take leave of its contents or vice versa. The disciplinary constraint raises subtle conceptual problems, and the discussion of symbolism and classification necessarily becomes technical and arcane. Those issues, however, cannot be avoided without falling into superficiality.

It would be an advance to clear thinking if scholars who are not going to use the license implied by the principle of cultural autonomy would refrain from saluting it. It is out of character for Peter Berger (in the light of his solid work toward the contrary view) to state the case, as he does in the following passage on Weber's conception of reciprocity between institutional processes and processes on the level of consciousness:

> Institutions, once established, develop a dynamic of their own and, in turn, have effects of their own on the level of consciousness. These effects are capable of autonomous development. Thus both institutional processes and processes on the level of consciousness are capable of developing autonomously, sometimes for considerable periods of time. . . . institutional carriers "discard" their erstwhile "baggage" of packages of consciousness. Conversely the latter can "go off on their own" and leave behind the institutional contexts to which they were originally linked.[29]

To assert that packages of consciousness can cut loose from any institutional anchorage and float off independently sounds very like writing a permit for one's own ideas about consciousness to fly high without empirical reference. Yet Berger is too clever to try to push this idea to its limits. The sociological underpinning of his 1973 analysis is strict and scrutinizable. He only makes use of the freedom in 1979 when he recommends that Christian theologians based in the West should consider the value to their modern flocks of the mystical forms in Indian religions.[30] Here he is writing *for* religion rather than about it. It is a very different exercise, and totally legitimate, to conclude a theological book by advising believers to remain open to all the possibilities of a future that lies in God's hands.

Let me choose Daniel Bell as the writer who has tried most systematically to supply a sociological argument for the disjunction between culture and society. In *The Coming of Post Industrial Society*[31] and *The Cultural Contradictions of Capitalism* he has developed an approach on which we can test the strength of the disciplinary formula I am proposing. He is not referring to any temporary dislocation due to modernization, but claims that all societies are at most times radically disjunctive. According to Bell, it is in the nature of both the social system and the cultural system to display different patterns of change. Everything depends, of course, on his idea of culture as expressive and symbolizing, compared with the social system, where, he says, the determinate principle is efficiency:

> If something is cheaper, more productive, provides greater extraction of energy or less loss, subject to cost, we use it. This is because the techno-economic realm is primarily instrumental. But there is no such determinate principle of change in culture. Boulez does not replace Bach or serial music the fugue. Where cultures are rooted strongly in tradition, one does not have repetition but the imminent development of stylistic forms and the absorption or rejection of new experiences as tested against the moral truths of the culture. Where cultures are syncretistic, as we find in the Hellenistic and Roman worlds and now in the contemporary world, strange needs and exotic modes jostle in the bazaars of culture, and individuals feel free to choose those varied combinations which define their self-created identities or life-styles.[32]

According to Bell, the present case of religion is to be explained by two separate causal chains, the one (institutional) leading to secularization, and the other (cultural) leading to profanation. First, let us adopt his excellent definition of secularization. It means disengagement of religion from the public sphere, from political life and from aesthetic life, "the retreat to a private world where religions have authority only over their followers and not over any other section of the polity or society."[33] The same word can be applied to the disengagement of art from public authority, as we shall see. Secularization has been caused by the trend to differentiation of institutional authority, a working out of the division of labor from industry to bureaucracy and politics. On the other hand, profanation, a result of a quite separate chain of causes, means disenchantment in the realm of belief and culture. Independent processes have produced the profane modernity whose features Bell identifies as antinomianism, anti-

institutionalism, moral laxity, endless pleasure-seeking, and the democratization of the erotic. He gives a very sour picture of modern culture.

Unfortunately for Bell's argument about the autonomy of culture, he
includes moral values and attitudes to life, death, and obligation. Music and
painting can be appropriately treated as symbolic modes, but in religious
studies, we are inevitably interested in whatever it is that the modes of
expression are being used to express.

As I have said, the concept of cultural autonomy varies according to which
aspects of culture call for our attention. Studying a grammar does not tell you
what stories the language is being used to narrate. If we intend to focus on
expressive modes that could properly be called autonomous, we must suspend
for the time any interest we may have in the moral or other motives of the
people who are employing the expressive symbolizing system. Referring to a
particular system of signs, and knowing all the possible transformations within
the system, Bell can develop a hypothesis about a human drive for innovation;
with these simple means he can construct a plausible swinging pendulum model
of cultural change, somewhat on the lines proposed by Kroeber.[34] Each new
cultural phase could be explained by exhaustion of possibilities in the previous
pattern.[35] Swings of the pendulum are the mechanism Bell invokes to explain
cultural change. But, alas for plausibility, he uses it to explain changes, not in
modality of expression, such as the change from Bach to Boulez, but in moral
values. Exhaustion, retreat, and reaction are the dynamics of the cultural
changes that Bell predicts will usher in new religious forms in the West: the
exhaustion of modernism and the emptiness of contemporary culture have
mitigated the harsh critical pressures from skeptical liberals, so that transcendentalist proposals are less likely to be derided. Redemptive religious doctrines
will have an appeal, because of the retreat from the excesses of modernity. He
also heralds a return to mystical thought as a reaction against the drab,
demystified world of modernism.[36] This kind of reasoning would work better if
mystical values, redemption, and transcendentalist theories were just modalities
of expression. It loses all cogency when applied to matters of morality and
metaphysics. Bell never makes sense of his claim that ideas about moral
obligation follow along one path of change, while institutions follow another.

Bell's central concept of the analysis of postindustrial society is that of axial
structure, not a causal system, but a central organizing frame and energizing
principle. For Tocqueville's view of the *ancien régime*, the axial structure was the
centralization of administration in the hands of the state. For his *Democracy in
America*, the axial principle was equality. Max Weber used the process of
rationalization as the axial principle for understanding the transformation of the
West from a traditional to a modern society. Marx used the production of
commodities as the axial principles of capitalism, and the business firm as its
axial structure. Bell divides any society into three parts: the social structure
(comprising economy, technology, and occupational system), the polity (regu-
lating the distribution of power), the culture (realm of expressive symbolism
and meanings), with each part ruled by a different axial principle. In modern
times the social structure is ruled by the principle of economizing; the polity, by
the principle of participation; and the culture, by the desire for fulfillment and
enhancement of the self. He emphasizes that the gaps between these disjoined

principles will widen. This assumption is declared in *The Coming of Post Industrial Society* but never explained beyond a few reiterative remarks in a Coda. He does, however, rely on it to justify treating culture quite separately in *The Cultural Contradictions of Capitalism.*

Whereas Tocqueville, Weber, and Marx could present whole periods under one single axial principle, Bell thinks he needs three for presenting the modern situation. This is his basis for declaring culture to be autonomous. It would run against his thesis to describe postindustrial society as governed by a single axial principle. Yet this is what Bell actually does, and very effectively. He starts from the change from a goods-producing to a service economy, with its concomitant change in occupational distribution, then to the new preeminence of the professional and technical class. The new axial principle is the centrality of theoretical knowledge as the source of innovation and policy formation;[37] the corresponding axial structure is organization around knowledge for the purpose of social control. As Bell develops, chapter by chapter, the remarkable synthesis of the new occupational structure, the new intellectual technology, and the new modes of access to political power, the initial project of explaining the three disjoined subsystems, each with its own axial principles, each moving farther away from the rest, is silently dropped. Cultural autonomy turns out to be quite irrelevant to the main thesis. The analysis, however, is so careful, that when the idea of cultural autonomy is reasserted (in "The Return of the Sacred?"), the natural place to look for refuting evidence is in *The Coming of Post Industrial Society*. To demonstrate his ideas about cultural autonomy, the main elements of modern culture should not in any way be explainable by the chain of events in the economic and political order. Yet when we examine the features of modern culture that he regards as characteristic, the whole case falls down.

Let us consider the alleged relaxation of moral standards in his argument that private morality is a part of culture that diverges from the principles governing the economy and polity. Imposed categories of analysis account for the confusion here between Protestant rationalizing ethics in business and family life. The most die-hard proponent of cultural autonomy would hardly maintain that sex has nothing to do with marriage and the family, or that these are independent of economic and social factors. Bell gives an excellent account of how changes in the economy and technology replaced inherited property with education as the necessary route of access to power.[38] As a supremely individual asset, education frees the individual from dependence on family control. The more that the axial principle of organization around knowledge dominates the politico-economic system, the more it lifts social pressure from the family unit. Another way of saying this is that the new organization of society no longer requires sexuality to be controlled. Moreover, when the whole economy moves toward services, it moves away from the sexual division of labor. When women can become bankers and scientists and enter the learned professions, the sexual division of labor is no longer the dominant metaphor for all classifications and meanings. Hence, as Bourdieu has pointed out, homosexuality tends to be more tolerated with increase in educational status.[39] Sexual morality has indeed relaxed, but the changed standards are actually entailed by the axial shift to control of power through knowledge. It is hardly necessary to say that a shift in moral focus does not imply a lowering of standards; nor does a breakdown of lawkeeping imply a sign of moral laxity. Prostitution was there before we heard an outcry against it. Wives and children have long been prone to be beaten, police defied, travelers terrorized by highway robbers. The causes of battered wives, child protection, workers' safety, minority rights, and the claims of vulnerable posterity have never been more on the public conscience. The bitter debate about abortion is a sign of moral concern. Consider where antinomianism—the effort of the self to reach out beyond, to become self-idolatrous—is located. Bell recognizes antinomianism in modern culture from an upsurge of the antibourgeois values of Baudelaire and Rimbaud.[40] Artists and performers have often been segregated away from the main avenues of power. When their location in the social structure positions them outside, over and against the central political and economic hierarchies, they see their role more as expressing protest and criticism than they do in periods when they depend on personal patronage from princes and rich individuals. Moreover, being relieved of the duties of affirming their country's grandeur, they are free to explore the inner recesses of consciousness, to reach beyond the self and comment in general terms about the human predicament. If one looked only at Left-Bank theatre and painting, one might get an impression of mild antinomianism—perhaps. But an anthropologist could not ignore the lowbrow mainstream culture. Soap opera, TV commercials, weekly magazines, musicals, mystery stories, and situation comedy give another impression altogether—of care for clean clothes and floors, love of good food and elegant service, concern for law and property, laughter at complex, entwined situations, and a passionate interest in individual freedom and individual success. One can concede to Bell a clear disjunction between the values held by segregated and structurally opposed sectors of the population. High culture, insofar as it is carried by a segregated category of people, may well express a widening disjunction from the rationalizing, economizing values of industry and corporate business. But this does not at all demonstrate autonomy for culture. The rationalized economy has segregated the producers of high culture; their segregation in turn entails a particular direction for their creative energies; low culture is still there as before.

The endless search for pleasure that Bell takes as a feature of modernism sounds like the familiar complaint against other people's mindless consumerism. To the consumers themselves, consumption is less like pleasure for its own sake and more like a pleasurable fulfillment of social duties—to one's child to have a horse or swimming pool, to one's wife to buy a laborsaving piece of domestic capital equipment, to one's health to eat proteins, to oneself to have a holiday. The same piecemeal thinking that separates cultural values from social structure tends to separate the demand for commodities from social life. Remember that one of the effects of organizing society around the axial principle of control of power through knowledge is to take the lid off social mobility. Aspirations have no obvious ceilings as they did in society controlled by inherited property. A stratified society imposes implicit sumptuary controls. I have tried elsewhere to show the connection between limitless consumer spending with competitive individualism,[41] and Bell has sufficiently shown how the new preeminence of scientists gives scope to individualist social ambitions. Whereas I can recognize and so explain most of his examples of modernist culture, I confess to being defeated by "the democratization of the erotic"—surely erotic pleasure has usually been an inexpensive and popular cultural resource.

The point is surely made that Bell's description of modern culture is highly selective, elitist, and unsystematic. His argument for the autonomy of culture fails. So does his account of modernism. His complicated model of culture as one of three subsystems, with three axial principles, each moving ever farther apart, is unjustified, unsustainable, and unhelpful for explaining modern religious behavior.

By contrast, Berger's account of the social structuring of modern consciousness is more consistent and perceptive. *The Homeless Mind* is in a direct line of descent from his earlier work. It is a cogent summary of how bureaucracy, work organization, and scientific ways of thought combine to isolate, confuse, and reduce the individual's subjective consciousness. In all his early work, the central idea of plausibility structure connects social life intimately with belief and knowledge and thus with culture. My criticism of *The Homeless Mind* is the passive role it gives to the knowing subject. As if in a rabbit warren, the mind runs in one direction, finds it closed off, burrows another way, only to find that closed off, too. Loops are cut, exits blocked, there is no space to turn around, all directions are closely regulated. According to Berger, modernization means that the mind cannot return upon itself to reflect or travel far enough to discover its limits, cannot confront others enough to find identity. The book convincingly exposes the insulating and isolating controls on responsibility and consciousness. Unfortunately, Berger's earlier book, *The Social Reality of Religion*, has raised expectations that his later work does not fulfill. The talk of plausibility structures should not have rested for so long at the epigrammatic, exploratory level without ever advancing even a tentative typology of the kinds of explanations that are plausible in different kinds of social structure. In the end we are left with the idea that the social order is not constructed, but received, as a set of external, mechanical constraints. There is not much scope for socially negotiated interpretation within limits strictly circumscribed by technology, productive equipment, bureaucracy, and science. Berger's modern man is always finding himself confronted by this or that. Even more contradictory—considering the emphasis in *The Homeless Mind* on the uniformity and reduced psychic space provided to modern society—when Berger comes to summarize modernity in *The Heretical Imperative*, he says that "modern consciousness entails a movement from fate to choice,"[42] and insists that the distinctive feature of modernity is to produce a plurality of options. Here he really seems to believe that differences in life-style are a result of personal preference, regardless of the evidence from market research that they are strictly predictable from occupational and income factors. But regardless of the evidence, to make the shift from fate to choice the pivotal point for interpreting modernization is an unwarranted conclusion from the relentless pressures to uniformity described in the earlier book.

In *The Heretical Imperative* Berger assumes that the Western religious vision has been discredited, and argues that it needs to be strengthened with grafts of Eastern religious wisdom. But a stricter discussion of how choice is possible in modern conditions would raise the question of whether the graft will take.[43] If consciousness is so constrained by bureaucracy and the rest of the modern social package, how can one be free to adopt the options of the Orient? At least we need a theory to explain the ability of large numbers of people to resist the attraction of something they are supposed to need, such as religion.

The tale of confusion, elitism, and bias interspersed with brilliance does more than explain why religious studies were not expecting certain religious forms to be preferred or traditional religion to come threateningly alive. Its work constitutes a self-referencing argument for the close connection between culture and society, since its scholars only saw possibilities that their own social constraints allowed them to see.

The real challenge of being modern is not so much in any reduced possibility of religious belief but in accepting the increased opportunities of inquiry. The privilege of modernization is for a culture to view itself, as Robin Horton puts it, from a meta-level.[44] To recognize the big problems and to anticipate the big surprises, a discipline needs to know that its

> body of knowledge does not determine unambiguously what are the self-evident areas to be explored next; since it is the consensus of the scientific elite which advises the individual scientist what to do next; since this consensus shifts with time, place, and state of affairs in the discipline and in related disciplines, *thus* it is very important for the scientist to understand the social and historical and philosophical context in which the consensus has been reached and how it has been reached."[45]

Here I stop. Everything is wrong because the stereotype of premoderns is wrong. It has been constructed to flatter prejudged ideas. Some premoderns are indeed organized according to the stereotype, in highly ascriptive social institutions. But some of them are as mobile, footloose, and uncommitted as any modern academic. Some have been gripped in the thongs of bureaucracy; some have been ruthlessly competitive individualists. In none of these variations do religious beliefs float free of social and moral pressures. When religious sociology modernizes, it will develop comparative empirical inquiry that does justice to the range of human experience, and will develop some systematic methods of asking how different moral principles become acceptable and different versions of reality plausible.

REFERENCES
    ¹For a literature survey, see Thomas Robbins, Dick Anthony, and James Richardson, "Theory and Research on Today's 'New Religions,' " *Sociological Analysis* 39 (1978): 2:95-122.
    ²Louis Dupré, "Marx's Critique of Culture and Its Interpretations," *Review of Metaphysics* 34 (1980): 1:91-20.
    ³B. Malinowski, *Crime and Custom in Savage Society* (London: Routledge & Kegan Paul, 1926).
    ⁴Margaret Mead, *Coming of Age in Samoa: A Psychological Study of Primitive Youth for Western Civilization* (New York: Morrow, 1928); and Mead, *Male and Female: A Study of the Sexes in a Changing World* (New York: Morrow, 1949).
    ⁵Peter L. Berger, *The Heretical Imperative* (New York: Doubleday, 1980), chapter 6.
    ⁶Ibid., p. 147.
    ⁷Peter L. Berger and Thomas Luckmann, *The Social Construction of Reality: A Treatise in the Sociology of Knowledge* (New York: Doubleday, Anchor Books, 1967); and Berger, *The Social Reality of Religion* (London: Faber and Faber, 1969; first published in the United States as *The Sacred Canopy*, 1967).
    ⁸Peter L. Berger, Brigitte Berger, and Hansfried Kellner, *The Homeless Mind* (New York: Random House, Vintage Books, 1974), pp. 102-3.

[9]Max Scheler, *Problems of the Sociology of Knowledge*, translated by Manfred S. Frings, Kenneth W. Stikkers (ed.) (London: Routledge & Kegan Paul, 1980): "By contrast, in all Asian cultures it was the 'sage' and a metaphysical mind that won over religion as well as science."

[10]Robert N. Bellah, *Beyond Belief: Essays on Religion in a Post-Industrial World* (New York: Harper & Row, 1970), p. 23.

[11]Jack Goody, "Religion and Ritual: The Definitional Problem," *British Journal of Sociology* 12(2) (1961): 142-62; and Robin Horton, "A Definition of Religion and Its Uses," *Journal of the Royal Anthropological Institute* 90(2) (1961): 201-26.

[12]Frances Fitzgerald, "A Disciplined Charging Army," *The New Yorker*, May 18, 1981, pp. 53-141.

[13]Bryan Wilson, *Patterns of Sectarianism* (London: Heinemann, 1967), p. 31.

[14]Berger, *The Heretical Imperative*, p. 38.

[15]Louis Dupré, *Transcendent Selfhood: The Rediscovery of the Inner Life* (New York: Seabury Press, 1976), pp. 18-26.

[16]Ibid., p. 26.

[17]Daniel Bell, "The Return of the Sacred? The Argument on the Future of Religion," in *The Winding Passage, Essays and Sociological Journeys 1960-1980* (Cambridge, Mass., Abt Books, 1980), pp. 333-34.

[18]Robin Horton, "African Traditional Thought and Western Science," *Africa* 37 (1967): 87-155. Kwasi Wiredu, in *Philosophy and an African Culture*, in the chapter "How Not to Compare African Thought," refers approvingly to Horton's work. (New York: Cambridge University Press, 1980). See also Paul Feyerabend, *Against Method* (1975; verso edition 1978), pp. 296-98; and Yehuda Elkana, "The Distinctiveness and Universality of Science: Reflections on the Work of Robin Horton," *Minerva* 15(2) (1977).

[19]Berger, *The Heretical Imperative*, p. 51.

[20]Berger, *The Social Reality of Religion*, p. 53.

[21]Ibid., p. 60.

[22]Ibid.

[23]Mary Douglas, *Cultural Bias*, Occasional Paper no. 35, of the Royal Anthropological Institute of Great Britain and Ireland, 1978; E. E. Evans-Pritchard, *Nuer Religion* (New York: Oxford University Press, 1956), p. 315; Mary Douglas, *Evans-Pritchard* (London and New York: Fontana, 1980).

[24]Dupré, *Transcendent Selfhood*, p. 24: "According to the teachings of Augustine, Luther and Kierkegaarde, is the feeling of being estranged in this world not in itself religious?"

[25]Claude Lévi-Strauss, *The Savage Mind* (London: Weidenfeld, 1966).

[26]Daniel Bell, *The Cultural Contradictions of Capitalism* (New York: Basic Books, 1976), pp. 148-49.

[27]Pierre Bourdieu, *Reproduction in Education, Society and Culture* (Beverly Hills, California: Sage, 1977); in original French, *La Reproduction* (Paris: Minuit, 1970).

[28]See Alan MacFarlane, *The Rise of English Individualism* (New York: Cambridge University Press, 1979), for the distortions of history to which the assumption of a pre-Renaissance or preindustrial European society of closed options gives rise.

[29]Peter L. Berger, 1973.

[30]Peter L. Berger, 1979.

[31]Daniel Bell, *The Coming of Post-Industrial Society* (New York: Basic Books, 1973), p. 330.

[32]Bell, "The Return of the Sacred?" p. 330.

[33]Ibid., pp. 332-33.

[34]A. L. Kroeber, *Configurations of Culture Growth*, (Berkeley: University of California Press, 1944).

[35]Claude Lévi-Strauss, This is only one of possible explanations for change in mythology or artistic forms given in *The Savage Mind*.

[36]Bell, "The Return of the Sacred?"

[37]Bell, *The Cultural Contradictions of Capitalism*, p. 20.

[38]Ibid., pp. 361-62.

[39]Pierre Bourdieu, *La Distinction: Critique Social du Jugement*, (Paris: Minuit, 1979).

[40]Bell, "The Return of the Sacred?"

[41]Mary Douglas, *The World of Goods*, (London: Allen Lane; New York, Basic Books, 1979).

[42]Berger, *The Heretical Imperative*, p. 10.

[43]Harvey Cox, *Turning East: The Promise and Peril of the New Orientalism* (New York: Simon and Schuster, 1977), p. 142, quoting Jâcob Needleman.

[44]Robin Horton, in *Second Order*, philosophical anthropological journal of the University of Ife, cited but not identified in Yehuda Elkana, "Two-Tier Thinking: Philosophical Realism and Historical Relativism" (*Social Studies of Science* 8 [1978] 309-26). The general principle has also been expressed by Horton, in "African Traditional Thought and Western Science."

[45]Elkana, "Two-Tier Thinking," pp. 309-26.

FRANK E. MANUEL

Israel and the Enlightenment

THIS MEDITATION ON ISRAEL IN THE ENLIGHTENMENT passes over the mass of eighteenth century Christian believers who dutifully performed their pre-scribed religious ceremonies, while in secret practicing pagan and primitive rites. It is engaged, rather, in converse with priests and bishops, doctors of divinity, professors of theology and ancient languages, and writers in various conditions of independence—literary men who lived on their estates or survived by their wits, philosophes who published journals and were occupied in remolding what Thomas Jefferson called the opinion of mankind. To this heterogeneous group a simple question was posed: What did they make of the ancient God of the Jews who lived among them, sometimes legally as in Holland, more often under murky arrangements as in France, but always on the margin of society? During the period of the Enlightenment there was a growing curiosity about the Jews and their God, as He and His chosen people were becoming more visible.

The responses constitute a reappraisal of ancient Judaism by Christians, many of whom were in the course of divesting themselves of the complex theological and dogmatic raiment of their own ancestors. The nature of Judaism—not only the physical existence of the Jews—has always been a prickly subject for Christianity. In the age of the Enlightenment new ways of ending the ambiguous position of Judaism in the bosom of Christendom were proposed. An attempt among certain literate elements of European society to cut the umbilical cord that had bound Christianity to Judaism from the moment of its origin was the most conspicuous break with tradition. More radical thinkers, reaffirming the historical tie with great fanfare, deliberately painted Judaism in gruesome colors to undermine the foundation of their own Christian religion. Others conceived of a new relationship between Judaism and Chris-tianity that allowed for their coexistence through a redefinition of the nature of religion itself.

I

The revolutionary character of the reexamination of Judaism may be communicated more fully if set against the background of Christian views of ancient Judaism that still prevailed on the eve of the Enlightenment. In seventeenth century Christian universal history, the binding of Jewish and

Christian experience was taken for granted. The survival of the Jews was conceived as an eternal punishment for the sin of deicide or as an everlasting witness of the Crucifixion. In the eyes of Catholic theologians, Jews had been burned by the secular arm after an inquisition, not because they were Jews, but because they were relapsed Christians or demons luring Christians to apostasy. The major state religions of western Europe—Catholic, Lutheran, Anglican, and Calvinist—taught that, although the Jews in their stubborn blindness had balked at accepting Jesus as the Messiah, there was one continuous sacred history from Adam through the present; with the insertion of pseudepigrapha, like the books of the Maccabees, and the inclusion of the histories of Josephus, it was possible to join the Old and the New Testaments in an unbroken narrative.

The universal history composed by Bossuet, the official churchman of Louis XIV, was really a history of Judaic experience joined to the history of Christianity, with the Roman Empire subordinate to the future needs of the Church, and the Chinese or other pagan histories ignored as having no intrinsic worth. This drove Voltaire in his passion to overturn Bossuet's universe and spitefully to start his world history with the Chinese. Anglican divines of all species—and there were many—adhered to a Bossuet-like central narrative. In his *Old and New Testament Connected*,[1] Humphrey Prideaux revealed the coherence of the divine plan in its totality. Isaac Newton, who devoted thousands of manuscript pages to the subject, many of them now in Jerusalem, fortified the structure with a new method of astronomical dating based on the precession of the equinoxes, and with proofs that in the great civilizing enterprises of mankind—architecture, the laws, the belief in the true God, writing—the Hebrews had preceded all other nations chronologically. Homer had derived his wisdom from Moses, as Clement of Alexandria had affirmed. In the seventeenth century there were many idealized portrayals of ancient Israel as the progenitor of Christianity. The Abbé Fleury's *Les Moeurs des Israélites* (1681) made of it a pastoral utopia that was a pendant to Fénelon's *Telemachus*. Moses was the great legislator of antiquity, far superior to the *nomothetai* of the Greeks.

In the political debates of the sixteenth and seventeenth centuries in northern Europe, it was common to draw on Old Testament biblical texts to find sanction for either monarchy, democracy, or aristocracy in a Christian polity; James Harrington in his *Oceana* even discovered a mixed establishment of the three in Moses' structuring of the Hebrew republic.[2] In the lively, often scratchy political pamphleteering of the English Civil War, there was a complete identification of the Commonwealth saints with Israel, and men busied themselves drafting law codes that would incorporate the rules of Deuteronomy down to the last tittle, or almost. The theocracy of Massachusetts was meant to be a literal implementation of the Mosaic code, with a few exceptions. The glorification of the Sabbath as the only day of the Lord and the rejection of Christmas as the residue of a pagan festival were symbolic of the Puritans' self-image as Israelites.

The hope of effecting the conversion of the Jews and moving on to the millennium was a common Protestant expectation that lasted well into the eighteenth century. Judah Monis, a rather enigmatic wandering Jew, who came from someplace in the Mediterranean, ended up at Harvard, was given a degree in 1722, and appointed an instructor in Hebrew after being duly baptized. His formal sermon celebrating that event dealt with the interpretation of the proof-texts in the Old Testament on the coming of Christ, supported by rather obscure rabbinic citations.[3] Increase Mather, as President of Harvard College, often lectured on the mystery of the survival of the Jews. Among Calvinists, it was only the failure of the Jews to accept Christ that stood in the way of a total approval of Jewish experience. Lutheran tradition was more tightly bound to the Judeophobia of its founder.

Christian preoccupation with Judaism became more intense in the Protestant world as the Old Testament, translated into the vernacular, was widely diffused. It was discovered to be veritably bursting with figures and types of the New Testament. Few verses could not be adapted to demonstrate a prefiguration of sacred Christian history that was later fulfilled. Catholic theologians had been engaged in such practices since the time of the Church Fathers; and if the texts illustrating concordances between the Old and New Testaments, such as those of Joachim of Fiore, are no longer commonly read, the idea of their linkage may be quickly grasped through visual examples. A medieval tapestry in the Metropolitan Museum in New York depicts on the lower level scenes representing the seven sacraments, while on the upper level are parallel Old Testament events: the anointment of David is a type for the sacrament of extreme unction.

Cotton Mather in his *Magnalia Christi Americana* of 1702 still saw a virtuous contemporary divine in New England as a Bostonian incarnation of an Old Testament figure. It was no burden on a young member of the Massachusetts Bay colony to go about with a weighty name such as Shearjashub. In the wilderness of New England, the colonists were reliving the sufferings of the Israelites. And a bit of rabbinic *gematria*—the translation of words into numerical equivalents—applied to prophecies in Daniel and Revelation, which conformed to each other, sustained the dating of the Second Coming.

The weaving together of pre-Christian Judaism and Christianity was constant in the centuries before the Enlightenment. It was perhaps most complete in the Swiss, Dutch, and English (including the American) scholarly worlds of the seventeenth century. And if hardworking believers could not themselves research the rabbinic commentaries for types, foretellings, and prefigurations, their pastors—usually chosen for their learning as well as their eloquence—poured something of this knowledge, garnered from the works of Christian Hebraists, into the willing and unwilling ears of members of their churches, who were subjected to a continuous round of sermons on the Holy Sabbath, on special fast days, and on days of thanksgiving.

II

Christian Hebraism of the seventeenth century occupies a corner in the cemetery of baroque learning, that magnificent age of scholarship when the production of a hundred volumes in a lifetime was considered a feat, but not an unsurpassable one. The grand folios of the Christian Hebraists were produced by the presses of Amsterdam, London, Venice, Leyden, Rome, and Frankfort, and are now preserved in university treasure rooms, rarely disturbed by intruders. Modern scavengers have hardly bothered to pick the bones of these worthies or plagiarize them, let alone savor the content of their works. An occasional essay on them has appeared, but few have ventured to encompass the writings of John Selden, John Lightfoot, John Spencer, and Edward Pocock in England, Johann Buxtorf, father and son, in Basel, the Dutchmen Jan van den Driesche, Adriaan Reeland, Antonius Van Dale, Pieter van der Cun, Wilhelm Surrenhuis, Philipp van Limborch, the heterodox Père Richard Simon in France, or the scholar who published in Leyden and bore the sonorous name Constantin L'Empereur van Oppick. The bibliographical zenith of this out-pouring of Christian Hebraism was reached in the Catholic world with the publication of Giulio Bartolocci's four-volume *Bibliotheca Magna Rabbinica de scriptoribus, & scriptis hebraicis* (1675-93) by the Sacred Congregation for the Propagation of the Faith.

Often the Christian Hebraists were helped by rabbis or converts, but sometimes they heroically confronted the rabbinic corpus alone, doubtless making egregious errors, but in solitude producing monumental works of interpretation that, in the prearchaeological world and in a primitive period of Oriental philology, transmitted rabbinic thought to Christian divines, littera-teurs, and even ordinary middle-class readers possessed by a desire to learn about the ancient religion of the Jews.

There was no consensus among the seventeenth century Christian Hebraists about what worth they should bestow upon the interpretations of the Talmud-ists and rabbinic commentators. But they were generally prepared to consult them, to learn Hebrew and, less frequently, Aramaic, and to accept their descriptions of the rites of the Hebrews at the time of Christ as indications of the Lord's meaning in difficult passages of the Scriptures. There was a general presumption that Judaism had been frozen for sixteen centuries and that the evidence presented by contemporary Jews and their writings was a fairly accurate reflection of belief and practice among the ancient Hebrews. If few would credit Lightfoot's long lists of parallel passages in the New Testament and in the Talmud,[4] and if others like Jacques Basnage saw no reason to appreciate a rabbi's explication of the Bible more than that of a Christian divine, there was rarely a scholar who would deny that he had profited to some extent from the linguistic knowledge of the rabbis. The Christian scholars might feel that the rabbis multiplied distinctions excessively and exaggerated their capaci-ty to deduce new laws and rules from brief texts in Scripture, but they could not reject them outright. Except for a minority of Christian mystagogues who were seduced by Christian Knorr von Rosenroth's potpourri, the *Kabbala Denudata* (1677, 1684), the Protestant sects of the post-Renaissance world were commonsensical and preferred to steer clear of the cabbalists. And, when in the eighteenth century the French Abbé Augustin Calmet published his gargantuan twenty-two volume commentary on the Bible,[5] he was careful to call it literal, to distinguish it from allegorical interpretations, which had gone out of fashion.

Seventeenth and early eighteenth century Christian commentators frequent-ly raised questions that involved matters of fact—the scientific and business spirit introducing mundane concerns into the realm of the sacred. Chorogra-phy—really, sacred geography—was ordered, biblical chronology set aright, and sacred chronology inserted into a world chronology of ancient peoples in such a manner that no gentile nation might appear to have priority over Israel. But meticulous historicization in the long run led to desacralization.

The trickle of printed Latin translations from the rabbis in the fifteenth century–incunabula like the *Aphorismi* of Maimonides and Rashi's commentary—had by the eighteenth swelled to a steady flow. In the years 1698 to 1700, under the direction of Surrenhuis, there had appeared in Amsterdam three vast folios containing the whole of the Mishna in Hebrew, a parallel Latin translation, along with Latin versions of the commentary of Maimonides and of Rabbi Obadia of Bonitera. The splendidly printed work of Surrenhuis—which was in Voltaire's library, now in Leningrad[6]—is enlivened with engravings illustrating the performance of rituals by noble Hebrews in Oriental (i.e., Turkish) costume, or depicting scenes that make vivid and realistic the intricate problems of Sabbath violations or the dietary laws. The postures of the Hebrew gentlemen resemble those of baroque saints, and the general impression conveyed is that of a civilized people with a highly developed legal system. The translator's introduction stresses the importance of the Mishna for understanding St. Paul, the disciple of Rabbi Gamaliel—a stock justification for Hebraic studies—and dwells on the significance of Paul's legal training as an element in his skillful propagation of the faith in Christ among the Romans. Talmudic and rabbinic Judaism served pre-Enlightenment Christianity in its scholarly attempt to understand itself.

The philosophes-litterateurs of the Enlightenment first saw ancient Judaism through the heavy lenses of the Christian Hebraists. Whenever they found them too weighty in their original form, Pierre Bayle and Jean Leclerc and Basnage, who spanned the two centuries and wrote in French, acted as guides or transmitters. The major French philosophes of the eighteenth century, educated before the expulsion of the Jesuits, read Latin fluently and did not always have to rely on *haute vulgarisation*. English Deists of the early eighteenth century who had gone to Oxford had available the Latin commentaries and treatises of their seventeenth century countrymen, whose texts they translated with a certain license. Thus the Enlightenment thinkers disseminated notions of Judaism that rested on information culled from respectable seventeenth century Christian Hebraists at first or second hand. What they did with the data effected a revolution in Christian Europe's perception of Judaism.

Many of the Christian Hebraist commentators had produced rather sympathetic accounts of the ancient Hebrews, even when peppered with derogatory asides about Judaic rites. Their studies of the chronology and the chorography of biblical literature, of surviving manuscript texts from all centuries, were intended to eradicate discrepancies among the variant versions, so that the proof of prophecies might be accurately demonstrated. They found the coming of Jesus the Messiah foretold in hundreds of Old Testament verses. The Deists and philosophes of the next century took these writings, with their profuse citations from rabbinic sources, as evidence that the whole postbiblical Judaic inheritance was a confused mess, and they quickly exploded the relevance of the Messianic proof-texts. Christianity was being loosened from its Judaic moorings in one breath, while in the next, everything that was muddled, miraculous, or counterfeit in contemporary Christianity was tarred as a derivation from

Judaism. In approaching the philosophes' attack on the God of the Jews, it would be futile to look for consistency. Just as nineteenth century Jews were denounced as subversive revolutionary communists and pillars of international capitalism at the same time, in the eighteenth century Judaism was at once proclaimed the progenitor of an absurd and iniquitous Christianity and denied as having any true connection with so universal and spiritual a religion.

III

The brazen reexamination of reality by men of the Enlightenment—including their radical revaluation of Judaism and Christianity—was based on a set of conceptions that they rarely doubted. It was assumed that the remote origins of a phenomenon, or the early history of a collective body such as the Hebrews, told what was most important about the thing itself. They thought it was possible to arrive at these origins by a procedure they often called unveiling. There was a Platonism unveiled, a Christianity unveiled, an antiquity unveiled, the human heart unveiled, nature unveiled. And to unveil Judaism was an undertaking of the same character. All collectives, like persons, had a quintessential core, an *esprit* that was their epitome. The idea is traceable to theories of humors and characteristics and psychologies that implied the existence of a dominant passion in individuals and in nations. Montesquieu's *Spirit of the Laws* and Herder's doctrine of the *Volksgeist* are examples of this conviction. The *esprit* of a nation or a religion was thought to be readily discoverable, definable, and identifiable in simple terms. It was held to be pervasive throughout the organism and relatively impervious to the ravages of time. In harmony with this presupposition, books on the *esprit* of various nations multiplied. In the twentieth century, the working out of the *esprit* of a religion or culture might become rather sophisticated in the hands of an anthropologist or a sociologist, but the fundamental conception has not changed much since the Enlightenment.

The French literary men of the eighteenth century, unlike the polymath philologists of the seventeenth, generally rendered pejorative judgments of ancient Judaism in terms that went far beyond a formal indictment of its principal theological beliefs. In the writings of one of the *patres majores* of the Enlightenment, Voltaire, aversion to Judaism assumed the proportions of an obsession, especially in the last fifteen years of his life. With the critical edition of the one hundred volumes of Voltaire's letters, it is possible to follow the constancy of his Judeophobia, from a shadowy period of his life in the 1720s—when he was flirting with Cardinal Dubois, with espionage, with court Jews in Germany deeply involved in the munitions business and thus having access to state secrets—through his last years, when this indefatigable defender of the rights of Protestants and freethinkers against the Catholic Church would never use the word "Jew" without prefixing it with the adjective "execrable." In a letter written toward the close of his life he burst out that a Jew was a man who should have engraved upon his forehead the words "fit to be hanged."[7]

Personal psychological explanations for Voltaire's fixation have been attempted since the eighteenth century, when it was first observed and his vituperative attacks on historical Judaism answered by a learned French abbé posing as a spokesman for Polish, Portuguese, and German Jews.[8] The "cause" of his hatred has been found in his money quarrels and lawsuits with court Jews, bankers, and speculators, some of whom had worsted him in business dealings. Jewish historiographers have toyed with the question at least since Heinrich Hirsch Graetz, and many have related it to his crusade against all positive religion. By some diabolical prefiguration of future events, one of Voltaire's nicknames in his select circle of friends was "Goebbels."[9] One might half-seriously venture the idea that Voltaire found in Jews and ancient Judaism a fetish into which he could pour those aspects of his being that he loathed in himself. François-Marie Arouet, a mere notary's son on the make, who had changed his name and became a rather sycophantic court Christian, hated the fawning court Jews who had also changed their names. One cannot read Voltaire's descriptions of massacres and buttocks-beatings in *Candide*—and his obvious enjoyment in describing Phineas the Levite entering the tent of the Jew lying with a Midianite woman, and piercing her belly and his private parts with one thrust of the spear—without being aware of the cruelty in the man, which expressed itself in his tirades against the cruelty of the Jews.

If personal psychological and socioeconomic motives are underplayed, left as a sort of grim obbligato, and the traditional Joshua-like bifurcation of Christians into Judeophobes and Judeophiles is avoided, there remains the broad question of the ways in which, on the overt level, the Enlightenment responded to ancient Judaism. Granted that the perception of ancient Judaism cannot be divorced from the realities of eighteenth century Jewish life, the portraits of the God of the Jews that were drawn during this period survived the Enlightenment and became dynamic historic forces in their own right. This was the first encounter of secular European intellectuals (emancipated or quasi-emancipated from traditional Christian angels and devils) with ancient Judaism, and new cultural stereotypes were fashioned that have endured for centuries.

IV

To attack with violence the barbaric customs and punishments of the ancient Hebrews as they were profusely recorded in the Bible, to lay bare the treacheries and butcheries of the kings of Judaea and Samaria, to expose the falsehood of pretensions to miraculous performances in violation of the laws of nature, was a primary mission of the philosophes. To neglect a commonsensical evaluation of the sacred writings of the Jews would have violated the very motto of the Enlightenment, Kant's *Sapere aude*.

The Enlightenment witnessed the falling apart of that uneasy Renaissance syncretism between the inherited traditions of Christianity and pagan Graeco-Roman philosophical conceptions. In some quarters it also meant the disengagement from each other of the Jewish and the Christian inheritances, which had once been linked with the bonds of Scripture and inveterate mutual loathing. As long as the Jews were condemned to continue their miserable lives as an eternal witness to the horror of deicide, they were a part of the world order with a role to play. Their existence had at least a satanic meaning. If the prophetic proof-texts of the Old Testament were miraculous demonstrations or prefigurations of the truth of Christianity, the Jews had deeper meaning, even if they refused to accept the plain evidence of their own Messianic writings. But what if philosophes or Deists showed that the essential moral truths of Christianity were as old as creation? What need was there then for Hebrews, ancient or modern? The later English Deists hoped to transform the existing orthodox ecclesiastical establishments into a Christianity even more watery than Herbert of Cherbury's original five tenets of religion. In this so-to-speak third dispensation, there was neither room nor need for Judaism as a prolegomenon to Christianity. If one believed that Christianity was as old as the Creation—to adopt the title of a well-known pamphlet by the Deist Matthew Tindal—Judaism had not fulfilled any special theological purpose in the past and was of no worth in the present. Judaism was, in effect, an outlandish example of the heavy incrustation of man-made ceremonials and priestly impositions on a pure and simple set of Deist principles. Since miracles were exposed as frauds, and prophecies shown to be superstitions or errors, what was the point of studying the texts of the Jewish prophets to prove the coming of Christ? The truths of Deism were engraved in the heart and mind of every man, and the rout of ceremonials and dogmas about which men disputed was so much arrant nonsense. Judaism had accumulated more ritualistic prohibitions than other religions, and was the more ridiculous for it.

One branch of the Enlightenment made Judaism useless: it was not necessary for a purified Christianity in Europe. The Jews lost their place in a Christian divine order of things, and they soon stood as naked aliens in a secular society. To the extent that Deism triumphed, it left Jews isolated, irrelevant, a sport in the history of Christianity. They became a mere remnant of ancient barbaric tribes, living on in the midst of civilized Europeans, preserving bizarre fanatical customs. Lessing is regarded as a Judeophile in popular Jewish historiography, and his relations with Moses Mendelssohn are a touching record of friendship; but if one reads carefully the hundred theses of Lessing's *Education of Mankind*,[10] Judaism is stage one, Christianity stage two, and the new Enlightenment supersedes them both in a stadial succession. Judaism has lost its reason for further existence.

When Voltaire played the Deist, his weapons were cruder. His underlying purpose—to attack Judaism and Christianity by conflating them—was plainly expressed in a letter of 1765 addressed to the Count and Countess d'Argental. He was writing a commentary on his own *Philosophie de l'histoire*, which had appeared pseudonymously as the work of the Abbé Bazin: "This book modestly shows that the Jews were one of the latest peoples to appear, that they took from other nations all their myths and all their customs. This dagger once dug in can kill the monster of superstition in the chambers of men of good will without the fools even knowing it."[11] On another occasion he had written: "It is good to know the Jews as they are and to see from what fathers the Christians are descended."[12]

Out of unheroic caution, which characterized many, though not all, the philosophes, the early history of the Church, the lives of Christ and the apostles, were considered off limits. Most of the philosophes were determined to illuminate mankind without being martyred by it, to adapt Beccaria's formula. As a result, the particular God of the Jews and his chosen people were often surrogates that the philosophes fashioned to their own purposes and then lashed.

Abbé Calmet's volumes of commentary provided the raw materials for Voltaire's biblical exegesis. Received as a prominent Royal Historiographer in Calmet's monastery, Voltaire stayed for almost a month in his workshop, and has left an amusing description of the monks scurrying up and down ladders to search out texts that ultimately fed Voltaire's bonfires of both traditional Christianity and Judaism. Beelzebub took the pious facts assembled by the monks and twisted them to fiendish purpose. But he also went to original sources. Even a cursory examination of the collection of Church Fathers in his library, kept intact from Catherine the Great through Brezhnev, bears witness to the assiduousness with which Voltaire consulted the sacred writings of early Christianity. In the dense forests of patristic literature, he carefully set up his own markers, little dabs of thin paper pasted on passages that might some day be useful in the anticlerical crusade. He set out to prove that the Jews had a material and anthropomorphic image of God: He spoke, the Jews maintained, ergo He had an actual voice. Judaism was carnal. By adhering to the literal, factual meaning of the Bible, Voltaire rendered it inconsistent and contradictory, even repulsive. Reading in the Book of Joshua that the victorious war leader circumcised all Jews who had been born during the decades in the wilderness and had been wandering about uncircumcised, Voltaire conjured up the spectacle of a veritable mountain of foreskins on Gilgal. What the Jews wrote was fiction and not to be believed. Then he turned about abruptly and uncritically accepted biblical statistics when they concerned the Hebrews on a slaughtering rampage of enemies and sinners, to illustrate the cruelty of the God of the Jews. To Isaac de Pinto of Amsterdam, who, in a respectful letter, had protested some of his remarks on the Jews, he wrote: "Remain a Jew since you are one, but don't massacre 42,000 men because they could not pronounce shibboleth right nor 24,000 because they slept with Midianites; be a philosophe."[13]

When literate freethinkers of the Enlightenment had to weigh the witness of the Old Testament on the nature of Judaism against the witness of their favorite Roman historian, Tacitus, in his famous excursion on the character of the Jews in Book V of the *Histories*, there could be no question that the scales would tilt heavily on the side of Tacitus. For them, he was a true, objective pagan historian, not involved in the quarrels of Christians and Jews. He was a first century civilized Roman official, who had sifted the tales about the Jews, the origin of their religion, their exclusiveness, the contempt in which they were held by all nations, and the hatred they reciprocated. Tacitus' account of how Moses instituted new religious rites to bind to himself the tribes of Jews driven out by the Egyptians was consonant with prevalent eighteenth century theories about the origin of Oriental religions: the religion was an invention of a leader or a priest and had no intrinsic meaning. The idiosyncratic idea of having an empty temple with no representation of the invisible god was for Tacitus a patent demonstration of Jewish absurdity. The Jews were contentious among themselves, but extraordinarily stubborn in clinging to their fatuous beliefs when the Romans attacked them. As a tribe in the Roman Empire, they were peculiar, obdurate, and troublesome, nothing more. Reading Tacitus, Enlightenment philosophes thought they recognized eighteenth century Jews. One had to be wary of them.

If the most relevant part of the Old Testament for theorists of the political state in Christian society was the history of kingship, particularly its cloudy inception under Samuel, for the theologians who were apologists of Christianity, as well as for those who would crush the infamous beast or at least cut its fangs, the heart of the matter was the nature of prophecy in ancient Judaea. It was here that the English Deists and French philosophes exerted their major effort in pulling Judaism and Christianity apart.

Among orthodox believers, Christianity was proved both by the miracles that Christ performed, witnessed by apostles and the people, and by the evidence of what were considered the prophetic passages of the Old Testament, verses in which the coming of Christ the Messiah had been foretold. In orthodox Christian theology of the seventeenth and eighteenth centuries, there was a growing apologetic movement in one direction: miracles were substantially underrated, especially in the non-Catholic world, and the main witness, proof, or demonstration of the truth of the Christian religion, inexorably shifted to prophecy. Protestants regularly mocked ongoing Catholic miracles such as the periodic liquefaction of the blood of St. Januarius in Naples. Locke and Newton, for whom miracles were a subject of some consequence during their frequent religious colloquies, had settled on a compromise: miracles had ceased after the first centuries of Christianity, because thereafter further demonstrations of divine will in the natural order would have been excessive, supererogatory, a violation of the scientific law of parsimony. Rationalism, skepticism about the accuracy of the senses, made reports of miracles that had occurred thousands of years ago weak reeds to lean on, since men of sound mind doubted even contemporary ones.

The written testimony of Old Testament prophets became the preferred battleground of both believers and unbelievers. In his customary manner, Baron d'Holbach once "abridged" a work by Rabbi Isaac Balthazar Orobio de Castro and entitled it *Israel vengé;*[14] in this polemic, Christian belief, which had found support in an interpretation of Isaiah 53 as foretelling the coming of Christ, was contradicted by a traditional Jewish reading of the text. Rabbinic Judaism was called to witness by Holbachian atheists to destroy prophecy as a persuasive demonstration of the truth of Christianity. As for the spirit of Judaism, the Holbachians took care of that in another context. The theological controversies over prophecy were a melee in which an observer from on high would often have had difficulty knowing on whose side the contenders were fighting. Did the proof-texts of Isaiah and Haggai and Malachi refer to Christ or to some more immediate political events in the history of Judaea? Or were they prophecies about a future Messiah who was yet to come? Ingenious commentators like Jean Le Clerc, the remonstrant Genevan popularizer who ended up in Holland editing universal libraries for the learned, held that Old Testament prophecy might be at once a prediction of some immediate event, like the Jewish release from the Babylonian captivity, and a foretelling of a more distant Messiah. Ultimately, Deist Christianity dispensed entirely with the philological refinements of rabbinic exegesis. Bereft of its primary function of prophesying the coming of Christ, the Old Testament lost much of its significance for Enlightenment Christianity.

What was an Old Testament prophet? Once Spinoza had answered the question in the *Tractatus Theologico-politicus* (1670), in what appeared to many to be naturalistic terms, the character of the prophet became a key to the judgment of Judaism. Christians like the Anglican professor John Spencer, who had codified the writings of Maimonides in a Latin work, *De Legibus Hebraeorum*,[15] adopted Maimonides' portrait of the prophet as a man learned, rational, of impeccable morals, probably rich, who after having shown himself worthy of divine inspiration, established a special relationship with God. Enlightened Anglicans with deistic leanings welcomed this portrayal of the prophet as a philosophical teacher, so totally unlike the tinker prophets and ranters who had spoken with tongues during the English Civil War, a horde of wild, mad enthusiasts, lechers, ignoramuses, living among the dregs of society. Maimonides, the respectable Moses of Judaism, was a welcome philosopher to rationalist Anglican clergymen.

But the Maimonidean portrait of a prophet was soon besmirched. Voltaire and the members of Holbach's atheist conventicle, perversely called the synagogue, drew a very different profile of a prophet. They read the biblical texts literally, and spread the image of Amos, the ignorant enthusiast, of Ezekiel running naked in the streets of Jerusalem. These prophets were blubbering lunatics who performed outlandish acts, married prostitutes. While orthodox believers took comfort in the wisdom of the prophets who had foretold the coming of Christ and sometimes naively talked of the "sons of the prophets" as sorts of universities of ancient Judaea, those Deists who wanted neither Christ coming once or twice, nor a future Jewish Messiah, made the biblical prophets sound like the Protestant "prophets of London," those persecuted Huguenots from the Cévennes who were afflicted with glossolalia and held scandalous séances predicting doomsday. For the Enlightenment, Spinoza, whose works had been translated into the vernacular, had relativized prophecy and divine inspiration. Prophecy had acquired a taxonomy: there were different types of prophets. Some heard voices, some had dreams. The Moses who saw God was the greatest, to be sure. But prophets were legislators of a particular people, and their admonitions had no universal applicability.

This rationalist and relativist attitude toward prophecy diverted the argument from God's nature and intent to the nation of the Jews. A Maimonidean theologian like Isaac Newton had gone to great lengths to show the absolute conformity of all prophetic utterances, Judaic and Christian. For him, the historic events of prophecy derived their unity from God himself, who could harbor no contradiction. Later in the century, ancient Judaic prophecies were still widely regarded as historic events, but for Voltaire and the Holbachians, they had become either the delusions of madmen or the planned deceptions of priestcraft.

V

Montesquieu taught that every nation had an *esprit* particular to itself that was the mainspring *(ressort)* of its whole being. For the Romans, it was a warrior spirit; for the Phoenicians, it was commercial; for the ancient Hebrews, it was religious. This conception of the dominant passion in a nation was complemented by another anthropomorphic analogy—that each nation experienced a stadial development that stamped a different *esprit* on its life in every particular period. Vico's three ages in the *Scienza Nuova* preceded Herder's *Volksgeist*, but despite marked distinctions in the definition and diagnosis of the stages, the idea itself is one of the most common and persistent notions of eighteenth century thought. Even skeptical philosophes like Diderot, Hume, and Voltaire, who were most reluctant to imprint a stadial pattern on the bewildering chaos of historical experience, distinguished at least two historical states among all nations, a condition of barbarism and a state of civilization. In passing judgment on the nation of the Hebrews and their God, the philosophes had to find a place for them somewhere in this implicit system. Was the ancient history of the Hebrew nation the account of a barbarous or a civilized people? The books of the Bible were opened to reveal harrowing delineations of the Jews and their priests and kings. For many philosophes, a barbaric Judaean kingship and a fanatical priesthood fitted together.

Travel literature described customs and habits of strange peoples in all parts of the world, many of them atrocious and cruel; but the question of whether the peoples were civilized turned on whether they had a system of laws. In this respect, once the Israelites had settled on both sides of the Jordan and occupied half of the Eastern Mediterranean littoral, it was difficult for even the most rabid Judeophobes of the Enlightenment to deny them a measure of civility. Diderot, perhaps with one eye cocked on the royal censor, included a dithyramb on Moses the legislator in the *Encyclopédie*. But there were those like Voltaire who were intent on likening the Jews to the early Picts and Celts of Europe and the primitive Greeks: the parallel sacrifices of Iphigenia and of Jephthah's daughter became the stereotyped example. They drew from the Bible the portrait of a barbaric, not a civilized, kingdom. David was their exemplar monarch of ancient Judaism.

In his *Histoire du Vieux et du Nouveau Testament* (1705), Basnage, the Huguenot exile and preacher at Rotterdam, who wrote what were probably the most popular eighteenth century source books of secular knowledge about Jews and Judaism, had dropped the more licentious episodes of King David's life or psychologized his misconduct, to the point where the story of his iniquities became a morality play about the dangers of giving free rein to the passions. Holbach and Voltaire took the same biblical narratives and presented them as a Tacitus or Suetonius might in writing about an emperor of Rome. Both the kings of the Jews and their God turned out to be grizzly characters if measured by the standards of Paris salon society or the club life of David Hume's London.

The French anticlericals reveled in shattering the image of David. The orthodox apologists of David had celebrated the piety of his Psalms; in *David, ou l'histoire de l'homme selon le coeur de Dieu* (1768), the Holbach circle turned to the simple facts narrated in the books of Samuel and Kings. In the previous century, Rembrandt, in a famous painting, had drawn King David as a resplendent Oriental monarch, repentant, deep in thought, listening to the admonitions of an emaciated Nathan. For the Holbachians, David, the murderous lecher, who had Bathsheba's husband Uriah killed at the front, and David, the disloyal harpist, made more plausible portraits. They pictured

David as the head of a gang of ruffians, and his God as a capricious creature who poured ointment about rather promiscuously. Pierre Bayle's article on David in the first edition of the *Philosophical and Critical Dictionary* had aroused such opposition, that he was forced in the second edition to suppress many of his acidulous comments; but they were later restored, and the philosophes had regular recourse to him. The brutal hacking up of King Agag by Samuel as graphically depicted in Voltaire's play *David* may tell something about the dynamics of Voltaire's personality; but whatever their motivation, Voltaire's Old Testament scenes had a convincing goriness that the most persuasive rabbinic apologies could not dispel. Not everything written in the Enlightenment about the first dispensation was false or even malicious in the light of a plain, straightforward reading of the Bible.

Comparison of ancient Hebrew rites with the religious practices of pagan neighboring nations revealed the polytheistic and idolatrous character of ceremonials described in the Bible, and diminished the reverence for Judaism as the first monotheistic religion. The philosophes quoted from the inflated volumes of Bishop Warburton's *The Divine Legation of Moses Demonstrated* (1742), which, in a crude fashion, propounded the thesis that the immortality of the soul was a conception introduced into Judaism only after the Babylonian captivity, and denied the very idea of a world to come among the ancient Hebrews. That the ancient Jews did not believe in the soul's immortality became a historico-religious dogma, and fed the timeworn notion that Judaism in its origins was carnal, dependent upon rewards in this world that were concrete, objective, and visible. It was but a step from there to the accusation that the Jews' absorption with accumulating money was derived from their religion and inextricably bound up with it—the worship of Mammon. While the carnal temper was often attributed to the absurd multiplication of rabbinic interpretations, an early tendency was discerned in the laws of Leviticus and Deuteronomy themselves.

On a more elevated plane, David Hume jumped to the conclusion that unphilosophical monotheism, by which he meant both institutional Christianity and Judaism, was incapable of holding to its lofty, abstract tenets, and inevitably lapsed into the worship of objects and idols, and into the fear of Hell reified as a place full of pitchfork-wielding devils.[16]

VI

In the clandestine publications of the Baron d'Holbach, one is confronted with frank, militant, blatant atheism. There was nothing in Christianity, Deist or positive, that he wished to preserve. As a consequence, in describing the relationship of Judaism and Christianity, he argued that Christianity was simply reformed Judaism—and not much reformed at that. Voltaire and d'Alembert shuddered at the prospect of atheism when they read Holbach's writings, and scribbled "dangerous work" on the flyleaves. Jefferson, who studied all three of them, vacillated, as his marginalia show.[17] What Voltaire and d'Alembert feared were ten-sou popularizations of Holbach's ideas that might corrupt the populace and lead to anarchy. Holbach, secure in his belief that society was protected by the hangman, not by God, let loose all the stops. The Holbachians assimilated Judaism to other primitive religions, generated and maintained by fear and terror. And fear, they had learned from the ancients, obfuscated truth and bred cruelty. The analysis of fear in primitive religion was pivotal in the attack on Judaism by Holbach and the engineer Nicolas-Antoine Boulanger, who frequented his salon. The fear of God in Judaism, the *Gottesfurcht* of sixteenth century Lutherans, the highest virtue in a man, became identified with cruelty in eighteenth century associationist psychology. And if the diverse branches of the Enlightenment were united in denouncing any single evil, it was cruelty.

The Holbachians reached the climax of their diatribes against the God of the Jews in *L'Esprit du Judaïsme ou examen raisonné de la loi de Moyse, & de son influence sur la Religion Chrétienne* (1770), a work often imputed to the Deist Anthony Collins. Actually, it is a composite in which one can recognize the rhetoric of Boulanger, Diderot, and Holbach. The twelfth chapter, "The Influence of Judaism on the Christian Religion," is an oratorical display in which the parallel between the God of Christianity and the God of Judaism is set forth with a passion rarely attained in anticlerical literature even by Voltaire and Nietzsche. The full force of the battering-ram is directed at the God of the Jews, of whom the Christian God is a mere replica.

> Christians, like Jews, worship a cruel and gory God; they proclaimed one who demands blood to appease his fury. But is not cruelty a sign of weakness? Did God create his creatures in order to spill their blood? Nevertheless these abominable principles have been invoked to justify the atrocious persecutions that Christians have launched a thousand times against those whom they falsely imagined were the enemies of their God. Having made of this God a veritable cannibal, they have honored him by avenging his cause with the fumes of human blood. It is in accord with these atrocious ideas that they imagined this same God demanded of the patriarch Abraham the blood of his only son and then demanded that to redeem men, the blood of a God, the blood of His own Son, be shed on the Cross.[18]

The Holbachians argued that, in belief, in *esprit*, in ecclesiastical organization, the Jews were the very model of Christianity. Where orthodox Christians had seen the sacrifice of Isaac as a type for the Crucifixion, the Holbachians saw it as a despicable Oriental precedent that was imitated:

> Blinded by their legislator the Jews never had any sound ideas of divinity. Moses devised an image for them with the characteristics of a jealous tyrant, restless and insidious, who was never restrained by the laws of justice and who owes nothing to men, who chooses and rejects according to his caprice, who punishes children for the crimes, or rather the misfortunes of their fathers. . . . What more was needed to make of the Hebrew people a troop of slaves, proud of the favor of their celestial Sultan, prepared to undertake anything without examination to satisfy his passions and unjust decrees. This ignorant, savage people, imbued with the idea that its God was amenable to gifts, believed that it was enough to please him to make him many offerings, to placate him with sacrifices, to enrich his ministers, to work in order to keep them in splendor, to fulfill scrupulously the rites that their cupidity dreamed up.

> These are the horrible features with which the legislator of the Hebrews painted the God that the Christians have since taken over.[19]

In this portrait, the God of love and mercy was completely stricken out.

Explaining the burning of marranos in contemporary Spanish and Portuguese autos-da-fé, the Holbachians returned Christianity to its origins—
Judaism. It was as if the Jews had willed their own eventual destruction. "In a
word, all the ferocity of the Judaic priesthood seems to have passed into the
heart of the Christian priesthood, which since it has established itself on earth
has caused barbarities to be committed unknown to humans before."[20]

VII

The last important Enlightenment interpretation of the spirit of Judaism
was made not by the enemies of religion but by a group of Christian believers. It
ended in emotionalizing and romanticizing the religion of Judaism as it was
embodied in the Old Testament. This novel religious conception assumed two
kindred forms in France and Germany: the romantic religiosity of the Vicar of
Savoy's confession of faith in Rousseau's *Emile*, and the exaltation by Herder of
the primitive Hebrew poetry of the Bible as the most sublime expression of the
religious spirit.[21] Together they generated a religion of feeling that was related
to moral beauty, and ultimately deflected traditional Western religions from
their doctrinal and historical pathways—in some instances, a departure so
radical that the whole nature of religious experience underwent a profound
change.

The effect on the view of Judaism was strongest in the German world,
where Jewish communities were more numerous than anywhere else in western
Europe. In 1753 the Oxford professor of poetry Robert Lowth, later Bishop of
London, whose Hebrew was in fact rather weak, had published his lectures *De
sacra Poesi Hebraeorum*. The German Hebraist Johann David Michaelis corrected
his errors and perfected his reading of much of the Bible as poetry. Their
discovery of the sacred poetry of the Hebrews was harmonious with Herder's
definition of the core of ancient Judaism as its poetic nature. The essential spirit
of Judaism had been made manifest in the earliest documents of the human race,
the Scriptures. Language revealed the secret soul of every religious people, and
the poetry of the Bible was the *Geist* of the ancient Hebrews in their very
beginnings, their creative moment. Among the Hebrews, early poetic language
was the vehicle for the most sublime religious feeling. The rationalist theologies
of all religions were secondary; it was the poetic language of religion in music
and in verse that was closest to the divine. When Herder, while remaining a
Lutheran, abandoned discussion of Jewish or Christian theology and identified
the religion of Judaism with the beauties of the Hebrew language, he freed the
spirit of Judaism from the contempt of the Voltaireans and the Holbachians.
But at the same time he opened the way to aestheticizing religious experience
among all peoples, which subtly robbed the Judaic dispensation of its
uniqueness.

One aspect of Moses Mendelssohn's defense of Judaism was deeply colored
by a perception that he shared with his friends Michaelis and Herder. In
aestheticizing the religion of the Old Testament, Christians and Jews could
have a common experience. They could read Psalms and prophetic works,
Mendelssohn wrote Michaelis, as poetry, without theological glosses and

debates over whether or not they foretold the coming of a Messiah. They could ignore the exegetical apparatus that discovered prefigurations of Jesus in what were poetic effusions of the Judaic religious soul.[22] In his book *Jerusalem*,[23] Mendelssohn likened religions to different languages in which the same universal humanity found a voice. Though he continued to observe Jewish rituals meticulously, he appeared no longer to hold to their absolute religious importance, regarding them as man-made, like commentaries on texts or theological deductions. It was then that the Swiss pastor Johann Kaspar Lavater summoned him to become a Christian—an invitation that Mendelssohn rejected with angry vehemence. Since the moral truths of Judaism were the same as those of natural religion without revelation, since each religion was a divinely inspired language, why should he forsake the religion into which he had been born? Proselytization was presumptuous, and conversion idiotic.

The consequences of this romantic, emotional transformation of Judaism into a religion of moral beauty were far graver than Mendelssohn imagined. The reduction of Judaism to an aesthetic-moral experience inflicted a more serious wound on traditional Judaism in the Germanic world than the sneering of a Voltaire intent upon its uglification. If Judaism and Christianity were equally appealing to the romantic imagination, why hesitate at the baptismal font? The convert Dorothea Schlegel, née Mendelssohn, was the visible outgrowth of this movement. The *raison d'être* for Judaism was being shattered by the celebration of the ancient God of the Jews as an inspirer of sweet and lofty poesy.

Despite his Judeophobia, Voltaire, too, was an admirer of the Old Testament as literature. He thought its dramatic incidents more gripping and vivid than those of the Homeric epics. Of course, like Shakespeare, the Bible violated the canons of good taste, and one spurned its wild coarseness in an enlightened age. The Bible was an incarnation of the barbaric spirit and vigor of antiquity, not a model for civilized Europeans.

Thus, after the rupture of the traditional union of Christianity and Judaism, in which Judaism had played the stock role of a prolegomenon to the dominant European religious culture, there were at least three principal positions on Israel assumed in the Enlightenment. Some thinkers maintained that the essence of a spiritualized Christianity was universal from the beginning of time, and they eliminated Judaism as a forebear. Others maximized the importance of Judaism, but saw it as the archetypal fanatical religion of which Christianity was a descendant, and piled up the evidence that it was unfit for any but barbarian peoples; the time had come for both Judaism and Christianity to be superseded by reason alone. Still others emotionalized or aestheticized religion, allowing for the appreciation on an equal plane of all religious languages, and the traditional belief in the Covenant between God and His chosen people evaporated.

VIII

Edward Gibbon once said of the religions of the Roman Empire that the mass of the people considered all the religions of the empire as equally true, and that the magistrates believed them all to be equally useful. This may apply well enough to much of present-day American society. Gibbon also remarked that philosophers thought all religions equally false.[24]

In the two hundred years since the triumph of the Enlightenment, the religious temper of Western society has changed more radically than in any period since the birth of Christianity. Present-day Christian views of Judaism would be incomprehensible to the heads of the established eighteenth century churches and to the theologians whose doctrinal positions have been outlined early in this essay. The pattern of distribution of Jews in the world has been dramatically altered. The Jewish inhabitants of Central and Eastern Europe have been wiped out, France has more than ten times as many Jews as it did in the eighteenth century, and North American Jews have become preponderant in the Diaspora. Christian belief has ceased to rest primarily upon miracles or proof-texts of Old Testament prophecy. Conversion of the Jews is not a major preoccupation of any Christian denomination. The acerbity of speech of many Deists and philosophes has generally been left behind.

Christian giants of scholarship no longer devote themselves to Hebraism. Nevertheless, the flowering of biblical studies worldwide among Christians and Jews (stimulated in part by the discovery of the Dead Sea scrolls) has bestowed a new dignity on ancient Judaism as a religion. Israeli bibliolatry has not brought about the neglect of the rabbinic learning of postexilic Judaism, and the multifarious forms of historical Judaism are alive in Israel. Hebraic studies flourish in Jewish theological centers in America and in Jewish secular universities. Judaism as a historical religion is now rarely treated pejoratively.

In Vatican II, the Catholic Church denied the collective responsibility of Jews in all ages for the Crucifixion. Though many American Fathers of the Council had favored an explicit rejection of the "infamous blasphemy" of deicide, the final text fell short of this demand.[25] Nevertheless, a call was issued in the 1965 declaration *Nostra aetate* for the opening of a fraternal dialogue between Christians and Jews, whose common spiritual patrimony "is so great."[26] Doctrinal reconstructions are evident in deeds as well as in words— Catholic priests have made forthright avowals of *mea culpa*. The gospel according to John cannot be amended, and teachings in some seminaries may perpetuate old ways of thinking; Jewish synagogues and cemeteries are the target of aberrant manifestations of Judeophobia as they have been through the ages. But the degree to which residual hatred of Jews draws sustenance from Christian theology has diminished. Contemporary Judeophobia has roots in racial and economic doctrines that are far removed both from the traditional arguments of the Church Fathers and from the caricatures of radical atheists of the Enlightenment. Antisemitism, the nineteenth century label for the latent malady of Christendom, has not been extirpated, and many Jews, believers and disbelievers alike, live in fear of its recurrence.

Protestants, loosely organized in a world council of churches, present a broad spectrum of attitudes toward Judaism, a few of which can be traced back to their eighteenth century origins. There are Jews who feel that some Protestant sects have lagged behind the Catholic Church in their inner reformation with respect to Judaism, that the venom of Luther's Judeophobia has only been diluted. Understandably, Protestant fundamentalists and believers in biblical inerrancy are more involved with the Old Testament texts than are other sects, often with paradoxical consequences. The return of the Jews to the Holy Land enjoys the active support of many biblical literalists and millenarians, for whom the in-gathering of Israel presages a fulfillment of prophecy. But at the same time they have questioned whether a Jew who does not recognize Christ can be saved. On occasion, the whole ecumenical position recently adopted in Christian churches has been muddled by the parochial contention that God does not listen to the prayers of a Jew.

On the commonsensical level, the forms and substance of Christian and Jewish religious life in America resemble each other. All Western Christian denominations have undergone the influence of eighteenth century emotional revivalism. Romantic effusiveness in religion is on the rise, and in this sense, Western Christianity and Judaism are associated in a common religio-aesthetic experience. The universal romantic religiosity of Rousseau—with more than a touch of nature worship—the pietism of Herder, and the expressive evangelical spirit of John Wesley have been victorious over the philosophical rationalism of Leibniz's conception of an ecumenical religion for all mankind. Jews who are neither Cabbalists nor Hassidim but belong to one of the three principal Jewish denominations in America—Orthodox, Conservative, and Reform—nevertheless draw the same kind of emotional sustenance from dalliance with the quasi-mystical Jewish sects. There are signs of increased religious observance among members of the three Jewish denominations, but the nature of their religious experience and their intensity of devotion are as varied as among their Christian neighbors. Memorable discourse on religious thought and feeling among Jews in twentieth century America is rare, as it is among their Christian compatriots.

Ecumenicalism has been so pervasive, that a Catholic church stripped of images looks much like a Protestant meetinghouse, and a Jewish sermon focused on current events is hardly to be differentiated from its liberal Protestant counterpart. Centuries-old Judaic moral admonitions to pursue justice and righteousness make it easy for a Jew to assimilate the social gospel of liberal Christianity; both religions at times seem to be turning into a kind of eighteenth century Deism shorn of anticlerical polemics. The hyphenated adjective "Judeo-Christian," which was not in common usage in the Christian world before the twentieth century, has come to symbolize shared moral values. This idea would have been preposterous to apologists who wove theological systems around the contrast between Jewish carnality and Christian spirituality. In North America, having some religion is still a social, if not a political, requirement for election to office, but fewer Americans care which religion is professed. Jews need not subject themselves to the humiliation of a conversion to Christ without conviction, as they did in nineteenth century Germany. Religious pluralism in American society is taken for granted even more than ethnic diversity. It was a stereotype of eighteenth century thought that religious intolerance was proportionate to zealotry and fanaticism, and that, conversely, nations like the Roman, which was rather indifferent in matters of religion, tended to be tolerant of the religious practices of others. If universal religious toleration was one of the wished-for human conditions in the Enlightenment, it has been largely realized in late twentieth century America.

Since World War II there has been one development in Judaism that is momentous. Messianism and the longing for the return to Israel have been potent forces in traditional Judaism, though the eighteenth century was probably a low point in the history of this sentiment. In our time, the existence of Israel as a state has been invested with religious meaning for a great number of Jews. Judaism, fervid or lukewarm, has been politicized. Reform Judaism of the nineteenth and early twentieth centuries, derived from Moses Mendelssohn, was long inimical to the commingling of religion and politics, and insisted on their complete separation, lest Jews be considered less patriotic than their fellow nationals in the lands where they lived. Today Reform Jews, once militantly hostile to Woodrow Wilson's approval of the Balfour Declaration, have joined Conservative Jews, Orthodox Jews, and other sects (except for tiny Jewish fundamentalist minorities that deny recognition to the state of Israel as a usurper of the Messiah's prerogatives) in moving the preservation of Israel as a political entity to a central position in their religious life. The prayer book of Orthodox Jews now includes a long text, promulgated by the chief rabbis of Israel, beginning: "Our Father who art in heaven, Protector and Redeemer of Israel, bless thou the State of Israel which marks the beginning of the flowering of our redemption." The careful phrasing still allows for the persistence of the traditional expectation of the coming of the Messiah at a future time. Conservative Jews have a briefer version that starts in the same way. And even Reform Jews, who in the nineteenth century eliminated from their devotions all references to Jerusalem and the resurrection of the dead, now pray for "the land of Israel and its people." This prayer for Israel is the only liturgical innovation on which the three Jewish religious divisions in America are in accord.

It may be difficult for Christians to comprehend the internal religious squabbles among Jews, to realize that there is no pope in Judaism, no world body that can speak for religious or secular Jews, no canonical law universally recognized by Jews. There is in fact great freedom in North America for any Jew to speak his mind on the orientation of the numerous religious synods and Jewish organizations of laymen that vie for his allegiance, or on the state of Israel and any of its wise, courageous, or foolhardy decisions. The persecutions of this century, however, have made Jews hesitant to alienate themselves from the general will of their community, ill-defined as it may be. Divergent interests of rich or poor, old settlers or new immigrants, belief in a false Messiah like Sabbatai Zevi or disbelief, Zionism or anti-Zionism, in their day have torn Jewish communities apart, and there is fear of divisiveness. The survival of Israel is now at the heart of spiritual existence among American Jews. Their religious institutions have been thrust into the maelstrom of American and Israeli party politics. But the needs of a beleaguered state like Israel may not always dovetail neatly with the requirements of an ancient religion like Judaism. And an Enlightenment prophet might hold that a second coming of the Holocaust is not reserved for Jews alone.

REFERENCES
    [1]Humphrey Prideaux, *The Old and New Testament Connected in the History of the Jews and Neighboring Nations from the Declension of the Kingdoms of Israel and Judah to the time of Christ*, 2 vols. (London: 1716-18).
    [2]The second book of Harrington's *The Art of Law-giving* (London: 1659) is described as "shewing the frames of the Commonwealths of Israel and of the Jewes."

[3]Judah Monis, *The truth, being a discourse which the author delivered at his baptism. Containing nine principal arguments the modern Jewish rabbins do make to prove the Messiah is yet to come; with the answer to each . . . and likewise with the confession of his faith. Prefac'd by the Rev. Increase Mather* (Boston: 1722).

[4]John Lightfoot, *Horae Hebraicae et Talmudicae in quatuor Evangelistas cum tractatibus chorographicis, singulis suo Evangelistae praemissis* (Leipzig: 1684).

[5]Dom Augustin Calmet, *Commentaire littéral sur tous les livres de l'Ancien et du Nouveau Testament*, 23 tomes in 22 vols. (Paris: 1707-16).

[6]Leningrad. Publichnaia biblioteka, *Biblioteka Vol'tera. Katalog Knig* (Moscow: 1961), p. 628, no. 2469.

[7]Voltaire, *Correspondence*, Theodore Besterman (ed.), vol. 93 (Geneva: *Institut et Musée Voltaire*, 1964), p. 140, no. 18819, Voltaire to Nicolas Toussaint Le Moyne dit Des Essarts, February 26, 1776.

[8]Antoine Guenée, *Lettres de quelques juifs portugais allemands et polonais à M. de Voltaire* (Paris: 1769).

[9]Voltaire, *Complete Works*, Theodore Besterman (ed.), "Key to Pseudonyms and Nicknames," in vol. 135 (Oxford: 1977), p. 985.

[10]Gotthold Ephraim Lessing, *Die Erziehung des Menschengeschlechts* (1780).

[11]Voltaire, *Correspondence*, vol. 58 (1960), p. 8, no. 11672, Voltaire to Charles Augustin Feriol, Comte d'Argental, and Jeanne Grâce Bosc Du Bouchet, Comtesse d'Argental, April 3, 1765.

[12]Ibid., vol. 52 (1960), p. 127, no. 10440, Voltaire to the Comte and Comtesse d'Argental, June 10, 1763.

[13]Ibid., vol. 49 (1959), p. 131, no. 9791, Voltaire to Isaac de Pinto, July 21, 1762.

[14]*Israel vengé, ou Exposition naturelle des prophéties hébraiques que les chrétiens appliquent à Jésus, leur prétendu messie* (London: 1770). Orobio's work was entitled *Prevenciones divinas contra la vana idolatria de las Gentes.*

[15]John Spencer, *De legibus Hebraeorum ritualibus et eorum rationibus, libri tres* (Cambridge: 1683–85).

[16]David Hume, *The Natural History of Religion* (1757), H. E. Root (ed.) (Stanford, California: Stanford University Press, 1957), p. 48.

[17]See Jefferson's copy of Holbach's *Le bon-sens ou Idées naturelles opposées aux idées surnaturelles* (London [Amsterdam]: 1772), with manuscript notes on the front flyleaf and in the margins (Houghton Library, Harvard University).

[18]Paul Henri Thiry, Baron d'Holbach, *L'Esprit du Judaïsme, ou Examen raisonné de la loi de Moyse, & de son influence sur la Religion Chrétienne* (London: 1770), pp. 175-76.

[19]Ibid., pp. 171-73.

[20]Ibid., p. 169.

[21]J. G. Herder, *Vom Geist der ebräischen Poesie* (1782).

[22]Moses Mendelssohn, *Gesammelte Schriften*, G. B. Mendelssohn (ed.) (Leipzig: 1844), vol. 5, p. 505, Moses Mendelssohn to Hofrath Michaelis in Göttingen, c. November 1770: "I feel certain that you will treat the Psalms as poetry, without regard to the prophetic and the mystical which Christian as well as Jewish expositors found in the Psalms only because they looked for them there; and they only looked for them because they were neither philosophers nor judges of literature." On the relations of Mendelssohn and Johann David Michaelis, see Alexander Altmann, *Moses Mendelssohn. A Biographical Study* (Philadelphia: Jewish Publication Society of America, 1973), pp. 242-44, where this letter is paraphrased. I owe the reference to Professor Altmann.

[23]Moses Mendelssohn, *Jerusalem, oder über religiöse Macht und Judentum* (Berlin: 1783).

[24]Edward Gibbon, *Decline and Fall of the Roman Empire*, chapter 2, section 1.

[25]*Commentary on the Documents of Vatican II* (New York: Herder, 1969), vol. 3, pp. 67-71.

[26]*The Sixteen Documents of Vatican II and the Instruction on the Liturgy* (Boston: Daughters of St. Paul, 1966), pp. 255-60. The official title of the document is: "Declaratio de Ecclesiae habitudine ad religiones non-Christianas."

WOLFGANG SCHLUCHTER

The Future of Religion[1]

IN 1927 SIGMUND FREUD published a short study on the future of religion. He gave it the revealing title *The Future of an Illusion*. Freud argued that illusions cannot simply be viewed as misperceptions and errors, even if they cannot be supported by reason. Rather, illusions express overwhelmingly powerful desires that human beings long to see fulfilled. Religious ideas represent such desires. They are meant to reconcile human beings with culture—that protective barrier against nature—which imposes deprivations and demands control over our instincts. Religious needs, therefore, arise from psychic repression, and religion itself appears as a kind of collective childhood neurosis. Although religion is a part of human culture and every human culture is repressive, this part and this repression can and should be left behind, for cultural prescriptions can be justified rationally. Therefore, Freud pleads for a revision of the relation of culture and religion. This revision ultimately aims at removing, through "rational intellectual effort," the repression constituted by religion and at replacing the religious with the scientific culture.[2]

More than fifty years have passed since Freud made his plea. Many reasons can be adduced for believing that today his own plea must be viewed as an illusion. It is true that especially in the advanced industrial societies of the West the end of religion has been proclaimed time and again since Freud's essay. In particular, the end of institutionalized religion has been asserted in the face of the ideological and institutional pressures of a secular culture and society.[3] But as early as the 1950s, some studies of the religious situation in the United States pointed to a paradox: Increasing this-worldliness in the secular spheres seems to go together with a strengthening of institutionalized religion.[4] Recently, a reversal was also asserted for the Federal Republic of Germany, a return of society to religion.[5] Moreover, in the countercultures of the Western industrialized societies, especially in the United States, the vanguard has apparently formed to lead a new religious movement, a nontheistic religion of this-worldly love, which combines secularized Christian with Buddhist and Hinduist traditions.[6]

Religion, however, has remained a major question not only in the First World. The vitality of religion has been demonstrated also in the Second and above all in the Third World. As the case of Poland shows, at least state socialism has not been able to solve the problem of religion in Freud's (and Marx's) sense. Furthermore, in parts of the Third World old religions have become political movements, especially in Islamic but also in Christian countries. Some Latin American developments have kindled the hope for a second Reformation in Europe itself. As the Catholic theologian Johann Baptist Metz, who has called for such a second Reformation, puts it: "This reformation would not come from Wittenberg or Rome, not from the Europe of the Christian Occident at all, but from the liberation movements within the poor churches of this world."[7]

Thus, fifty years after Freud we face a complex and ambivalent religious situation not only in the Third and Second World but also in the First. The two large Christian churches in Germany, for instance, the Catholic and the Protestant, which have been threatened with the prospect of turning from mass churches into churches without masses, seem to approach the reversal of a trend that was characterized less by an exodus than by passivity. Passive members are like Gogol's dead souls—they bring in money but no interaction. Many people remain church members in order to preserve the abstract option of participation, and many use it only "when it is too late for interaction—during their funeral."[8] It is true that a church that has some success in reversing the trend toward passivity among its members does not necessarily reform itself by this very token and compensate for its integrative weakness toward certain social groups, especially workers, intellectuals, and youth. Moreover, it is a matter of dispute what this return to religion means—whether it indicates merely a religious fashion or the need for a religious reformation.[9] In the Federal Republic of Germany the alleged reversal of the trend does not seem to affect the relatively harmonious relations of the two major churches to one another or to their social environment. We can thus ask with Metz: Does Christianity in West Germany remain, after all, a bourgeois religion? Its social value may be high and at present even rising. But does it have a messianic future and hence a specifically religious value for the future?[10]

If we want to answer this question, we should take leave of one aspect of Freud's theory of religion. As a sociologist I assume with many theologians that we have left behind certain historical configurations of religion but not religion itself.[11] Like many others before him, Freud stood in a tradition of the Enlightenment that wanted to replace religion by science, either by asserting that religious statements could be translated into scientific ones or by claiming that religion was a prescientific stage of knowledge destined to be succeeded by it. If we want to answer this question, we should, however, retain one aspect of Freud's theory of religion, at least as long as we want to provide a sociological and not a theological answer. Freud belongs to a tradition of the psychology and sociology of religion that interprets religion as the result of human action that creates and preserves the world as a meaningful cosmos. Like Ludwig Feuerbach, Karl Marx, Emile Durkheim, and Max Weber before him, Freud proceeds from the anthropological turn of the religious question.[12] Sociologically, this anthropological or, more accurately, anthropocentric perspective can be viewed as being itself a partial result of religious developments. But this perspective does not replace the theological—better, the theocentric— perspective. There is also no simple compatibility. At best the anthropocentric perspective provides a starting point for theological arguments, just as it uses the latter for its own purposes.

If we want to answer the question of the messianic future of Western Christianity, we should furthermore follow Freud's advice: We can improve the always risky assessment of the future of a cultural phenomenon if we base our judgment on a diagnosis of the past and present of the civilization of which it is a part.[13] I will attempt such a diagnosis of our religious situation. Of course, this can only be done in a very sketchy fashion, and I must dare to draw the picture with broad strokes. I will then proceed to examine the function of religion today and to speculate about its messianic future. I shall limit myself to the traditions of institutionalized Christianity, not because of any ethnocentric leanings and not because I consider Christianity to be the highest and last stage of religious development, as some philosophers of religion still believed in the nineteenth century. For pragmatic reasons I will leave out alternative world religions, among which I count not only Buddhism, Hinduism, and Islam but also Judaism.[14]

Every scientific investigation must approach its subject not only pragmatically but also analytically. In my case this requires a definition of religion. From a sociological perspective religion is the product of that "world-forming" action of human beings through which they constitute a sphere of the sacred, which is at the same time a realm of superior power. Religious action establishes and reinforces the distinction between a sacred and a profane sphere. The sacred appears as a reality that exists beyond or above the profane but that also remains connected with it. This is demonstrated especially in individual and collective extremities. Then it becomes clear that individual and collective action depends on circumstances beyond control.[15] For Max Weber, therefore, religion requires the construction of a world behind or above the world, which is usually populated by demons and gods. Ordering the relationship of demons and gods to human beings constitutes "the realm of religious action."[16] After a certain developmental level has been reached, this realm is organized by religious associations. They administer external or internal, this-worldly or otherworldly goods of salvation. They protect their order through the application of psychic coercion. They grant or deny those very goods for which they are responsible.[17] The structure and content of religious world views and of religious associations vary within and among religious traditions. A historical sociology of religion has the task of discovering these variations and their consequences. Its analytical subject, however, is religious action—that action which establishes or maintains a sacred cosmos by trying to control uncontrollable contingencies.

What is the constellation within which religious action takes place today? What are the most important characteristics of our contemporary religious situation? If we follow the familiar analyses of some theologians and of many sociologists, our present religious situation appears as the result of a process of secularization that has been going on for centuries. Secularization replaced religious values by secular values on the value level, an otherworldly by an inner-worldly orientation on the level of consciousness, and the primacy of the religious institutions by that of the political and economic ones on the institutional level.[18] The concept of secularization, however, has a dubious analytical status, because for a long time it was not a scientific notion. Like many other concepts employed by sociologists, secularization was at first a concept with which historical actors attempted to define their situation. It was a battle cry in the war of ideas. In the nineteenth century, in particular, it was used to demand the abolition of the allegedly illegitimate clerical domination, but it was also used for the opposite purpose. Thus, secularization was one of the central slogans in the church-state conflicts of the time. At the turn of the century Ernst Troeltsch and Max Weber attempted to neutralize the word.[19] Since then, secularization has denoted that dialectical historical process through which the Christian religion furthered the rise of modern industrial capitalism, of the modern state, and of modern science at the same time that it was increasingly weakened by these very inner-worldly powers. According to this definition, secularization is a historiographic and sociological category of a process, a summary term that describes a historical development that should be understood neither one-dimensionally nor one-sidedly. The concept refers to profound changes on the level of ideas and of the world views enveloping them, to basic changes on the level of material and ideal interests and of the attitudes corresponding to them, and to crucial institutional transformations within which individual and collective action takes place. Secularization, however, also refers to the fact that religion lost its power not only for external but also for internal reasons. In Max Weber's view, secularization, which he terms a process of disenchantment, originated in the pre-exilic Torah and the pre-exilic prophecy of ancient Israel and found decisive support in ascetic Protestantism, as it developed in the northwestern corner of Europe from the Reformation to the Westphalian Peace.[20]

I am using secularization in this neutralized sense when I ask: What is the function of Western Christian religion after secularization has largely run its course? In view of the desirable differentiation of the concept, I am primarily interested in two dimensions—the world views and the institutional arrangements. I would like to suggest two theses: (1) As far as the world views are concerned, largely completed secularization means that religious beliefs have become subjective as a result of the rise of alternative interpretations of life, which in principle can no longer be integrated into a religious world view. (2) As far as the institutions are concerned, largely completed secularization means that institutionalized religion has been depoliticized as a result of a functional differentiation of society, which in principle can no longer be integrated through institutionalized religion. I will draw on Max Weber's diagnosis of modern culture, mainly from his sociology of religion, to support the first thesis.[21] I will use arguments of recent systems theory to justify the second thesis.[22] Two questions can now be asked on the basis of the two theses. (1) Is there a legitimate religious resistance to secular world views that is more than a refusal to accept the consequences of the Enlightenment? (2) Is there a legitimate religious resistance to depoliticization, a resistance that is more than a clinging to inherited privileges? Both questions are linked to that of the messianic future of Western Christianity. Our answers should permit at least a rough estimate of the developmental tendencies in Western industrialized societies.

I now turn to the first thesis, the claim that the religious world view, in our case the Christian, is today confronted with alternative world views that it can no longer integrate, thus becoming a matter of subjective preference. This thesis is true of the relation of Christianity to the other great world religions. Ever since the disintegration of classical evolutionism, since the results produced by an empirically and historically oriented comparative study of religion, cultural anthropology, psychology, and sociology, it has become clear that these religions can no longer be ranked simply according to a sequence of stages.[23] (Today the various versions of neo-evolutionism in social science contrast with those of comparative historical sociology according to the different assessment of the role played by stage schemes for the reconstruction of historical processes.) Our thesis applies, however, primarily to the relationship of Christianity and secular humanism, as it was shaped by Hellenism, the Renaissance, and the Enlightenment.[24] It is true that Western Christianity has always lived in tension with the orders of the world and their values, especially with the economic, the political-legal, the aesthetic, and the sexual-erotic spheres, since it was a salvation religion based on the construct of a transcendental and personal creator God and a universalist ethic of brotherhood (both at least as tendencies). This tension grew the more the religious world view was intellectually rationalized and the more its claims were sublimated in the direction of an ethic of conviction, but also the more the "worldly" goods themselves were rationalized and sublimated by this religious development or for immanent reasons. This interpretation is central to Max Weber's comparative studies in the sociology of religion.[25] He discusses the ways in which these tensions were dealt with, in principle, not only by Christianity but also by other great world religions. Weber emphasizes, however, that in the Christian case the rise of secular humanism adds a new dimension to the tension between salvation religion and the world. The Enlightenment is the high point at which the integrated religious world view is confronted with an integrated secular world view, the presuppositions of which are mutually exclusive. Whereas before it seemed possible to achieve a direct unity, well-founded mutual recognition, or at least indifference between religious and secular values and goods, now a fundamental tension prevails that can no longer be hidden by some compromise formula.

What are the reasons for this fundamental tension? Wherein lies the heterogeneity, the "inescapable disparity" of the ultimate presuppositions of Christianity and secular humanism?[26] If we follow Weber—and I for one am ready to go a long way with him on this score—the Christian religion and the discipline that rationalizes it, theology, are forced to make two assumptions if they do not want to abandon themselves: The world is "willed by God and therefore somehow ethically meaningful," and its comprehension requires "certain revelations that must simply be accepted on faith as facts of salvation."[27] Only the idea of God can justify meaningful Christian conduct. Its foundation is a belief not in a kind of knowledge but in a kind of possession, the charisma of "illumination" or inspiration. Only those human beings who have been transfused with this experience can be positively religious and adhere to a positive theology. In spite of the cognitive component that is part and parcel of the belief in religious salvation, this spiritual possession involves "at some point the *credo non quod, sed quia absurdum*, the 'sacrifice of the intellect.' "[28] Secular humanism, too, and the disciplines rationalizing it—philosophy and the empirical sciences—are forced to make at least two assumptions if they want to remain true to themselves. The world is not merely in the grip of natural causality but also subject to ethical control, and for this purpose the continuous improvement of our knowledge about the world by means of the rational concept and the rational experiment is a necessary, if possibly insufficient, condition.[29] Meaningful secular humanist conduct can be based only on the idea of humanity. Its foundation is a belief not in a kind of possession but in a kind of knowledge, "an ultimate intellectual knowledge about the is and the ought"—the charisma of reason. It is true that this charisma of reason, which proved its historical efficacy during the Enlightenment and the democratic revolutions of the eighteenth century, has in the meantime largely disappeared. For a long time the dialectic of Enlightenment, and the paradox of the rationalization caused by it, has replaced the glorification of reason by disillusionment, indifference, and even hostility, and the idea of world mastery through empirical knowledge pursues us like a nightmare in view of the world's potential self-destruction with the means of science. Moreover, although the empirical disciplines depend on value presuppositions, they have turned away from the problem of the world's meaning. At any rate, no empirical science that is aware of its limitations tries to promise a way to true happiness. Philosophy, too, finds it difficult to interpret the value presuppositions of the individual sciences, to develop them systematically, and to integrate them into a coherent world view appropriate to the post–Enlightenment period. Thus, it is not surprising that some prefer to become trumpeters of the counter-Enlightenment instead of carrying on the no longer rosy heritage of the Enlightenment under the changed conditions. Furthermore, as in the past, we hear today not only the voices of the counter-Enlightenment but, especially among academic youth, the voices of those who search for the kind of experience ("kicks") that can be had only by turning against modern science. Nevertheless, the disenchantment of the world through modern science is an irreversible fact. Those who want to lead a secular humanist life must claim that modern science is for them "the only possible form of thinking about the world."[30] In spite of the recognition of the paradox of unintended consequences of their own actions they must also believe that there "are in principle no mysterious unpredictable forces" and "that all things can in principle be controlled through calculation."[31] At the same time, secular humanism is committed to purely this-worldly individual or collective goals of perfection, which must be outright unacceptable to religion and even to that theology that has participated in the anthropological turn. Therefore, there must be a fundamental tension and conflict between a religious and a secular world view, between religious and secular humanist conduct, rather than unity, recognition, or indifference. This is true even if modern science, with its humanist orientation, largely abandons its interest in unmasking religion, which it pursued for a long time, in view of its recognition of its own historical preconditions and limitations. Among other reasons, this fundamental tension arises from the fact that secular humanism has pushed religion out of "the realm of the rational": Religion appears to it not necessarily as "the irrational or anti-rational" power, but as the nonrational power.[32] Even more, secular humanism, with the support of some sectors of theology, helps to make religion subjective through its idea of a world that can in principle be controlled through calculation and is thus without surprises. Religion is translated from an external fact into a component of individual consciousness.[33]

Thus, the religious and the secular world views confront one another today. Both claim to be total world views. Irrespective of all variations, the one can be called theocentric and the other anthropocentric. Both suggest an ultimate position through which they attribute meaning to the world with its value spheres and institutional realms. In the one case the world is understood as a process of salvation driven by the dialectic of sinfulness and redemption; in the other, primarily as a natural and cultural process caught up in the dialectic of dependency and emancipation.[34] If the carriers of these ultimate positions do not avoid each other, if they face one another without neutralizing their fundamental conflict on the level of ideas through so-called "liberal" interpretations and on the level of action through opportunism, they will relativize each other. Each will define the other as the carrier of a partial world view, which at best can offer a limited interpretation of the world. In this struggle the secular world view has been on the offensive for a long time. In fact, it has displaced the religious world view as the dominant one. Of course, the religious world view was never without competition, not even in the Middle Ages after the transition from the Carolingian to the Gregorian church. This transformation aimed not only at creating a culture controlled by the church but at a whole Christian society.[35] But then and for a long time to come, the competition took place in a setting in which the religious world view was dominant and the religious institutions were dominant, that is, "regulatory agencies for both thought and action."[36] This situation has changed radically. Although the two Christian churches in West Germany count the majority of the population among their members, the carriers of a religious world view are today a "cognitive minority."[37] They represent no longer a dominant interpretation of the world, but at best a partial world view among many others. Apparently this partial world view does not modify and specify the dominant one but deviates from it and therefore is faced with special problems of legitimation. Of course, this is not merely a matter of changing relations among ideas on the level of world views but also among church, state, university, and the like on the institutional level.

This brings me to my second thesis: In a functionally differentiated society institutionalized religion is depoliticized and society can no longer be integrated through it. Sociologists distinguish societies, among other criteria, according to the form of primary differentiation—whether it is segmental, stratified, or functional. In this sequence, transitions from one to the other form are related to processes of external and internal differentiation. In the first case (that of external differentiation), new tasks come into being or old ones are newly defined. This leads to changes in the kind and relationship of the social orders of a society. In the second case new environmental conditions demand from the existing social orders as a rule a reorganization of their internal structure.[38] Beginning with the Middle Ages, but definitely since the French Revolution, institutionalized religion has had to deal with the consequences of functional differentiation.[39] Apparently it is very difficult for it to find a place in a society whose contexts of individual and collective action are shaped to a significant degree by functional differentiation.

How has functional differentiation affected the kind and position of the religious sphere in society? To answer this question, it is useful to describe very briefly the institutional constellation out of which this process arose—medieval society, which in ideal-typical simplification can be seen as a society with stratified differentiation. Medieval society already knew spheres characterized by selectivity, particularity, and specialization, but these were coordinated in such a manner that an all-inclusive hierarchical structure came into being, at least as a tendency. In this structure the church played a particularly important role. It monopolized the religious tasks and, in contrast to the ancient Christian church, endeavored to penetrate the whole world. It aimed to be a universal church and no longer to be a regional one. The goal of the medieval church was "to transfuse all of mankind with sacramental grace."[40] To accomplish this, the church gave precedence, at the latest since the Gregorian reform, to the papal over the episcopal principle and strove to subordinate the secular to the sacred power. It was the duty of the church to mediate between God and the world, since it perpetuated God's incarnation in Christ. Through this mediation the church must protect as well as support the secular power (imperium). Political authority, too, was considered an instrument for the Christianization of the world. As the Investiture Conflict and its consequences show, the religious order did not succeed in imposing an unequivocally vertical coordination of universal church and empire, religious and political domination.[41] But religious values and institutions were ranked above the secular ones. The actual institutional arrangements reinforced the dominance of the religious world view. In Ernst Troeltsch's sense, medieval society can be regarded as the institutional articulation of a "relatively unified Christian culture" embodied in both the universal church and the empire.[42] It is true that next to the religious culture, which was primarily one of monks and priests, a secular culture arose, especially a knightly and courtly feudal culture and increasingly the culture of the urban citizenry. But, according to Troeltsch: "Only the church reigned supreme, not the state, economic production, science or art. The transcendental values of the Gospel might encounter worldliness, hedonism, sensuality and violence, but it was not confronted by competing ideals, a secular culture that would have been independent of the church and capable of creating an autonomous order."[43]

The central position of the religious sphere in the hierarchical structure of medieval society and the dominance of its world view are reinforced by the internal organization of this very sphere. The claims to autonomy and autocephaly toward the outside are combined with a centralist and hierarchical organization, with a relatively advanced bureaucratic structure.[44] The relatively unified Christian culture of the society at large rests on a relatively unified ecclesiastic culture of the religious sphere.[45] For Max Weber, the institutional backbone of the religious sphere is the church as a bureaucratic organization that administers grace through priestly sacraments. Of course, this church had to contend long before the Reformation with heterodox religious movements, which challenged her religious monopoly of interpretation and organization. In particular, these movements opposed the ecclesiastic model of organization with the alternative model of the sect, which from the earliest Christian beginnings constituted part of the realization of the Gospel. The universal church absorbed many of these currents through internal differentiation, by recognizing special organizations in which religious virtuosi could act upon their heightened needs for salvation. This had positive consequences for the church and did not compel a basic reformation of its organization.[46] Just as externally the church ranked above the empire and the other secular institutions, so internally the priest, who had the powers of the keys and the monopoly of the sacraments, took precedence over the laity, whereas the religious virtuoso, the monk, stood above the priest, who as mediator between the sacred and the profane was in closer touch with the this-worldly orders and their autonomous values. The externally and internally important ideal of a hierarchic structure was formulated in the most impressive manner in the Thomist ethic. "The architecture of instrumental stages" and the notion of a "crowning stage of ecclesiastic sacramental grace in which mankind is unified and finds its fulfillment" permitted this Thomist ethic to conceive of the unity of the system as a whole and yet to grant to every stage its relative autonomy.[47]

Medieval society, then, was a religious society dominated by a Christian world view and deeply influenced by a bureaucratic universal church, which successfully monopolized the dispensation of grace. In this society the individuals were not given the choice of whether they wanted to have religion. They must have it. The question was merely how much or how little religion they had. The answer was given not by the individual but by the church, which decided the salvation of every individual, since there is no salvation outside of it. Its most severe sanction was exclusion from the sacraments, excommunication, which involves not only the loss of "salvation chances" but also of worldly life chances. Although the religious sphere is differentiated from the other spheres to such an extent that the latter can develop varying degrees of internal differentiation, the laity cannot disengage the political from the religious role. Membership in society depends on belonging to a political and a religious association.[48]

Modern society has broken this connection, since it is a society based primarily on functional differentiation. This form of differentiation forgoes the integration of the social spheres into a hierarchical whole and enormously increases the selectivity, particularity, and specialization of the spheres. The rigid and permanent hierarchy is replaced by the flexible and open competition of the spheres. Of course, a functionally differentiated society too must be integrated through the coordination of the social spheres. This is, however, a negative rather than a positive integration. The rules of coordination are not meant to establish a permanent rank order among the spheres, which would be legitimated through the "unity of a highest value or through a value system or value hierarchy." Rather, the rules are supposed to make it impossible "that the operations of a partial system lead to insoluble problems in another partial system."[49] When difficulties arise, the regulatory needs are satisfied by recourse to secular values, especially political ones. The latter may have a religious origin, as Georg Jellinek showed with the example of the Rights of Man and of Citizens, but they themselves are not religious.[50] The functional differentiation of the religious and political order leads to the separation of state and church, to the transformation of the Christian state into the "free state." This change has been treated especially by the left Hegelian critique of religion in the nineteenth century as a political emancipation from religion.[51] It has influenced the state-church conflicts until far into the twentieth century. Moreover, the functional differentiation of the religious and the political spheres has also led to the privatization of religious life. As the state and bourgeois society are separated, religion is assigned to the latter and thus "depoliticized" for structural reasons.[52] When religious freedom became a Right of Man, instituted in the wake of the democratic revolutions of the eighteenth century, this involved not only the right to adhere to one's own religion but also the right to be free of religion. For laypersons the religious role becomes a private role and their access to society is regulated through the secular role of citizenship.[53]

The depoliticization of religion as a result of functional differentiation does not mean, of course, that religious associations forgo politics. As before, they attempt to make the political order instrumental for the religious world view. In comparison with other associations, religious associations also retain a number of institutional privileges in spite of advanced secularization. In sociological perspective, some religious associations appear today as "separatist" churches that try to retain their past role. But in spite of the importance that religion still has for political decisions, especially in matters of education and family life, it cannot be denied that outside of the religious sphere itself the areas subject to penetration by religious values continue to shrink. The European Christian parties, too, which endeavor to bridge the religious and the political sphere, must follow the imperatives of a functionally differentiated political order, which can no longer be exclusively oriented—in fact, not even primarily oriented—to religious values. Religion is today not only privatized, its claims are also considerably restricted by the relative autonomy of the other social spheres. This forces religion to be highly selective, particularized, and specialized. Given the state of the social environment, religious specialization cannot choose areas for which other spheres were differentiated, that is, the areas of politics, economics, science, art, and leisure. Although the mass churches tend to react today to their changed position in society through the assumption of tasks that belong in these areas, their specialization must focus on the three central functions of the Christian tradition: spiritual communication, charity, and the reflection on these internal and external functions, theology.[54]

In contrast to medieval society, then, modern society has structurally changed the relation of the religious sphere to the other spheres and thus brought about a depoliticization and privatization of religion. But this is only one aspect that emerges with advanced secularization on the institutional level. Another is that the religious sphere itself has been differentiated segmentally. This process began with the Reformation, which broke the spiritual monopoly of the medieval church: internally through the new doctrine of the sacraments, which put a community of believers next to the church as a sacramental institution and the teacher of faith next to the priest as the dispenser of grace; and externally through the split of the church, which led to denominationalism.[55] Therewith arose a religious pluralism that reinforced the depoliticization and privatization of institutionalized religion. The religious believer must cope not only with secular but also with other religious world views.[56] This makes it difficult to regard one's own beliefs as the only road to salvation. Universal church and sect are replaced by partial or quasi churches and denominations, which only claim to offer one road to salvation among others.[57] It is true that the claims of universal church and sect persist and that religious pluralism can justify at least Christian ecumenism. But religious pluralism weakens the institutional position of the individual religious association, both in relation to other spheres as well as in relation to members by birth if not by conversion, who may come to feel that their membership is accidental.[58]

Our contemporary religious situation is thus characterized by two tendencies that are part of advanced secularization. The first is the tendency of modern culture to treat the religious world view as a partial one and to make religion subjective, and the second is the tendency of modern society to depoliticize institutional religion, to privatize it, and to specify its social function in such a way that it serves the exclusive purpose of interpreting and organizing the relation of human beings to the sacred. Both tendencies have been directed against the traditional structure and position of religion and have forced a response. Catholicism replied primarily with the institutional strengthening of the universal church as a sacramental institution, Protestantism with a greater effort at theological reflection.[59] There have been attempts at a countersecularization, but in the meantime the old front lines have largely crumbled. Religion and the secular world have reconciled themselves to one another. This is not accidental, for modern culture and modern society can tolerate religion as long as it limits itself to a specific sphere. The secular world view recognizes an open pluralism of individual and collective ideals of perfection, which can include religious goals; functional differentiation as the primary form of differentiation recognizes an open pluralism of functions, which includes also the religious function. In the last analysis, however, religion cannot accept this placement. It represents a total world view and must raise total, and hence also political, claims.

In conclusion, I can now answer my two questions: (1) Is there a justified religious resistance to the secular world view that is more than a denial of the Enlightenment? and (2) Is there a justified religious resistance to depoliticization that is more than a clinging to inherited privileges?

The secular world view grew out of the charismatic glorification of reason. It is based on the idea of the self-sufficiency of the intellect. The belief has waned, but the idea has remained and with it the ideal of inner-worldly self-perfection. This ideal lies at the root of the rationalism of world mastery, which shapes our lives. For religion this ideal must be meaningless, since it cannot come to terms with what is perhaps the most difficult problem of life—death, which negates the ideal of inner-worldly perfection.[60] Death is, however, not the only uncontrollable contingency with which we are faced. It is true that today we can control some forces that appeared uncontrollable in the past; and some things that elude us today will become manageable in the future. Nevertheless, our lives will remain subject to inescapable contingencies. The secular world view reaches its limits when it asks for the meaning of these uncontrollable contingencies. The experience of this dependency is not yet a religious experience, but it reveals the reasons for the existence of religion. As Hermann Lübbe has put it, speaking in religious terms means to realize the contingencies of the world and of our lives within it. Religious practice is the recognition of this fact, but only if it is linked up with the notion of salvation.[61] Recognition of the fact of dependency and acceptance of a certain interpretation of it are two different steps. The second requires, in the case of religion, the sacrifice of the intellect. Whoever cannot take this step will remain unmusical in matters religious. But recognition of the fact of contingency may make a person feel friendly toward religion.

Thus, the carriers of religious world views have good reasons for resisting the secular view. The recognition of nonrational, transcendental powers, upon whom our lives depend, is not tantamount to denying the Enlightenment. There are questions of meaning that cannot be answered without going beyond an inner-worldly attitude. This remains true even if the majority of human beings no longer tries to face these questions. It is the task of religion to transcend the existing world and to remind it of its contingency. Therefore, institutionalized religion also has good reasons to resist the depoliticization that results from its being pushed back into a sphere of its own. Still, if religion today insists on a total view, it can at best be politically relevant but no longer politically dominant.

Does such a religion, however, still have the power to transcend the existing world? Is it still capable of a turnabout that would be a precondition for not just complementing the secular life but for breaking out of it and with it? Is such a religion still able to offer the charisma of inspiration? Has not its bureaucratic constitution ruined its ability to change hearts? This is the opinion of Johann Baptist Metz and probably of other political theologians from both Catholicism and Protestantism. Metz sees a future for this religion only if it turns around and regains its messianic dimension. Metz regards the turnabout as a new understanding of salvation and of the life of the church. He thinks of salvation in terms of palpable, concrete, visible, and liberating grace and of the life of the church as a solidary community united around the eucharist, a group that is no longer necessarily guided by a permanent official. Metz therefore pleads for the transition from the tutelary church to the liberation church, a church that is no longer a church for the people but a church of the people.[62]

What are the chances of institutionalized religion finding its way back to its messianic dimension? After all, this dimension has been largely lost. The path proposed by Metz might indeed lead to a new Reformation, but with consequences that cannot be intended by political theology. From a sociological perspective, Metz's proposal amounts to an abandonment of the church as a large-scale bureaucratic organization in favor of a small democratic group or even a charismatic community. This would be quite compatible with a functionally differentiated society, but also without much political importance. Similar to the family, such a "church" would likely become part of the background structure of society, a realm of perhaps private but hardly of political revolution. For in a functionally differentiated society, a sphere that wants to revolutionize not only itself but above all its social environment must resort to generalized media of exchange and complex organization. For this, Christian love and the small eucharistic group are insufficient. The proposal of such a political theology indirectly supports Max Weber's diagnosis of the present: The disenchantment of the world has deprived charisma and religious messianism of a good deal of their once revolutionary impetus.[63]

Does this mean that Christianity has no messianic future? I do not doubt that the prospects for a new prophetic inspiration (*Pneuma*) that could revolutionize a functionally differentiated society are not good. We live in a culture and society that are in part a product of religion but that largely emancipated themselves from it. If they do not face it with hostility, they do so with indifference. It was once again Max Weber who in his famous study of the Protestant ethic and the spirit of capitalism penetratingly analyzed this connection with regard to the modern occupational culture. No one knows, Weber wrote, who will live in the housing of our technological and scientific civilization "or whether at the end of this tremendous development entirely new prophets will arise, or there will be a great rebirth of old ideas and ideals, or, if neither, mechanized petrification, embellished with a sort of convulsive self-importance."[64] If this is the alternative, and much speaks for it, then we should wish religion a messianic future, even if we are unmusical in matters religious.

REFERENCES

[1]This article appeared in slightly different form under the title "Über die Zukunft der Religionen" in *Kölner Zeitschrift für Soziologie und Sozialpsychologie*, 1981, Issue 4. I am grateful to Guenther Roth for translating it from the German, and to Ottmar Olhausen for his assistance in translating the footnotes and locating their English references. The quotations from Weber's writings are re-translated, but the references are to the standard English translations.

[2]See Sigmund Freud, *The Future of an Illusion*, New York, Doubleday Anchor, 1964.

[3]See, among others, Peter L. Berger, *A Rumor of Angels: Modern Society and the Rediscovery of the Supranatural*, New York, Doubleday, 1969, p. 1: "If commentators on the contemporary situation of religion agree about anything, it is that the supranatural has departed from the modern world. This departure may be stated in such dramatic formulations as 'God is dead' or 'the post-Christian era.' "

[4]See Will Herberg, *Protestant-Catholic-Jew: An Essay in American Religious Sociology*, New York, Doubleday Anchor 1960, especially chap. 1.

[5]See Johann Baptist Metz, *The Emergent Church*, New York, Crossroad, 1981, Munich, Matthias-Grünewald.

[6]See Talcott Parsons, *Action Theory and the Human Condition*, New York, Free Press 1978, pp. 253 ff. and pp. 312 ff. As to the religious components of the American counterculture, see Günther Roth, "Religion and Revolutionary Beliefs," in Günther Roth and Wolfgang Schluchter, *Max Weber's Vision of History: Ethics and Methods*, Berkeley, University of California Press 1979, pp. 144 ff., especially pp. 159 ff.; Robert Bellah and Charles Glock, eds., *The New Religious Consciousness*, Berkeley, University of California Press 1976; and Robert Wuthnow, *Experimentation in American Religion*, Berkeley, University of California Press 1978.

[7]Metz, *Jenseits*, p. 82.

[8]See Niklas Luhmann, *Funktion der Religion*, Frankfurt, Suhrkamp/KNO 1977, p. 300.

[9]This depends not only on the intellectual and social relevance of the religious movements but also on structural factors of the modern societies. See Peter L. Berger, *The Sacred Canopy: Elements of a Sociological Theory of Religion*, New York, Doubleday Anchor 1967, and Daniel Bell, *The Cultural Contradictions of Capitalism*, New York, Basic Books 1976, especially pp. 146 ff.

[10]Metz, *Jenseits*, p. 9

[11]See Hermann Lübbe, *Philosophie nach der Aufklärung: Von der Notwendigkeit pragmatischer Vernunft*, Düsseldorf, Econ 1980, p. 59.

[12]This anthropological turn in regard to religion is stated by Feuerbach and the early Marx. See Ludwig Feuerbach, *Grundsätze der Philosophie der Zukunft* (1843) and Karl Marx, *Zur Kritik der Hegelschen Rechtsphilosophie: Einleitung* (1843-44). As to the impact of this turn on the sociology of religion, see especially the quoted writings of Peter L. Berger.

[13]See Freud, *Future of an Illusion*.

[14]See Max Weber, "The Social Psychology of the World Religions," in Hans H. Gerth and C. Wright Mills, eds., *From Max Weber: Essays in Sociology*, New York, Oxford University Press 1958, pp. 267 ff. As to the place of the Jewish tradition in this connection see Wolfgang Schluchter, "Altisraelitische religiöse Ethik und okzidentaler Rationalismus," in Wolfgang Schluchter, ed., *Max Webers Studie über das antike Judentum: Interpretation und Kritik*, Frankfurt, Suhrkamp/KNO 1981, pp. 11 ff., especially pp. 54 ff. See also Peter L. Berger, *The Heretical Imperative: Contemporary Possibilities of Religious Affirmation*, New York, Doubleday Anchor 1979, chap. 6.

[15]Here I am grounding my view on the work of Emile Durkheim in connection with proposals developed by Berger, Luhmann, and Lübbe.

[16]Max Weber, *Economy and Society: An Outline of Interpretive Sociology*, Berkeley, University of California Press, 1968, p. 403.

[17]Ibid., p. 54.

[18]This notion of secularization is developed in Parsons, *Action Theory*, pp. 240 ff. See also Luhmann, *Funktion der Religion*, chap. 4.

[19]See Hermann Lübbe, *Säkularisierung: Geschichte eines ideenpolitischen Begriffs*, Freiburg, K. Alber 1965, especially chap. 4.

[20]About this point of view, which is derived from Weber, see Berger, *Sacred Canopy*, chap. 5, and Talcott Parsons, *The System of Modern Societies*, Englewood Cliffs, N.J., Prentice-Hall, 1971, chaps. 3 and 4.

[21]Important in this context are Max Weber's studies on the world religions and his speech "Science as a Vocation," in Gerth and Mills, *From Max Weber*, pp. 129 ff. For an interpretation, see Wolfgang Schluchter, "The Paradox of Rationalization: On the Relation of Ethics and World," in Roth and Schluchter, *Weber's Vision of History*, pp. 11 ff.

[22]See especially the quoted writings of Parsons and Luhmann. See also Niklas Luhmann, *The Differentiation of Society* (New York: Columbia University Press, 1982), chap. 10.

[23]One feature that distinguishes sociological neo-evolutionism from comparative historical sociology is its use of stage-concepts for the reconstruction of historical processes.

[24]I adapt the concept of secular humanism from Talcott Parsons. He identifies four main cultural movements in modern societies, especially in the United States: Catholicism, Judaism, Protestantism, and secular humanism. See Parsons, *Action Theory*, pp. 249 ff. and 308 ff.

[25]See Max Weber, "Religious Rejections of the World and Their Directions," in Gerth and Mills, *From Max Weber*, pp. 323 ff. Already Karl Mannheim regarded this text as an elucidating example for the generalizing apprehension of Weltanschauung. See Karl Mannheim, *Strukturen des Denkens*, Frankfurt, Suhrkamp/KNO 1980, p. 139.

[26]Weber, "Religious Rejections," p. 352.

[27]Ibid., p. 351, and Weber, "Science as a Vocation," p. 154.

[28]Weber, "Religious Rejections," p. 352.

[29]See Weber, "Science as a Vocation," pp. 139 ff.

[30]Weber, "Religious Rejections," p. 355.

[31]Weber, "Science as a Vocation," p. 139.

[32]Weber, "Religious Rejections," p. 351. It was Talcott Parsons who in his early writings emphasized the importance of the distinction between the irrational and the nonrational in sociological theory. See also Parsons, *Action Theory*, pp. 233 ff., and Wolfgang Schluchter, "Gesellschaft und Kultur: Überlegungen zu einer Theorie institutioneller Differenzierung," in Wolfgang Schluchter, ed., *Verhalten, Handeln und System: Talcott Parsons' Beitrag zur Entwicklung der Sozialwissenschaften*, Frankfurt, Suhrkamp/KNO 1980, pp. 119 ff.

[33]Berger, *Sacred Canopy*, p. 166. See also Thomas Luckmann, *The Invisible Religion*, New York, Macmillan 1967.

[34]See Wolfgang Schluchter, *The Rise of Western Rationalism: Max Weber's Developmental History*, Berkeley, University of California Press 1981, p. 52.

[35]As to this point see the classical study of Ernst Troeltsch, *The Social Teaching of the Christian Churches and Sects*, New York, Macmillan 1949, pp. 223 ff., and, partly in reference to Troeltsch, Parsons, *Action Theory*, pp. 243 ff.

[36]Berger, *Sacred Canopy*, p. 134.

[37]Ibid., p. 152.

[38]See Luhmann, *Funktion der Religion*, p. 89 ff.

[39]Ibid., pp. 231 ff.

[40]Troeltsch, *Social Teaching*, p. 234.

[41]This is related to an institutional invention, which had a great relevance for further development. See M. Rainer Lepsius, "Modernisierungspolitik als Institutionenbildung: Kriterien institutioneller Differenzierung," in Wolfgang Zapf, ed., *Probleme der Modernisierungspolitik*, Meisenheim am Glan, Hain, 1977, pp. 17 ff.

[42]Troeltsch, *Social Teaching*, p. 247; also pp. 235 ff., 246, 257 ff.

[43]Ibid., p. 252.

[44]See Weber, *Economy and Society*, pp. 828 ff., 1163 ff.

[45]See Troeltsch, *Social Teaching*, pp. 223 ff. In Weber's view, however, the Occidental Middle Ages are largely lacking the character of a unified culture. See his *Economy and Society*, pp. 1192 ff.

[46]See Weber's analysis of hierocracy and monasticism in his *Economy and Society*, pp. 1168 ff.

[47]Troeltsch, *Social Teaching*, p. 273.

[48]See Parsons, *Action Theory*, pp. 243 ff.

[49]Niklas Luhmann, *Zweckbegriff und Systemrationalität: Über die Funktion von Zwecken in sozialen Systemen*, Frankfurt, Suhrkamp/KNO 1973, p. 38, and Luhmann, *Funktion der Religion*, p. 242.

[50]See Günther Roth, "Charisma and the Counterculture," in Roth and Schluchter, *Weber's Vision of History*, p. 133.

[51]See Bruno Bauer, *Feldzüge der reinen Kritik*, Frankfurt, Suhrkamp/KNO 1968.

[52] See Hegel's classical analysis in his *Philosophy of Right* (New York: Oxford University Press, 1967) and Marx's critical analysis of it in his *Critique of Hegel's 'Philosophy of Right'* (Cambridge: Cambridge University Press, 1970).

[53] See Lübbe, *Philosophie nach der Aufklärung*, p. 60.

[54] According to Niklas Luhmann, these are the central functions of religion. See his *Funktion der Religion*, pp. 54 ff.

[55] See the analysis of Parsons in *Action Theory*, pp. 244 ff. and 304 ff.

[56] See Berger, *Rumor of Angels*, pp. 55 ff., who sees secularization as generally connected with the pluralization of socially accessible worlds.

[57] There is a broad discussion and no consensus on an adequate typology of religious organizations. A good overview, combined with an interesting suggestion, can be found in Roland Robertson, *The Sociological Interpretation of Religion*, New York, Schocken 1972, pp. 113 ff., especially p. 123. I modify Robertson's suggestion somewhat and distinguish four religious forms of organization: universal church, partial church, sect, and denomination.

Typology of Religious Organizations

Legitimation based on / Membership based on	the only way to salvation	one way to salvation
ascription	universal church	partial church
achievement	sect	denomination

[58] See Lübbe, *Philosophie nach der Aufklärung*, p. 84.

[59] One of the crucial attempts by Catholicism to counter secularization was connected with Vatican I. Papal infallibility became dogmatized, which makes some observers believe that this meant the apotheosis of the emerging idea of a church. See Thomas O'Dea, *The Catholic Crisis*, Boston, Beacon Press 1968, pp. 18 ff., whose analysis, however, is focused on Vatican II. Protestantism countered secularization by developing liberal theology. According to Berger, this led to a theological synthesis, which is matched only by Thomism. See Berger, *Sacred Canopy*, p. 158.

[60] See Weber, "Religious Rejections," pp. 355 ff.

[61] See Lübbe, *Philosophie nach der Aufklärung*, pp. 79 ff.

[62] Metz, *Jenseits*, pp. 87 ff.

[63] See Weber, "Science as a Vocation," p. 155.

[64] Max Weber, *The Protestant Ethic and the Spirit of Capitalism*, New York, Scribners 1958, p. 182.

STEVEN M. TIPTON

The Moral Logic of Alternative Religions

WIDESPREAD INTEREST IN "NEW RELIGIONS," now a decade old, has yet to yield a clear overview of their relation to traditional norms and values, their appeal to specific social groups, and their resonance with broader changes in American culture. Instead, we find ourselves still awash in exotic ethnographic detail, buffeted by membership statistics, or swept away by generalizations on modernity that new religions as an undifferentiated class are supposed to reflect. To clarify our overview of these movements and their ideas, we need to look more closely at the cultural dynamics of conversion to them. Youth of the sixties have joined alternative religious movements of the seventies and eighties basically, I will argue, to make moral sense of their lives.[1] Their conversion may be an intensely personal and subjective change of heart, but it is also a change of mind that draws on and transforms the public, objectified resources for moral meaning carried by our culture.

To trace the process of conversion as a shift in moral outlook, we must inquire into the ways Americans understand right and wrong, into how they think out their morality, and how they live it out. What shape do moral ideas take in individual lives and in the life of a society? Why at times do they weaken and break down? How do they undergo change and find renewal? What results from attention to such questions is a kind of moral anthropology, built around descriptive ethics and interpretive sociology. It uses philosophical categories to analyze the inner logic of moral ideas, and then probes the social conditions that make these ideas particularly plausible to the people who hold them. This approach assumes that the coherence of social life rests on the convictions we share about its moral meanings. We can act and experience momentarily without conscious reference to these meanings, but we cannot *know* what we're doing or feeling without thinking about it in their light. Social and economic conditions influence our thinking, but they do not do it for us. Instead, they intersect with culture in speech to provide the crux of social action. The moral sense we make of our lives, and of one another, takes the form of discourse about what is good, which acts are right, and who is virtuous. Concern for the actual content of this moral discourse and respect for its integrity as a living text mark the starting point of this paper. It will take what people say about how they see, judge, and make sense of their lives as raw evidence for the way they make and change their culture.

Table 1. Styles of Ethical Evaluation

	Oriented to	Mode of Knowledge	Discourse	Right-making Characteristic	Virtue
Authoritative	Authority (God)	Faith/ Conscience	What does God command?	Commanded by God	Obedience
Regular	Rules	Reason	What is the relevant rule, principle?	Conforms to rules	Rationality
Consequential	Consequences	Cost/benefit calculation	What do I want? What will most satisfy it?	Produces most good consequences	Efficiency
Expressive	Self and situation	Intuition/ feelings	What's happening?	Expresses self/responds to situations	Sensitivity

Adapted from Ralph Potter, *Nuclear Dilemma* (see Ref. 3).

Understood in ethical terms, the ideas we hold give us a model of and for social reality.[2] They tell us what is so and what we ought to do about it. They mirror the world we enter every day, and they point out the path we ought to take through it, so that we can justify self and society only in relation to each other. To hold moral discourse central to the study of conversion, and of social life generally, is not to imagine ordinary persons as moral philosophers writ small, but rather to recognize that they, like us, ask themselves, "What should I do now? Why?" and that their answers matter just as much to them as do ours to us.

This approach enables us to address to ideologically and socially distinct movements the same fundamental ethical questions: *What is good in itself? What makes an act right? What makes a person worthy of praise or blame? What concrete cases decisively test these general views?* We can, then, ask philosophically unified questions both of different traditions in our culture and of individuals in different movements allied with given traditions. We can also analyze their answers in light of ethical theories tied to the sweep of Western high culture, now being re-created or changed through the concrete experience of persons who live in a particular generation, time, and place in American society.

Interpreted as a shift in moral outlook, the process of conversion begins with problems of right and wrong that an earlier view cannot resolve and a later one can. Such problems are couched in the social situation of those who face them, and their solution turns on changes in that situation. The conflict of values between mainstream American culture and counterculture during the 1960s framed problems that alternative religious movements of the 1970s and 1980s have mediated and resolved. Whether conservative Christian, neo-Oriental, or psychotherapeutic, these movements are successors to this conflict. In its terms they have acquired their special significance for the sixties youth who make up their core membership. These youths were raised on traditional ethics they came to deny in favor of countercultural values, only to find these, too, impossible to live out. At the end of their youth, and the decade, they converted to religious movements that resolved their moral predicament by recombining elements of its opposing sides into unified ethics that have given new meaning to their experience and new purpose to their lives. Contrasting styles of ethical evaluation have shaped this conflict and its mediation. These styles distinctively characterize the romantic tradition of the counterculture and, as well, the two traditions that underpin mainstream culture, biblical religion and utilitarian individualism.[3]

Styles of American Moral Culture

Biblical religion traditionally conceives of reality in terms of an absolute objective God who is the Creator and Father of all human beings. God reveals himself to them in sacred scripture and commands them to obey him. Biblical morality embodies an "authoritative" style of ethical evaluation. This means it is oriented toward an authoritative moral source whose will is known by faith, conscience, and scriptural exegesis. The moral question, "What should I do?" is posed by asking, "What does God command?" An act is right because divine authority commands it. It is to be done in obedience, the cardinal virtue of this ethic. (See Table 1 for the styles of ethical evaluation typified here.)

In addition to this revelational aspect, biblical religion includes a rationalist line of development, characterized by a rule-governed or "regular" style of ethical evaluation. It is oriented to rules and principles of right conduct as discerned by dialectical reason. It poses the moral question, "What should I do?" by asking, "What is the relevant rule or principle?" An act is right, not solely by virtue of its consequences, but because it conforms in itself to rules of action taken as relevant by reason. It also accords with the regularity of nature and human existence. To do the act, therefore, is a matter of rationality, defined by canons of consistency and generalizability, the cardinal virtue of the regular ethic. In this sense, the rationalist believer holds that God commands an act because it is right, not that an act is right because God commands it.

Utilitarian individualism begins with the individual person as an actor seeking to satisfy his own wants and interests. He asks first, "What do I want?" and second, "Which act will yield the most of what I want?" "Wants" are taken as given, suggesting notions such as happiness, pleasure, or self-preservation as the good. Good consequences are those that most satisfy wants. Right acts are those that produce the most good consequences, as reckoned by cost-benefit calculation. Thus the chief virtue of the "consequential" style of evaluation employed by utilitarian culture is not rationality or obedience, but the efficiency of actors in maximizing the satisfaction of their wants.

Because right action follows from the determination of self-interest, "freedom" for the utilitarian is freedom *from* restraint, freedom to pursue his own ends, whatever they may be. This stands opposed to the biblical or humanist freedom *to* do the right act specified by divine commandment or dialectical reason. For utilitarian individualism, self-interest replaces biblical commandment as a moral starting point. "Technical reason"—the rationalization of means to maximize given ends—replaces conscience as a moral guide. Because the utilitarian's right act is that which *maximizes* good consequences, choosing the right act becomes an empirical question of accurately calculating consequences, not an evaluative question of conscientiously judging acts in themselves.

The counterculture of the sixties arose out of the romantic tradition to repudiate these two conceptions of reality in America, biblical religion and utilitarian individualism, especially the latter. The counterculture begins with the individual, not as an actor efficiently pursuing his own self-interest, but as a personality that experiences, knows, and simply *is*. "The way to do is to be." Self-awareness is the touchstone of moral motives, not self-preservation. Neither a logic of following rules nor of maximizing consequences predominates in the counterculture's ethic. What does, is the idea that everyone ought to act in any given situation in a way that fully expresses herself, specifically her inner feelings and experience of the situation. This situational and "expressive" style of evaluation is oriented to the feelings of the agent, those of others around the agent, and to their present situation, as discerned by empathic intuition. This style shapes an ethic of impulse ("do what you feel") and *self*-expression ("let it all hang out"), on the one hand; on the other, it shapes an ethic of situational appropriateness ("go with the flow; different strokes for different folks"). The moral question, "What should I do?" is posed by asking, "What's happening?" An act is right because it "feels right," most simply; or because it expresses the inner integrity of the agent and responds most appropriately to the situation here and now. The chief countercultural virtue is sensitivity of feeling. "Be here now," this ethic exhorts. "Get in touch with yourself." By contrast, the utilitarian's maximizing calculus and his technical reason are always aimed toward calculating future consequences, while biblical commands and rules often look back to the past in prescribing, for example, that we keep the promises we have made. For both utilitarian and counterculture, "freedom" refers to external conditions of nonrestraint, but now it is freedom to "do your own thing" impulsively rather than to pursue your own interest efficiently.

Biblical, utilitarian, and countercultural views of society differ sharply. In Protestant Christianity, each person becomes an individual. Unlike her classical or medieval forebears, she stands alone before God, abstracted from all social relations, and makes moral choices as a sovereign agent. Yet she faces unconditional moral demands revealed as God's will, to be fulfilled by autonomous action within society. Society is seen as a holy community dedicated to building God's kingdom on earth and bound by God's objective moral judgment. Utilitarian society is a collection of individuals whose relations rest on the mutual advantage of exchange, not on duties given by reason or revelation. The social order is defined by the sum of the individual wants and interests of its constituents, not by fixed moral ends and rules. In the ideal Christian community, social relations manifest the virtue of charity; in utilitarian society, refereed by the state, social relations manifest the contingent fact of reciprocity. One gives in order to get, or because one has already gotten. One does not give in order to give. The romantic counterculture sees the ideal society as an organismic community of persons who "encounter" each other face-to-face in an intimate confluence of feelings and wills. This vision assumes the substantive and evaluative identity of human feelings, as opposed to the utilitarian's formal and instrumental identity of human interests. In the counterculture's community, persons are to "be" with each other (*a la* the "be-in"), rather than do anything in particular together, freeing them from the mediation of roles ("role playing") and unequal status ("power tripping"). They relate to one another as ends in themselves, not as reciprocal means to the satisfaction of their own individual ends. Possessed of benignly congruent selves, they reach decisions collegially, without recourse to fixed rules, authority, or cost-benefit calculation.

Biblical morality affirms that there are features of an act itself (being commanded by God or conforming to rules of reason), besides the good or bad consequences it produces, that make it right. Such an ethic is called "deontological." Utilitarianism, on the contrary, is a "teleological," or consequential, ethic. It defines right acts solely by their good consequences. This puts it at odds with any ethical system that uses rules and direct commands ("thou shalt not kill") to specify that a particular act is itself right or wrong, to be committed or omitted for its own sake. For utilitarianism, doing the right thing is a matter of choosing whatever means effect a given end. Utility displaces duty, and it does not direct the individual to do or not do any particular act for its own sake. In the expressive ethic, the intuited sense of those involved in a given situation suggests the most appropriate feeling about it and the most fitting action in response to it. If an individual persists in feeling otherwise, however, no act-specific commandments or principles can be invoked to sway him against his feelings. Neither can these be invoked to sway the utilitarian who has calculated consequences accurately but defined their goodness by reference to peculiar interests of his own. Insofar as rules and commands prescribing acts and intentions in themselves do, in fact, shape norms in social life, utilitarianism and, to a lesser extent, the expressive ethic lead us toward moral normlessness. The utilitarian's almost exclusive concern with outcomes, and the hippie's with inner feelings, break down the autonomous structure of moral rules.[4]

The counterculture challenged utilitarian culture at the most fundamental level. It asked what in life possessed intrinsic value, and to what ends ought we to act. It rejected money, power, and technical knowledge, mainstays of "the good life" of middle-class society, as ends good in themselves. Instead, it identified them as means that did not, after all, enable one to experience what is intrinsically valuable—love, self-awareness, intimacy with others and nature. Utilitarian culture grew away from biblical morality in a modernizing America, but it could not generate autonomous moral rules by itself. This opened space for the counterculture to emerge. Because the counterculture relied on unregulated feelings to realize its values, it could not institutionalize them stably. Further, utilitarian culture fits with the structural conditions of modern society: technological production, bureaucratic organization, and empirical science. This blocked the counterculture's growth and bound its revolutionary impulse to failure. But in the process, utilitarian culture was stripped of moral authority, especially in the eyes of the young. The conflict of values during the 1960s left both sides of the battlefield strewn with ideological wreckage. In this atmosphere of disillusionment, many youths sought out alternative religious and therapeutic movements. Here they found a way both to cope with the instrumental demands of adulthood in conventional society *and* to sustain the counterculture's expressive ideals by reinforcing them with moralities of authority, rules, and utility. Changes in the ethical outlook of sixties youth involved in the human potential movement, specifically in *est*, describe one aspect of this larger transformation. Comparing this case to the moral logic of conservative Christian and neo-Oriental movements will enable us in conclusion to grasp the dynamics of conversion and cultural change as interrelated processes of ethical recombination.

est *and Ethics: Rule-Egoism in Middle-Class Culture*

Erhard Seminars Training *(est)* describes itself as an "educational corporation" that trains its clients "to transform [their] ability to experience living so that the situations [they] have been trying to change or have been putting up with clear up just in the process of life itself."[5] The standard training program takes over sixty hours spread across four days. A single "trainer" delivers it in a hotel ballroom to groups of two hundred or so persons, mostly urban, middle-class young adults, at a cost of $350 per person. Werner Erhard gave the first *est* training in a friend's borrowed apartment in 1971. Today the *est* organization is a model bureaucracy, molded by a former Harvard Business School professor and Coca-Cola company executive, which coordinates the efforts of some two hundred fifty paid employees and twenty-five thousand volunteers in twenty-nine cities. At a rate peaking above six thousand per month, *est* has trained more than three hundred thousand persons through 1981, a quarter of whom are concentrated in California. In the San Francisco Bay area, where *est* is based, one out of every nine college-educated young adults has taken the training.[6]

Compared to the larger population, *est*'s clients include proportionately more women and fewer men, more whites and fewer blacks, more divorced and fewer married persons, more young adults and fewer persons under twenty or over forty.[7] The mean age of *est* graduates is 33.7, with sixties youth (now twenty-five through thirty-four) comprising nearly half their total. This is two and one-half times their fraction of the Bay Area's population, and four times that of the nation. Most sixties youth in *est* saw themselves as members of the counterculture while going to college and for several years afterward, often living in modestly hip, drop-out style during this time (living communally, working intermittently at casual jobs, using marijuana regularly and psychedelics occasionally). They have since moved into apartments, tapered off their drug use, and entered full-time white-collar jobs, around which their lives are now organized. *est* graduates span the range of the middle class, with their educational level higher than average but their income lower. Nine out of ten *est* graduates began college; less than six (57%) finished. Relatively few hold jobs as technically specialized professionals or blue-collar workers, perhaps 10 percent in each case. For example, only 0.4 percent of all graduates are lawyers, 1.4 percent doctors, 0.8 percent laborers, as opposed to 11.7 percent in clerical work, the largest single occupational category. The great majority of *est* graduates (some 70%) work primarily with other people, not physical objects or abstractions. They do mainly white-collar work—clerical, sales, managerial, official, educational, and social work.

Almost two thirds of all *est* graduates are now unmarried. More than a quarter have never been married. Another quarter are now divorced or separated, a rate three times that of San Franciscans and seven times that of Americans generally. Some 26.7 percent of *all* graduates—four of ten ever married—have gone through such breakups within the year before or after taking *est*. The unreliably fluid, short-lived pattern of graduates' marital relationships carries over among sixties youth in *est*, whom one most commonly finds in nonexclusive, sexually active "dating" relationships or "living with someone." One out of three *est* graduates is affiliated with a conventional religious denomination, but less than one of ten participates weekly. Conventional religious affiliation among sixties youth in *est* is almost nonexistent.

A CONSEQUENTIAL THEORY OF RIGHT AND AN EXPRESSIVE THEORY OF GOOD

Youthful *est* graduates look back on their earlier moral views as a patchwork of love and self-interest, whose confusion *est* has dispelled.[8] Coming from relatively secularized middle-class backgrounds, they report themselves little influenced by the authoritative ethic of revealed religion. They felt ambivalent toward a conventional morality of rules, usually favoring a consequential ethic of self-interest. Recalls one,

Right was whatever benefited me. Wrong was what didn't benefit me. . . . There were rules and regulations from my parents, but I never felt they were right or wrong in themselves. They were just something I had to follow, or I was gonna get punished. . . . Maybe I felt there *was* a moral code up there in the universe. But it was special for me. I was immune from other people's rules.

Utilitarian concepts of the individual's natural rights and his freedom from restraint clash with the constraining bureaucratic regulations of modern society, which also conflict with expressive ideals of loving others and expressing oneself. "All through school I always felt hassled by the rules and regulations," continues the graduate. "I'd always rather be a martyr and stand out—'Fight for the right, for idealism. Fight for the truth.' Loving your brothers and sisters and grooving with them was right. And the establishment was wrong, and the rules and regulations were wrong." From this countercultural viewpoint, love and noninjury take on the obligatory weight of rules, justifying opposition to American institutions and public policy in the 1960s. The same youth who rejected rules in his personal life defended them as "idealism" in the political realm, with the value of the individual's freedom from restraint providing the denominator common to both stances. These sixties youths professed an expressive ethic, but acted according to a utilitarian one when the situation called for responses contrary to their own interests.

Youthful graduates of *est* see it as enabling them to enact expressive values idealized but unattained in the counterculture, while at the same time meeting the demands of mainstream life. *est* mediates the moral conflict between mainstream and counterculture with a consequential ethic that justifies compliance with conventional rules for the sake of one's self-interest, which is defined in forms integral with self-expression and situational responsiveness. Like utilitarian culture, and in contrast to biblical views, *est* sees acts as neither right nor wrong in themselves. Acts are right only by virtue of the goodness of their consequences. What are good or intrinsically valuable, according to *est*, are the individual's experiences of well-being and satisfaction. Acts of rule-compliance and agreement-keeping are right, because they produce such experiences in the agent. Thus the human potential *est* promises to realize is "your true potential for producing aliveness and satisfaction in your life."[9] Let us proceed through this reworking of utilitarian individualism with reference to its felt meaning for sixties youth.

Young graduates see *est* as enabling them to "act appropriately" on a reliable basis at last, realizing expressive ideals held earlier. "Now I can actually *be* open to whatever comes up," affirms a graduate, "instead of *having* a position called openness that makes me right and everyone else wrong. Being open is being appropriate. It means being here now, with nothing added." Expressive terminology permeates *est*'s moral discussions. "Appropriateness" is the right-making characteristic of actions, while "right" and "wrong" are used derogatorily to designate authoritative and regular moral judgments as unsupported by experiential fact. *est*'s idea of what it means to act appropriately, however, differs from that of the counterculture, since it continues to rely on the ends-means logic of utilitarian culture. A graduate considers the question, "What does acting appropriately mean? Why should I do it, anyway?" He replies,

Acting appropriately means "playing for aliveness" and getting what you want in life. When you act appropriately, your life works. You experience satisfaction and aliveness. You experience completeness. . . . The reason why is because it works, not because it's right or wrong.

The appropriate action is the one that "works," that "plays for" and produces the fullest experience of "aliveness" for its agent. In other words, the right act is the one that produces the greatest amount of good consequences for the agent. Which consequences are good, and what makes them so? Ultimately, goodness inheres in certain experiences that the individual feels: aliveness, satisfaction, spontaneity, naturalness, and the like.

According to *est*, an individual can assess not only her actions, but also the point of view from which she acts by the cost-benefit calculus and the consequential logic of utilitarianism. Does a given point of view I hold yield me the greatest "payoff" of aliveness for the least "cost"? *est* promises that "getting it" in the training will enable each individual to pose and act on this question to transform her life:

> Each context or point of view we hold can be said to have a "cost" (reckoned in terms of aliveness) and a "payoff." "Getting it" means being able to discover that you are holding a position (a context) which costs you more in aliveness than it is worth *and* being able to choose to give up (or transform) that position. Living becomes a continuing and expanding discovery of positions or barriers to your and others' aliveness and the attendant opportunity to give up (or "get off") those positions. The results of this continuing process of choosing or "getting it" is an expanded experience of happiness, love, health, and full self-expression.[10]

Here *est* states its consequential theory of right in explicitly economic terms. The "worth" of a viewpoint lies not in its truth or falsity, no more than the worth of an act lies in its moral rightness or wrongness. The worth of each lies only in the consequential payoff it makes to its holder or agent. As in classical utilitarian culture, the agent is calculating "costs" against "payoffs" in order to maximize or "expand" the satisfaction of his wants. But *est* has carried this calculating activity inward, from the marketplace to the psyche. It is "reckoning" costs and payoffs "in terms of aliveness," not money. It is analyzing points of view, not economic transactions. And it is seeking to expand experience, not capital.

est shares the consequential theory of right action held by utilitarianism, which it revitalizes by using a more modern psychology to answer the questions of what makes consequences good, and how do actions produce these good consequences. Traditional utilitarian definitions of the good fasten on notions like "pleasure and the absence of pain," derived from a mechanistic psychology and tending toward objectification in economic terms—material comfort and consumption, social status, and power. Tangible economic means displace relatively intangible psychic ends. Money comes to count for happiness. This displacement was cast in a harsh light for sixties youth by the counterculture's excoriation of utilitarianism and the contrast of its own self-consciously experiential definition of intrinsic value, which was drawn in specifically religious and psychological terms. Erhard makes a similar point: "Material success isn't all that bad a thing: however, it's only what people thought they wanted. When they have it, they often realize it's not what they thought it would be, and doesn't in itself bring them satisfaction."[11] *est* defines what is intrinsically valuable in a form more compatible with countercultural ideals, namely the individual's experiences of satisfaction and aliveness. Maximizing these values justifies participation in *est*'s moral enterprise. "We *do* need to master life," Erhard concludes. "As you master life, what happens is that there's more living in life, more aliveness; more experiencing *here now*."[12]

Given this definition of ends, which is an evaluative claim, *est*'s ethic devolves on questions of aligning actual means to these ends, questions that are presumed to be exclusively empirical. "*est* doesn't tell you what you should want," a graduate distinguishes, "it tells you how to get what you *do* want." Psychology and epistemology explain how and why actions produce certain experiential states as a consequence, thereby indicating which acts are to be performed in any given situation. Once one knows that right actions are those that produce the fullest experience of aliveness for the agent, further recourse to moral standards or principles becomes pointless. One simply "plays for aliveness," by doing whatever maximizes this experience.

RULE-EGOISM

What sort of acts produce those states of experience that constitute the good? How do we come to do such acts? According to *est*, the individual's feelings of well-being depend on, and follow from, the functional condition of his life, the state of "having your life work," which in turn results from "realizing your intentions and achieving your goals." "Love or money, you name it, whatever goal you set up in life, go for it!" urges a youthful graduate. Intentions and goals refer to concrete events or conditions of self-orientation, interpersonal relationships, work, education, and life-style. By this logic, feelings of individual well-being depend on achieving one's goals. They cannot be arrived at simply by "turning on, tuning in, and dropping out." For sixties youth who have tried and failed to enact the expressive ethic by such direct means, this consequential reformulation of its idea of intrinsic value has a powerful appeal. *est*'s ethic explains the failure of the counterculture's drop-out life-style to realize its own ends of self-gratification, and it justifies dropping back into middle-class life to do so. Personal and expressive ends justify impersonal and instrumental means. Aliveness justifies goal-achievement.

What must one do to achieve his goals? In answering this second question, *est* departs from both the expressive ethic and the usual utilitarian tactic of doing whichever particular act best serves one's self-interest. It posits that "following the rules and keeping your agreements" are necessary to achieve your goals. "Your life is based on breaking the rules. Cheating. Lying to yourself and conning your 'friends' into buying your lies," charges the trainer. "And then you wonder why you're never satisfied."[13] The individual cannot satisfy his "real" self-interest, as *est* defines it, by violating the rules and agreements bearing on him. Rule-breakers experience no satisfaction. Even when they go uncaught, they feel tense and uneasy, fearful of discovery and punishment or of being cheated on in turn. On these premises, the consequential ethic itself drives the self-interested individual to follow rules and keep agreements.

For *est*, "the rules" possess no authoritative source, as they do for revealed religion. Nor do they reflect in themselves the essential reality of existence, as in Western natural law theory or its analogue in Eastern thought. *est* justifies following rules and keeping agreements because these practices produce good consequences for the agent: Follow the rules if you want to experience aliveness.[14] This constitutes what I will call "rule-egoism." Compliance with rules is justified on egoistic grounds. This formulation is consistent with utilitarian culture, since it adheres both to a consequential ethical style—right acts are those that yield the most good consequences—and to an effectively egoistic reply to the question of whose good is to be sought—one's own. It invests with utility the practices of following rules and keeping agreements, thereby rerationalizing ethical elements of biblical religion in a way consistent with utilitarianism. It defines utility with reference to an ultimate good, consisting of experiences such as aliveness and spontaneity, whose subjective content seems compatible with countercultural ideals, even if the objective means to having those experiences is goal-achievement on the job instead of dropping out and "grooving."

What are the rules to which *est* refers? Their identification outside the training itself is not precisely bounded. They are "the rules of life," and examples range from codes of dress and etiquette through bureaucratic regulations to laws against murder and the law of gravity. By contrast, the "ground rules" by which the training itself proceeds are extraordinarily explicit, precise, and comprehensive. The *est* training is impressively and instructively overorganized. Its procedural rules prescribe schedule, performance, seating, interaction protocols, physical movement, posture, and ideal attitudes in concrete detail. The trainees are told that, with respect to the rules as in every other respect, *est* parallels life. "If you follow the ground rules, you'll get value from the training. If you follow the rules of life, life will work for you." Taking this parallel concretely, the rules that govern *est* as a bureaucratized voluntary association mainly reflect the bureaucratic regulations that govern life in modern society, especially middle-class life centered on white-collar work. And indeed, it is from this social setting, as we have seen, that *est* draws almost all its clients.

For the white-collar worker, in particular, bureaucratic regulations possess an external, objectively given quality. He does not take part in their formulation, and they act over against him, constraining his behavior. They exist as "social facts" in Durkheim's sense. But neither a divinely revealed, authoritative source nor the status of laws of nature are claimed for such regulations to legitimate their power. Instead, they are justified by utilitarian efficiency. By following bureaucratic regulations, persons will be able to coordinate their activities most predictably to maximize productivity and its proceeds. Each individual should "go along to get along." The individual's compliance is warranted because it promises to yield him the largest possible share of the profits that accrue from the collectivity's efforts.

Just as the rise of a market economy provided the social genesis and plausibility structure for the development of a utilitarian morality of action in general, so the rise of modern bureaucracy provided the social genesis and plausibility structure for a utilitarian morality of following rules. Classical economic man could pursue his self-interest directly, just like his profits, assessing each act according to its maximal market utility in satisfying his wants.[15] The modern organization man pursues his self-interest by complying with the rules of the bureaucracies that assess and reward his actions. Rule-egoism, in its vintage corporate formulation, advises the organization man to "go along to get along." *est*'s counsel to "follow the rules to get what you want in life" implies conventional social and economic success as a desideratum, but it makes clear that it is not the only good nor, more important, the ultimate good. What are ultimately and intrinsically valuable are individual experiences of well-being—aliveness. Thus *est* takes an idea of the right (rule compliance) that is usually associated with the regular ethic, and an idea of the good (feeling alive and natural) that is usually associated with the expressive ethic, and subsumes them into the consequential ethical style of utilitarian culture in its bureaucratized version, rule-egoism.

MORAL KNOWLEDGE AND MORAL RESPONSIBILITY

est speaks of the individual's felt aliveness and naturalness as the ultimate good toward which appropriate action aims, and also as the motivational source from which it arises. "When you come from aliveness," testifies a graduate, "you always act appropriately." In advocating this motive, *est* sponsors a facsimile of the counterculture's idea of appropriate action always arising from and expressing the individual's true inner self. Hip self-expression squares with the bureaucratic constraints of rule-egoism in light of *est*'s subjectivist theory of knowledge and its related idea of moral responsibility as "the willingness to acknowledge you are cause in a matter." Social norms are interpreted as expressing the intentions and "choice" of each individual. He himself is seen to be the "total cause" of his experience, including "the rules" of society. The individual has "created" the rules by a process of self-expression and "communication" leading to interpersonal "agreements," from which the rules have evolved. Once each person has intuited his own subjective interests and empathically communicated them to another, the two are then able to make agreements with each other that will serve the self-interest of each and will, therefore, be kept by both.

Here we have reached a moral locale resembling the marketplace of classical economics and the focal situation of social contract theory. Mutually disinterested agents are each seeking to serve their own interests by mutual exchange. But in *est*, the approach to this situation has been psychologized in a way echoing the expressive ethic, and the contract itself has been placed primarily at the level of interpersonal relationships instead of social structure. John Locke has entered therapy. *est*'s teaching on "communication" resonates with countercultural ideals of self-expression, interpersonal honesty, intimacy, and sensitivity as ends good in themselves. In the consequential logic of *est*'s ethic, they appear, on one hand, as means to making viable agreements with others, to achieve one's goals and feel aliveness. On the other hand, *est* points out that satisfying interpersonal relationships, which may themselves be chosen as goals, require the participant to keep agreements and follow rules. In this latter respect, *est* reinforces expressive values with elements of a regular ethic. As a result, sixties youth experience relationships idealized by the counterculture to be realized reliably for the first time in *est*.

est sees moral disagreement as a fundamentally psychological failure of two persons to intuit and communicate their subjective interests. Translating these interests into generalized judgments of right and wrong only exacerbates the conflict. Instead, *est* calls for disclosure of the real causes of one's "upset" at another's behavior, which are located in one's own conditioned feelings. "Instead of running your 'that's wrong because' tape," suggests a graduate, "why not just tell the truth and say 'I've got an upset on that.'" This leads ideally to accepting others and going on to make relevant agreements or recognize relevant rules in relation to them. A graduate affirms this strategy:

Q: What do "right" and "wrong" mean to you now?

A: They're ideas people have. Beliefs. They depend on where people are coming from, and everybody's coming from someplace different. I used to judge people on whether they were right or wrong, but it's a waste of time. Judging means putting extra bullshit on top of what's so. It's like lying.

Q: Are there any acts that are right or wrong in themselves?

A: Sure there are, in my little universe, lots of them. Like if someone comes to my dinner table and farts, I consider that wrong.

Q: What happens now when you disagree with someone about what he and you should be doing?

A: Right after the training I was coming from a place where I was right and everybody else was wrong. Then I got that, and saw that when other people do stuff that's not OK with me, it's OK with them. And it can be OK with me. At the time maybe I feel angry, then afterwards I look and see what was going on inside of me to make me feel that way. I just have to confront whatever's going on with me, get in touch with it, and get off it, so that whatever they're doing is OK with me. When I relate to people now it's more for aliveness, instead of being right, so it's easier for them to be OK with me. They're not wrong if they're gay or something. It depends on whether it works for them or not, and that's up to them.

Q: What if it's really not OK with you?

A: If it's really not OK, if it's just their act, well, that's beautiful, too, and I'll tell them that and give them the space to get off it.

Q: What happens if they don't get that it's their act, or they just don't want to get off it?

A: That's OK, too. I acknowledge that's what's so for them, and all I can do is let them be the way they are.

Q: Even if they're hurting you?

A: *You're* hurting you, they're not. When you let it be, they're just doing what they're doing. That's what the training is about, getting that nobody's doing anything *to* you. You're doing it to yourself. *You're* creating it.

Q: All right. I guess I mean, what if it feels like you *are* the victim? What if you get robbed and shot, or you're a black kid and you can't get a job. And you can't just let it be and go someplace else, because there's no place else to go?

A: Look, if you're talking about murder or something, that's what the rules are for. *And* people get murdered anyway. We all know "Life ain't fair," and that doesn't change who's responsible for *your* life. You are.

From the emotivist viewpoint *est* adopts, the bases of moral judgment inhere not in any descriptive characteristics of acts or persons but in the subject's own psychologically conditioned beliefs and feelings. Attributing them to this latter source, disclosed by therapeutic introspection and communication, fosters interpersonal acceptance. To represent objects of moral judgment, *est* favors examples relating to standards of life-style, fashion, etiquette, or taste that tend to leave out considerations of overt injury or injustice (for example, homosexuality and table manners instead of murder or race discrimination). Indeed, the training's conclusive depiction of moral choice centers on the example of choosing to eat chocolate or vanilla ice cream, a matter of taste manifestly without moral value or reason. Such examples imply that the usual wisdom in matters of taste, *de gustibus non disputandum*, is to be followed in matters of moral choice as well.

Effectively, then, *est*'s memorable dictum that "standards are bad" supports tolerance of various codes of personal behavior and life-style, thereby encouraging self-acceptance and acceptance of others in a pluralistic society, rather than licensing the amoralist to break laws. *est*'s critics charge that it also lends itself to toleration of injury and injustice to persons other than oneself and those with whom one interacts face-to-face, especially when these others hold interests not shaped by social experience specific to the middle class.[16] Where the behavior of others threatens one's interests, these are to be asserted in the process of communication and agreement described above. If a mutually satisfactory agreement is not forthcoming, withdrawal of one's emotion, interest, and involvement is justified. The interpersonal mobility implied by such an ethic characterizes the social milieu in which most of *est*'s youthful graduates live— urban, middle class, white collar, and "singles" oriented—where decoupling from lovers and spouses, and leaving behind friends, neighbors, and co-workers, are familiar facts of life. The relative economic security of this milieu, where most individuals can fend for themselves materially, likewise lends plausibility to the laissez-faire aspect of *est*'s ethic.

est conceives moral responsibility as each individual acknowledging that he is the total cause of his own experience. "You're God in your Universe," writes Erhard. "You caused it."[17] The responsible person attributes whatever happens to him to his own ultimate doing instead of blaming others. He introspects his own consciousness to disclose the hidden motives for his difficulties. He "acknowledges" and "experiences out" these ultimate causes, thus allowing them to "disappear," and causing his problems to "clear up just in the process of life itself." The responsibility each person bears toward others is to "assist" each of them in taking responsibility for himself in the abreactive fashion just described. *est* argues that the paradox of its psychological theory of change— "trying to change an experience makes it persist; accepting it and being with it makes it disappear"—applies as powerfully to social institutions as to the individual mind. By heeding it first with themselves, then with others, then everyone, individuals can "transubstantiate" social institutions, altering their essence while leaving their structural accidents unchanged. Thus psychologism defines both the mode and sequence of social change for college-educated sixties youths now stuck in white-collar jobs within the system they had hoped to change. Says one, resignedly, "I found out you can't worry about saving the world. You have to just live your own life." This shift in outlook—from seeking to save society to surviving in it, from making it over to making one's way in it—fits with America's political cooling-off and economic tightening since the 1960s. It also reflects the speaker's age-related shift of position in the society: from studying in an age-segregated youth setting while being supported by others, to working in an age-integrated adult setting to support oneself. Following the line of such shifts, *est*'s ethic holds out hopes for social change, outside the context of radical or liberal politics, in a form compatible with a conventional career and life-style.

est's concept of moral responsibility is, finally, binocular, because its beginning assumptions are radically individualistic on one side and monistic on the other. *est* posits that each individual is the total cause of all his own experience, implying that he is totally *and exclusively* responsible for his situation and its difficulties. But *est* also posits that each individual exists ultimately as a "being" coextensive with all existence, implying that he is responsible for everyone else. *est*'s critics see such monistic universalization of responsibility for social problems as obscuring their institutional causes and dissolving into pure consciousness any politically focused effort to resolve them. From either point of view, the subtlety of *est*'s ethic in practice and the socially specific power of its appeal only become fully evident in considering what *est* has to say about love and work as well as politics.

PLAYING THE GAME OF LOVE AND WORK

After the training, *est* graduates continue to marry, divorce, and switch lovers and friends at much the same high rates, yet they credit *est* with critically assisting them in choosing to leave old intimates, find new ones, and renew existing relationships. The high frequency of these interpersonal changes, coupled with their diverse directions, are significant in themselves. *est*'s ethic serves its clients in a social setting (the cosmopolitan city), social stratum (white-collar middle class), and age cohort (young adult), all characterized by extremely fluid relationships between spouses, lovers, friends, co-workers, and neighbors. *est*'s clients are not social atoms or isolates of the sort often attracted to conventional cult movements. But neither are they persons bound to one another and a place by a religiously weighted marriage, children, house ownership, compelling careers, extended families, or a cohesive community. They are persons making their way through a large number of social contacts and relationships, many of short duration or low frequency of interaction, and searching in their midst for intimacy and honesty with others. "We're all looking for the fairy princess," laughs one of them.

In an associational society like our own, the differentiation of social roles makes common purposes and meanings hard to arrive at with other persons. In place of such shared meanings, it permits the reciprocal exchange of instrumental support in a greater variety of interpersonal relationships, among which the individual can move and choose more freely. *est*'s ethic fits such social conditions, lending to its adherents new insight into their touch-and-go experience on the "singles" scene. A young graduate reflects on his marriage and divorce:

My old position on love was about "giving" and "needing" and having common goals. That's a myth. You can't make another person have your goals. *est* talks about "allowing." You have to allow them to be who they are and want what they want. You support them in *their* goals, not yours.

Unlike hippie communes, conservative Christian sects, and neo-Oriental ashrams, *est* offers no communal contrast to an associational society. "You can't *belong* to *est*," comments a trainer. "There are no members." Instead, *est* teaches its clients, including the living partner of two out of every three graduates,[18] an interpersonal ideal of "powerful relationships": two persons exchange power supporting each other's achievement of individual goals. This generalizes the market model of exchange to all social interaction, and at the same time psychologizes the content and medium of that exchange. Reports a young graduate:

In the training, I got in touch with how I actually felt and what I actually wanted to do. Not what I'm *supposed* to do, not what somebody else wants me to do. *est* made it OK for me to do what *I* want to. . . . I'm more forceful in the world. I see the people I want to see, I don't see the people I don't want to. I'm living my life more for myself, whereas before it was harder for me to say No to people. Now that I accept who I am, I can't be had anymore.

est proposes a unified model of interaction—affectively expressive yet detached, therapeutically poised, and assertively self-interested—to apply equally to friends and lovers, to associates, clients, and strangers. This conflation of feelings and interests points to the merger of a utilitarian ethic based in public life and an expressive ethic based in private life. The bureaucrat's logic defines interpersonal relations more calculably with reference to individual satisfaction, a function welcomed in a world where spouses, lovers, and friends circulate without the reliability of fixed rules, circumstances, and living groups to anchor impulse. Emotional fluency and detachment produced by therapeutic techniques are required in "risking" oneself to initiate tentative relationships, develop them into deep ones, and accept their failure to so develop, not merely to enjoy casual relationships.

The all-or-nothing dilemma of romantic love leading to marriage has been replaced by a flexible openness to the sort of less-committed, encompassing, and reliable relationships that have become the norm in the social world that *est*'s clients inhabit. Says one, "I used to feel strange saying 'I love you.' I was always wondering whether I meant it, or they meant it. Now I can just say it. It's just another word in my vocabulary." Marriage itself takes on some of the same attitudinal openness and contractual structure that permeate modern public life. To explain "what it looks like when a relationship works," an *est* trainer describes his marriage:

First of all, when L— and I got married, we set out a carefully created set of agreements, including an operating procedure and a divorce agreement. . . . In order to have a workable marriage, it seems to me that you have to be willing not to have one. So we have already set up the whole divorce, as well as the whole marriage, to include all possibilities. It's a condition in which whatever happens is appropriate and OK. Out of that condition, in which all possibilities are all right, we have created a strength in our relationship that allows us to be together at choice.[19]

A graduate concludes: "We're getting into more honest, open relationships, where you're free to choose to give each other support." Two individuals exchanging "support" to maximize the satisfaction each feels: this utilitarian model achieves its interpersonal plausibility largely by making love, the heart of modern private life, more adaptable to the conditions of bureaucratic public life that impinge upon it. In light of this adaptive function, *est*'s claim to enhance interpersonal sensitivity through the standardized techniques of a mass training no longer seems so ironic. For it is increasingly in such bureaucratically standardized settings that middle-class urbanites must exercise this virtue.

Seen conversely, the most obvious dimension of *est*'s merged ethic is the public utilization of private emotions and expressive behavior in bureaucratic and services-oriented work. In such occupations, the intimate side of one's personality becomes part of the impersonal means of his livelihood. The individual must sell his smile, not only his time.[20] *est*'s central idea of the omnicausal agent relies, in a peculiarly concrete way, not on the mystical experience of the monist, but on the interactive experience of the white-collar worker, especially the salesman, for its plausibility. Erhard's prior experience training door-to-door encyclopedia salesmen was applied directly, during the first years of *est*, to a franchise operation, owned by his wife, selling soap products, cosmetics, and vitamins door-to-door. The business was run strictly according to *est* principles and staffed exclusively by *est* graduates. A former employee recalls,

When you went door to door, they said you only met one person behind every door—yourself. "There's nobody out there. It's all you." Whatever happened, you made it like it was. So if no one was home, it was because you weren't home. You could never say, "No one was home on my route today." It had to be, "Today all I did was create no one being home for me." Then they'd ask you, "Well, what's going on for you not to be home?" The idea that you created everything was like a law.

est showed me that I didn't have an outside life. It all entered into the job. How I felt, my relationships, everything. If I got angry, then people would come to the door already angry, before I'd even said a word. You're forced to look at that. The guy who delivered the soap said he could tell who had sold it without knowing, just from the way our customers were with him.

The door-to-door salesman incarnates *est*'s idea of the omnicausal agent. He sells products whose purchase is entirely discretionary. His customers either have some on hand, have no specific need for it, or if they do, can purchase it more cheaply at a store. Thus, their purchase depends on how effectively the salesman sells himself. The client buys in response to him, not the product. By modulating his relation to others—that is, by first selling himself—the salesman makes the sale. From actually influencing the purchaser's behavior at the door, it is a short symbolic leap to "creating" him behind it. The door-to-door salesman creates from intrapsychic resources, through interpersonal means, the conditions of occupational success. In this sense, the individual's inner state determines his external achievement, which in turn mirrors it. *est* has recast the classical Protestant ethic, after inheriting it through the hands of American evangelical religion (where success, once the *sign* of election, became the *result* of an experience of perfection) and a secularized commercial culture (where the believer who strives for salvation became the striver who believes in salvation on earth).[21]

"Work," by *est*'s definition, is "a game" to be played, not labored at or "efforted," but played for mastery as well as fun.[22] The individual detaches himself from his social activity to accomplish it more effectively, not to devalue its accomplishment. In advising this sort of instrumental detachment, *est* folds a new wrinkle into the program of positive thinking, if not into the history of religious renunciation. Says Erhard on the subject of "making relationships work":

> No matter what comes up, just absolutely be willing to let it be. Give it space and just continue moving on through the course. Whatever you can let be, whatever you can give space to, you've begun to master. What you can let be, allows you to be, and that's the beginning of mastery.[23]

A graduate puts it more succinctly: "When you let go of it, you get it all."

est adapts the entrepreneurial ideal of the salesman, that last American dreamer, to the corporate reality of middle-class work by emphasizing the need for bureaucratic cooperation and rule-compliance to get the job done. *est* makes explicit the individual's contractual agreement to comply with bureaucratic rules, invests them with the binding power of personal promises, and sanctions their violation accordingly. To a generation of youth bred by liberal education and countercultural personalism to mistrust the rationale and moral claims of bureaucratic work, yet now faced with the need to perform it for a living, *est*'s lessons carry a startlingly persuasive force. One former dropout testifies, "Assisting at *est* is like [attending] a school for learning to keep your agreements. I always used to be the artist-hippie-weirdo doing my own thing. I'd cheat and lie to make the job someone else's problem. Now I take responsibility for me being the whole *est* organization and getting the job done."

Accused by critics of being an authoritarian army, the *est* organization is, in fact, a bootcamp for bureaucracy. Hierarchical, tightly rule-governed, and meritocratic, it trains its young volunteers and staff to answer phones, write memos, keep records, promote and stage public events, and deal smoothly with clients. It explains organizational authority by locating its genesis within the psyche. "You created your boss to tell you what to do," explains a volunteer. "The same with the rules and Werner. The way you get power is by giving power to a source of power." By following this schema, sixties youth who have outlived their years of schooling, the summer of love, and the Revolution come to accept and "own" the bureaucratic organizations for which they now work, not by controlling an economic share of them nor politically formulating their rules, but by psychologically appropriating those rules.

For committed *est* graduates, the meaning of mundane work has been redeemed as a means to the sacred end of "expanding your aliveness." The idea of work as a game goes hand-in-hand with the notion of one's own life as a work of art. "The picture I'm painting of me is a masterpiece," observes a young real-estate broker of his career. "Because now each brushstroke I do, each step I take, I'm experiencing it much more." The enterprise of self-perfection, passed down from philosopher and monk to bohemian dandy and hippie, now takes therapeutic form in "working on yourself." Exploded by the counterculture, the old economic myth of the self-made man is recast into the new consciousness myth of the self-made Self.

est's ethic responds to the predicament of sixties youth exposed to the expressive values of the counterculture and conventional private life, yet now faced with the instrumental demands of adult middle-class public life. Its psychologized reintegration of personalism and utilitarianism also appeals, with different felt emphases, to older graduates moved by the same contrary cultural impulses. *est* uses expressive ends to justify the workaday routine and their disenchantment with it. Follow the rules and work hard to achieve your goals, it advises, and then you will feel alive and natural. This formula justifies sixties youth in giving up their utopian expectations of political and personal change, and dropping back into middle-class social and economic life. *est* motivates them to lead this life effectively, with an eye to inner satisfaction as well as external success; and it trains them in the face-to-face fluency and emotional self-management this life requires in a white-collar singles milieu. Rule-egoism makes sense to these exiles from youth, still seeking self-fulfillment and hoping for a better world, yet needing to consolidate a career and relationships within the existing order.

Engaging, yet detached, *est*'s therapeutic ideal responds adaptively to the social conditions permeating urban bureaucratic life, especially, but not only, for young adults. Largely secularized, college-educated, white-collar singles and divorcees, *est*'s clients embody religious, educational, occupational, and marital characteristics now spreading through our society. Expressive, yet utilitarian, *est*'s ideas claim legitimate kinship with recognizable moral traditions long contained in our culture but now strengthening their hold on what we recognize as common sense. *est* presents a powerfully convincing model of and for interpersonal behavior in the urban office, schoolroom, sales conference, and singles bar. The appeal of this model, whatever its merits, suggests how deep and troubling are the questions *est* addresses in contemporary American middle-class culture. *est* appeals, says a psychiatrist-graduate, "because it's so middle class, so all-American—like the Chevrolet."[24] Indeed, it *is* such an ideological vehicle, but one redesigned for a society unsettled in new ways and now picking up freeway speed toward an end that may leave us far from home.

Conversion as Ethical Recombination

Alternative religious movements have not overturned tradition and replaced it with something entirely new. Rather, they have drawn out strands from traditional moralities and rewoven them into a fabric that ties into American culture as a whole yet differs in pattern from any one of its traditions. As a romantic successor to modernism, the hip counterculture carried on the iconoclastic injunction "Make it new!" in more radical form. The attempt to make life new in day-to-day experience and action, not just in art, poses problems for that side of the human condition that calls for order and regularity, for a measure that lasts. Though ever-present, this need grows stronger as youth turns toward adulthood, and alternative religious movements of the 1970s and 1980s have answered it as the counterculture could not. In doing so, these movements sustain expressive ideals by recombining them with moralities of authority, rules, and utility. The human potential movement recombines the expressive ethic of hip culture with the consequential ethic of utilitarian individualism, with particular plausibility for the middle middle class. Conservative Christian groups recombine the expressive ethic with the authoritative ethic of revealed biblical religion, with particular plausibility for the lower middle class. Neo-Oriental groups recombine the expressive ethic with the regular ethic of rationalized religion and humanism, with particular plausibility for the upper middle class. Today's alternative religious movements are not rehearsing a new version of sixties iconoclasm, aimed at knocking over their predecessor along with its targets. Instead, these movements draw from the old targets of biblical religion, rational humanism, and utilitarian culture itself, as well as from non-Western traditions, to synthesize their ethics. In this respect they are "religious" in the literal sense that they "bind together" heretofore disparate elements within a pluralistic culture, revitalizing tradition as they change it. They are engaged in a constructive process of mediating and recombining existing meanings, not in the sort of prophetic "breakthrough" that began the great historical religions or that triggered modern revolutions. From diverse moral meanings, these religions form alternatives to utilitarian culture—or variations of it, in *est*'s case—better adapted to survival within utilitarian society than was the counterculture, because their ideas are more coherent, their movements more stably institutionalized, and their members' lives more regulated.

The stock answers of utilitarian individualism begin to unravel when its adherent asks, "Why don't I feel happy?" This question presupposes, of course, the individual's right to possess happiness, not merely to pursue it, a shift in American expectations nowhere more dramatically visible than between sixties youth and the generation of their parents. Already possessed of much that money can buy, and still unsatisfied, these youths found the ultimate meaning of conventional values and their logic of action undercut by the counterculture. It attempted to replace the instrumental values of wealth, power, and technical knowledge with the ultimate values of love and self-awareness. It sought to fill the subjective form of "happiness," left empty by utilitarianism, with the expressive content of its own deeper feelings and closer intimacy with others and nature. It sought to intuit right action from whatever expressed one's inner self and fit the situation here and now, instead of calculating it from future costs and benefits to maximize want-satisfaction. Yet these expressive alternatives too proved unable to stand up to experience on their own terms. "Money can't buy you love," it is true, but that does not mean that "love is all you need." You also need moral rules to live by, authority to respect, and contracts to keep—even to sustain—your love. Alternative religions resolve this predicament by recombining elements of its opposed romantic, biblical, and utilitarian sides into unified ethics. By mapping out moralities of loving authority, antinomian rules, and rule-egoism through the middle of a conflicted culture, alternative religions have saved sixties youth caught between the devils of self-interest, law-and-order authority, and heartless rules on one side and the deep blue sea of boundless self-expression on the other.

As represented most literally by pentecostal and fundamentalist sects, the conservative Christian offers to the utilitarian question, "Why don't I feel happy?" the radically authoritative answer, "Because you are sinning. You are disobeying God's will because you have turned away from God and are being possessed by the Devil." By repenting his sins and being ritually reborn as a child of God, a person comes to recognize God's love and His power to command right acts. An authoritative theory of right replaces a consequential theory: that act is right in itself that God commands. Good consequences follow on doing right acts. They do not *define* right acts. Obey God's will and you will be a good person. As an aftereffect, affirms the Christian, you will feel good. Seek only to make yourself feel good, and you will disobey God and be an evil person. Thus a theory of good follows on an authoritative theory of right. Relativism is rejected. God's will is read as an absolute in scripture, likewise proclaimed by prophetic leaders, and recognized by the church as an orthodox unit.

At the same time, the Christian's authoritative ethic embraces expressive elements. He experiences the goodness of an intimately personal Jesus in such devotional or ecstatic rites as pentecostal tongue-speaking; he responds to Him with love and follows Him with gladness. Religious faith is the necessary condition of moral virtue. One must know and love God within a given church, and intend to obey Him to do right. Sect members obey God not only because God is good, but, finally, because God is God. They imitate the loving example of Jesus out of love for Him. This morality of expressive aspiration based on love intertwines with a morality of regular obligation that is based on a covenant of reciprocal duties and rights between God and sect members as His "chosen people." If they keep this covenant, God will reward them with everlasting life. If they break it, He will punish them with death.

Neo-Oriental religions—for example, Zen Buddhism—usually share the deontological structure, but not the content, of the Christian answer to the utilitarian question, "Why do I feel unhappy?" The Zen student replies, "Because you cannot get what you want. You cannot satisfy your desires because, by the very nature of desire, they are inexhaustible and insatiable." He proposes practicing Zen meditation according to its orthopractical rules to bring release from desires and thus from suffering. In the course of such practice, a regular theory of right replaces a consequential one. Release from suffering as the good consequence that makes acts right becomes release from delusion as the good state of consciousness that arises from acting rightly—that is, in accord with rules that follow the nature of reality. What does the Zen student advise us, then? Practice Zen (according to its rules) and you will become a good person who naturally acts rightly (as Buddhism's moral precepts describe). Thus a theory of good both follows from, and leads into, a regular theory of right.

The regular ethic of neo-Oriental religions can resolve itself into expressive terms. Acts are right or wrong in themselves, and they are so specified by moral precepts. Ultimately, however, acts appropriate to the moment arise directly from the ideal agent's "nonattached" state of mind and feeling of compassion for others and life itself. The good person idealized by the Bodhisattva or Krishna, for example, and embodied by the Zen Master or guru, feels and acts intuitively in response to the situation, as did the ideal hippie. But now the agent's feelings are shaped by meditation and monastic life. Through this experience, his actions come to reflect the true nature of existence conceived as a spiritual unity and identified by such terms as Buddha Mind. Moral relativism is rejected, albeit within a paradoxical dialectic that both recognizes moral rules and calls for nonattachment to them.

As represented by *est*, the human potential movement offers an analysis of the question, "Why don't I feel happy?" within the consequential logic of utilitarian moral argument. Persons do not feel happy because they have not figured out what they "really" want, which are experiences of aliveness and satisfaction. They mistake material success—that is, conventional utilities—for these feelings of well-being. They try to manipulate themselves, others, and social rules to maximize their own possession of such utilities. Psychological self-clarification will enable persons to identify their real subjective interests and those of others. Then they can act directly to maximize their own felt well-being by playing for aliveness, and they can contract more effectively with others to do likewise. *est* brings to bear a subtler psychology on the utilitarian theory of good, and further subjectivizes it: what is good in itself is experiencing aliveness, not having money. *est* meanwhile retains utilitarianism's consequential theory of right: that act is right that yields the most good consequences to its agent.

Thus *est* merges an expressive theory of good with a consequential theory of right, in which rules play an instrumental part. Acts of rule-compliance and agreement-keeping are right because they enable the agent to achieve his goals and thereby feel aliveness. The expressive value of self-fulfillment justifies following the bureaucratic rules that govern the instrumental activity of middle-class adult life. *est* squares hip self-expression with the bureaucratic constraints of rule-egoism by positing that each omnicausal individual should take responsibility for the rules that bind him. He acknowledges himself as their cause and complies with them as means to satisfy his own wants. He likewise engages others: individuals are to intuit their own subjective wants, empathically communicate them to each other, and then make contractual agreements that will serve the self-interest of each and will, therefore, be kept by both. In these ways, *est* personalizes utilitarian exchange, while it invests rules and expressive values with utility.

CONVERSION AND CULTURAL CHANGE IN A MODERNIZED SOCIETY

As long as technological production, bureaucratic organization, and a massed urban population remain central to the structure of American society, outright rejections of the instrumental behavior rationalized by utilitarian culture are likely to flourish only within small subcultures or for short periods in the life cycle of their carriers. Otherwise, Americans must respond to the practical demands exerted on adults by the modernized society in which they live. Yet they must also respond to the integrity of meaning exerted by the different moral traditions with which they think. In this double-edged process, members of alternative religious movements carry nonutilitarian perceptions, assumptions, loyalties, and styles of evaluation out into a utilitarian culture, which absorbs these contrary elements even as it dilutes and makes them over. Awareness, too, becomes a commodity to be merchandised for consumption. The good becomes still another "goodie." Yet in the process, the goodness of experience becomes less identified with the good *things* of life. The possession of happiness and the unrestrained freedom to pursue it become more elusive not only in fact but in meaning. This process of reciprocal cultural change will go on for as long as utilitarian culture cannot justify by itself the dedicated work, cooperative behavior, and distributive justice that its political and social structure requires. It will continue, too, for as long as utilitarian culture cannot symbolize the enchantment the human mind finds in the world around and within itself.[25] Alternative cultural views will rise up against the current of the utilitarian mainstream. They will be swept up in it and will influence its course in turn.

For the present, alternative religious movements influence the culture more directly than they inform the society's structure. They reintegrate the meaning of social life for sixties youth more directly than they reintegrate these youth into society. The cultural changes carried by alternative religions do help them to adapt to adulthood in conventional society, but they also enable their alternative visions of that society to endure within it. In some regards, these movements find alternative grounds to justify conventional patterns of response to existing structures of opportunity: *est* graduates play the "game" of work for inner self-fulfillment; millenarian Christians marry and raise a family to prepare for their theocratic responsibilities; neo-Oriental devotees leave off political struggle because "you are one with your opponent." But in other regards, these movements back unconventional patterns of response to conventional job, education, housing, and other opportunities: live alone or coupled in a communal setting, serve people instead of a career, work on and off to buy time instead of things and space, learn from a master instead of a professor. In both ways, alternative religious movements may signal wider trends in our culture.

Unconventional life-style patterns have begun to stake their public claims to normality, especially in metropolitan areas like San Francisco and its suburbs.[26] But in Des Moines, too, sixties youth have carried expressive life-styles from the counterculture into mainstream institutions.[27] Having dropped back in and begun to interact as adults with their elders, they have introduced other generations to new attitudes toward marriage, work, and politics (not to mention sex, drugs, and dress). Meanwhile, more structural changes are underway. The stable nuclear family with the husband at work and his wife at home with the kids has ceased to be the modal household unit.[28] Indeed, only an estimated 7 percent of all American households now fit this pattern.[29] Singles, divorcees, those "living with someone" or serially monogamous, childless marriages, parents without partners, and working women have all increased.

Changes in household formation and the family are tied to changes in the world of work. As working women become freer to lead lives of their own and to negotiate egalitarian relationships with others, economic dependence no longer reinforces marital stability so strongly, a fact with important implications for changing patterns of marriage, divorce, fertility, and child-rearing. Moreover, the labor force directly involved in industrial production continues to shrink in relation to technological means and their management.[30] As a result, the influence of traditional work and its ethic continues to ebb, drained by structural unemployment at the bottom of the job ladder, overeducation and underemployment in the middle, and at the top, an increase of fluidly interpersonal and knowledge-oriented jobs that require ongoing innovation, mobility, and learning. Emerging ideals of work and love characterize both as ever-unfolding processes of choice instead of once-and-for-all commitments. They counsel each of us to communicate sensitively and to respond intensely in the present, taking as fully as we give. Over time they advise us to be flexible, to learn and "grow" through crisis and change. They also encourage us to relax our demands for permanence and fidelity to past choices, whether it be our own fidelity or others'. Self-expression instead of self-restraint, self-realization instead of self-sacrifice: the counterculture has passed, but in the postindustrial mainstream, personalist values continue to make headway against Protestant ones.

In general, the average person is now likely to spend much less of his life within a nuclear family than he was in generations past; and he is likely to undergo more changes in residence, income, job, and marital status with less linearity than before. As the course of work, marriage, and community life becomes less continuous, people grow more aware of themselves as individuals apart from their commitments to job and neighbors, spouse and children. They become more concerned with their own development—responding to their individual "needs" and "rhythms," setting their own "priorities" and values. Yet their selfhood simultaneously becomes less secure, since it is less surely fixed by social institutions and less faithfully upheld by commitment to them. The individualist self, at once isolated and imperial, can look to no authority beyond itself for confirmation. We have glimpsed how alternative religions rejoin the self to the rest of reality by conceiving it as a child of God, part of Buddha Mind, or a transpersonal "being." These ideas of the self, backed by a movement's rules and authority, retie the individual to some form of moral virtue and obligation not of his private making. Whether he wants to or not, he *ought* to obey God, live in accord with Buddhist precepts, or follow "the rules of life." Duties rejoin rights. Authoritative and regular judgment of ends rejoins consequential calculation of means. Individual wants are not enough to justify action. They must be tested against common needs.

The quest for self-fulfillment seen sweeping across America in the "Me Decade" carries with it questions about the ultimate usefulness of utilitarian goods and thus about the ultimate meaning of utilitarian happiness. This has reopened to an audience well beyond ex-hippies the question of what is good in itself. Alternative religions have carried through the counterculture's recognition that getting the goods of affluence does not add up to feeling good. Nor does feeling good, they add, necessarily mean being good. The hip insight that "money can't buy you love" has been deepened by the religious truth that "man does not live by bread alone." These lessons have sharpened since the 1960s with the discovery that the goods of affluence may not grow ever more available to everyone in the society, not even to the middle class; and that getting such material goods may now confer fewer of the benefits of superior social position (such as the freedom to enjoy material goods in relative peace and solitary splendor) than before. In a society where material goods and positional goods become divorced, there is a loosening in the utilitarian linkage between getting the things you want and doing or feeling as you like.[31] Alternative religions respond to these problems with feelings and ideas, not things. The immediate personal experience they induce by ritual anchors a view of reality that gives substance to shared moral values.

The ultimate values of Christian salvation, neo-Oriental enlightenment, and even *est*'s rule-egoist aliveness deny radical subjectivism and materialism in defining what is good. These values justify following social norms regardless of whether a person feels like it or reckons it advances his interests in a given case. Christian and neo-Oriental forms of alternative ethics oppose head-on the utilitarian tendency to see rules and law itself merely as means to advantage oneself or everyone at best and someone else at worst. *est*'s rule-egoism seeks to redefine the instrumental identity of social rules so that their self-interested violation can yield a person no real (psychic) good, though it may promise him material gain. The ultimate values of alternative ethics also support personal virtues—Christian charity, neo-Oriental compassion, and *est*'s "at cause" responsibility—that help to objectify personal character in moral terms and likewise extend it into social relations.

However little direct difference alternative religious movements may make to existing social or governmental structures, their political impact cannot be dismissed without gauging the secondary effects of the changes in moral and cultural meaning that they carry. The nature of selfhood and virtue, the individual in relation to the group, (inexhaustible) wants in relation to (limited) needs, rights in relation to duties, the legitimacy of moral authority and rules— redefinition of such ideas occurs at the foundation of social values and eventually makes itself felt in public policy. It does so by relocating the good ends at which policy aims and by reshaping the criteria of justice that policy seeks to satisfy. Giving each person his due assumes that we know what a person is, what things are good, and what a person should do to deserve them. When such moral knowledge changes, so does the political exercise of social justice.

For those outside of alternative religious movements, even more than for those inside, the present importance of these movements lies chiefly in the ideas they carry, not in the social models they embody. Chances are it will be an unforeseeable while before American society turns into a Christian theocracy, a monastic ecotopia, or one vast encounter group. This is just as well, given the nondemocratic structure of each. But the ideological upsurge of conservative Christianity, neo-Oriental and ecological monism, and psychologized individualism throughout American culture is already unmistakable. So is the weakening of liberalism, that synthesis of rational religion and humanism with utilitarian views that has long held sway over the moral middle ground in

America. This weakening has created a vacuum of meaning these other ideologies are expanding to fill, echoing from the political podium as well as the religious pulpit. We are witnessing the beginnings of a postliberal culture, rooted in personal life-style, but reaching through social values into the polity. Whatever direction this new culture takes, however far it advances or is reversed, the lines between the would-be successors to liberalism have been drawn.

Looking back over our inquiry, we recognize that styles of ethical evaluation by themselves are empty analytical categories. They take on substance only when they are applied in turn to the different layers of moral meaning that make up social life. These include (1) cultural historical patterns of morality like biblical religion, which support (2) the norms of social institutions like the family, and underlie (3) the formal ethics of ideological organizations like *est*, which inform (4) the ethical outlook of persons in a particular place in society at a particular time in their own lives and in history, like middle-class sixties youth. Only when styles of ethical evaluation link the other elements that make up moral understanding—that is, perceptions of facts, loyalties to others, and axial assumptions about the nature of reality—do these analytical categories reveal a living ethic by which persons make particular judgments.[32]

Without considering styles of evaluation, on the other hand, we are left with nothing but the particular judgments persons make. These appear as discrete "opinions" presumed to follow from the interests their adherents' social conditions define. When persons act contrary to their interests, it can only be because they have miscalculated them. This pragmatic view of moral behavior has practical drawbacks that a more interpretive strategy can address by relating the process of evaluation to its outcome. How a person thinks about right and wrong bears powerfully on what he judges to be right or wrong, and what he decides to do about it. How a person justifies his moral positions and actions bears on how he may be persuaded to change them. Styles of ethical evaluation are the necessary link between cultural and social conditions (which give these styles substance and plausibility) and particular moral positions and actions (which these styles generate and defend). Without taking ethical styles into account we cannot understand moral behavior nor can we change it, except by coercion or by the manipulation of interests. This is because we *think* our way to moral actions. Circumstances influence our thinking, but they do not do it for us. Recognizing this fact makes it possible to enrich research that neatly correlates social and economic data with discrete opinions on concrete issues, by exposing the interlocking assumptions, arguments, and modes of discourse that hold together these particulars within a cultural matrix. It also makes it possible to honor the commonsense conviction we have of our own moral views—that they come from our understanding, not our circumstances.

Looking from our inquiry to ourselves, we recognize that every one of us must find a way to regulate our own conduct and our relations with others. When this breaks down, as it did for many sixties youths, we are driven to recover our moral balance, even if it means "getting saved" or becoming world-savers. Converts to alternative religions are people who experienced ethical contradictions of unusual intensity and as a result looked for unusually coherent solutions to them. Their conversions provide a particularly vivid picture of how moral ideas come together and change, but one that depicts a cultural process in which we all participate. If every person faces the need for self-regulation, so does every society. In traditional societies and even now—less visibly, but no less essentially—in our own, religion makes morality possible. It does so by molding the fundamental order of reality—our deepest convictions about nature, self, and society—and deriving from it a feeling of commitment and a sense of intrinsic value and obligation.[33] We *ought* to act in accord with the way things actually are, conceived and symbolized in particular forms, no less than *est* graduates ought to take total responsibility for a world they totally created. What do *we* go by? How do we think it out, and live it out? If we inquire into our own moral views, as we have the views of sixties youth in alternative religious movements, will we find traditional answers still clear and powerful? If so, then their voices may seem curiously confused, their lives odd or obscure. But if instead we find ourselves unsure of what to go by, unmoved by our received ideas and symbols, then we cease to be observers safely watching others search to get saved from the sixties. Eager or unwilling, we have already joined them in a cultural drama where their efforts to renew tradition or transform it offer us cues. Whether we take their example as paths to follow or avoid, possibilities to test, or puzzles to solve, the answers they give us about how we should live cannot simply be dismissed. For the questions are our own. Let us face them.

REFERENCES

[1]For fuller development of this thesis, applied to conservative Christian, Zen Buddhist, and human potential movements, see my *Getting Saved from the Sixties* (Berkeley: University of California Press, 1982).

[2]See Clifford Geertz, "Religion as a Cultural System," in his *The Interpretation of Cultures* (New York: Basic Books, 1973) for the classic statement of this view. Max Heirich points to the need for some such interpretation of conversion in "Change of Heart: A Test of Some Widely Held Theories about Conversion," *American Journal of Sociology* 83, 3 (1977): 658-80.

[3]This interpretation rests on Robert N. Bellah's argument in "New Religious Consciousness and the Crisis of Modernity," chapter 15 of *The New Religious Consciousness*, C. Y. Glock and R. N. Bellah (eds.) (Berkeley: University of California Press, 1976). I have developed its specifically normative dimension, using a taxonomy of styles of ethical evaluation taken from Ralph B. Potter, "The Structure of Certain Christian Responses to the Nuclear Dilemma, 1959-1963" (unpublished Th.D. thesis, Harvard Divinity School, 1965), pp. 363-98. The discussion of utilitarian and counter-cultures also draws on Alvin Gouldner, "Utilitarian Culture and Sociology," chapter 3 of his *The Coming Crisis of Western Sociology* (New York: Avon Books, 1970).

[4]See Robert K. Merton, *Social Theory and Social Structure* (Glencoe, Illinois: Free Press, 1957), p. 157; and A. Gouldner, *Coming Crisis*, pp. 65-73. Utilitarian culture, not utilitarian philosophical theory, is the object of analysis here. I have interpreted it as closer in practice to the philosophical position of general impersonal ethical egoism ("Everyone ought to act so as to produce the greatest balance of good over bad consequences for her or him, and any choice that does not affect her or him is morally indifferent.") than to any other, notably the universalistic utilitarianism of Bentham and Mill.

[5]From "What is the purpose of the *est* training?" *est* pamphlet #680-3, 13 January 1976.

[6]*est, The Graduate Review*, February 1978, p. 3; June 1978, p. 2; and personal communication with staff, 1980.

[7]The following data are drawn from Robert Ornstein et al., *A Self-Report Survey: Preliminary Study of Participants in Erhard Seminars Training* (The *est* Foundation, 1975, pp. 25-27, 34-36, 59); supplemented by reference to Ornstein data sets in File SYS8, 10/11/74, Variables W29-88; and by twenty sixties youths formally interviewed by the writer. Average age data come from *est*'s own records (see *The Graduate Review*, February 1978, p. 3). Occupational data come from Ornstein File SYS8, Variable W88, pp. 76-78.

[8]These data come from formal taped interviews averaging three hours each with twenty sixties youths who are *est* graduates, done in the San Francisco Bay Area during 1975-78; and informal interviews with thirty or so others done over a year's participant-observation, during which period the writer took the *est* training and two "graduate seminar series," and worked as an *est* volunteer. Youths formally interviewed averaged 28.3 years of age in 1976, were equally divided by sex, and were all Caucasians. Fourteen of twenty held B.A. degrees, of whom seven also held advanced degrees. Fourteen of twenty did white-collar work, one blue collar; four were professionals, and one a law student. Two of twenty were married and another four were divorced. Six of twenty were living with someone when interviewed; four were regularly dating one person; five were dating more than one person; three dated only occasionally. Fifteen of twenty had lived with someone for at least several months in the past, and only two were still living with their first such partner. None were affiliated with conventional churches. Eighteen of twenty had used marijuana, fourteen LSD. All reported using drugs less now than in the past. (Ornstein's sample [File SYS8, 11/22/74, pp. 27-30] shows that 39.5 percent of *all est* graduates had used marijuana, but only 14.4 percent had used LSD. Since *est*, 49.8 percent reported using less marijuana and 56 percent reported using less LSD.) Nine had been in political demonstrations; none were active in politics at present. Eleven of twenty had lived communally; three now did so. Fifteen of twenty had worked irregularly since school; three were now unemployed, one by choice.

[9]*est*, "Questions People Ask about the *est* Training," brochure #1474-1, 1977.

[10]*est*, "Questions People Ask."

[11]*PSA Magazine* (Pacific Southwest Airlines), June 1978, p. 13.

[12]*est, The Graduate Review*, July 1976, p. 5.

[13]Trainer R. McNamara, day 1, San Francisco "A" Training, September 1975.

[14]A deontological ethic prescribes, for example, "Keep your promises." Why? "Because promise-keeping is right." Why? "It is God's will." Or, "It accords with the true nature of existence." *est*'s consequential ethic asserts, "*If* you want to feel aliveness, keep your promises." The imperative is conditional upon particular desires or goals of the agent. In Kant's terms, there are no unconditional or "categorical imperatives" for *est* ("Keep promises!"). There are only "hypothetical imperatives" ("*If* you want to feel aliveness, keep promises.").

[15]To be sure, the classic utilitarian (an "act-utilitarian") followed the "rules" of the cost-benefit calculus, just as the classic economic man followed the "rules" of the market in *rationally* pursuing his self-interest.

[16]By "*est*'s critics," I refer, among others, to Peter Marin, "The New Narcissism," in *Harper's*, October 1975, pp. 45-56; Edwin Schur, *The Awareness Trap: Self-Absorption Instead of Social Change* (New York: Quadrangle, 1976); and Tom Wolfe, "The Me Decade," in *New York Magazine*, August 23, 1976.

[17]Werner Erhard, "Up to Your Ass in Aphorisms," 1973, booklet published by *est*.

[18]Ornstein, "A Self-Report Survey," p. 26.

[19]*est, The Graduate Review*, June 1977, pp. 3-4.

[20]See C. Wright Mills, *White Collar* (New York: Oxford University Press, 1951), p. xvii.

[21]See Max Weber, "The Protestant Sects and the Spirit of Capitalism," in *From Max Weber*, Hans Gerth and C. W. Mills (eds.) (New York: Oxford University Press, 1958), pp. 302-22; and Weber, *The Protestant Ethic and the Spirit of Capitalism* (New York: Scribners, 1958).

[22]J. Palmer, "Special Guest Seminar," San Francisco, March 1976.

[23]From "Making Relationships Work II," quoted in graduate information briefing notebooks in use April 1976, San Francisco.

[24]*The Graduate Review*, June 1977, p. 12.

[25]Cf. Weber, *The Protestant Ethic*, pp. 181-82; also "Science as a Vocation," pp. 155-56 in *From Max Weber*.

[26]For survey research evidence of substantial change in these directions, see Robert Wuthnow, *The Consciousness Reformation* (Berkeley: University of California Press, 1976), especially pp. 11-57, 215-24.

[27]*The New York Times*, August 12, 1979, "Spirit of 60s Generation Still Alive in American Society," pp. 1, 38.

[28]See Larry Hirschhorn, "Urban Development and Social Change: The Demographic Dimension" (unpublished essay, Childhood and Government Project, Earl Warren Legal Institute, School of Law, University of California at Berkeley, 1976), especially pp. 73-79.

[29]See *The New York Times*, April 10, 1977.

[30]See Fred Block and Larry Hirschhorn, "New Productive Forces and the Contradictions of Contemporary Capitalism: A Post-Industrial Perspective," *Theory and Society* 7 (1979): 368-71. See also Ann Swidler, "Love and Adulthood in American Culture," in *Themes of Work and Love in Adulthood*, Neil Smelser and Erik Erikson (eds.) (Cambridge: Harvard University Press, 1981). This paragraph and the one following draw on these sources.

[31]For an economist's analysis of this predicament, see Fred Hirsch, *Social Limits to Growth* (Cambridge: Harvard University Press, 1976), especially pp. 1-12, 117-58.

[32]See Ralph Potter, "The Logic of Moral Argument," pp. 93-114 in *Toward a Discipline of Social Ethics*, Paul Deats (ed.) (Boston: Boston University Press, 1972).

[33]See Clifford Geertz, "Religion as a Cultural System."

II. Weighing the Religious Moment

DAVID MARTIN

Revived Dogma and New Cult

AFTER THE DISINTEGRATIONS AND ANARCHIC ENTHUSIASMS of the sixties, there
has been a recovery of strong religious identities, ambiguous as yet in Roman
Catholicism, obvious in evangelical Christianity. Alongside this we have
another version of strengthening religious identity to be found in some of the
cults. This last is not a phenomenon of the same size. Nevertheless, the cults
attract a remarkable amount of comment, and they are, arguably, a side effect of
the same thrust toward a renewed and more definite religious persona. So what
we have to consider is the firming-up of the religious frame and a sharpening of
the edge which faith presents to the world. After the dissolution comes the
resolution.

This essay will be concerned initially and primarily with the Protestant
world and with evangelical revival.[1] It will, in the first instance, set that revival
against the kind of liberal, half-radicalized context which runs *pari passu* with the
decline of the state Churches of Northwest Europe, especially England,
Holland, and Scandinavia. Next it will set the evangelical revival against the
background provided by the cultural disintegration and anarchy of the sixties.
Here the starting point will be the United States. It then considers various other
recoveries of the seventies, which have produced the more insistent voice of the
"moral majority" and other expressions of traditional feeling. The final two
sections of the essay are briefly concerned with parallel indications in the cults
and in the Roman Catholic Church.

We have to begin with a distinction between evangelical revival and any
general recovery of religion. The two may, on occasion, go together, but it is
perfectly possible for evangelicals to expand and the universe of religion as such
to shrink. It is not unknown for evangelicals to get warmer as the overall climate
gets colder. For a start, the eighteenth century saw the appearance both of the
cold, deistic universe and of the ardent enthusiasm of the evangelical counterat-
tack. The Baron d'Holbach, archmaterialist, and John Wesley were contemporaries. For that matter, as the eighteenth century drew to a close, the
Southcottians and other rough equivalents of the much publicized cult groups
of today made a dramatic appearance.

That is by way of a preliminary warning, which immediately directs
attention to the general situation of religion within which evangelical revival and
cultic expansion take place. Old-fashioned religion and morality may have

111

recovered nerve and energy, but what is the broad contour of organized practice and belief? Where stand the mainline churches which provided the staple of liberal Protestantism? On the eastern side of the Atlantic, that question leads to a query about the very notion of a state church and its viability for the future in England and Scandinavia. The situation of liberal Christianity and of the state churches is the context which complements both the evangelical revival and the expansion of the cults.

One can say that in the sixties the liberal denominations and state churches, which are, of course, different if related things, lost out to radicalism on their leftward margin, and that in the seventies they lost out to evangelicals on their theologically conservative margin. Liberalism was first not adequate for real revolution, and then not adequate for real religion. In any case, liberalism was confused by the similarity between the rhetoric recommending personal liberation and the rhetoric of social liberation, whereas in fact the two point in totally different directions. Only in the West could liberals be so nicely cushioned against social reality not to know the difference.

The particular condition of the Protestant state churches in Northwest Europe provides the first set of indicators within which to locate evangelical revival. The sixties and seventies were a time of contraction for the historic state churches of European and English Protestantism. The imposing shell of a state religion was held up by the performance of the rites de passage at birth, death, marriage, and (in Scandinavia) confirmation. There is a slow erosion of these rites, but they still cover some four fifths of the population in Scandinavia, and in England nearly half the population is at least christened and married in the Church of England.[2] But the actual weekly practice of Anglicans, Lutherans, and the Dutch Reformed is startlingly similar. It varies between 3 and 5 percent on any given Sunday. There are, of course, wider circles of monthly or intermittent practice in England, so that perhaps 10 percent attend in the course of a month, and 20 to 25 percent in the course of a year. Parallel figures could be given for the other countries, with Denmark and Sweden somewhat lower than Norway and Finland.

Indeed, Denmark and Sweden can be designated the heartlands of secularized modernity. The world capitals of secularity are Copenhagen, Stockholm, London, and Amsterdam. Underneath this institutional laxity lies an inchoate belief in God, which is still held by a majority in all these countries except, perhaps, Sweden, even though the profile in the younger age groups suggests that the level of belief will drop somewhat as the older generations crumble. Then, too, there is widespread evidence of what Scandinavians call "personal Christianity," which sometimes surfaces in small group activity, but also lives on as a form of individual private commitment to the idea of living a Christian life. In Copenhagen, a majority pray even though most people are absent from weekly worship.[3]

This icy thinness of religion in the cold airs of Northwest Europe and in the vapors of Protestant England is highly significant, because it represents a fundamental difference in the Protestant world between North America and the original exporting countries. In all those countries with stable monarchies and Protestant state churches, institutional vitality is low.[4] In North America, lacking either monarchy or state church, it is high. Indeed, in the United States, the latest Gallup polls show 51 percent of teenagers in church on any given Sunday. The reasons for this difference cannot be gone into here, though they are discussed in the author's "A General Theory of Secularisation," but the current situation places a fundamental question mark, though not a final negative, against the ancient and historically potent idea of *cuius regio eius religio*.[5] The partial coincidence of church and nation now remains only at the level of diffuse identification and public ceremonial. The sacred ecology of these countries, where spire or tower or bulbous dome defines the genius loci of landscape and townscape, is now a latent, unactivated symbolism, apart from life crises, public formalities, and state occasions. This is a momentous development, however slow paced, and it has brought about a crisis of identity in the clerical guardians of the state religion. So great is the crisis, that often they no longer appreciate the virtue or latent power of national churches.[6] What has happened in Poland, Lithuania, and Iran seems aberrant, or at least alien and distant.

The crisis is essentially a separating out of any single religion from the sense of communal unity. It is a weakening of historic links between the parallel hierarchies of religious and secular power both at national and local level. The seat of the Bishop no longer exists in symmetrical alignment with the seat of the Senator. This can, of course, be overstated, and the links of religion with elites, and the solidarities of nation and local community, may yet revive, but the clergy are especially sensitive to the change. They no longer feel it is sufficient to occupy the formal role of chaplain to various local activities and to provide the religious aspect of natural solidarities. Very many clergy feel footloose, castaways without proper moorings. Some of them seek new anchorages in social work, in specialist ministries, or even in political activism. They try to discover a social role which can be justified on secular grounds. They want to relate to a social reality of tight-knit believers which is supportive and dynamic. Hence the preference for the language of relevance and dialogue. Such language codes the longing for vital contact and the shared kiss of warm *gemeinschaft*. Hence, too, the dissatisfaction with distinctive clothing and with liturgical forms which seem to cut them off from an outside world they deeply desire to enter on ordinary terms.

Consider, for example, the role of guardian of the sacred. This suggests (though it does not absolutely require) a sacerdotal, or at least a separated, character. It usually implies a local enclosure or sacred emplacement, providing a focus for a cluster of human habitations. It offers the cleric a distinctive profile, a defined set of duties which are unproblematic, and a settled niche in the community. Of course, such communities remain in their thousands, but they are not the context experienced by the majority of clergy, and even less of the majority of people they aim to serve. The equation of church-place-community is dislocated.

This is hardly new, but until relatively recently the state Churches were weighted in the direction of village and small town, where indeed their support is most dense, visible, and active. With the progressive tilt of modern society away from such settled locations, the draining of the countryside—apart from some commuter resettlement—and the bringing of small towns within the corrosive scope of the megalopolis, this no longer seemed able to provide a comprehensive context for the activity of the Church.[7] No doubt it is a possible option for some whose vocation is to serve in settled communities, but the Church must have other strategies as well. Moreover, since the Church has to provide a specifically religious justification for such strategies, they easily acquire a more than pragmatic sanction. They are not merely practiced as useful ways of coping with the plural, mobile, privatized aspects of modern social life, but are preached as the true, contemporary forms of the everlasting gospel.

The point of departure for the new breed of clergy involves, then, a farewell to the sacred, at least as embodied in the genius loci, whether that is a birthplace or a native country. The Church is no longer to be a stronghold sure, built like a sacred fort in some local bower or emplacement, but a movable tent for God's people as they travel in convoy through the secular desert. This notion of the tent is supposed to correspond to the journeying of St. Paul, who was by profession a tentmaker, and also to the journeyings of the chosen people as they made their exodus from Egypt in search of milk, honey, and liberation. In the same way, these ancient images of movement are linked to contemporary social mobility. Such a linkage is highly characteristic of the Church today, since it seeks for images in its tradition which appear to be appropriate for the modern situation.

These New Testament journeyings and Mosaic images of social movement involve an attempt to rejoin the whole society and to be in solidarity with mankind as such. The old role of priest or minister was restrictive in conferring special sacred roles and duties. Also, it was restrictive because as society became more plural, ministry had to be carried on in the confines of a particular voluntary association, Methodist, Congregationalist, Anglican, or whatever. In Northwest Europe and in England, the historic free churches were well used to this restriction and even thought it normal, but the clergy of the state churches chafed at such confinement, and they chafed the more when the confines of their local congregations became smaller. They felt trapped in a declining religious industry, with irrelevant skills, out-of-date roles, restrictive notions of their activity and proper work.

So significant numbers of them retranslated the *Opus Dei* as a call to live and work in the wider community, and some felt a positive dislike of the local parishes. They saw them as constricting enclaves of privatized piety, religious reservations for the practice of conservative and familial mores. Their own call was to leave boring, slow-paced parishes and find themselves anew in the real world of industry, or even in the global concerns of politics. They therefore sought fresh vocations, where they could strip down the fixed capital of ecclesiastical organization and cast away all the confining symbols, like vestments and distinctive buildings, sacred spaces and sacred times, which separated a declining church from the world.[8]

This was then the radical direction: the parson no longer chained to altar or pulpit, but moving as a man among men, sharing their concerns, accepting their definition of what was relevant. Industrial mission, for example, was partly based on such ideas.[9] A branch of the theory of church architecture was also based on them, and such ideas were built into some of the more avant-garde notions of liturgy. In a rather extreme form, liturgy was conceived as a movable feast with an entirely open-ended content. It might be celebrated in any place, at any time, and with almost any intention. A church was a people, not a sacred enclosure, and the Christian tent might be used for any and all the secular purposes that people might desire. The church was to be built on an open plan, with little or no attempt to set aside distinctive spaces. Or, alternatively, there was no necessity to build a church at all, because any space in the secular desert might be temporarily converted overnight. In short, the regulation of time and space, with its careful segregation of Sunday and its distinctive focus for the sacred, was to be comprehensively disrupted as part of an overall strategy aimed at sharing in the life of the world. There was to be no distinction of holy and profane places, nor any special rhythm of sacred time, nor any special dress to cut off the man of God (or woman of God) from humanity at large.

This implies two further rejections, both of them cutting at the supports of church-state religion. The first rejected folk religion, partly because it was not really Christian, and partly because it no longer offered a supportive context within which the Church might propagate its message.[10] Folk religion was to be set aside as a matter of those residual rites and ceremonies of the life cycle, as mixed up in the ancient underground continuity of paganism, and also as part of conventional morality. The second rejection concerned civic (or civil) religion. Many clerics saw this as a matter of asking for an official divorce to confirm a de facto separation. They felt less and less at ease in maintaining a public face for a form of religion which lacked any body in the form of everyday practice.[11] Civic religion seemed at best a decent facade; at worst archaic farce and flummery. In more malignant forms it required a sanctification of the social hierarchy, a benediction for military violence, and an unthinking legitimation of local or national patriotism.[12]

All these shifts of role and redefinitions of Christianity were quite plausible revivals of primitive faith, and could therefore be regarded as authentic. Indeed, the whole Constantinian "interlude," from the fourth century to the twentieth, could be seen as a distortion, though no doubt a rather large one. The dynamic of the New Testament had been incarcerated in Greek thought-forms, and the radicalism of Christianity expropriated by its adoption as the imperial religion. The *state* and the *static* went together. The very idea of the sacred was an importation from Roman religion, and the numinous character of traditional Christian worship was a pagan snare and delusion. *Sacer* and *numen* were not part of the original Christian vocabulary, even though traces of both might be found in the Old Testament.[13] (It is interesting that those who seek to reactivate Old Testament prophecy are appalled by Old Testament social solidarity.)

So here we have a whole group of themes whereby a selective analysis of "original" Christianity could be placed alongside a selective analysis of modernity. The small, mobile groups of early Christians, at odds with hierarchy and empire, with violence and wealth, corresponded to the radical grouplets of contemporary Christians dispersed incognito in the world, like the spies of God. The really far-out spies could become truly incognito, dropping not only their denominational identity, but the specific name of Christian and the otiose and distinctive concept of God. A "Christian" atheism was developed in which every characteristic of the modern world, godlessness and secularity, relativism and eternal change, could be baptized as the final, long-term working out of the faith. The distinctions between Church and World, between God and Man, and between Grace and Nature might be dissolved. The old Eucharist, set apart and celebrated by the sacred hierarchy in the name of an alien God, above and beyond, was now the shared feast of the poor, liberated from the alien transcendence of the divine, and celebrating *"Gott mit uns."*

There is no need here to work out the obvious transpositions whereby a religion which sought to convert might itself be converted to serve purely radical purposes, emptying its illusory transcendence into the active dynamism of the real world. Not all radicals pushed the analysis to such lengths, and an orthodox Christianity could perfectly well become implicated in the radical movements of Latin America, Korea, or South Africa, provided only that it shed its contaminating social attachments. In the Nicaraguan Revolution, for example, the collaboration between the Church and the Revolution generally involved no derogation of orthodox Catholic Christianity. The People of God simply aligned themselves with "people power."

In most of the Anglo-Saxon world the Marxist element has been subordinate to the existentialist one, in keeping with the general resistance which Anglo-Saxon Protestant cultures have to Marxism. Existentialist philosophy is quite adequate to sustain the rejection both of the specific sacerdotal and ministerial role, and cultural Christianity. What Kierkegaard said about the Grundvigians of nineteenth century Denmark can be transferred to all manifestations of folk religion and cultural Christianity. On the whole, the *soi-disant* radicals propagated the personalist and existential version of liberation, and only kept socialist liberation theology as an additional rhetorical flourish best indulged in overseas by charming and fiery Latins—or effervescent Africans. The real problems of authority, coercion, and hierarchy in collectivist regimes were never faced. Indeed, the reality of society itself was never faced. They took on board just enough sociology to be enthused and not enough sociology to be chastened.

This free-floating embrace of the world and denial of every distinctive enclave of time, space, and social role is quite unrealistic. The human desire for a location of religion, in place and in time, and for easy recognition of ministers of religion, is not necessarily a distortion. What has no locus in time and space and name, may indeed purport to exist universally and anonymously, but in practice it just does not exist. In practice, the embrace of "the world" was secularization under another name, a retrospective baptism of what was believed to have already occurred in the advance of social evolution, and a suicidal destruction of distinctive categories disguised as an affirmation of life. So the whole secularizing tendency within the Church follows its own logic, and is lost in the sands of secularity. What is *Sine Nomine* ceases to be.

What, however, is of crucial interest, when we consider revived dogmatism and renewed evangelical fervor, is the way certain of these themes have been taken up by evangelicals, but given a different transposition. *Evangelical fervor is in part a specific translation of certain themes shared with radicals, and a strong reaction against the kind of translation which the radicals have produced.* Evangelicals, whatever else may be said about them, recognize the unrealistic and self-deluding character of the radical translation. They know it doesn't work, and they are, above all, unprepared to "empty" God into history, and evacuate the Church in favor of the world.

What then of the evangelical alternative and the renewed, strongly defined religious persona which it represents? In the first place, it offers a more plausible reworking of primitive Christianity, since whatever else may have been true of the early Christians, they had a strong sense of the distinction between the Church and the World. The cells of early Christians operated in the body politic without loss of identity or definition. They were militant if not yet triumphant. They stood as *milites Christi* in an alien environment, *not* in solidarity with the world, but in solidarity with each other.

Thus, in England, at least, the evangelicals have mostly given up civic and folk religion for lost, and reject any rich and positive relation to culture. The situation in America is somewhat different, and I want now to speculate as to what the differences may be. As I do so, I think I should enter a caveat to the effect that some people express skepticism about the extent of contemporary evangelical revival, at least outside the United States. In Canada, for example, Dr. Reginald Bibby, of Lethbridge University, Alberta, has argued that what we observe is the capacity of evangelicals to retain rather than positively to expand. Certainly Canada has experienced a general secularization in the last two decades, without the recent upturn indicated by Gallup in America.

Let us speculate by devising a continuum which runs from Scandinavia, through England and thence via the white Commonwealth (Canada, Australia, New Zealand) to the United States. Two points are to be noted. One is that weekly practice increases all along this continuum. It is about 5 percent in Scandinavia and about 10 percent in England. In Canada, according to an unpublished report by Dr. Reginald Bibby for the United Church of Canada, it is about 30 percent.[14] This takes into account the concentration of relatively high Roman Catholic practice in Quebec; though there have been sharp declines since the sixties among the Quebecois, according to an unpublished paper by M. Guy Coté of St. John's College, Oxford. In Australia and New Zealand weekly practice is higher than in the United Kingdom, but less than 20 percent. In the United States weekly practice is about 40 percent, which is higher than anywhere in Europe, excluding Ireland and Poland. Moreover, belief also is higher in the United States when we make comparisons with countries like England and Sweden. If one takes belief in the Devil, only Greece rivals the United States for commitment to his diabolic existence.

The next thing to notice is that the evangelical religion grows in relative strength roughly along the same continuum, and exists in increasing detachment from the state Church (or the ex-state Church). In Scandinavia, the free evangelical churches, which mostly ceased expansion in the thirties (apart from the Pentecostals) are quite small. Evangelical religion has remained *inside* the state church as one particular type of established religiosity. In England the free churches, though also in the doldrums (apart from the Baptists and Pentecostals) are much larger. There is also a very lively, if somewhat defensive, evangelical sector inside the State Church paralleling the Scandinavian situation. When we come to the United States, the free churches are much the largest Protestant bodies, especially the enormous Baptist Church in its various manifestations, and the ex-state Church, the Episcopalian, a mere two to three million strong, has only a small evangelical component. In the culture at large, evangelicalism is very strong.

Now these shifts in the density of practice, of belief, and in the size of free churches and the influence of evangelicalism are not precise all along the continuum and are affected by various historical factors, such as the situation represented by Quebec. But all the same the profile is clear enough, and it is collateral with the growth of religious pluralism and voluntarism over against the monopoly exercised by the state church. Once churches shift free from the state connection, which is also the link with high culture, they can swing along with the tides of social change, proliferating and adapting as they do so. This is *not* to say, however, that if the state churches of Scandinavia and England (or Scotland) abandon the link with the state and/or with high culture, that they then acquire the advantages of the American situation—that is, vulgarization and popularity. History is not turned round so easily. More likely they will lose richness without gaining popularity, as happened to the unhappy Episcopalians in America, once they cut their ties with long-term liturgical continuity and the richness of their tradition.[15]

These differences, systematically varying over the whole continuum from the United States to Scandinavia, are connected with differences in political culture. Thus we see state provision at its highest in Scandinavia—that is, the state providing wholeness and health where once it provided holiness. Again in Scandinavia there has been, until quite recently, a political monopoly, exercised by Social Democracy, and emerging out of a cultural matrix characterized by religious monopoly. If we follow through the continuum from the United States to Scandinavia, we find a steady increase first in labor parties, and in Scandinavia the existence of significant communist enclaves, expecially in Iceland and Finland, where communist voting is nearly one in five. I would also add into this continuum certain cultural traits, such as the importance attached to sincerity in the evangelically influenced culture of the United States, and the importance attached to formal manners, at least until recently, in the cultures of England and Scandinavia. Formal manners are an analogue of the rich formal liturgies characteristic of the state church. Sincerity is an analogue of the Methodist emphasis on experience, an emphasis absolutely crucial to the development of American culture.

This same continuum is important, indeed crucial, since it relates to the quite different level of confidence and influence enjoyed by evangelicals in the United States. In the United States they comprise a huge sector of Protestant churchgoers, in a churchgoing nation, and a nation moreover, which is nearly two thirds Protestant in its religious identity. They are—almost—the majority in the majority. In England, Scandinavia, Holland, and even in West Germany, they are the minority in the minority, though they are probably the active, aggressive sector and the point of growth. In Britain, the three leaders of the main political parties do *not* declare themselves "born-again" Christians, though as it happens, they all come from strong evangelical backgrounds. In Britain such connections must remain implicit. In America, of course, they are trumpeted from the rooftops. And in Scandinavia, they barely exist, and if they do remain irrelevant.

I should here remind readers of what has been argued hitherto, and why it has been argued, before proceeding to the next step in the argument, which brings us back to the sixties and its aftermath. We are interested in the firming-up of the religious persona within the Protestant (or North Atlantic) cultural sphere, expressed principally in evangelical revival and marginally in the influence of the so-called cults. We have outlined various movements in the liberal and radical wing of the Christian Churches. We have suggested that these movements exhibit a corrosive, dissolving tendency. They lack form and a realistic sociological basis and are inclined to break down the frames which defend faith against secularity and/or politicization. This is not *all* that may be said, but it remains an important part. Then we have tried to indicate how the evangelical revival has reacted against these breakdowns and dissolutions, and also how that revival starts from a different cultural situation in America as compared with Northwest Europe.

But why, given that American evangelicals have been, and remain, so well placed (Northeastern seaboard snobbery apart), should they "react" at all? Here we have to put the argument into reverse, and consider how the student movement was very influential in the United States and less so in Northwest Europe. The student movement is a term used here to designate a cultural syndrome which surfaced most dramatically in the universities, but which was not at all confined to them. I mean the cult of openness and of letting it all hang out, of liberty defined as license. I also refer to the radical repudiation of frames, limits, borders, institutions, organizations, and especially of hierarchy, authority, and bureaucratic governance.

I think it is reasonable to argue that this radical repudiation, essentially anarchic in its thrust, went furthest in the United States, and remained fairly marginal in Britain and Scandinavia.[16] America, above all California, was *fons et origo* of the anarchic contagion. The laissez-faire principle in American culture experienced its most radical development by being transferred from the material economy to the economy of the psyche. Protestant individualism toppled over into post-Protestant anarchy by taking its logic one further and self-destructive step.

This meant the liberalized mainstream of American Protestantism (and by a spillover, the liberalizing mainstream of American Roman Catholicism) experienced an inundation. The frames, limits, and mechanisms of containment, both in the personality and at the level of organization, were overrun. And they could be overrun precisely because the established rhetoric of individualism and sincerity could be deployed against "the establishment." In Northwest Europe, by contrast, there was less of such rhetoric to utilize. The stiffer frames and tighter modes of cultural manners, integrally related to elite universities, elite state churches, and to respect for law, were softened, but they did not collapse. The radicals only managed to establish bridgeheads, notably in the expressive professions and the media, that is, the key sectors for sending out signals and messages. Only after that, as Bernice Martin has argued, was there a steady widening out of anti-institutional ideology.[17]

Thus evangelicals in the United States were better placed to face a greater threat: the Protestant base of American culture made possible both the extensive dissolution and the eventual massive response of the moral majority. Evangelicals in Northwest Europe were worse placed to face a smaller threat. But both in America and in Northwest Europe, they incorporated some of the themes spread abroad in the sixties and reset them in tight, defensive frames. They protected the core of faith within distinctive, well-marked borders. A semifundamentalist Christianity revived, and did so to such an extent that many people began to equate Christianity with evangelicalism. Just how it revived may be briefly illustrated by the situation in Britain and Holland.

The broad contours of evangelical revival in Britain have been documented by Dr. Steven Bruce of the Queen's University, Belfast, in an unpublished article, "The Resilience of Religion: Conservatives, Conversions, and Conversionism." He surveys Scotland, Ulster, and England to show the relative resilience of conservative bodies. He also quotes a Baptist Union Report which says that the smaller Baptist churches are both more conservative and more resilient than the larger ones. Even within Methodism and the Church of Scotland conservative associations have emerged with increasing support. Dr. Bruce comments on the notion put forward by Kelley that this conservative success is due to conversions from the heathen. On the whole, he inclines to those critics of Kelley who do not stress conversions but rather efficient childhood socialization, social control, and organizational transmission. Crusades have an impact mostly on the twelve-to-twenty age group, and crystallize what is already there in the background, as well as increasing the cohesion of those who run and promote them.

It is very instructive to observe the fate of the liberal Student Christian Movement in the sixties in Britain, as compared with the fate of the evangelical student organization. This also has been analyzed by Dr. Stephen Bruce.[18] The SCM, a flourishing body at the commencement of the decade, declared itself "open" in accordance with advanced opinions about embracing the world and realizing the political potential of the faith. No sooner was the world well and truly embraced than it proved a veritable Thaïs, more capable of seducing than of being reformed. Meanwhile, the evangelical cells, sharply defined and conservative, proliferated and became the main carriers of Christianity and almost its defining image in the university context.

The other illustration is provided by Holland. Evangelical revival there has been analyzed by G. Dekker in *"Opkomst der evangelischen."*[19] It takes place in a situation where even the stricter Calvinist body, standing on the theological right of the Dutch Reformed, is subject to liberal incursion, and where the Roman Catholics have gone some distance toward the liberal cultural center, as they have in America. So evangelical revival represents an expanding ghetto of ethical rigorism, much of it active in house churches entirely outside the organized bodies. It has, as in Scandinavia, a minor expression in small Christian political parties; and, as in England, there is a touch of evangelical political radicalism mixed in with the general cultural conservatism. They have their own TV, a move which may be made in England, and this is actually preferred by conservative-minded Catholics to their own rather lax TV. What is interesting for this argument is that when the old Roman Catholic hierarchy and liturgy weakened, there was no point of attachment and reference around which religious resistance might rally. In Calvinism, however, the elect remnant reformed themselves around the Bible. I should add here that the Dutch Churches and the English Churches have taken up anticonservative attitudes on the nuclear issue, migrants, and aid to the Third World. The Dutch Inter-Church Peace Movement is notably radical.

It remains only to show how certain themes which evangelicals shared with the counterculture were reset in a muted form. One theme was personal contact and subjective experience. This was, of course, always an evangelical motif, but it now provided a point of overlap with the counterculture. The sixties hungered and thirsted after subjective reality, and the evangelicals offered the bread of life and living water. For evangelical religion, there is no need of any objective medium of experience, whether it be liturgical form or hierarchical authority, since Christ is the one Mediator between man and God. The difference between evangelicals and liberals is the capital "p" in Person. Indeed, much of evangelical sentiment is simply a personalism about Jesus and a free-floating invocation of being "in the Spirit."

This dispenses at one blow with the constrictions of form and liturgical sequence, and establishes a radical egalitarianism in every respect except with regard to the divine Word. An evangelical service or prayer meeting was a participating democracy to which the individual might contribute his own experience, even if that experience is organized according to a fairly uniform Biblical pattern. Thus participation is given some scope and, at the same time, checked and stabilized by an established stereotype. This enables evangelical religion to survive the storms of the student movement, and then to pick up a sizable proportion of the shipwrecked survivors.

Two secondary themes of evangelical religion which received increasing emphasis were the "house church" movement and charismatic fervor, though the latter also made a dramatic appearance in the traditional Anglican and Roman Churches. The informality of house churches and the spontaneity of charismatic worship enabled faith to ally with, and simultaneously to resist, the psychic anarchy then abroad. Indeed, the invocation of the spirit and the expulsion of daemonic forces ran alongside the almost daemonic spirituality found in many of the young. Evangelicalism was a form of spiritual "conjuring" within an established paradigm.

That paradigm constantly reproduced a firm and resistant frame, rooted in biblical authority and having no truck with "the world." The frame was provided by the cohesion of the group itself, not by any external ecclesiastical organization, though no one would deny that evangelicals were also efficiently organized. Sometimes this frame could be restrictive, at least intellectually. For example, the sixties even saw the expansion of "creationist science," a neo-fundamentalist manifestation which—oddly—appealed to the authority of believing scientists to underpin the credentials of Genesis.[20] But on the whole, the firm core of cohesive sentiment did not require such a degree of intellectual restriction, and could even allow some evangelicals to pursue social and radical goals, such as we have noted in Holland. The Anglican Bishop of Liverpool, David Sheppard, sometime England Cricketer, is a noted evangelical and also a social radical. At the same time, evangelicalism maintained its traditional strongholds in the engineering, medical, and business professions, providing a religious analogue of secular individualist striving and supporting a firmly conservative view of the world. Yet, whatever their political divisions, the evangelicals acknowledged above all else the overarching bond of common faith.

It could also support various movements for moral regeneration along traditional lines. The "new morality" of the sixties, which gave fresh and engaging names to sin, alerted the watchdogs of morally conservative nations like England and America, and even brought forth reactions in Scandinavia. Nobody knew how far the radical penetration of the media and expressive professions had eaten into the moral majority, but the citizen crusades in America were paralleled by the organization run by Mrs. Whitehouse in Britain, called the National Viewers and Listeners Association.[21] In Scandinavia and Holland, as we have already noted, specifically Christian parties either appeared or expanded, though their overall impact was not large.[22] The moral crusades endeavored to set up safe corners in the modern media, where impulses and signals might be morally monitored. The "Electric church" was invented as just such a corner.

Occasionally, countercultural themes and evangelical religion can achieve odd and unexpected symbioses. There was, as is well-enough known, a Christian version of rock. Eldridge Cleaver found the light, and so did Bob Dylan. The most consistent performer in the charts was the evangelical Cliff Richard. Elvis Presley has been, since his death, the focus of a huge cult, which proclaims he is now singing for the Lord. When John Lennon died, the assemblies in Central Park and in Liverpool immediately had resort to Christian paradigms of mourning. In Catholic Liverpool, the evangelical Anglican bishop was a major figure in a huge public act of grief, and he expressed the Lennon philosophy in explicitly Christian terms. Too much should not be made of such examples, or of their semi-Christian character, but the semiotic relation between the pop music scene and religion exists, and can surface dramatically. A careful analysis of this has been provided by Bernice Martin in "The Socialisation of Disorder."[23]

The radical thrust and evangelicalism have important points in common. For example, they can both operate in an ecumenical, nondenominational way. This is because they leap over the bounds of denominational difference, and also because they can define the crucial distinction as existing between liberals and evangelicals, not as between (say) Methodists and Anglicans. However, it now seems that the conservative recovery in religion begins to include some recovery of denominational distinctiveness. There is some questioning of the value of compromises which blur the integrity of genuine and important differences. It is recognized that the pragmatic success of ecumenical unions, such as that of the Methodists in 1932 and of the English Presbyterians and Congregationalists quite recently, is very equivocal. Organizational ecumenism is now in the doldrums, as distinct from grass roots unity "in the Spirit."

The clearest instance where liberal and evangelical are conjoined is in the sphere of liturgy. This is not the place to discuss the final phase of the liturgical movement, which is, in my view, destructive, but it is worth indicating how the shared elements of otherwise opposed trends have worked against the traditional liturgy, and against the poetry of traditional religion, whether liturgical or biblical. The traditional liturgy of the Anglican Church was marked out for destruction for a number of reasons, nearly all of them relevant to the argument of this essay. In the first place, it was an objective form which aimed to shape and inform a distinctive, disciplined spirituality, not to "express" subjective feelings. And just because it was distinctive, it was held to militate against ecumenical aspirations. Common texts were devised in international and national ecclesiastical bureaucracies, and though these were wretched examples of sham antique posing as modernity, nevertheless they were promoted because they were shared interdenominationally. But more than that, the English

Prayer Book (and the King James Bible of 1611) had uniquely powerful alignments with English-speaking culture in England, Australia, and America, and that was a negative asset for clerics fearful of involvement in the wider culture. Even the sheer power and quality of these masterworks was a negative asset, because it was held to appeal, in particular, to the elite. The Anglican liturgy was, therefore, stigmatized as part of that rich interpenetration of traditional culture and religion, which involved the ideal of uplifting a *whole* community. This was regarded as no longer viable, for some of the reasons outlined above.

The opposition was led by a sociologist—myself—who was convinced that these reasons, however plausible, had been misapprehended by a panicky sector of the clergy.[24] Gallup showed in the United States and in Britain that more of the faithful preferred the traditional language; and the secular newspapers in Britain (and in the United States) gave united and vigorous support to the traditional liturgy, indicating that the sense of the link between nation and Church was not so dormant as many churchmen thought. A petition was presented to the General Synod of the Church of England, prepared by the author, which was the most distinguished ever presented in England, beginning with the names of the Foreign Secretary, the Home Secretary, and backed by a commendation from Mr. Michael Foot, now the Labor leader. Twenty-one heads of houses at Oxford and Cambridge signed, indicating the clear attachment of the academic community to the traditional forms of scripture and liturgy. The most recent expression of feeling has been a symbolic vote by both Houses of Parliament in favor of a Prayer Book Protection Bill. This is very unlikely to become law, but it is a warning signal of some significance. The reaction of certain clerics to the petition was interesting, and often paradoxical. They objected to the presence of atheists among the petitioners, though they had previously desired to embrace the secular world. They objected to the challenge to the remnants of clerical authority, though they had previously called for a desacralization of the clerical role. The subsequent controversy between journalists and academics, on the one hand, and a powerful group of clergy, on the other, underlined the clerical promotion of the new forms, including the elements borrowed from the counterculture such as the mandatory spontaneity represented by the Kiss of Peace. "With it" clergy recognized that the classic liturgy was not easily utilized for an open-ended, folksy get-together or for ecclesiastical versions of the encounter group. Neo-clericalism is a clear component in current changes, however much disguised by the rhetoric of the "people of God."

This extraordinary demonstration of affection for poetic and traditional forms is not identical with the recovery of conservative religion. As has been argued, the main revival of conservative religion took place in the semisectarian enclave set up by evangelicalism and cutting itself off from traditional culture. Nevertheless, it is one form of conservation which had been previously written off, and turns out to be unexpectedly alive. Nor was it an isolated phenomenon simply sparked by a clericalist manipulation of liturgy. The University of Cambridge produced vigorous contributions by Edward Norman and Maurice Cowling dedicated to the cause of the Established Church, and directed against what was seen as the superficial and morally self-indulgent liberalism in parts of the Church leadership, including the British Council of Churches and the World Council of Churches.[25] The criticism of the latter for selective moral indignation has been as widespread in America as in Britain. But the British criticism, as developed in Cambridge, drove the needle relentlessly into the soft, pink liberal flesh, claiming to expose it as no more nor less than a reach-me-down version of the social worker-cum-educationalist ideology, supported by an inflated vocabulary with very little substance. Actually, there were genuine questions at stake which the liberal conscience, however indulgently, endeavored to face, but the critique made by Edward Norman had great negative power, even if his positive alternative was less clear. It is worth pointing out in parenthesis that there was no great overlap between this right-wing critique and the traditionalist feeling mobilized behind the Prayer Book. Nor for that matter was there a necessary link between objections to female ministry and either the Prayer Book agitation or the right-wing attack on inspissated liberalism, though individuals might well connect them together. In America, such linkages may well be much stronger than in Britain. Indeed, they have to be given the social locus of the Episcopalian Church in America.[26] It is a fact that the Church of England, at least in theory, embraces a people, which enabled the whole issue to resonate through large networks of traditional feeling.

In case this seems a parochial matter, it is worth emphasizing what is implicit above, how a rich and profound expression of Christianity, embedded in the racines of life, thought, imagination, and poetry, and uplifting "true religion and virtue" in society at large, is attenuated. What Hooker stood for in his invocation of a godly Commonwealth is undermined, and the positive evaluation of form and art rejected. The imaginative life of Christians is pushed aside into children's books and into music. If they want poetry, let them read Tolkien, C. S. Lewis, and Madeleine L'Engle. Anyone who enters the new-style church today will have to emulate the hero in Gide's *La Porte Etroite*, who gave up his Pascal, and castrated himself intellectually and imaginatively.

Two other manifestations of a firming-up of religious defenses are found in some of the contemporary cults and in the Roman Church at large. These manifestations are such large subjects in themselves, that no more than one or two aspects can be indicated. Indeed, so far as Rome is concerned, one can snatch only at straws in the wind.

The expansion of cults has been the object of considerable press concern and comment.[27] However, not all of them firm up the boundaries of belief and reinforce religious cohesion. On the one hand, there are those which do just that, and they are of primary concern here—the Unification Church, for example, or the Children of God, or (in rather different style), the Hare Krishna devotees.

On the other hand, there are other groupings which are diffuse and ill-defined, such as Transcendental Meditation. These are much more undefined as to their boundaries than even the liberalized denominations. Where the conservative evangelicals and certain of the cults are highly visible, such movements as TM are almost invisible. So far as the various personal therapies are concerned, the sanctity of a discernible religious collectivity and the reality of a God "out there" have dissolved. Adherence to TM and other therapies is often compatible with other more "normal" religious commitments, and the therapeutic method may be promoted as a technique rather than as a faith. However, the various cults combine different elements. Scientology, for example, is certainly a technique, but it is also authoritarian and hierarchical in its organization, and has gradually built up a theological edifice. The Divine Light Mission is a technique, and has created a distinctive community, but it allows degrees of commitment—that is, a graduated slope between the inside core and the world outside.

The fallout from the anarchic enthusiasms of the sixties may land, like the ash from Mount St. Helens, in any one of these religious territories, both those which are strongly demarcated and those which are highly diffuse. TM or Scientology are likely to have acquired a somewhat older clientele, concerned one way or another to improve themselves, whereas the Unification Church and the Children of God captured youthful idealism anxious to change the world. Again, one cannot draw distinctions too sharply, since even TM has harbored ideas of a restored world to come.

If, however, one takes, by way of instructive example, the Unification Church, one has a millennial movement which maintains a strict frontier with the world and has built up a considerable body of doctrine. Such a movement receives more public notice (though it has less than a thousand adherents in Britain and some ten thousand in the United States) than does (say) TM in Scandinavia, where practitioners are supposed to be numbered in six or seven figures. The point is worth emphasizing, since whenever a strictly demarcated group undergoes expansion, the countervailing pressure of society creates the false impression of serious inroads into societal "normality." Noise and friction are equated with genuine danger.

Nevertheless, some of the characteristics of the Unification Church are worth scrutiny, as studied by Eileen Barker and others, because they are both expected and unexpected. Barker shows that recruits present an age and sex profile which is almost exactly the inverse of the mainstream churches.[28] They are young and male, whereas the numbers of mainstream bodies tend to be older and female. On the other hand, they are well-educated and tend to come from comfortable, satisfactory families, which have provided them with a religious upbringing. In short, they have conventional and comfortable, often religious childhoods, and then have passed into a period of "seekership," which may well have led through the various paths of alternative life-styles and counterculture. In this respect, they resemble recruits to other movements, like the Jesus People, the Children of God, and the devotees of Hare Krishna. Roy Wallis says that "the principal early following of each of these movements was drawn from among the hippies, drop-outs, surfers, LSD and marijuana users among the American and European young, and many more from those who sympathized with, and shared aspects of, the same sub-culture as these groups."[29]

Since these movements present such a sharp edge to "the world," and draw the young into comprehensive, total loyalties, they experience certain gains and losses. The main advantage is their capacity to attract the idealists who seek a purpose to life, and even to history. Like the evangelicals, but to an even greater extent, they mobilize those who seek a wider meaning and a deeper service than self can provide. By running in parallel to evangelicals, at a more acute angle to society, they are unlikely to draw many of those young idealists who have already been drawn to evangelical religion. The only exchange between evangelicals and the cults has been a tendency at the margin for some of the more experimental evangelicals to adopt certain items from the "alternative" life-styles, the better to "save" the young from the appeal they might otherwise exercise.

On the debit side, the extreme demands they make are likely to ensure a following as small as it is totally committed and unremittingly enthusiastic. Only as the "edge" presented to society dulls somewhat is a wider expansion likely, and this indeed is what is happening in some degree. Categories of commitment are allowed which permit believers to sojourn partway between the religious universe and the wider secular world. Until that happens there will be a spiral of suspicion, and of claim and counterclaim between the media and the organs of the new movement, especially where young people are taken out of their families of origin into the wider fellowship of faith.

This can also happen to other movements than those mentioned, if they enter a phase of social withdrawal, such as occurred in the case of Synanon, or if they try to exercise authoritarian controls on members even when they remain in their ordinary avocations. Scientology, for example, appeals to the search for greater personal potency to be found within the world, and not apart from it.[30] Nevertheless, the pressure which some say is exercised on the individual to fulfill the required psychic trajectory evokes considerable outside criticism and even, in some places, a measure of governmental restraint. There appears to be a group of movements, exemplified by "Moonies" and "Scientologists" in particular, which are very different one from another, yet nevertheless attract intense negative comment on the ground that they are not really "religious." Where Bahais or Anthroposophists can be seen as a religion, Moonies are regarded as quasi-political, and Scientologists as exploitative and commercial. Hence the rise of anticult movements designed to present as sharp an edge to the cults as they have presented to society. The objective rights and wrongs in this war between society and cult are very difficult to determine, and it is clear that many of the features objected to manage to exist relatively uncriticized within the wider society and in (say) the Roman Catholic Church. The essence of the complaint seems to lie in the violation of the normal social definition of what is "genuinely" religious.

The broad matrix out of which idealistic collectivities emerged and flourish, however modestly, has been set out in thumbnail caricature by Barker.[31] She sets out on the one hand "the achievement-oriented world of the materialistic ratrace" and on the other "the antinomian world of the amorphous countercul-ture." These are, if you like, the two alternatives which movements like the Children of God and the Unification Church insist on rejecting, even though an antinomian strain has remained amongst the Children of God, particularly when it comes to recruiting new members by "flirty fishing." Alongside these alternatives, Barker sets a Marxist viewpoint, "The Mystified World of alienated cogs"; a Weberian viewpoint, "The Disenchanted World of rational-ized cogs"; and what she calls "The Secularized World of the spiritually inarticulate." The themes of alienation and rationalization are familiar enough, but the lack of a language to articulate spirituality has its own importance. What new religious movements do is to provide a language and vocabulary within which spiritual experiences and comprehensive meanings can be framed. The old languages of religion were felt to be damaged by hypocrisy and compromised by compromise. Hence, the new mintage within which the world is, literally, re-formed.

This is not to say that this sequence from secular counterculture to religious counterculture characterized the seventies in general. In broader ways the seventies were times of economy, retrenchment, and recession, accompanied by widespread political apathy in the young and by privatization. The moral majority might reassert themselves, but the atmosphere in universities was simply a hedonism seeking private satisfaction, which might occasionally include some personal spiritual therapy, provided economic stringency had not placed it financially out of reach. A movement like *est* perhaps symbolized one aspect of the change by emphasizing getting one's act together rather than letting it all hang out.

As to the mood within the Roman Catholic Church, one can only append a codetta.[32] The new mood repeats certain of the themes noted above in the evangelical revival and in certain of the new religious movements or cults. In the person of Pope John Paul II, a new force emerged at the centre of authority, willing to use his power and convinced of the rightness of using it.[33] John Paul is both religiously conservative and dedicated to social justice, and in that respect resembled some of the new breed of evangelicals. He finally broke the old and already fading stereotype which related religious to political conservatism. However, his social convictions were less those of liberation theology than a further extension of the social teaching of the Roman magisterium delivered *de haut en bas*.

This is not surprising. The pope came out of a society where religious and political authority remain deeply entrenched. He regards the hedonistic liberalism of the West as effete and slack. "Social Justice" for him is full of hard sayings and proceeds out of a hard school. Perhaps the paradoxes of John Paul were illustrated, as Peter Hebblethwaite has argued, during his visit to Brazil. On the one hand, he offered symbolic and verbal solidarity with the reforming, radical bishops. On the other, he denounced class warfare, and by implication showed disapproval of the "base Communities" and the concept of "people power." His aim was both to distance himself from unrestrained capitalism and from Marxism and to reassert the discipline of Rome and the specific, special role of the priest. The pope remains Vicar of Christ, and the priest is set apart for a task which is primarily religious.

Not only is the reassertion of discipline impressive, but the direction in which that discipline is exercised remains religiously conservative. This is particularly the case on the issues of marital regulation and sexual mores. "Remains" is perhaps the right word, since the previous pontificate was, after all, responsible for *Humanae Vitae*. Paul VI spoke of the corruption and degeneracy present in those countries which had legalized divorce. All the same, John Paul II applies the traditional discipline with renewed vigor. The diocesan tribunals in the United States, which have speeded the process of obtaining annulments, are not likely to remain for long "at ease in Zion." Indeed, the whole process of loosening which affected the Roman Church in the

United States is likely to be repugnant to the pope. It was in the United States that the pope was challenged by a group of liberated nuns. Even in England, where Roman Catholics are hardly contumacious, a survey in 1980 showed that three quarters of the Catholic community see nothing wrong in artificial contraception, about half would accept married priests, and a quarter would accept women priests.

In morals, politics, and also theology, the disciplinary powers of the magisterium have been reasserted, and in ecumenical relations, the specific claims of Rome vigorously maintained. Ecclesiastics of conservative mind have received key promotions at Rome, and theologians of radical tendency, like Hans Küng, have been rebuked. Observers in Rome say that the pope favors the conservative-minded *Opus Dei*, and that in Spain he does so in a way which sides against the Spanish bishops. This is not to say that the Second Vatican Council from 1962 to 1965 has been repudiated, since, after all, the present pope was enthusiastically in the middle of it. It is to say, however, that the Council's decrees were capable of a fairly conservative interpretation, and the personalistic radicalism which followed, particularly in North America, was a euphoric, unjustified extension of it.

This is not to attribute the change to one man, since even popes reflect shifts as well as cause them, and the choice of a pope is in part the reflection of a mood. The Catholic charismatic movement, for example, probably reached a plateau in the mid-seventies, and has recently shown signs of increasing ethical rigorism. The charismatic movement may itself have been a search for a more personal inner authority, once the external point of reference in Rome appeared to have weakened. Now, however, that external point of reference has been signally reinforced, perhaps producing a fortress—Catholicism which is analogous to the recovery of *ein feste Burg* in evangelical Protestantism and the minibastions of religious rigor found in the small cults.

REFERENCES

[1]On evangelicalism in general I have derived particular profit from G. M. Marsden, *Fundamentalism and American Culture* (New York: Oxford University Press, 1980).

[2]J. K. Hadden (ed.), *Religion in Radical Transition* (Rutgers, New Jersey: Transaction Books, 1971). For a discussion of Church-State tensions in Sweden, see G. Gustafsson, *Religion och Politik* (Lund: University Press, 1979). For the most recent summary of the English situation, see A. Gilbert, *The Making of Post Christian Britain* (London: Heinemann, 1979).

[3]P. Salomonsen, *Religion i dag* (Copenhagen: C. E. Gad, 1971).

[4]I know, of course, that it is misleading to describe the Church of England as Protestant. But England as a culture is so Protestant in the negative sense, that worship hardly seems necessary.

[5]Oxford: Blackwell, 1978.

[6]A. J. Russell, *The Clerical Profession* (London: S.P.C.K. 1980), and R. Towler and A. P. M. Coxon, *The Fate of the Anglican Clergy* (London: Macmillan, 1979).

[7]According to the 1981 British census, there is now a noticeable return to rural areas.

[8]J. G. Davies, "The Influence of Architecture upon Liturgical Change," *Studia liturgica* 9 (1973): 230-40.

[9]The *locus classicus* in Britain remains E. R. Wickham, *Church and People in an Industrial City* (London: Lutterworth 1957).

[10]R. Towler, *Homo Religiosus* (London: Constable, 1974). This contains a discussion of what the author calls "Common Religion."

[11]Baptism, for example, was seen as contaminated both by an autocratic and "natural" acceptance of the child after the manner of Church-State Christianity, and also by notions of magical efficacy.

[12]For an account of a civil religion still going strong, see T. Dunbar Moodie, "The Afrikaner

Civil Religion," in *Identity and Religion*, H. Mol (ed.) (Beverly Hills, California: Sage Publications, 1978).

[13]J. G. Davies, *Every Day God* (London. S.C.M. Press, 1973).

[14]R. Bibby, "Why Conservative Churches *Really* Are Growing: Kelley Revisited," *Journal for the Scientific Study of Religion* 17 (1978): 129-37. Cf. R. Bibby, "The State of Collective Religiosity in Canada," *Canadian Review of Sociology and Anthropology* 16 (1) (1979). Bibby's wider work documents a rapid decline in overall Canadian practice, which includes Quebec. Canada does not seem to exhibit the recoveries which Gallup seems to indicate for the United States. For England, see *Prospects for the Eighties*, a conspectus of the 1979 religious census (London: Bible Society, 1980). Parallel manifestations of evangelical vigor (and cultic expansion) may be observed in other parts of the English-speaking world, but they are very much united compared with what is observed in the United States. For example, only a tiny ripple reaches New Zealand. See M. Hill, "Religion and Society: Cement or Ferment," in J. Veitch and C. Nichol (eds.), *Religion in New Zealand* (Wellington: Victoria University, 1980).

[15]Over the 1970s, the Episcopal Church lost a very sizable proportion of its membership.

[16]There were important eruptions in Holland and West Germany arising in contexts that cannot be discussed here.

[17]B. Martin, *A Sociology of Contemporary Cultural Change* (Oxford: Blackwell, 1981).

[18]S. Bruce, "A Study of the S.C.M.," Ph.D. thesis, Aberdeen University. This is very much an analysis of the vulnerability of liberal theology.

[19]G. Dekker, privately circulated, Free University of Amsterdam. Dr. Dekker, in another unpublished paper, "Power and Powerlessness of the New Clergy," written for the Oxford Symposium at Blackfriars, Oxford, January 1981, concludes that vocal clergy are a new kind of pressure group, with some force, but not really carrying their constituencies with them.

[20]E. Barker, "In the Beginning: The Battle of Creationist Science against Evolutionism," in *On the Margins of Science*, R. Wallis (ed.), Keele: Sociological Review Monograph no. 27.

[21]M. Tracey and D. Morrison, *Whitehouse* (London: Macmillan, 1979), and Tracey and Morrison, *The National Viewers' and Listeners' Association* (London: Macmillan, 1981). Cf. L. A. Zurcher and R. G. Kirkpatrick, *Citizens for Decency* (Austin: University of Texas Press, 1976).

[22]J. T. S. Madeley, *European Journal of Political Research* 5: 268-86.

[23]B. Martin, "The Socialisation of Disorder, Symbolism in Rock Music," *Sociological Analysis* 40 (2) (1979): 87-124, and B. Martin "Symbolism and the Sacred in Contemporary Rock Music," in Arts of the Fourteenth Conference of the International Conference of the Sociology of Religion (Paris: CNRS/CISR, 1977).

[24]D. Martin, "Crisis for Cranmer and King James," *Poetry Nation Review* no. 13 (Manchester: Carcanet Press, 1979); D. Martin and P. Mullen, *No Alternative* (Oxford: Blackwell, 1981); B. Morris, *Ritual Murder* (Manchester: Carcanet Press, 1980); and D. Martin, *The Breaking of the Image* (Oxford: Blackwell, 1980).

[25]M. Cowling, *Religion and Public Doctrine in Modern England* (Cambridge: Cambridge University Press, 1980); E. Norman, *Christianity and the World Order* (New York: Oxford University Press, 1979); and D. Martin, "The Revs and Revolutions," *Encounter* 52 (6) (January 1979).

[26]D. Mills-Parker, *The Prayer Book Issue*, SPBCP, Box 120206, Acklen Station, Nashville, Tennessee 37212. This is a lively account of the American situation.

[27]For general work on cults (or "alternative religions"), see T. Robbins and D. Anthony, "New Religions Movements and the Social System," and I. Richardson, "An Oppositional and General Conceptualisation of Cults," both in *The Annual Review of the Social Sciences of Religion* 2 (The Hague: Mouton, 1978). See also R. Wallis, "The Rebirth of the Gods," Queen's University, Belfast, New Lecture Series, no. 108, and B. Wilson, "The New Religions," *The Japanese Journal of Religious Studies*, Summer 1979.

[28]E. Barker, "Who'd Be a Moonie?" in *The Social Impact of New Religious Movements*, B. Wilson (ed.) (New York: Rose of Sharon Press, 1981).

[29]R. Wallis, "The Elementary Forms of the New Religious Life," a manuscript available from Queen's University, Belfast.

[30]R. Wallis, *The Road to Total Freedom* (London: Heinemann, 1976).

[31]E. Barker, "Whose Service is Perfect Freedom," in *Spiritual Well-Being: Sociological Perspectives*, D. Moberg (ed.) (Washington, D.C.: University Press of America, 1979).

[32]I am not discussing here the kind of Roman Catholic conservatism associated with Archbishop Lefebvre of Lisle. His conservatism is a Romanist traditionalism of the nineteenth century kind based on religio-political *intégrisme* and bitter opposition to the progeny of the French Revolution. He believes Rome to have departed from the faith in a Marxist and Protestant direction.

[33]Cf. J. Hitchcock, *Catholicism and Modernity* (New York: Seabury Press, 1979); W. McSweeney, *Roman Catholicism: The Search for Relevance* (Oxford: Blackwell, 1980); S. Campbell-Jones, *In Habit: An Anthropological Study of Working Nuns* (London: Faber, 1979). All three books are studies in a changing Roman Catholicism up to the advent of Pope John Paul II.

WADE CLARK ROOF

America's Voluntary Establishment: Mainline Religion in Transition

THE FIRST THING TO CATCH HIS ATTENTION upon his arrival in America in the early nineteenth century, commented Alexis de Tocqueville, was the religious character of the nation. He was struck, among other things, by a seeming paradox: religion in America was in constant flux, ever changing and taking on new forms, yet it seemed to have an established character, to be widely accepted and fundamentally rooted in the mores and values of the people. "In the United States there are an infinite variety of ceaselessly changing Christian sects," he wrote, "but Christianity itself is an established and irresistible fact which no one seeks to attack or to defend."[1] American religion was striking for its remarkable blend of institutional qualities—stable, yet fluid, in structure; morally unified, yet pluralist, in character.

Had Tocqueville been around during the past two decades, he would no doubt have been amazed at religious developments in America. Ceaselessly changing sects, Christian and otherwise, dominated the scene. On college and university campuses, in downtown plazas of large cities, and in major airline terminals across the country, strange cults and sects in distinctive garb could be found, often chanting versions of religious truth alien to that accepted by most Americans. Diverse, often esoteric religious movements—Eastern mystical cults, religious communes, occult and pagan practices, resurgent evangelical and fundamentalist faiths, and others—all proclaimed it a time of widespread spiritual experimentation. This considerable spiritual vitality and ferment, especially among youth, gave rise to many new and different religious expressions. It was, as put by Robert Wuthnow, a period of "consciousness reformation" for a broad sector of young Americans.[2]

But what, Tocqueville might inquire, was happening to the more traditional religious faiths during this period? Did the established institutions, the mainline churches and synagogues, experience similar ferment and vitality? To be sure, whatever was happening in the traditional institutions caught less public attention than did the so-called new religions, and by comparison, seemed less dramatic and eventful. Although less apparent and more subtle, the developments are hardly less significant for the future of American religion. Almost 90 percent of Americans identify themselves as Protestants, Catholics, or Jews, and it is therefore unlikely that these faiths would not in some way reflect the climate of religious change and experimentation. The established faiths are almost always in flux, and most certainly so in times of rapid cultural change.

130

Indeed, to a considerable extent, these faiths tend to mirror the broader currents of social and cultural change within the society. Thus it is inconceivable that recent events and developments would not significantly alter the shape of American religious institutions.

Commentators on America's religious life generally agree that the last two decades have been a time of critical transition. Although various aspects of the period are singled out for attention, a good deal of concern has focused on the established religious institutions. Martin E. Marty, in describing the changing institutional patterns, speaks of a "seismic shift" in the nation's religious landscape.[3] Sydney A. Ahlstrom likewise ponders the possibility that we may have reached the end of a distinct quadricentennium—a unified 400-year period—in Anglo-American experience: the end of the great Puritan cultural epoch.[4] As always in times of major transition, the institutional shifts and religious experimentation that we see are but surface manifestations of a larger, underlying spiritual ferment.

This essay will examine the changing shape of the American religious establishment in this period, especially that of the mainline traditions. "Mainline" here means simply the dominant, culturally established religious faiths that are closely associated with prevailing social values and mores. Because of the variety of traditions involved and the wide scope of changes, attention can be given only to general trends and patterns. We shall look first at recent developments in institutional religious life, and then turn to an interpretation of the present realities and future possibilities of American religion.

Trends in Institutional Commitment

As Tocqueville understood so well, American religion is flexible and adaptable because of the nation's distinctive heritage of voluntarism: no single circumstance affected the shape of religious life more than the principle of religious freedom. When combined with strong and widespread democratic values, this has meant that religious styles are to a large extent molded by forces of public opinion and popular sentiments. Prevailing social attitudes and views at any given time play an important role in shaping and sustaining institutional religious loyalties. When these forces shift, so do religious styles and commitments. As a consequence, religion in America operates as a "voluntary establishment"—an institution whose strength rests upon those freely consenting to it,[5] and whose form tends to reflect the moods and sentiments of the time.

Three discernible trends of the recent significant shifts in religious commitment are: (1) the privatization of religious commitment; (2) the growth of conservative religious forms; and (3) the decline of liberal mainline institutions.

PRIVATIZATION

The trend toward greater individualism in religious choice and practice— the privatization of faith—is important in the modern period. Historically, individualism has been an important value in Western culture, and in contemporary society, fundamental social and psychological transformations have made it more so. Modernization brings about greater institutional differentiation and societal complexity, which individuals experience as the pluralization of life-worlds. Individuals confront life in the modern world as a fragmented reality, often lacking in those shared aspects that make a common universe of meaning and interpretation possible. Consequently, unless they take on meaning and motivational significance in an individual's life, traditional religious affirmations often lose plausibility. Religion becomes "invisible," to cite Thomas Luckmann, a private affair, something to be worked out within the boundaries of one's life experiences,[6] each individual fashioning, from the sources available, a system of sacred values and meanings in keeping with personal needs and preferences. Such privatized religion knows little of communal support, and exists by and large independent of institutionalized religious forms; it may provide meaning to the believer and personal orientation, but it is not a shared faith, and thus not likely to inspire strong group involvement.

Of interest in this regard is the emphasis, both religious and quasi-religious, placed on the various techniques employed by individuals to cultivate spiritual growth or, in less religious terms, to awaken inner experience. Whether religious or humanistic in inspiration, self-fulfillment is the primary goal of such activity; the major concerns are obtaining spiritual enlightenment and how a particular technique or discipline can lead to greater self-realization. What is important in judging a method's worth are not theological or institutional standards of evaluation, but its utility. The appeal of the many contemporary religious and quasi-religious therapies thus lies in the explicit attention they give to the benefits to be gained through participation. By focusing on rewards, the traditionally "latent" consequences of religion are redefined as "manifest" positive identity functions; that is, the instrumental value of the therapy becomes the reason for choosing it. In this respect, today's spiritual therapies are similar to the positive-thinking movement of the fifties, which was also concerned with techniques and results in the religious life.

Many of the new spiritual techniques have been prepared for mass consumption, and thus "packaged" and "marketed" to a wide audience. How much is "consumed," as measured by actual participation, is not huge by statistical standards, yet it is large enough to warrant serious attention. A 1976 Gallup survey of a representative sample of Americans revealed that 4 percent of the adult population professed involvement in Transcendental Meditation, 3 percent in yoga, 2 percent in mysticism, and 1 percent in Eastern religions.[7] By projecting the percentages to estimate the approximate number of devotees in each movement, we find there are surprisingly impressive constituencies. For example, 4 percent participation in TM projects into approximately 6 million people—roughly the size of the Jewish population in the United States and larger than the memberships of most Protestant denominations. When we add to these the many Americans involved in more secular therapies—psychotherapy for example—it becomes evident just how sizable a body of Americans adhere to privatized faiths of one form or another. An even larger number have been meaningfully exposed to them, and thereby possibly influenced as well.

The trend toward privatization has important implications for institutional religious commitment. Aside from the observation that privatization thrives on freedom from pressures of conformity and of individual choice, and thus tends not to inspire strong religious group involvement, two further points should be noted. One is that these therapies have their greatest appeal among youth, especially those more highly educated. Wuthnow's Bay Area study, for example, shows the college-educated, twenty-one-to-thirty-five-year-old age group most likely to be attracted to movements like TM, Zen, yoga, Scientology, and *est*.[8] This group may well be lost forever to established religious institutions, for their more individualized, privatistic religious commitments appear to be firmly entrenched, and may well persist without strong institutional attachments. A second point is that many *within* the religious establishment are turning to the spiritual therapies: both laity and clergy are among the growing numbers of people taking part in workshops on personal growth and meditation techniques. Concern for experiential religion and cultivation of the inner life are high priorities, especially for charismatics who have found a home within the established institutions. What the effects of this diffusion of spiritual concerns and techniques will be remains to be seen. It could conceivably result in a lessening of institutional loyalties, as energies become more inner-directed, or possibly, in a restructuring of the institution to accommodate more experiential religious forms. Either way, the shape of traditional religious institutions will be affected for the future.

CONSERVATIVE GROWTH

Another and quite opposite trend is the growth of conservative churches and the appeal of evangelical and fundamentalist faiths, Marty's "seismic shift" in American religion. The conservative religious presence in the media and their direct involvement in the political process serve to heighten public awareness of this shift. The emergence of the "Electronic Church," with its vast network of religious programming, popular television preachers, and broad-based viewer participation and support, has been welcomed by some, but feared by others, as a new religious form. Although the audience is probably less than claimed, evangelical and fundamentalist groups have used the media very successfully. Through its creative use, religious conservatism has not only spread, but has become more respectable and socially acceptable in contemporary America. Also, popular-based movements like Moral Majority and Religious Roundtable have thrust the religious Right into the public arena. On a wide range of issues—most notably, the Equal Rights Amendment, abortion, gay rights, pornography, and school prayer—the conservative voice is heard loud and clear. With the politicization of these issues, religious conservatism has taken on a greater presence in American public life.

Yet its presence is not simply a creation of the media or the outgrowth of political activists. The rising tide of religious conservatism has deep religious roots, best demonstrated by recent church membership trends. The churches that grew in membership in the late sixties and seventies were virtually all conservative—namely, Protestant evangelical and fundamentalist—with growth rates often exceeding the rate of population growth for the nation. Among these were Seventh-Day Adventists, the Church of the Nazarene, Jehovah's Witnesses, the Salvation Army, the Christian Reformed Church, the Pentecostal Holiness Church, the Assemblies of God, and Mormons.[9] Two of these, Mormons and Jehovah's Witnesses, actually increased at a rate of 5 percent a year, an astounding rate of growth, as church membership trends go. Southern Baptists and Missouri-Synod Lutherans also gained, though at a somewhat lesser rate. Although most of the rapidly growing Protestant bodies have small memberships, the major exception to this is the Southern Baptist Church, which in 1967 emerged as the largest Protestant denomination, and since then has continued to grow. The rate of growth has slowed down somewhat in recent years, but it is still the largest Protestant body in the United States.

As for American Judaism, there are no trend data available for the several branches, and thus growth patterns here cannot be documented as easily. There have, however, been various indications of a growing interest in Orthodox Judaism throughout the seventies. These include gains in membership, greater attendance at worship services, increased financial contributions, institutional proliferation, and expanding seminary enrollments.[10] This resurgence is all the more striking, considering that the Conservative and Reform branches have not experienced similar trends.

Despite obvious differences between the growing faiths, there are important similarities in religious and cultural motifs. Generally, they all share what Dean M. Kelley describes as "traits of strictness"—demanding and absolutist beliefs, social and moral conformity, and enthusiasm and missionary spirit[11]—that arise out of intense religious meanings and inspire rigid psychic boundaries and strong group loyalties. Unlike "private" religion, conservative religious energies are channeled in the direction of recovery of faith *within* the religious tradition, and of reaffirmation of religious and life-style boundaries within the dominant culture. Boundaries are drawn by means of belief and practice, and are embodied in group identity and loyalty. Participation within the institution and a sense of belonging are essential, providing as they do a matrix of shared experience in which religious meanings take on personal and social significance. Growing churches and synagogues are usually exclusive in character, capable of drawing both social and religious boundaries.

LIBERAL DECLINE

A third major trend is the decline of liberal mainline religious institutions. Though less visible a trend than conservative growth, religious decline has nonetheless been very much a part of the American religious scene of the past two decades. During the seventies, many churches suffered from a widespread malaise brought on by a loss of institutional vitality and direction. As institutions, they were somewhat unprepared for the spiritual and ideological climate emerging at the time. Trends toward more experiential religion and absolutist belief left many liberal churches with shrinking appeal and support. As a consequence, a number of large, well-established Protestant denominations not only failed to grow, but actually reported significant membership losses in this period. Protestant traditions with long-standing records of sustained membership growth and prosperity, some dating back to Colonial times, experienced their first major downturn in membership. For still other Protestant groups, the rate of membership growth slowed considerably. To a

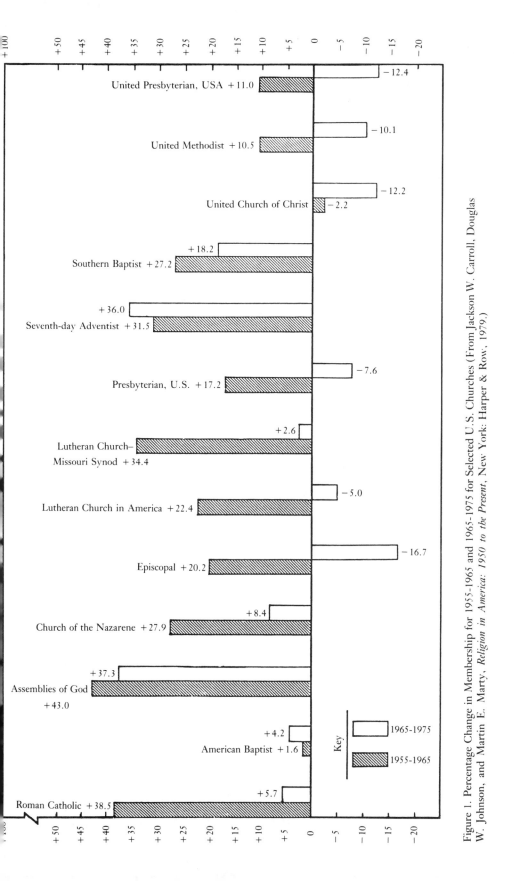

Figure 1. Percentage Change in Membership for 1955-1965 and 1965-1975 for Selected U.S. Churches (From Jackson W. Carroll, Douglas W. Johnson, and Martin E. Marty, *Religion in America: 1950 to the Present*, New York: Harper & Row, 1979.)

lesser extent, Catholic and Jewish faiths have also experienced disruptions. Although their memberships losses are not as apparent, the patterns of religious change and the ideological shifts within these religious communities are much the same as for Protestantism. The established faiths have undergone an undeniable major transition in their relation to the culture during this period. Out of the turmoil and upheaval of these years has come a fundamental reordering of religious and cultural values, manifested most directly in a retrenching liberal mainline.

For liberal Protestants, the turnaround came in the mid-sixties. Beginning about 1966, most of the large moderate-to-liberal Protestant denominations stopped growing and began to lose members.[12] The losses were sizable and steady, continuing year after year throughout the sixties and much of the seventies. It became increasingly apparent that the downturns were pointing not to a brief dip in the trendline, but to a major break with the earlier growth era. Figure 1 shows net percentage gains and losses in membership for selected denominations for two ten-year intervals during this period, for twelve Protestant denominations, liberal as well as conservative, and for comparative purposes, for Roman Catholics.

In the earlier growth era, all but one of these denominations enjoyed membership gains. The exception was the United Church of Christ, which was formed out of merger during this period; that some congregations refused to join the merger contributed to an overall membership loss. Liberal growth in these years, although less than that for the conservative, was still substantial. The Episcopal Church, for example, grew by 20.2 percent. The rate of growth for most liberal churches, however, began slowing down in the early sixties, and by the latter half of the decade, many were beginning to show membership declines. In the second period, the net losses stood out in stark contrast to the gains of the previous decade. Some of the nation's most established Protestant bodies—Episcopalians, Presbyterians, United Methodists, and United Church of Christ—reported losses of 10 percent or more.

There were similar trends in religious participation. Attendance at worship services declined steadily throughout the sixties and well into the seventies, after a period in the fifties when institutional participation was quite high.[13] Declines in attendance have been greatest for the moderate-to-liberal Protestant denominations, and even higher for Catholics. The over 75 percent attending mass in 1957 dropped to 54 percent by 1975[14]—a spectacular shift in a religious tradition undergoing enormous change and adaptation in the modern era. Converging trends in attendance across religious traditions suggest the place that Catholicism now holds in the American religious mainline and the manner in which patterns of institutional participation are responsive generally to societal conditions.

Several features of the decline point to a widespread cultural shift for the established faiths. One has to do with the simple matter of timing. The drop in membership and participation rates occurred at about the same time for all the affected churches, the mid-sixties. This implies that the sources for the decline originated primarily outside any single denomination or faith, and cut across all the major liberal traditions. Second, the declines were a result mainly of decreasing numbers of new members rather than an increase in "dropouts."

Proportionately fewer were joining these churches and synagogues in the sixties and seventies, and among those joining, fewer were becoming active participants and faithful supporters. This was true especially among the young. Fewer youth and young adults under thirty-five were recruited into membership—too few to keep the membership rolls constant, much less to grow—and participation among this age group was less than in the past. "Believers" perhaps, but "belongers," not.

Collapse of the Middle

America's religious establishments are flourishing on the fringes but languishing in the mainline. Growth and prosperity are occurring among two kinds of religious expressions. On the one hand, conservative religious belief and ideology flourish, advocating traditional morality and life-styles; evangelical and fundamentalist faiths are the most rapidly growing religious expressions in America. On the other hand, growth is also evident in the various nontraditional, often non-Christian religious movements and in related quasi-religious movements concerned with spiritual therapies. These movements are largely outside of the churches and synagogues, although they include participants from the established institutions. While conservative and nontraditional religious forms prosper, the institutions in the middle—the more liberal mainline Protestant, Catholic, and Jewish bodies—are losing appeal and support.

In a religious context such as this, liberal mainline institutions are likely to become quite vulnerable. Caught in the middle, they can easily suffer collapse on both sides, losing adherents both to religious conservatism and to the nontraditional, more secular modes of commitment. Indeed, there is a good deal of evidence pointing to defections of both kinds during the sixties and seventies.[15] Many persons brought up in the mainline faiths either switched to more conservative affiliations or opted for no institutional affiliation at all. Liberal Protestants suffered more than any other from such moves, a far cry from the fifties, when liberal denominations were the major beneficiaries of religious switching. Traditionally religious and highly committed members often chose to transfer to more conservative churches; and a considerable number of the less traditional and less committed abandoned institutional affiliation altogether. Increases in both types of switching among Protestants were substantial, and particularly so for the latter. Striking gains among the "nones"—those rejecting institutional affiliation—were made in this period, especially at the expense of the liberal Protestant establishment. Evidence points to a somewhat similar realignment occurring within American Judaism. The Conservative branch, the religious majority representing a peculiarly American religious and cultural synthesis, appears to be losing members at present, with the larger, less traditional component moving to the Reform or ceasing to affiliate denominationally, and the smaller, more traditional component moving into the Orthodox.

Not surprisingly, much concern has been expressed about the mainline religious future. The term "mainline" came into use as a means of distinguishing the well-established institutions from the esoteric cults that drew so much attention in the early years of the decade, and from the rapidly growing evangelical and fundamentalist faiths.[16] Theologically, these institutions, despite differences of doctrine and of polity, have generally stressed nurturing more than conversion, and have sought to incorporate in their outlook a vision of public order alongside that of personal belief and commitment. In actual practice, they have served as "bridging institutions," by mediating religious meanings and values broadly in the culture, and by expressing concern for society as well as the cure of souls. In some historical periods, such as the 1950s, this bridge was strong and nurturing, and provided a synthesis of religious and cultural meanings widely shared throughout the society. The mainline faiths flourished during this time, providing as they did a meaningful, transcendent vision embracing personal as well as social existence. But by the 1970s this synthesis of the religious and the cultural had lost much of its plausibility. The bridge was no longer as meaningful and sustaining, no longer as widely shared in the society. Lacking a sense of a strong and integrated whole, the mainline faiths seemed to languish in a world that was vastly different and vastly more indifferent.

The seventies were characterized not by unity, but by growing cultural polarization. Conservative ideologies of the religious right clashed increasingly with secular humanism, and out of this confrontation came a greater awareness of fundamental differences in values and outlook in contemporary America. In a most basic sense, the culture is grounded in two major foci of meaning: the traditional Judeo-Christian and the secular humanistic. The first is institutionally supported in traditional churches and synagogues; the second is based primarily in the scientific, communications, and educational establishments. Although secular humanistic values were originally derived largely from the religious, the two meaning systems coexist today in some degree of tension. Over the decades, the secular humanistic culture has become increasingly dominant. Values originally rooted in Judeo-Christian tradition such as individualism, tolerance, and rationalism are now regarded as part of secular humanism without any reference necessarily to their religious underpinnings. The prevailing ethos is, in Robert Bellah's terms, "utilitarian individualism,"[17] a complex of secular values based essentially on individual self-interest, and upon which rest the modern structures of science, technology, and capitalism.

As scientific understanding and outlook permeated the modern world, secular humanism, with its recognized achievements in the scientific and technological realms, became more influential. At the same time, conservative evangelical faiths enjoyed great appeal by their virtual monopoly of a strict supernatural religious perspective; by offering a highly personal meaning system, definite expectations about moral standards, and a supernatural frame of reference, the "right-wing" faiths have prospered as a religious alternative. This clear-cut, absolutist religious challenge generated for both a vitality and identity they otherwise might not have had, and as they flourished, the gap between them widened.

For the liberal religious traditions, however, this polarization has wrought theological and ideological disarray. As the gap widens between religious and secular world views, it becomes more difficult for the liberal faiths to bridge the two by means of creative synthesis. The result, the "collapse of the middle,"[18] involves a loss of credibility and persuasiveness within the larger context of religious and ideological alternatives. Lacking a unified transcendent vision of personal and social existence, the culture-affirming faiths suffer an identity diffusion and loss of appeal.

Sources of Religious Change

Why has the middle collapsed? Why are the liberal, mainline churches declining while others are prospering? If there is any consensus in the various interpretations of the contemporary American religious scene, it is that institutional trends are complex and far-reaching, and cannot be accounted for by any single cause or circumstance. As tempting as it is to try to identify a major explanatory principle—for example, secularization of Western culture and its accompanying religious reactions—to do so vastly oversimplifies the situation and fails to offer much in the way of specific insight. The religious changes can be traced to numerous sources, partly from within the institutions themselves, partly from the broader societal and cultural context of modern America. At least four major factors, or set of factors, help in explaining the trends: demographic change, value change, institutional policies and activities, and religious styles and identity.[19]

DEMOGRAPHIC CHANGE

In a most basic sense, religious involvement is affected by the age structure of the population. If there are large increases in the school-age population, there will likely be increases in religious membership and participation; if the school-age population declines, so will institutional religious activity. The reason for this is quite simple: religious involvement is related to the family life cycle, with a peak in institutional activity occurring during the parenting phase when children are in the home. In the years of late adolescence and early adulthood, young Americans are usually less involved religiously; but as they form families of their own and become parents, they tend to become more involved. Most want their children to have religious instruction, and they are apt to affiliate, or reaffiliate as is often the case, with a church or synagogue out of a feeling of responsibility to participate in the institution to which they send their children. The presence of young children old enough to attend Sunday School or instructional classes thus often results in the parents' decision to join the religious institution. Since parental involvement generally tends to be closely associated with the religious socialization functions of the young, the parents' continued participation depends to some extent on how satisfied they are with the activities available for children and youth. Hence a shift in the size of the school-age population is a good indicator of institutional patterns to follow.

The period since 1950 offers a good example of how demography has been destiny for the churches. Throughout the fifties, the "baby boom" after World War II swelled the size of the school-age population. There was a massive expansion of schools and churches, especially in the suburbs, where many middle-class Americans moved during the postwar years. The age groups from whom church members are drawn—children and their parents—grew considerably; those age groups least likely to join or attend—older youth and young adults without school-age children—grew less. In effect, numbers were on the side of the established religious institutions. Church and synagogue attendance in the late fifties reached an all-time high, and church extension, or organizing new congregations, became a major priority for virtually all the mainline Protestant, Catholic, and Jewish faiths. Religious membership rolls expanded to accommodate an expanding religiously active population.

But in 1958 the birth rate peaked, and began a downward trend that would last for some years to come. The under-twenty age group continued to grow during the sixties, but by less than a third of its fifties rate, and by the first half of the seventies, it was declining in absolute numbers. Furthermore, by the seventies the "baby boom" children were reaching the age levels at which active religious participation is least likely. They constituted the largest number of youth ever in the history of the American population, a cohort impressive in its sheer size but foreboding in its implications for the American religious establishment.

Both churches and synagogues were affected by the drop in the number of children and the large sector of youth and young adults not inclined to religious participation. The demographic shifts were felt particularly in the traditional suburban strongholds of liberal Protestantism. Birth rates dropped more rapidly for the white upper-middle-class constituencies of these denominations. Since most of their new members are the children of present members, to a great extent their future rests on those born within the fold. Thus, especially among white upper-middle-class Protestants, where pressures seem to be greater for affiliating on behalf of their children's religious upbringing, the consequences of declining numbers become all the more significant. Conservative evangelical churches were less affected, because they gain converts more through proselytizing and rely less on additions from their own communities.

VALUE COMMITMENTS

Of great significance too were the changing values and attitudes in this period. As always, cultural change reflects the impact of historical circumstance and events, which for many young Americans of the sixties and seventies were momentous and, at times, traumatic. Broad changes in values and orientations, along with distinctive cohort experiences, coalesced to create a climate among the young more supportive of spiritual experimentation and introspection than that of the established religious faiths. The new religious and quasi-religious movements flourished largely among middle-class youth, as they turned to religious alternatives to find an ultimate grounding for their lives that was meaningful and purposeful—which says something about the peculiar mode of estrangement that many felt. Although affluent and socially privileged, they yet found themselves spiritually unnourished by the dominant belief system.

The major religions of course reflect the cultural ethos of a given time and the extent to which alienation and conflict are experienced. In times of broad value consensus, the established faiths enjoy great appeal; in troubling times, these institutions bear the brunt of dissatisfaction and disillusionment. This is well illustrated by contrasting the value climate of the fifties with that of the late sixties and early seventies. Such comparison helps in understanding how the cultural context of American religion has changed, and how culture and religion interact to create meaningful—or not so meaningful—modes of believing and belonging.

Many commentators have pointed to the fifties as a time when American religious and cultural values were highly integrated. The postwar economic boom, an upwardly mobile population, life in the suburbs, and above all, the cold war ideology, all served to create a setting in which affirmations of solidarity and value consensus were important. Along with an emphasis on religious belief, many value commitments and attitudes were widely shared: conformity to social norms and other-direction, fear of subversion and communism, commitment to traditional family life, acceptance of military duty and war, and a favorable view toward patriotism. In such a climate, churchgoing was an expression of belongingness and civic loyalty. As Will Herberg described so well at the time, to identify oneself as Protestant, Catholic, or Jew was to identify as an American and to celebrate a way of life.[20] Public piety offered a means of affirming core American values.

A quite different cultural milieu obtained in the sixties and seventies. Among young Americans there was little fear of communism or subversion, but instead considerable expression of concern about the evils of the capitalist system; little emphasis on social conformity and far greater emphasis on personal freedom; less commitment to traditional family life and much more willingness to experiment with new sexual styles and family forms; more refusal of military duty and opposition to an unpopular war; and widespread criticism of major institutions of the society. It was not a value climate in which mainline religious-belonging flourished. Churches and synagogues were viewed by many as part of the problem, not the solution. Closely identified with the establishment, these institutions were often blamed for the ills besetting the larger society.

Alienation was, of course, a major motif of the so-called youth counterculture, and helps to explain why many youth of the period turned away from the churches. Wuthnow's research convincingly demonstrates that there was a "generational unit" countercultural impact felt by these institutions.[21] Probably more important than cultural alienation, and certainly more widespread, was the growing indifference toward institutional religious authority. The broad shifts in value orientations underway—stress on personal freedom and choice, individual autonomy and self-fulfillment, and tolerance of diversity—tended to erode loyalty to the religious establishment. Underlying these was a more basic shift in the locus of moral authority, away from traditional sources to more personal, relativistic considerations. Not only were religious values affected, but views on many aspects of life, including notions about sex and marriage, war and patriotism, and the inherent good or evil in the democratic capitalist state, as well. Changing religious views were part of a much larger cultural change that involved differing ideas about authority and decision-making in personal and social life.

The era of countercultural protest and institutional alienation has passed, yet the themes of personal freedom and individual fulfillment are very much alive. These values are not only part of contemporary youth culture, but more important, are becoming highly diffused in American life. Among the majority of college-educated adults under thirty-five, according to pollster Daniel Yankelovich, the pursuit of personal fulfillment and the right life-style for expressing psychological potential are now major goals.[22] Likewise, the so-called "new morality" values have spread into sectors far beyond the student populations where they originated. As such values have become more common, the effect has been to undermine institutional religious loyalty. The result is a more privatized mode of religiosity, more and more focused around individual needs and preferences, and less and less anchored in a congregational setting. Believing without belonging is an increasingly popular form of religious expression.

INSTITUTIONAL POLICIES AND ACTIVITIES

In addition to demographic and cultural change, both of which are external to the churches, there are internal factors to consider in interpreting religious trends. These have to do primarily with policies and activities within church bureaucracies, and unlike external considerations, are matters over which the institutions have some control. Three important institutional themes during this period were social activism, liturgical reforms, and the prohibition against birth control.

During the mid-sixties, many churches became engaged in civil rights and antipoverty activities, with attention shifting later in the decade to the war in Vietnam. Throughout the period, many clergy and concerned laity participated in social action programs—the civil rights march on Selma, the Delta Ministry, the Angela Davis Legal Defense Fund, and antiwar marches on Washington—that were highly visible and controversial. Attention was centered particularly around the various activities undertaken by the National Council of Churches, an ecumenical agency of liberal mainline Protestants. Among other things, the NCC recruited and trained volunteers for voter registration, lobbied for civil rights legislation, spearheaded efforts at economic and social development among rural sharecroppers, assisted draft-evaders, and channeled church funds into various grass-roots organizations within minority communities and among the poor. In addition, the major denominations all had bureaucracies of their own for dealing with programs, of one sort or another, concerned with racial justice, assisting the poor, and in opposing the war in Vietnam.

The impact on the churches was widespread and at times divisive. Within denominational constituencies there was a good deal of negative reaction, particularly to programs that were highly visible and widely publicized. Reactions ranged from letters of protest to attempted withdrawals of entire congregations from parent religious bodies. Intense feelings were aroused in the South more than elsewhere, but were by no means limited to that region. Perhaps the most common reaction was the withholding of funds to denominational and ecumenical agencies. Despite such withholdings and much negative sentiment, membership and attendance declines were probably not great. Some membership loss occurred in instances of congregational schism, but this seems not to have amounted to very much. The mainline Protestant declines were fairly constant over the years after 1965, in times that were relatively calm as well as in times of stormy protest. Furthermore, the declines for some denominations had set in before social involvement became highly controversial in many parishes and congregations.

Another theme for some of the faiths in the period were the liturgical reforms. The Second Vatican Council initiated vast reforms within Catholicism in the early sixties, the most encompassing and controversial being the translation of liturgy from Latin to the vernacular, an institutional transition of enormous significance. For many faithful members, the liturgical changes were regarded as a serious break with the past, and as potentially undermining the whole structure of traditional Catholic religious practices. Among Protestants, there is nothing quite like this, although the prayer book revision for Episcopalians is similar in some respects. In 1976 the General Convention of the Episcopal Church authorized the revision of the Book of Common Prayer, prompting much internal dissension among both clergy and laity. Lines between revisionists and traditionalists were sharply drawn, and forces mobilized within the church on both sides. Conflict was intensified by the decision at the same time to ordain women priests, a decision that represented still another radical break with tradition to many.

It is difficult to assess the consequences of these reforms, since so many institutional changes were bound up together and cannot be easily sorted out. In a major attempt at unraveling the various sources of contemporary Catholic change, Andrew Greeley found little evidence that declines in attendance at mass were related to reactions to the Second Vatican Council and to the liturgical reforms it brought about.[23] Contrary to what many feared, Greeley's findings suggest that the liturgical changes have had little negative effect. Episcopalians in dissent because of the prayer book revision and ordination of women priests did break away to form the Anglican Church of North America. About a dozen parishes and perhaps as many as fifty priests left in the aftermath of the 1976 General Convention. Again, although some members chose to leave or to become inactive, the overall effect of these reforms appears not to have been very substantial. At best, these reforms are but supplementary factors insofar as mainline Protestant and Catholic declines are concerned.

Finally, there is the issue of birth control that has figured so prominently within Catholicism. Of all the issues that have provoked reaction in the modern era, none has triggered more within the Catholic faith than the 1968 papal encyclical of Paul VI, *Humanae Vitae*, which reaffirmed traditional proscriptions against birth control. Among young Catholics, the encyclical was met with much dismay and disfavor, and on the part of many, avowed rejection. In subsequent years, the number of Catholics rejecting, or simply ignoring, the teaching has risen considerably in the United States. In keeping with the trend toward greater privatization of belief and personal morality, more and more Catholics regard the issue as beyond the boundaries of the church's authority or as irrelevant to their own personal religious faith and practice.

In this instance, it is quite evident that church policy has resulted in a turning away from institutional belonging and loyalty. Greeley's research shows that the sharp declines in attendance at mass among the young were very much related to rejection of the church's teachings on sex. Disagreement with the church's stand on this issue appear, in fact, to have undermined papal authority more generally and to have precipitated questioning of other aspects of the church's teaching and practice. As Greeley and his colleagues put it, "The decline in Catholic religiousness . . . is in part the result of a joint decline in the acceptance of the pope as a leader in the church and acceptance of the church's sexual ethic."[24] If this is indeed the case, the church's position on this particular matter may in the long run have significant implications for the future shape of Catholicism in this country.

RELIGIOUS STYLE AND IDENTITY

A final consideration is that of religious style and identity. The growing faiths are those that convey a distinct religious and cultural style; those declining generally lack such identity. Whereas the former appear to "stand" for something clear and positive, the latter are more diffuse in what they represent. Reasons for this are varied and diverse, partly due to differences in theological heritage and polity, partly a result of the vast changes in American community life of recent times. Both types of factors—institutional and contextual—combine to generate quite contrasting congregational styles, some seemingly more attractive than others in the contemporary religious milieu.

Transformations in community life have played a great part in creating a context for religious change. Churches and synagogues usually are community-based institutions that draw their members from the immediate area in which they are located. This means that as communities change, so do congregations. Enormous changes have occurred over the past several decades in how Americans experience local community life, brought on by high rates of geographic mobility, greater diversity of life experiences, and mass cultural trends. The result of weakened local social ties and heterogeneous cultural styles is a community life that has lost much of its traditional stability. The effects of such changes on religious institutions are numerous and complex, but the most far-reaching has perhaps been the pluralization of life worlds. With this has come a diminished shared social world and a diminished sense of belonging and community solidarity. Even the choice of becoming involved—or not—in local community institutions is afforded so many in a large-scale society, that any possibility of a shared community-wide religious affirmation is thereby undermined. For those faiths concerned with integrating the private and public aspects of life, it has become more difficult to fashion a set of religious meanings that are plausible across a wide spectrum of life experiences.

Socially and economically, congregations—like communities—are fairly homogeneous. Religious institutions tend to mirror the status distinctions of the social order and to develop a style or ethos that reflects somewhat the particular characteristics of the dominant membership. While recognizing this to be a social reality in a pluralistic denominational society, some faiths are more concerned than others about the exclusiveness and separation that result. The liberal mainline institutions have been forthright in calling for boundaries of faith that transcend racial, economic, and social lines. In preaching, if not always in practice, they have sought to bear witness to the ideals of equality and inclusiveness. Conservative churches, in contrast, tend not to be as openly concerned theologically, and are more inclined to accept the social and cultural styles of their congregants. Rather than being in tension with the local culture, these churches tend to adapt to the realities of the social situation.

Mainline congregations are thus somewhat more diverse internally than conservative ones. This diversity is most evident in more pluralistic religious styles. Members within a congregation often have quite different expectations of a church or synagogue, and vary considerably in how they choose to express religious commitment. Distinct religious "audiences" can be identified in most mainline congregations, such as a group that gives top priority to fellowship needs; another, to evangelistic concerns; and still another that emphasizes social ministry, and so forth. These congregations often deliberately offer alternative programs and activities, in an attempt to provide a religious mode for everyone. Such diversity would seemingly facilitate religious adaptability and growth, but this appears not to have happened. Too much pluralism erodes institutional boundaries and creates a void. In trying to provide something for everyone, many mainline congregations seem to have lost the central focus of meaning or a distinctive religious style with which to identify.

Conservative churches have been more successful in developing a single focus, or a "one-audience" congregation. In religious emphasis and belonging, conservative congregations often express the sentiments of a single constituency, especially when the basis of solidarity is that of similar life-styles, common perceptions of the world, or strong feelings and experiential needs. Usually this results from the happenstance of group formation, but sometimes it comes about by means of deliberate planning. For example, the Institute for Church Growth, a conservative agency that assists local congregations, emphasizes the "homogeneous unit principle" as a major axiom of church growth.[25] According to this principle, a church maximizes its growth potential by reflecting as nearly as possible in its composition the social patterns and life-styles of the community it serves. Growing churches are likely to be those that embody natural communities, wherein social and religious bondings, by reinforcing each other, create a strong sense of identity.

Contemporary conservatism is diverse, so much so that it almost defies generalization. Yet evangelical and fundamentalist faiths give wide expression to the sentiments of the upwardly mobile lower middle class. In outlook and values, this class, with its strong affirmation of traditional life-styles, celebration of the American way of life, and commitment to the entrepreneurial, capitalist spirit, is the embodiment of "Middle America." Mobilization of this sector represents a reactionary, traditionalist movement within the larger culture on the part of those who have much at stake in preserving the old order. Ideologically, the class finds itself at great odds with the more liberal, secular "knowledge" classes, locked into a struggle over power and influence in the public realm.[26] Appeal to the "old-time religion" gives legitimacy to a way of life, and serves to integrate the religious and cultural identity so important to a large number of Americans today.

Recovery of the Transforming Middle?

Whatever the reasons for the hard times that have befallen the religious establishment, the important questions are: Is recovery of the transforming middle possible? Can we expect the mainline religious institutions to engage the culture creatively in the eighties? Given the complexities of the situation, there are no easy answers to these questions. Yet, if the notion of a "voluntary establishment" for religion means anything, it is that the religious impulses of Americans are highly adaptable and resilient. American religion is capable of taking on new institutional form as times and conditions change, even those that on occasion come quickly and decisively. Sensitive always to shifting values and sentiments, the mainline faiths are responsive institutions in every age, and hence we should not prejudge their potentialities for the decade ahead.

The period of widespread religious upheaval and change seems to have passed, giving way to greater institutional stability in the present. Recent evidence indicates that the rate of expansion of the rapidly growing conservative faiths is slowing, and that the declines for liberal Protestant denominations may be bottoming out.[27] In many respects, emerging signs are pointing toward a new religious equilibrium of sorts. Indeed, developments of the past couple of decades underscore the ebb-and-flow character of American religion. In times when the culture is secure and expansive, the mainline churches flourish; in times of cultural turmoil and strain, they suffer, and often fringe religious phenomena thrive in their stead. The sixties and seventies will probably be remembered somewhat like the "religious depression" of the twenties, when many major Protestant churches experienced a loss of morale and mission, but sectarianism enjoyed remarkable vitality and growth. Both periods will stand out in sharp contrast to the fifties, a time when the established religious institutions generally reached a peak of prosperity. Viewed in this historical perspective, American religion's "voluntary establishment" may be seen as changing over time, in keeping with its highly secular and populist character.

In every major transition period, the complexion of the mainline religious institutions undergoes something of an alteration toward a more prophetic public, or a more accommodating private, stance. The alteration comes as a result of the changing moods and dispositions of the American people. Within all the major religious bodies there are conservative evangelical fundamentalist constituencies, as well as those that are more moderate-to-liberal, one or the other predominating at any given time. A "two-party" system has prevailed in liberal Protestantism since the early days of the modernist-fundamentalist controversies at the turn of the century to the present.[28] Throughout this century the churches have been riddled with internal conflict and have lacked consensus over doctrinal and social ethical issues. At present there are a lingering sense of unease and a lack of resolve about biblical literalism, the "born-again" phenomenon, and charismatic outbreaks, even in the most liberal Protestant denominations. In addition, there are the pressing issues of abortion, homosexuality, and women's ordination, over which much spiritual blood has been shed of late. Particularly on matters of personal ethics and life-styles, the institutions are currently groping for direction and vision, as they attempt to relate to the modern world.

The dilemma the churches face is that of trying to be true to their heritage as "bridging institutions" in the culture in a time when religious energies have turned inward. They are being pressured to abandon a public posture and to retreat into more privatistic religious concerns. There is the temptation to accept the complete individualism of religious choice and practice that modernity urges, and to adopt a theology of personal and self-fulfillment tailored to private religious tastes. Liberal Protestantism especially is vulnerable to privatism, because it allows for greater freedom of choice than do the more conservative faiths. To give in to privatism in its fullest sense, however, is to lose sight of the communal character of faith and the strength, which comes from a shared religious and moral commitment, that these churches have traditionally known. Temptations are also strong to turn toward evangelical, fundamentalist religious styles in search of more absolutist claims. Impressed by the appeal of the conservatives, mainline churches are easily led into believing they should mimic their strategies for growth and influence. Yet to do so is to embrace a form of religious and cultural traditionalism offering little inspiration for creative confrontation with modernity. As Marty observes, the crucial need in this time is for a "public church," one that will engage the culture, transcend rigid, exclusivist boundaries, and give witness to the social dimensions of the religious presence.[29]

Quite clearly, even if the churches hold onto a public mediating posture, they will emerge in the eighties as quite different institutions. The complexion of the mainline churches is undergoing change, and will most assuredly reflect a more conservative mood and outlook. Theologically and socially conservative constituencies within the religious traditions are mobilized, and they are exerting a great deal of influence over public as well as personal religious styles. Yet, as Richard Quebedeaux points out, the evangelicals now becoming a part of the mainline represent something of a new breed.[30] Many evangelicals today are committed to a social gospel of sorts, are open to theological dialogue, and perhaps most significant of all, are closely wedded to such dominant cultural values as worldly success, middle-class respectability, and economic and political laissez-faire ideology. The affinities of the new evangelicals with the establishment are so striking, that Quebedeaux is led to question: "Are today's evangelicals tomorrow's liberals?" Certainly, it is the case, historically, that centripetal forces in American religion run deep—that is, the tendency for sectarians over time is to become more churchlike in style and ideology. Peripheral religious groups seem to be propelled toward the middle, toward core values of the culture, particularly those groups advancing evangelical, conversionist beliefs. Today's evangelicals are well into this developmental process, and it is still too soon to know what the institutional implications will be.

Several aspects of mainline religious life in America may find renewed vigor in the years ahead. One is the recovery of the experiential dimension of religious life. In many liberal churches, the cure of souls is almost a lost art, but it may well be that the widespread concern with personal and spiritual fulfillment will offer new opportunities to address the psychological needs of individuals. Greater attention to people's concerns for themselves may help bring about a new synthesis of personal and social identity, of private and public faith. Another possibility for renewal lies in the creative potential of liberal theology. Stress upon experience is a key feature of liberal theology, which gives the tradition an affinity with current concerns of experiential faith. Explorations into experience are reaching farther outward and inward in human life than ever before, including cross-cultural as well as Western modes of expression; in the future, experience, rather than doctrine or ecclesiology, is likely to set the agenda for theological reflection. Peter Berger's call for an "inductive" mode of reflection rooted in human experience represents a major effort at redirecting theology along this line.[31] Finally, the religious situation at present may well give rebirth to the ecumenical spirit. Awareness of a common plight among many major religious bodies, plus a growing sense of the need for broader spiritual unity, may facilitate a new vision of a concerted religious presence in a divided world. If the public church Marty envisions emerges in the eighties, it will be ecumenical, deeply concerned with the bonds of theology and tradition, yet open to alliances across lines of ideology and heritage.[32]

By virtue of their heritage, mainline faiths are uniquely equipped to reach out to other traditions and simultaneously to explore the depths of their own faith affirmations. Among those who respect universal human religious quests and feel responsible for both the care of souls and for the welfare of society, to engage in one need not threaten the other. In a time when so many boundaries are drawn and so many particularistic claims are heard, the need is greater than ever for the recovery of religion's transforming middle. It will not come by mimicking the styles of others nor by adopting a sectarian Christ-against-culture stance; rather, it will come out of honest and constructive confrontation with the culture, by means of wrestling with the enduring human quests for meaning and belonging in this particular time and place. Therein lies the challenge, and maybe even the continued survival, of a culture-transforming religious presence in the American future.

REFERENCES
    [1]Alexis de Tocqueville, *Democracy in America*, J. P. Mayer and Max Lerner (eds.) (New York: Harper & Row, 1966).
    [2]Robert Wuthnow, *The Consciousness Reformation* (Berkeley: University of California Press, 1976).
    [3]See his foreword to *Understanding Church Growth and Decline: 1950-1978*, Dean R. Hoge and David A. Roozen (eds.) (New York: Pilgrim Press, 1979).
    [4]*A Religious History of the American People* (New Haven: Yale University Press, 1972), p. 1079.
    [5]The phrase is suggested by Elwyn A. Smith. See his "Voluntary Establishment of Religion" in *The Religion of the Republic*, Elwyn A. Smith (ed.) (Philadelphia: Fortress Press, 1971), pp. 154-82.
    [6]The thesis is set forth in *The Invisible Religion* (London: Macmillan, 1967).
    [7]Reported in Jackson W. Carroll, Douglas W. Johnson, and Martin E. Marty, *Religion in America: 1950 to the Present* (New York: Harper & Row, 1979), p. 25.
    [8]See Robert Wuthnow, "The New Religions in Social Context," in *The New Religious Consciousness*, Charles Y. Glock and Robert N. Bellah (eds.) (Berkeley: University of California Press, 1976), pp. 276-93.
    [9]These trends are summarized in *Understanding Church Growth and Decline*, pp. 21-38.
    [10]Reported in *The New York Times*, July 6, 1980.
    [11]See Kelley's *Why Conservative Churches are Growing* (New York: Harper & Row, 1972).
    [12]See *Understanding Church Growth and Decline*.
    [13]Gallup Opinion Index, *Religion in America, 1977*, Report No. 145, 1977, p. 32.
    [14]Andrew W. Greeley, William C. McCready, and Kathleen McCourt, *Catholic Schools in a Declining Church* (Kansas City: Sheed and Ward, 1976), pp. 29-30.
    [15]For evidence on religious switching, see Wade Clark Roof and Kirk Hadaway, "Denominational Switching in the Seventies: Going beyond Stark and Glock," *Journal for the Scientific Study of Religion* 18 (December, 1979): 363-77.
    [16]Usage of the term is described in Martin E. Marty, *A Nation of Behavers* (Chicago: University of Chicago Press, 1976), chapter 3.
    [17]See Robert N. Bellah, "New Religious Consciousness and the Crisis in Modernity," in *The New Religious Consciousness*, pp. 333-52.

[18]The phrase is attributed to James I. McCord of Princeton Theological Seminary, and has been used by Hoge and others quite extensively. See Dean R. Hoge, *Division in the Protestant House* (Philadelphia: Westminster Press, 1976), p. 120.

[19]The discussion of factors underlying the religious change draws heavily from Carroll et al., *Religion in America*, chapter 5, and *Understanding Church Growth and Decline*.

[20]*Protestant-Catholic-Jew* (Garden City, N.Y.: Doubleday, 1955).

[21]Robert Wuthnow, *Experimentation in American Religion* (Berkeley: University of California Press, 1978), chapter 6.

[22]See *New Rules: Searching for Self-Fulfillment in a World Turned Upside Down* (New York: Random House, 1981).

[23]Greeley et al., *Catholic Schools in a Declining Church*.

[24]Ibid., p. 129.

[25]See C. Peter Wagner, *Your Church Can Grow* (Glendale, California: Regal Books, 1976).

[26]Peter Berger calls attention to the ideological conflict between the old business class and the new knowledge class, the latter composed mainly of intellectuals, educators, planners, and bureaucrats. See his "Class Struggle in American Religion," *The Christian Century* 98 (6) (February 25, 1981): 194-99.

[27]See membership trends reported in *Yearbook of American and Canadian Churches 1981*, Constant H. Jacquet, Jr., (ed.) (Nashville: Abingdon, 1981).

[28]For a discussion of the "two-party" system, see Martin E. Marty, *Righteous Empire* (New York: Dial Press, 1970), pp. 178 ff.

[29]For the latest of Marty's statements, see *The Public Church* (New York: Crossroad Publishing Company, 1981).

[30]*The Worldly Evangelicals* (San Francisco: Harper & Row, 1978).

[31]*The Heretical Imperative* (New York: Doubleday, 1980).

[32]See *The New York Times*, November 8, 1981, for coverage of the recent National Council of Churches convocation in Cleveland. Described as an "Ecumenical Event," the meeting urged liberal Protestants to seek stronger theological and activist alliances with Roman Catholics and evangelicals.

GEORGE M. MARSDEN

Preachers of Paradox: The Religious New Right in Historical Perspective

IF HISTORY HAS LAWS, the first is that it is usually unpredictable. Who in the 1950s anticipated the upheavals of the 1960s? Or who in 1970 clearly projected the conservative religious resurgences of the next decade? So when we look at the religious New Right in America today we cannot say whether it marks the dawn of a new spiritual era, a phase in recurrent cycles of social and spiritual anxiety, or the last gasp of an old order. All we can agree on, perhaps, is that theories of secularization that predicted correlations of scientific-technological advance and spiritual decline are in deep trouble.

Such theories themselves combined a violation of history's first law with the biases of secularist scholars. In America such prejudice has been directed particularly against revivalist evangelicalism. During most of this century scholars had difficulty taking this tradition seriously and integrating it into their understandings of the American past. Theory and wish converged to suggest that traditionalist Protestantism would wither in the bright sun of modern culture. During the late nineteenth and early twentieth centuries, secularist intellectuals were locked in a bitter struggle to free themselves from religious control and review. Evangelicalism was the semi-official religion of the old order and had controlled much of academic life. Secularists, when freed from the repressive features of evangelical ideology and mores, completed their revolution by eradicating evangelicalism from academia and public life altogether. During the first half of the twentieth century the history of the nation was rewritten accordingly. Previously the Protestant roots of the nation had been uncritically lauded and sentimentalized; now they were presented as repressive[1] or, more often, were simply ignored. Evangelical religion was regarded as though it had been peripheral and hence all the more dispensable to American culture. To choose a relevant example, generations of American students learned of the nineteenth century with no intimation that, as Perry Miller later observed, "the dominant theme in America from 1800 to 1860 is the invincible persistence of the revival technique."[2]

The recent public appearances of a widespread "born-again" evangelicalism and then of a formidable fundamentalist political front have been puzzling to many observers partly because of this neglect of evangelical history.[3] Not only were these resurgences unanticipated, but among secularists nuanced interpretations have been rare because of lack of appreciation of the complexities of the traditions represented. During the past twenty-five years the groundwork for an improved understanding has been laid. A number of historians have redis-covered evangelicalism as a major force in the American past and have begun to view it as a complex phenomenon not to be simply condemned or championed. Such integrative scholarship, however, has not penetrated far beyond the spe-cialists. Consequently, the recent fundamentalist political activities are often viewed simplistically, sometimes as little more than sinister exploitations of the tensions of the moment.[4]

The purpose of this essay is to understand the religious New Right more clearly by looking at it from the perspective of the history of evangelicalism and fundamentalism in America. So considered, we find in current fundamentalism the amalgamation of a fascinating variety of traditions. Some are highly intellec-tualized and some highly emotional, some elitist-establishmentarian and some directed toward outsiders, some concerned with public policy and some pri-vatistic, and all are mixed with various American assumptions and folklore. During the twentieth century these were fused together, transformed, and sometimes fragmented by intense efforts simultaneously to fight American sec-ularists and to convert them. The result is a movement fraught with paradoxes that have made it sociologically mystifying. By employing a historical perspec-tive we can perhaps sort out some of those paradoxes and show how the move-ment has the potential to point in more directions than is usually perceived.

Fundamentalism and Evangelicalism in America

Protestant fundamentalism forms the core of the religious New Right. Fun-damentalists are evangelicals in the revivalist tradition who crusade militantly against certain features of modern theology and culture. Fundamentalism as an identifiable movement began to emerge in America in the late nineteenth cen-tury.[5] It appeared first in premillennial prophetic conferences that stressed the literal interpretation and complete accuracy of the Bible. It soon appeared also among traditionalist Northern Presbyterians and Northern Baptists who were alarmed at modern theological trends. Many of the adherents of the emerging movement were loosely associated with Dwight L. Moody (1837–1899). Moody himself, more interested in winning souls than in doctrinal controversy, helped establish an important structural feature of the movement. As was already true in nineteenth-century American revivalism, fundamentalism built its strongest centers on a free-enterprise principle. Effective evangelists, working indepen-dently of major denominations, built empires around evangelistic associations, Bible institutes, summer conference grounds, and affiliated ministries that could mobilize support for various causes.

Militancy against what was then called "modernism" in theology and what is now called "secular humanism" in the culture set fundamentalism apart as a movement in the early decades of the twentieth century. The growing sense of alarm concerning theological and cultural trends and the need for nationally organized holy warfare to combat these trends distinguished fundamentalism from revivalism generally, although the widespread nineteenth-century revival-ism had many similar tendencies. The revivalist tradition, however, simulta-neously pointed in a variety of directions: Three parallel movements emerged out of American revivalism in the decades spanning the turn of the century as the Protestant religious-moral consensus began to wane. First was the holiness revival in the Methodist tradition that led to the formation of a number of new holiness denominations such as the Church of God (Anderson, Indiana), the Pilgrim Holiness Church, the Nazarenes, and (from England) the Salvation Army. These met the challenges of modern living by stressing separation from the world in ethics, marked by a dramatic experience of "second blessing" and a subsequent life of perfect holiness. In the first decade of the new century another distinct movement, pentecostalism, appeared. Developing partly out of the holiness heritage, pentecostalism even more strongly emphasized super-natural experiences as marking the believer's separation from the world. Such pentecostal experience was signaled both by spiritual strength for holiness and by special spiritual powers such as speaking in tongues or healing.

Although parented by the same American revivalist movement, fundamen-talism was distinct from each of its two siblings. Sometimes the three squabbled bitterly, with fundamentalists opposing both perfectionist holiness and speak-ing in tongues. Their common revivalist parentage, however, gave them many similar traits. All emphasized the central evangelical doctrines of the complete authority of the Bible, the necessity of a conversion experience, and the impor-tance of a holy life, freed particularly from barroom vices such as drinking, dancing, cardplaying, and lasciviousness. They preached basic Protestant doc-trines and opposed modern substitutes other than their own innovations. Holiness and pentecostal groups, however, tended to respond to modern worldliness with more stress on experiential and practical signs of personal separateness from evil. Fundamentalists, with more ties to scholastic Protes-tantism, stressed more the necessity of right doctrine (the "fundamentals") and especially the importance of organizing warfare against modernist theology and the worldly trends.[6]

Fundamentalism coalesced as a distinct movement in the wake of the cul-tural crisis following World War I. The spectacle of Germany, the cradle of Protestantism, having succumbed to the barbaric "might is right" evolutionary philosophy of Friedrich Nietzsche suggested that America's alleged Christian heritage was a tenuous legacy. Preachers made the most of such analogies after the war when the nation seemed threatened by labor unrest, a "Red menace," and revolutionary outbreaks of public displays of sexuality in new dances, movies, tabloid newspapers, and advertising. Worse still, some Protestant de-nominations were embracing these modern trends. Such apostates were virtu-ally dispensing with the Bible as a norm for modern people, incorporating evolutionary doctrines into their theologies and looking for the Kingdom of God in the social and political progress of modern culture.

In this atmosphere a "fundamentalist" coalition developed, the name being first used in 1920 by a group of conservative Baptists fighting modernism in the Northern Baptist Convention. Religious people alarmed by the recent trends soon rallied to the fundamentalist cause on two fronts. They joined in battles to combat modernism in major denominations, particularly the Baptists and Pres-byterians in the North. They also enlisted behind William Jennings Bryan under the banners of the anti-evolution crusade, the chief political expression of the movement. Because evolution simultaneously seemed to substitute natu-ralism for the Bible and to support a philosophy that eventually would undermine morality, opposition to Darwinism surpassed fears about Bolshevism and Catholicism as a focal point in efforts to preserve the Christian republic. The anti-evolution campaign was also an early step toward bringing a southern component into the fundamentalist coalition. A large potential was already there. The South preserved a strong revivalist heritage plus a deep-seated resentment of Yankee culture, which included most of the modern ideas such as evolution and biblical criticism that had been disseminated in the northern United States since 1861. As southerners in the 1920s were beginning to participate more in the national culture, one group of congenial allies were the northern fundamentalists.[7]

Fundamentalism's first era of public prominence lasted about half a decade, the movement fading precipitously from national press coverage after the Scopes trial and the death of William Jennings Bryan in 1925. About the same time it became clear that the conservatives' campaigns to stop modernism in the major northern denominations had been lost. Nevertheless, fundamentalists were regrouping more than retreating. The centers of the movement were shifting to individual congregations, often independent (with names like "Calvary Independent" or "Calvary Baptist"), virtually independent but still in a major denomination, or in smaller (sometimes new) denominations. Such fundamentalists were united through networks such as transdenominational agencies, schools, and publications. Fundamentalism was a segment of American Protestantism that was growing vigorously during the so-called religious depression of the 1930s.[8] Fundamentalists were particularly adept at employing the modern technology of the radio, as best exemplified by the "Old-Fashioned Revival Hour of Charles E. Fuller." By the early 1940s this was by far the most popular radio program in America, surpassing Amos 'n' Andy, Bob Hope, and Charlie McCarthy.[9] Despite such a huge constituency, fundamentalism was virtually overlooked or ignored by liberal culture and academics during this era. No doubt this reflected both the prejudgment that religion must be peripheral to modern culture and the tendency, particularly strong in the press, to act as though movements are of little significance unless they have a prominent political program. After World War I a number of fundamentalist preachers, such as Billy Sunday, William B. Riley of Minneapolis, or Frank Norris of Texas, had laced their messages with political pronouncements, featuring patriotism and Prohibition and attacking Bolshevism, socialism, and Catholicism. Nonetheless, during the period of rebuilding in the 1930s, positive emphases on revival and growth were more prominent.[10]

Success, however, had its problems. As is true of all coalitions united by opposition to common enemies, fundamentalists were finding themselves divided concerning the direction they should take in establishing a distinct movement. The chief question was that of separation from unbelief. Should fundamental Christians remain associated with denominations that taught un-Christian doctrines and that sent out missionaries who did not preach the gospel? As more fundamentalists left traditional denominations to form independent churches, separation often became an important test of faith. This stance was supported by the most important doctrinal innovation, widespread though not universal among fundamentalists, "dispensational premillennialism." Dispensationalism originated in nineteenth-century Great Britain and had been taught in American prophecy conferences since the late nineteenth century. Presenting a scheme of world history including the future, dispensationalists saw the present dispensation, or "church age," as marked by the corrupt illusion of so-called Christian civilization and the apostasy of the large churches of that civilization. Reflecting further such anti-establishmentarian impulses, dispensationalism taught that only a remnant of true believers would remain pure. The Kingdom of Christ was not to be expected at all in churches or the church age (nor did any modern nation foster it); rather it would appear only when Jesus personally returned to rule the nations from Jerusalem. Dispensationalism was therefore congenial to the doctrine of separation from apostate denominations. However, not all fundamentalists, including many of the dispensationalists, pushed the implications of the teachings this far. Many fundamentalists remained within major denominations, insisting that their more respected positions gave them a more effective base for witness to the gospel. Others both separated and condemned all who continued to consort with apostasy.[11]

The clearest indication of this split was in the formation of rival fundamentalist national organizations—the strictly separatist American Council of Christian Churches, founded in 1941, and the National Association of Evangelicals, founded in 1942 to try to cultivate a less militant evangelicalism among the heirs to fundamentalism.

Paradoxically, Carl McIntire, the founder of the ecclesiastically separatist American Council of Christian Churches, was among the fundamentalist leaders most deeply concerned about politics. During the next thirty years he was the most influential spokesperson for the fundamentalist Right, including among his sometimes associates or protégés Billy James Hargis, Verne Kaub, Fred C. Schwartz, and Edgar C. Bundy, all of whom developed vigorous fundamentalist political organizations of their own.[12] McIntire's career is illustrative of the development of fundamentalist political interests during this era. Having been forced out of the (Northern) Presbyterian Church in 1936, McIntire maintained a typically fundamentalist central focus on church battles. This was expressed in the American Council, which kept up a barrage of attacks on the ecumenical National Council of Churches and World Council of Churches. McIntire was also avidly anti-Catholic, as late as 1945 stating that the Catholic threat outweighed even that of communism.[13] Such ecclesiastical concerns, however, had strong political overtones, the National Council subverting America by promoting the "social gospel" of New Deal socialism and the Catholics plotting world rule by the Pope. Conspiracy to undermine America at home became the chief theme of such political fundamentalists, and communism became by far their chief concern.[14] McIntire himself thrived on exaggerating the numbers of both his friends and his enemies, constantly portraying himself at the center of a fight to the death between the powers of light and darkness. He and his imitators fit well what Richard Hofstadter characterized in the early 1960s as a "Manichean" mentality.[15] Fundamentalist political concerns may have seemed inconsistent with their world-denying dispensationalism and their condemnations of the social gospel; but, whether in theology or politics, their world view had the unity of accounting for everything as part of organized forces for good or for evil.

By the early 1960s the work of the various fundamentalist political organizations reached something of a peak as it coincided with that of nonfundamentalist anticommunism that had been growing since the McCarthy era. The impact of fundamentalism on other strains of American anticommunism is difficult to assess, but by this time concerted anticommunist-conspiracy-at-home forces were strong enough to raise strong opposition to the Kennedy administration and to augment the nomination of Barry Goldwater for the presidency in 1964.

Hard-line fundamentalists were not nearly as unified in these political efforts as such accounts might suggest. Leaders such as McIntire were too cantankerous to maintain large coalitions, so fundamentalist efforts were fragmented into various empires. More important, many fundamentalists, while personally very conservative politically, were more consistent with their dispensationalist and separatist principles, seeing communist threats and American declines as signs of the times and keeping away from politics or at least keeping politics from a major role in their ministries. So Jerry Falwell in 1965 was still typical of this apolitical fundamentalism, declaring, "I would find it impossible to stop preaching the pure saving gospel of Jesus Christ, and begin doing anything else—including fighting Communism, or participating in civil-rights reforms."[16]

While hard-line separatist fundamentalism was fragmented, it was also bitterly separated from the wing of the old fundamentalist coalition that had moved toward a more moderate "evangelicalism." This movement, signaled by the formation of the National Association of Evangelicals in 1942, consolidated in the early 1950s around the work of Billy Graham. Graham was willing to accept the support of even some liberal church leaders in his evangelistic crusades and so by the late 1950s became anathema to the strict separatists. By now only the separatists kept the name "fundamentalists," while a much larger constituency sympathetic to Graham began to be known as "evangelicals."

Behind Graham was a group of leaders with fundamentalist backgrounds attempting to forge a new postfundamentalist coalition of America's evangelicals. These leaders, known during the late 1940s and the 1950s as "neo-evangelicals," wanted both to place the fundamentalist heritage at the center of American evangelicalism and to change that heritage in two basic ways. First, they wanted to abandon some of the cultic aspects of fundamentalist militancy in favor of a broader evangelism. This moderation involved dropping the innovations of dispensationalism that had set fundamentalists apart from other conservative Protestants. Second, the new evangelicals redirected the fundamentalist attack on modern theology and modern culture, particularly making it intellectually much more sophisticated. Emphasizing apologetics, the new evangelicals developed substantial philosophical critiques of the secular and humanistic presuppositions that dominated Western culture and its modern theologies. Fuller Theological Seminary, founded in 1947 in Pasadena, California, became a center for an impressive array of neo-evangelical leaders during the 1950s. In 1956 Carl Henry moved from Fuller to found *Christianity Today*, which for about the next decade gave a sense of unity to the new evangelical coalition by combining intellectual critiques of modern secularism with conservative theology, zeal for evangelical outreach, and moderately conservative anticommunist politics. Politically the movement leaned strongly toward conservative Republicanism, but generally its spokespersons were careful to separate evangelism and church work from the explicit political activities of individuals or *ad hoc* political organizations.

By 1960 one might classify as "evangelical" anyone who identified with Billy Graham and as "fundamentalist" those who thought him too liberal. Nevertheless, by no means all American conservative evangelical Protestants would have been comfortable being classified in either of those movements. Holiness and pentecostal churches had traditions of their own. So did ethnic groups with Reformation origins such as Missouri Synod Lutherans, Christian Reformed, or Mennonites. Black evangelicals had little contact with their white counterparts even though their concerns were often parallel. Even Southern Baptists, despite leaders such as Graham, often remained regional in outlook and had little contact with the broader national evangelical or fundamentalist coalitions. Conservative evangelicals estimated their church membership in the late 1950s at about half of all Protestants, or 24 million.[17]

The cultural crisis of the 1960s proved a boon to evangelicalism as it did to many religious groups. The crisis was, in an important sense, a spiritual crisis. The ideals, the belief system, and the eschatology of the mid-twentieth-century version of liberal culture were proving vacuous. The attacks as expressed first by the counterculture were directed against the ideals of a centralized, liberal, nationalistic, scientific, sociological, service, and consumer culture. The failures of the value system of this technological establishment opened the door to vast varieties of new spiritualities. Religion of almost any sort was accepted on campuses by the early 1970s to an extent that was unthinkable in the late 1950s. In this setting, evangelicalism still did not get the headlines, which were reserved for more bizarre movements. The evangelicals, however, had a great advantage over most other spiritual beneficiaries of the upheavals of the 1960s. They had already in place a vast network of institutions, ready to absorb and direct the new enthusiasms.[18] Moreover, evangelicals were also prepared for these new opportunities by their skills in modern techniques of promotion, organization, and communication. The movement had always depended on these for its survival.

Evangelicalism benefited from the upheavals of the 1960s in paradoxical ways.[19] On the one hand it capitalized on the decline in prestige of the liberal-scientific-secular establishment, a value system that evangelicals had already proclaimed as illusory and doomed. The decentralizing emphases of counterculture readily could be appropriated to evangelicalism, which already was a hodgepodge of *ad hoc* structures. More important, the people-community impulses of the era were readily translated by evangelicals into personal contacts and small-group meetings, such as groups for Bible study and prayer, that contributed substantially to evangelical growth during the 1970s.

On the other side of the paradox, evangelicalism gained from the deep reactions against counterculture ideals. The instinctive impulses of much of the evangelical constituency were of the Spiro Agnew variety. Translated into spiritual terms, what they saw first in the protests of the young was a more virulent sort of Godless secularism and lawlessness. To many conservative evangelicals such vices were extensions of the permissiveness of the New Deal liberal culture rather than protests against it. Such impressions were indeed reinforced by liberalization of the laws in the direction of permissiveness, such as toward homosexuals or abortion, and enforced secularization of schools and public places. During the Vietnam era, however, attacks on the nation and on authority commanded the most attention, so many evangelicals defended with fierce patriotism the nation that they nonetheless regarded as disastrously corrupt.[20]

As is well known, evangelicals benefited also from the uncertainties of the Vietnam era and its aftermath by offering decisive answers. The fundamentalist militancy in the heritage encouraged polarized thinking. The metaphors of warfare that dominated that movement suggested that battle lines could be clearly drawn on almost any issue. Confronted with the crisis in authority in a changing and pluralistic society, evangelicals could point to the sure certainty of the word of God. The "inerrancy" of the Bible became an increasingly important symbolic test of faith for much of the movement.[21] Evangelicals generally could draw on the immense residual prestige of the Bible in America as a firm rock in a time of change.[22]

These circumstances—a deeply rooted ideological-spiritual heritage, vigorous institutions, skills in promotion, and an era when people were open to spiritual answers to national and personal crises—combined for the evangelical resurgence of the 1970s. Jimmy Carter's presidency was an appropriate symbol of the new status of the movement, which was growing in fact but also growing much faster in media attention. Carter-as-evangelical suggests some of the variety within evangelicalism at a time when forty or fifty million constituents were attributed to the movement. Carter was a Southern Baptist and was outside of the movements that claimed to speak for evangelicalism generally. His political stance, moreover, illustrated that one did not have to be politically conservative to be a full-fledged "evangelical." By now the movement had vigorous wings that tended toward liberal democratic politics and a significant, more radical, Anabaptist political voice.[23] Political conservatism, however, was no doubt the most widespread inclination.

The Moral Majority arose in this situation in 1979, capitalizing on the unfocused but conservative political sentiments of many evangelicals and some others. From the viewpoint of the history of evangelicalism, a striking feature of the Moral Majority was that its leadership proudly called itself "fundamentalist." Up to this time the hard-line fundamentalists might have seemed unlikely candidates for exercising national leadership on a large scale. Having split from the larger body of evangelicals, their avowed separatism seemed sufficiently extreme to make any widespread cooperation, even among themselves, appear unlikely.[24] Those who dealt with politics tended to do so in several ways, although these were not mutually exclusive. They might, like Carl McIntire or Billy James Hargis, continue to beat the drums of simplistic anticommunist crusades that dated back to the McCarthy era. All the nation's problems were reduced to communist infiltration of the nation's liberal ecclesiastical, political, and intellectual establishments. Such views attracted a numerically solid but limited constituency. Second, consistent with a long revivalist tradition, fundamentalists occasionally organized in moral campaigns, such as to clean up textbooks or to fight pornography. Third, like the early Jerry Falwell, many fundamentalists tended to view politics primarily as signs of the times that pointed toward the early return of Jesus to set up a political kingdom in the land of Israel. The sorry moral state of the nation was seen primarily as an impetus for repentence. The new Jerry Falwell and the Moral Majority mobilized not so much the political impulse that had been distinctive to fundamentalism but rather the moral-political impulse that had been one part of the revivalist tradition more generally. Although Falwell comes from a fundamentalist background and is pastor of a fundamentalist church, his national moral crusade involved too broad an alliance with "Mormons, Jews, Roman Catholics, Adventists, apostates, New Evangelicals"[25] to suit the strict fundamentalists. Falwell in their view was a "pseudo-fundamentalist" or, worse, a "neo-evangelical" in disguise.[26] In this dispute, the stricter fundamentalists are probably correct that Falwell's movement is similar to the neo-evangelical movement of the 1940s and 1950s. He is, as Frances FitzGerald has observed,[27] torn between doctrines that demand separation and ambitions for acceptance and influence that demand compromise. While condemning in good fundamentalist fashion the compromises of Billy Graham, Falwell is moving in the same direction away from strict fundamentalism as did Graham.

In terms of the history of American evangelicalism, Falwell and the Moral Majority perhaps can best be seen as a recombination of some elements drawn from the neo-evangelical and fundamentalist heritages since 1950. From neo-evangelicalism comes the conception of "secular humanism" as virtually a religious force threatening to displace Christianity entirely from the culture. This critique was articulated around midcentury by a number of neo-evangelical theologians and philosophers who spelled out the incompatibilities of the world views derived from Christian presuppositions drawn from Scripture and world views founded on atheistic-naturalistic assumptions.[28] Following in a general way the sophisticated suggestions of the Dutch theologian-politician Abraham Kuyper (1837–1920), the neo-evangelicals viewed Western culture as locked in a struggle between these contending world views. By the 1970s such ideas in simplified form had filtered to some fundamentalist leaders through, for instance, the immensely popular film series *How Should We Live Then?* (1976) by evangelicalism's well-known quasi philosopher and evangelist Francis Schaeffer.[29] The fundamentalists further transformed these ideas by putting them into the characteristic fundamentalist paradigm of a simple warfare between the forces of light and darkness. Just as typical of fundamentalist thought, the struggle between contending ideals was personalized as a carefully orchestrated conspiracy. So in the view of Moral Majority spokesman Tim LaHaye, humanists (whom he defines as everyone but Bible believers) have been "planted" in strategic places in the United Nations, they teach children in public schools "to read the words *scientific humanism* as soon as they are old enough to read," and 275,000 humanists control American government, education, and media.[30]

The "secular humanist" idea has revitalized fundamentalist conspiracy theory. Fundamentalists always have been alarmed at moral decline within America but often have been vague as to whom, other than the Devil, to blame. The "secular humanist" thesis gives this central concern a clearer focus that is more plausible and of wider appeal than the old monocausal communist-conspiracy accounts. Communism and socialism can, of course, be fit right into the humanist picture; but so can all the moral and legal changes at home without implausible scenarios of Russian agents infiltrating American schools, government, reform movements, and mainline churches. As many analysts of modern society have observed, secular humanism *is* an ideology with a quasi-religious character and involves a number of naturalistic beliefs to give it a rough-hewn unity.[31] The fundamentalists' simplified version of this observation, while extreme, nonetheless points to a real secularizing trend in a large area of the culture, so that their claims carry more force of plausible evidence than do most conspiracy theories.

The Paradoxes of the Fundamentalist New Right

The first thing to notice in considering the New Right in light of this fundamentalist and evangelical history is the diversity of the religious movement and hence its sometimes self-contradictory stances toward culture. Fundamentalism from the outset was both a distinct movement or impulse and a coalition of a number of movements. Nineteenth-century American evangelicalism, from which fundamentalism grew, was itself a coalition of several denominational traditions. Similarly, today we can identify at least fourteen varieties of evangelicalism.[32] While these evangelicals share many doctrines, their diversities in inherited stances toward culture and politics are especially pronounced. So on the issues of culture and politics generalizations about evangelicalism are particularly hazardous.

Central to the fundamentalist heritage is a basic tension between positive revivalism and polemics. Fundamentalism developed largely within the revivalist tradition, in which the highest goal was to win other souls to Christ. Controversy could aid revivalism for a time, but in the long run too much controversy and too much cantankerousness could hinder evangelistic efforts. This was one of the issues that divided neo-evangelicals from hard-line fundamentalists after 1940. Fundamentalist separatism, insistence on strict doctrinal purity, and incivility toward persons with other beliefs seemed to the new evangelicals to hinder the spread of the Gospel. The evangelism of Billy Graham well represented their impulse. Despite his traditionalist message and his efforts to change individuals, Graham was willing to live with American pluralism. Hard-line fundamentalists were unwilling to accept such compromise with pluralism and so continued the warfare on modern society from the position of strict separatists. The price of such polemics was that they remained on the fringe where fewer people would take their message seriously.

The tensions between positive revivalism and controversialism are complicated by a second tension that pulls evangelicalism simultaneously in two directions. Simply put, this is a tension between being and not being politically and culturally oriented. This division cuts differently than does the positive revivalist versus polemicist division. Some evangelicals with political-cultural concerns are militant controversialists (fundamentalists) and others are not. Moreover, many evangelicals who stress positive revival also have political-cultural programs; but many others do not. So these two types of tensions produce four combinations of basic ideal types (positive-nonpolitical, positive-political, polemicist-nonpolitical, and polemicist-political).[33]

The tension between emphasizing political-cultural implications of the Gospel or eschewing them is also deeply rooted. It is inherent in Christianity itself, which always has wavered between Old Testament and New or between redeeming the city of the world and thinking of the City of God as wholly spiritual or otherworldly. Such ambivalence is particularly strong in American evangelicalism. This is so both because American evangelicalism and fundamentalism fuse so many traditions and because in America itself evangelicals have been cast in vastly different roles in different eras.

The most immediate heritage of fundamentalists comes from their twentieth-century experiences of being a beleaguered and ridiculed minority. Sin and secularism had run rampant over some key parts of American culture. Like twentieth-century sociologists, most fundamentalists believed in laws that declared that the process of secularization was irreversible. In the fundamentalists' case these laws were drawn from dispensational premillennialism, which posited the steady decline of the modern era in preparation for a final world calamity resolved only by the personal return of Christ with avenging armies. Fundamentalists in this world view were outsiders.[34] They were outsiders from the power centers of society, its politics, and its cultural life; they viewed themselves as separated from these worldly powers. This separation was indeed selective, not precluding full participation in the nation's economic life and usually not thwarting impulses to patriotism. Some fundamentalists stood as lonely prophets warning of the destruction that was to come and that could be seen in the growing strength of demonic world forces such as Catholicism or communism. More typically, however, fundamentalists and many other evangelicals, sensing themselves to be essentially outsiders, drew on those considerable strands in their revivalist and New Testament heritage that forsook political and cultural aspirations.

If one looks a little further back, however, one finds an almost opposite strand in the heritage. Throughout the nineteenth century, revivalist evangelicalism was the dominant religious force in America, strong enough to be a virtual establishment in this most religious of modern nations. Though often submerged, the images of this historical tradition retained a residual power through the hard days of the twentieth century. When in eras such as the early 1920s or 1980s when the nation was in the midst of a conservative reaction and unfocused anxiety, this establishmentarian side of the tradition could be readily revived.

This political-cultural side of the heritage reflects not at all the premillennialism that was taught in twentieth-century fundamentalism but rather a residual postmillennialism that had dominated nineteenth-century evangelicalism. In this view America has a special place in God's plans and will be the center for a great spiritual and moral reform that will lead to a golden age or "millennium" of Christian civilization. Moral reform accordingly is crucial for hastening this spiritual millennium. Fundamentalists today reject postmillennialism as such, but genetically postmillennial ideals continue to be a formidable force in their thinking. Such ideals now appear not so much as Christian doctrine but as a mixture of piety and powerful American folklore. This folklore is a popularization of a version of the Whig view of history, in which true religion and liberty are always pitted against false religion and tyranny. America, in this view, was founded on Christian principles embodied in the Constitution and has been chosen by God to be a beacon of right religion and liberty for the whole world.[35]

Puritanism is another powerful source of fundamentalist cultural views. Almost always, Puritan social doctrines are mixed with the Whig version of American history and folklore. One clue to the Puritan connection is the constant use of the jeremiad form. The light of true religion and liberty has dimmed, though only rather recently—sometime since the end of World War II.[36] Up to that time "America has been great because her people have been good," as Jerry Falwell puts it.[37] Her recent moral decline coincides with her recent international humiliations. These are, in fact, simply cause and effect. While the connections might not seem apparent to human wisdom, we can be sure that God is punishing America for her depravity, an idea inherited directly from the Puritan covenantal tradition. God's blessings and curses are, in Old Testament fashion, contingent on national righteousness or sinfulness. Falwell constantly repeats this theme, suggesting, for instance, that the spread of pornography is causally related, through God's providential control, to national distresses such as the oil crisis.[38] "Our nation's internal problems," he says, characteristically, "are direct results of her spiritual condition."[39]

The continuing strength of this combination of Whig and Puritan views in the religious outlook suggests that it is misleading to characterize the fundamentalist-evangelical heritage as generally "private."[40] One important strand of the revivalist heritage, drawn from pietism, Methodism, and Baptist zeal for separation of church and state, has tended to eschew identifications of the Kingdom of God with social-political programs. Evangelicalism has always been divided within itself on this point, however. During the nineteenth century the Puritan heritage was still a formidable force in shaping evangelicals' quasi-Calvinist visions of a Christian America. Such Puritan culture-dominating ideals persist in the Moral Majority today. Much of evangelicalism accordingly has been of two minds on the question of personal versus social applications of the Gospel. Even the Methodist-holiness tradition, certainly a center for some strongly privatistic impulses, has sometimes supported postmillennial visions of social reform. Fundamentalism has sometimes resolved its internal dilemma on this point by making distinctions between public "moral" questions that it supports as opposed to illicit mixing of "politics" with religion by liberal church leaders.[41]

A related point is worth noting: Fundamentalists are reputedly highly individualistic. Indeed, fundamentalists are individualistic in the sense of advocating classical liberal economics and in emphasizing the necessity of an individual's personal relation to Jesus. Moreover, their view of the church is nominalistic; they see it essentially as a collection of individuals. Early in this century theological liberals who were building the Social Gospel movement were quick to point out such individualistic traits and to contrast them with their own more communal emphases. Ever since, this individualistic-privatistic image has dominated views of fundamentalism. Despite the substantial truth to this characterization, there is another side. In fact fundamental churches and national organizations are some of the most cohesive non-ethnic communities in America.[42] Certainly the fundamentalist churches offer far stronger community for their members than do their moderate-liberal Protestant counterparts.

Moreover, despite the profession of individuality, fundamentalist churches and organizations tend to be highly authoritarian, typically under the control of one strong leader. Although fundamentalist preaching sometimes stresses making up one's own mind, in fact the movement displays some remarkable uniformities in details of doctrine and practice that suggest anything but real individualism in thought.

Returning to the persistence of the quasi-Calvinist vision of cultural dominance, we can see yet another paradox within fundamentalism. Fundamentalism usually has been regarded as essentially anti-intellectual. Again, there is some truth to this accusation. A considerable tradition within American revivalism has always viewed higher education with suspicion.[43] Early Methodists, many Baptists, and other American groups considered an educated clergy a stumbling block to true spirituality. Today some fundamentalist groups insist that education beyond high school be confined to their own Bible schools. Moreover, bitter opposition to the American intellectual establishment and accusations that too much learning has corrupted liberal and neo-evangelical Protestants are commonplace.

Nonetheless, as we have seen, fundamentalism also reflects the persistence of the Puritan heritage in the American Protestant psyche. This heritage includes a cultural vision of all things, including learning, brought into the service of the sovereign God. Fundamentalists accordingly retain vestiges of this ideal. Schools, including colleges and "universities," are central parts of their empires. Although they may only rarely attain excellence in learning, they seek it in principle and sometimes do attain it. No group is more eager to brandish honorary degrees. Perhaps more to the point, genuine degrees are more than welcome when in the service of the Lord. Nowhere is this clearer than in the creation-science movement, a predominantly fundamentalist effort. While decrying the scientific establishment and people who blindly follow the lead of "experts," the Creation Research Society emphasizes the hundreds of Ph.D.'s who make up its membership.

Even more centrally, fundamentalists are among those contemporary Americans who take ideas most seriously. In this respect they reflect, even if in a dim mirror, the Puritan heritage. For the fundamentalist, what one believes is of the utmost importance. They are, as Samuel S. Hill, Jr., observes, more "truth-oriented" than most evangelical groups.[44] The American intellectual establishment, in contrast, has a tendency to reduce beliefs to something else, hence devaluing the importance of ideas as such. So, for instance, fundamentalist ideas themselves have long been presented as though they were "really" expressions of some social or class interest. It seems fair to inquire in such cases as to who is really the anti-intellectual. To reduce beliefs to their social functions is to overemphasize a partial truth and so to underestimate the powers of the belief itself. Consider, for instance, the important fundamentalist belief that God relates to the nation convenantally, rewarding or punishing it proportionately to its moral record. This is a belief, deeply held on religious grounds, about some causal connections in the universe. Throughout the history of America this conception about causality has survived through a number of revolutionary changes in the class and status of its adherents. While, as suggested earlier, social and cultural circumstances strongly influence the expressions of this belief, there is no doubt that the belief itself is sometimes a powerful force in determining the way people behave.

Fundamentalist thought often appears anti-intellectual because of its proneness to oversimplification. The universe is divided in two—the moral and the immoral, the forces of light and darkness. This polarized thinking reflects a crass popularizing that indeed is subversive to serious intellectual inquiry and a world view that starts with a premise that the world is divided between the forces of God and of Satan and sorts out evidence to fit that paradigm. Another influence on this thinking reflects a modern intellectual tradition that dates largely from the Enlightenment. Fundamentalist thought has close links with the Baconian and Common Sense assumptions of the early modern era. Humans are capable of positive knowledge based on sure foundations. If rationally classified, such knowledge can yield a great deal of certainty. Combined with biblicism, such a view of knowledge leads to supreme confidence on religious questions.[45] Despite the conspicuous subjectivism throughout evangelicalism[46] and within fundamentalism itself, one side of the fundamentalist mentality is committed to inductive rationalism.

This commonsense inductive aspect of fundamentalist thinking, rather than being anti-intellectual, reflects an intellectual tradition alien to most modern academics. What is most lacking is the contemporary sense of historical development, a Heraclitean sense that all is change. This contemporary conception of history invites relativism or at least the seeing of ambiguities. Fundamentalists have the confidence of Enlightenment philosophies that an objective look at "the facts" will lead to the truth.[47] Their attacks on evolutionism reflect their awareness that the developmentalist, historicist, and culturalist assumptions of modern thought undermine the certainties of knowledge. Correspondingly, persons attracted to authoritarian views of the Bible are often also attracted to the pre-Darwinian, ahistorical, philosophical assumptions that seem to provide high yields of certainty.

It is incorrect then to think of fundamentalist thought as essentially premodern.[48] Its views of God's revelation, for example, although drawn from the Bible, are a long way from the modes of thought of the ancient Hebrews. For instance, fundamentalists' intense insistence on the "inerrancy" of the Bible in scientific and historical detail is related to this modern style of thinking. Although the idea that Scripture does not err is an old one, fundamentalists accentuate it partly because they often view the Bible virtually as though it were a scientific treatise. For example, southern Baptist fundamentalist Paige Patterson remarks: "Space scientists tell us that minute error in the mathematical calculations for a moon shot can result in a total failure of the rocket to hit the moon. A slightly altered doctrine of salvation can cause a person to miss Heaven also."[49] To the fundamentalist the Bible is essentially a collection of true and precise propositions. Such approaches may not be typical of most twentieth-century thought, but they are more nearly early modern than premodern.

Fundamentalist thought is in fact highly suited to one strand of contemporary culture—the technological strand. Unlike theoretical science or social science, where questions of the supernatural raise basic issues about the presuppositions of the enterprise, technological thinking does not wrestle with such theoretical principles. Truth is a matter of true and precise propositions that, when properly classified and organized, will work. Fundamentalism fits this mentality because it is a form of Christianity with no loose ends, ambiguities, or historical developments. Everything fits neatly into a system. It is revealing, for instance, that many of the leaders of the creation-science movement are in applied sciences or engineering.[50] The principal theories of creation science were in fact designed by an engineer, Henry Morris. Morris, in typically fundamentalist Baconian terms, describes his quest for scientific confirmation of the Bible: "In trying to lead others to Christ, I needed answers and this led me to research. And being an engineer, I looked for solid evidence."[51]

Fundamentalists in more general ways have proved themselves masters of modern technique. Again, the creation-science movement provides a prime example, this time of effective techniques of promotion. The Creation Research Society and related agencies have convinced some state legislatures to require in public schools the peculiar teachings of their "scientific creationism" (including that the geological contours of the world are explained by a worldwide flood). Such views of creation, which are disputed by most evangelical scientists and are certainly not held by most Catholics and other Christians who have addressed the subject, have nonetheless been sold as "creationism"; so many laypeople have been led to believe that this is the only alternative to evolution. Such a result reflects a marvel of shrewd promotional technique. The skillful use of organizational mass mailing and media techniques by the fundamentalist New Right during the 1980 election similarly demonstrates this mastery of an aspect of modern culture. Such expertise in rationalized technique should hardly be surprising in a Protestant American tradition. Moreover, evangelicalism has long depended for support on effectively mobilizing masses of potential constituents. Evangelist Charles Finney in the early nineteenth century was in fact one of the pioneers in rationalized techniques of modern advertising and promotion.[52]

The fundamentalist message is also peculiarly suited for large segments of society in the technological age. Fundamentalists have been particularly adept at handling mass communication.[53] If there is a rule of mass communications that the larger the audience the simpler the message must be, fundamentalists and similar evangelicals came to the technological age well prepared. Television ministries flourish best when they provide answers in simple polarities.[54] By contrast, one could hardly imagine a widely popular neo-Orthodox television ministry; subtleties and ambiguities would kill it immediately.[55] Such aptness of the message to the age is not confined to TV. Although not often acknowledged by the controllers of public opinion, evangelicals have also dominated the actual best-seller statistics during the past decade.[56] The key to such success is again a simple message. Such simplicity itself bears a paradoxical relationship to contemporary life. On the one hand, it is a reaction against the tensions, uncertainties, and ambiguities that surround modern life and always shape the human condition. At the same time, the ancient simplicities have been given a contemporary shape by the same forces that produce the efficient production and sales of, let's say, McDonald's hamburgers. As the Cathedral at Chartres symbolized the essence of the medieval era, so perhaps the McDonald's golden arches may symbolize ours. For better or worse, fundamentalism is a version of Christianity matched to its age.

Fundamentalism, then, is fraught with paradoxes. It is torn between uncivil controversialism and the accepting attitudes necessary for being influential and evangelizing effectively. Often it is otherworldly and privatistic; yet it retains intense patriotism and interest in the moral-political welfare of the nation. It is individualistic, yet produces strong communities. It is in some ways anti-intellectual, but stresses right thinking and true education. It accentuates the revivalists' appeal to the subjective, yet often it is rationalistic-inductivist in its epistemology. It is Christianity derived from an ancient book, yet shaped also by the technological age. It is antimodernist, but in some respects strikingly modern. Perhaps most ironically, it offers simple answers phrased as clear polarities; yet it is such a complex combination of traditions and beliefs that it is filled with more ambiguity and paradox than most of its proponents, or its opponents, realize.

REFERENCES

[1]Particularly striking, for example, are some of the harsh treatments of the Puritans. See, for example, Brooks Adams, *The Emancipation of Massachusetts* (Boston: Houghton, Mifflin & Co., 1887), pp. 1–2, 42 and passim; James Truslow Adams, *The Founding of New England* (Boston: Atlantic Monthly Press, 1921), pp. 66, 174, and passim; and Vernon Parrington, *The Colonial Mind, 1620-1800* (New York: Harcourt, Brace & Co., 1927), pp. 5, 15, 29 and passim. The Puritans, safely in the past, were the first religious group to be rehabilitated by secularist scholars, beginning around 1930. R. Stephen Warner, "Theoretical Barriers to the Understanding of Evangelical Christianity," *Sociological Analysis*, 40, No. 1 (1979), 1-9, documents the persistence of such biases among sociologists of religion.

[2]Perry Miller, *The Life of the Mind in America: From the Revolution to the Civil War* (New York: Harcourt, Brace & World, 1965), p. 7.

[3]An excellent bibliography is Richard V. Pierard, "The New Religious Right: A Formidable Force in American Politics," *Choice* (March 1982), 863-79.

[4]Popular instances of such approaches are found in the literature of the American Civil Liberties Union, which describes the Moral Majority as, for example, planning "to establish a nightmare of religious and political orthodoxy." From an ACLU mailing from Norman Dorsen, president, fall 1981. Many similar statements are found in the literature of groups opposed to fundamentalist-supported causes such as anti-abortion or creation science.

[5]The following survey is based largely on George M. Marsden, *Fundamentalism and American Culture: The Shaping of Twentieth-Century Evangelicalism, 1870-1925* (New York: Oxford University Press, 1980).

[6]Since fundamentalism was a coalition of antimodernist militants, it included holiness and pentecostal representatives.

[7]Southerners, however, still generally remained aloof from the national movement. As progressive ideas spread in the South during the next decades, so did fundamentalism. See *Review and Expositor*, 79, No. 1 (Winter 1982), an issue devoted to "Fundamentalism and the Southern Baptist Convention" and David E. Harrell, Jr., ed., *Varieties of Southern Evangelicalism* (Macon, Ga.: Mercer University Press, 1981).

[8]Joel A. Carpenter, "Fundamentalist Institutions and the Rise of Evangelical Protestantism, 1929-1942," *Church History*, 49, No. 1 (March 1980), 62-75.

[9]Daniel P. Fuller, *Give the Winds a Mighty Voice: The Story of Charles E. Fuller* (Waco, Tex.: Word Books, 1972), pp. 140, 149-50.

[10]This is the conclusion of Joel Carpenter, "Tuning in the Gospel: The Fundamentalist Revival of Revivalism, 1930-1942," a paper delivered to the Harwichport (Mass.) Conference on American Religious History, June 29-July 1, 1982.

[11]This dispute is summarized from the separatist side by Robert Lightner, *New-Evangelicalism* (Findley, Ohio: Dunham, 1962), and Charles Woodbridge, *The New Evangelicalism* (Greenville, S.C.: Bob Jones University Press, 1969). For the nonseparatists, see Ronald H. Nash, *The New Evangelicalism* (Grand Rapids: Zondervan, 1963).

[12]Erling Jorstad, *The Politics of Doomsday: Fundamentalists of the Far Right* (Nashville: Abingdon, 1970).

[13]James Morris, *The Preachers* (New York: St. Martin's Press, 1973), p. 199.

[14]Jorstad, *Politics*, p. 44. Anti-Catholicism was revived during the Kennedy election of 1960, but

McIntire repudiated it as a factor when Goldwater's running mate in 1964, William Miller, was a Catholic (ibid., p. 119).

[15] Richard Hofstadter, *Anti-Intellectualism in American Life* (New York: Random House, 1962), p. 135.

[16] Quoted from a sermon, "Ministers and Marchers," by Frances FitzGerald, "A Disciplined, Charging Army," *The New Yorker*, May 18, 1981, p. 63. Falwell since has repudiated this sermon.

[17] James DeForest Murch, "The Evangelical Year," *United Evangelical Action*, January 1, 1957, p. 5, cited in Louis Gasper, *The Fundamentalist Movement, 1930-1956* (Grand Rapids: Baker Book House, 1981, p. 30. Presumably the supporting community would be somewhat larger than this number of actual members.

[18] This point is suggested in Jeremy Rifkin, with Ted Howard, *The Emerging Order: God in the Age of Scarcity* (New York: G. P. Putnam's Sons, 1979), p. 104.

[19] David Martin, "Revived Dogma and New Cult," in this volume, makes some similar points.

[20] See, for example, the chapter "The Bible Fundamentalist is A GOOD CHRISTIAN CITI-ZEN" in John R. Rice, *I Am a Fundamentalist* (Murfreesboro, Tenn.: Sword of the Lord Publishers, 1975), pp. 151-79. Rice, editor of *Sword of the Lord*, with a circulation of about 250,000, was not heavily political but adamantly for law and order.

[21] A leading signal in the revival of this issue was the publication of Harold Lindsell's *The Battle for the Bible* (Grand Rapids: Zondervan, 1976). By 1980, 100,000 were in print.

[22] On the role of the Bible in the evangelical tradition and in American culture see Nathan O. Hatch and Mark A. Noll, eds., *The Bible in America: Essays in Cultural History* (New York: Oxford University Press, 1982).

[23] These movements are studied in Robert Booth Fowler, *A New Engagement: Christian Evangelical Political Thought, 1966-1976* (Grand Rapids: Eerdmans, 1982). They are also covered, sometimes more impressionistically, in Richard Quebedeaux, *The Worldly Evangelicals* (New York: Harper & Row, 1978).

[24] George W. Dollar, *A History of Fundamentalism in America* (Greenville, S.C.: Bob Jones University Press, 1973), p. 248, estimated the total number of separatist fundamentalists at about four million.

[25] "The Moral Majority: An Assessment of a Movement," by Leading Fundamentalists, compiled by James E. Singleton, ca. 1981, p. 16. Cf. "The Fundamentalist Phenomenon or Fundamentalist Betrayal," compiled and edited by James E. Singleton, ca. 1981. These pamphlets are produced by persons sympathetic to Bob Jones University.

[26] Jerry Falwell, with Ed Dobson and Ed Hindson, eds., *The Fundamentalist Phenomenon: The Resurgence of Conservative Christianity* (Garden City, N.Y.: Doubleday, 1981), pp. 160-63.

[27] "A Disciplined, Charging Army," *The New Yorker*, May 11, 1981, p. 103. FitzGerald sees this same tension in Falwell's people, who aspire both to separation from the world and to worldly success.

[28] These themes are developed, for instance, in Carl F. H. Henry, *Remaking the Modern Mind* (Grand Rapids: Eerdmans, 1946), and Edward J. Carnell, *Introduction to Christian Apologetics* (Grand Rapids: Eerdmans, 1948).

[29] Tim LaHaye, *The Battle for the Mind* (Old Tappan, N.J.: Fleming H. Revell, 1980), cites Schaeffer extensively. Falwell, in turn, cites LaHaye for his definition of *humanism*, in *Fundamentalist Phenomenon*, p. 199. The critique of "humanism" and "secular humanism" is not prominent in earlier fundamentalist literature, but does appear especially in connection with non-Christian influences in public schools. For instance, opponents of teaching evolution typically have argued in court cases that it was part of a humanistic religion.

[30] LaHaye, *Battle*, pp. 27, 74, 97, and 179.

[31] For example, cf. Peter L. Berger, "From the Crisis of Religion to the Crisis of Secularity," in this volume.

[32] Robert E. Webber, *Common Roots: A Call to Evangelical Maturity* (Grand Rapids: Zondervan, 1978), p. 32. Cullen Murphy, "Protestantism and the Evangelicals," *The Wilson Quarterly* (Autumn 1981), 105-17, identifies twelve varieties.

[33] A more refined version of this sort of categorization is found in Richard J. Mouw, "The Bible in Twentieth-Century Protestantism: A Preliminary Taxonomy," in Hatch and Noll, *Bible in America*, pp. 139–62.

[34] R. Laurence Moore, "Insiders and Outsiders in American Historical Narrative and American History," *American Historical Review*, 87, No. 2 (April 1982), 390-412, provides a helpful account of this outsider theme and its inherent ambiguities.

[35] Ronald A. Wells, "Francis Schaeffer's Jeremiad: A Review Article," *The Reformed Journal*, 32, No. 5 (May 1982), 16-20, suggests the combination of Whig history and the jeremiad.

[36] For example, John R. Price, *America at the Crossroads: Repentence or Repression?* (Indianapolis: Christian House Publishing Co., 1976), pp. 3-7. Cf. Jerry Falwell, *Listen America!* (Garden City: New York: Doubleday, 1980), and LaHaye, *Battle*, passim.

[37] Falwell, *Listen America!* p. 243.

[38] Jerry Falwell, interview, *Eternity* (July-August 1980), 19.

[39] Falwell, *Listen America!* p. 243. Cf. Price, *America at the Crossroads*, pp. 109-58 and passim, who details at length the covenant parallels between modern America and Old Testament Israel. Also cf. the ideas of Bill Bright, president of Campus Crusade, who at least for a time advocated evangelical political action based on covenantal principles of God's judgments or blessings. See John A. Lapp, "The Evangelical Factor in American Politics," in *Evangelicalism and Anabaptism*, ed. C. Norman Kraus (Scottdale, Pa.: Herald Press, 1979), pp. 91-94.

[40] Unfortunately, the identification of evangelicalism and revivalism as "private" in contrast to "public" Protestantism has been widely promoted by one of the most consistently astute interpreters of American religion, Martin Marty. See, for example, his *Righteous Empire: The Protestant Experience in America* (New York: Harper Torchbooks, 1970). Marty has recently refined his distinction to take into account fundamentalist political activities. These he calls "political" but not "public." A "public theology" must allow for some acceptance of the secular-pluralistic order as a domain through which God may work positively. See Marty, "Fundamentalism as a Social Phenomenon," *Review and Expositor*, 79, No. 1 (Winter 1982), 24-25. This definition solves the immediate problem but ultimately confuses the issue. I fail to see how it is helpful to describe the long history of fundamentalist political activities as "private." Concerns about abortion, pornography, public schools, prohibition, growth of government, and so forth are as much public issues as are progressive social causes. Since the rise of the Social Gospel, however, politically progressive Christians have been reluctant to admit that conservative political stances were expressions of social concern at all. Furthermore, Marty's version of a "two-party" scheme (private evangelical and public nonevangelical) fails because not only the evangelicals but also the nonevangelicals are divided on these issues. An interesting confirmation of the difficulties of the scheme is suggested by a finding of the 1978-79 Gallup–*Christianity Today* poll. On the question of the importance of religious organizations stating what they believe to be the will of God in political/economic matters, evangelicals scored well above liberal Protestants or any other group. See James Davison Hunter, "Contemporary American Evangelicalism: Conservative Religion and the Quandary of Modernity," Ph.D. dissertation, Rutgers, The State University of New Jersey, New Brunswick, 1981, pp. 207-09, 255-60.

[41] Carl McIntire, for instance, characteristically responded to accusations that he had made the Gospel too political with statements such as "What men call politics, to me is standing up for righteousness." Morris, *Preachers*, p. 190.

[42] Lowell D. Streiker and Gerald S. Strober, *Religion and the New Majority: Billy Graham, Middle America, and the Politics of the '70s* (New York: Association Press, 1972), pp. 139-40. Most fundamentalists are of northern European descent, but the unity of their communities is not usually based on more narrow ethnic ties.

[43] According to the 1978-79 Gallup–*Christianty Today* survey, evangelicals (who include many persons from the rural South) are the least educated of the groups surveyed. Only 9 percent completed university education, while 37 percent had not completed high school. Hunter, "Contemporary Evangelicalism," pp. 123-24.

[44] Samuel S. Hill, Jr., "Popular Southern Piety," in *Varieties of Southern Evangelicalism*, ed. David Edwin Harrell, Jr. (Macon, Ga.: Mercer University Press, 1981), p. 100.

[45] Charles W. Allen documents this tendency in southern Baptist fundamentalist Paige Patterson, who says of liberal views: "The Subjectivism of their epistemology reduced easily to a formula, T = P − C, i.e., Truth = my Perception minus Certainty. I for one cannot build faith on such a quivering foundation." Quoted from Patterson, "Inerrancy—and the Passover," *The Shophar*, 4 (May 1980), A-1, in Allen, "Paige Patterson: Contender for Baptist Sectarianism," *Review and Expositor*, 79, No. 1 (Winter 1982), 110.

[46] James Davidson Hunter, "Subjectivism and the New Evangelical Theodicy," *Journal for the Scientific Study of Religion*, 20, No. 1 (1982), 39-47, documents the subjectivist side of evangelicalism.

[47] For example, the apologetics of Josh McDowell, *Evidence that Demands a Verdict: Historical Evidences for the Christian Faith* (San Bernardino, Calif.: Campus Crusade, 1972). Such objectivist apologetics were dominant in nineteenth-century American evangelicalism.

[48] Martin E. Marty makes some valuable comments on this theme in "The Revival of Evangelicalism and Southern Religion," in Harrell, *Varieties of Southern Evangelicalism*, pp. 7-22. Among other things, Marty observes that evangelicals' modernity is reflected in their emphasis on *choice*. Here is another paradox, since evangelicals speak much about both choice and absolute authority.

[49] Patterson, *Living in the Hope of Eternal Life* (Grand Rapids: Zondervan, 1968), p. 26, quoted in Allen, "Paige Patterson," p. 110.

[50] Dorothy Nelkin, *Science Textbook Controversies and the Politics of Equal Time* (Cambridge: MIT Press, 1977), p. 72.

[51] Quoted in Nelkin, *Science Textbook Controversies*, pp. 71-72.

[52] Hunter, "Contemporary American Evangelicalism," pp. 171-92, provides many examples of

current evangelicalism's obsession with technique and how such interests have changed parts of the evangelical message.

[53]This side of evangelicalism makes it unclear exactly how the movement fits the scheme suggested by Peter Berger, who argues that the real conflict within American Protestantism is a "class struggle" between two elites, the "new knowledge class" and "the old business class" (Berger, "The Class Struggle in American Religion," *The Christian Century*, February 25, 1981, p. 197. Cf. his "From the Crisis of Religion to the Crisis of Secularity," p. 14 in this volume). If the knowledge class is "a new elite composed of those whose livelihood derives from the manipulation of symbols—intellectuals, educators, media people, members of the 'helping professions,' and a miscellany of planners and bureaucrats," then many conservative evangelical media people, educators, evangelists, pop psychologists, and so forth would seem to qualify admirably ("Class Struggle," p. 197). Manipulation of symbols has long been an evangelical forte. A simpler explanation for the conflict is preferable. The conflict is at root ideological, a version of avowed secularism versus a version of Christianity. Some secularists have championed a "new class" and helped create it; but they approve only of secularist manifestations of it. Berger's recognition of secularism as a "denomination" (in "From the Crisis of Religion to the Crisis of Secularity") would fit this interpretation but does not have to be tied to the sociological bias of reducing the ideas to the social functions they sometimes have.

[54]Many of these ministries were enhanced also by salting the Gospel with promises of personal success and healing, often by implication related to contributions to the ministry. Such themes have been relatively stronger among evangelists with pentecostal heritage or ties. Throughout much of evangelicalism, traditional themes of sin and judgment have been muted. This latter point is well documented in Hunter, "Contemporary American Evangelicalism," pp. 99-206.

[55]This point is suggested in Falwell, *The Fundamentalist Phenomenon*, p. 172, regarding the media advantage of fundamentalists versus "left-wing Evangelicalism."

[56]Rifkin and Howard, *Emerging Order*, p. 112.

EDWIN SCOTT GAUSTAD

Did the Fundamentalists Win?

IN JUNE OF 1922, Harry Emerson Fosdick gratified many and alarmed more when he preached a rousing sermon entitled "Shall the Fundamentalists Win?" The congregation of New York City's First Presbyterian Church and soon newspaper editors all across the nation recognized that a gauntlet had been thrown down, a line had been drawn, a *hier stehe ich* stand had been taken. And at no small cost to Fosdick himself. Treated with gravest suspicion where not actually villified, Fosdick found himself challenged in the next General Assembly of the Presbyterian Church. Continuing maneuver and uneasiness within the upper echelons of that denomination led Fosdick, ordained a Baptist, to accept an invitation to become pastor of the Park Avenue Baptist Church, eventually developing that institution into the famous Riverside Church. There Fosdick for many years attempted to define the position of liberal Protestantism and to bring about some mediation and conciliation. He had even dared to hope that his 1922 sermon would heal wounds rather than open them, but in that hope he had been sharply disappointed. "It was a plea for good will," he later wrote, "but what came of it was an explosion of ill will, for over two years making headline news of a controversy that went the limit of truculence. That trouble was, of course, that in stating the liberal and fundamentalist positions, I had stood in a Presbyterian pulpit and said frankly what the modernist position on some points was—the virgin birth no longer accepted as historic fact, the literal inerrancy of the Scriptures incredible, the second coming of Christ from the skies an outmoded phrasing of hope."[1]

Now two full generations after that sermon was preached (has any one paid as much attention to any sermon since?), it may be time to rephrase Fosdick's question in order to ask: *Did* the Fundamentalists win? To move in the direction of an answer, it is necessary to examine American religion in its cultural context at that time and to compare those circumstances with the current scene. How did Protestantism relate to and interact with other cultural forces earlier in the century and how does it do so now?

I

In the 1920s, and for some decades before, science had come into striking prominence as oracle of truth, molder of minds, and midwife of the future. As

169

geologist John Wesley Powell observed in 1898, the schools used to be "devoted to philosophy and disputation. But little by little the disciplines of science, when they could no longer be ignored, were introduced into the seats of learning." And from that time on, science spread to the point where "finally governments were enlisted in the work of research," while metaphysics, Powell added with ill-concealed relief, was relegated to a single year or even a single term in one's total educational experience.[2]

Charles Darwin and Herbert Spencer marched on to victory after victory as theologians, philosophers, social reformers, and military theorists enlisted in the ranks. Evolution was not God's rival, only his method. Science, moreover, was not to be argued with. The notion of evolution, Lyman Beecher reported, was being accepted "by a steadily increasing number of scientific men. I recognized that they were as honest as I, as eager to learn the truth, and much more intelligent than I was upon all scientific subjects."[3]

So the clergy could retreat from biology and geology to more proper spheres of sin and salvation, of human aspiration and universal ideals. But other sciences, more social and more personal, also rode on waves of the new authority. Men "more intelligent" in matters of guilt and innocence, of sickness and health, of urban evil and public repentance began to speak with authority, addressing subjects that had long been thought to be a ministerial preserve. Sigmund Freud might not have been heralded all over the Austro-Hungarian Empire, but his popularity in America was enormous and his voice was heard. Elwood Worcester, Episcopal founder of the Emmanuel Movement, wrote in 1908 that "we are surely safe in accepting . . . the weight of scientific opinion" in our own healing effort "to a field in which it is known to be efficacious."[4] Science was on the march, its blessings were manifold, its horizons were unlimited. Yet modern "religious man" at that time, liberal Protestant humankind, had nothing to fear and certainly nothing to criticize in this ebullient march toward a better life for all. One should trust those who know, yield to those "more intelligent."

Philosophy in this period was not really on the march, but it had not yet begun its large-scale retreat. Great questions, universal concerns, and human values still occupied the philosopher. And if moral philosophy was no longer what most college presidents taught to most students, and natural philosophy was no longer the context in which the physicist and chemist moved, the whole world was still kept in view. William James, trained in medicine, contributing clarity and definition to psychology, moved on to philosophy because that was where the really vital questions could be found. And James probed and tussled with those questions in such a way as to excite lawyers, doctors, students, housewives, clergymen, and practitioners of every art or of none. The strength of science lay in its power to predict and thereby shape the future. So it must also be with philosophy as it learned that the power of an idea, indeed the truth of an idea, lay in its potential, in its consequences. If there was no potential, if there were no consequences, then one was not discussing philosophy, only making humanoid noises. James did not thrust religion aside, but embraced it as an arena of human activity in which ideas clearly had consequences. Faith did move mountains.

If James was influenced in part by a Swedenborgian father, Josiah Royce was greatly swayed by a Protestant mother. Religion drove him to philosophy,

Royce reported, but philosophy did not pull him away from religion. Religious questions occupied Royce from his *Religious Aspect of Philosophy* (1885) through his *Problem of Christianity* (1913). And as philosopher he saw it as equally appropriate to unfold the mysteries of Pauline theology and to unpack the complexities of Hegelian philosophy. All this was not in the seventeenth century, much less in the midst of medieval scholasticism, but only two generations ago, when Fosdick saw an alliance with all learning as the cresting wave of the Protestant future.

From the time of the Renaissance, literary critique and analysis had been enlarging their scope and refining their tools. Such tools were applied first to long-standing papal claims (for example, the Donation of Constantine), thereby winning Protestant praise and emulation. So also the drive for a return to the sources, a scraping away of centuries of barnacled tradition, became the defining essence of Protestantism. By the nineteenth century, the techniques of this literary enterprise began to challenge the Protestant sources themselves. The Bible was not that rocklike foundation behind which or beneath which it was impossible to go. Much-scorned tradition, moreover, turned out to be responsible for the very canonization of sacred Scripture, as the early Church—long after the apostolic age—stumbled its way slowly to an "approved list." By that time who possessed the original holographs? Where was the authentic, official, infallible copy of the Gospel of Matthew? Of the New Testament? Of the entire Bible? Textual criticism in the nineteenth century turned from a light industry to a heavy one, but the literary critics had only begun. Having located the best text of Matthew (which, it turned out, was based on a collection of texts in various languages and with variant readings), they faced still tougher questions. How much did Matthew himself actually write, and when? How much had been modified, edited, revised, or mishandled?

"Higher criticism" ("was there ever such an unfortunate label?" Fosdick asked in 1924)[5] seemed to be dedicated not to securing the best Bible but to undermining the destiny of any Bible at all. The Bible had been the Protestant icon; now iconoclasts were everywhere. Yet it was still possible in 1922 to hold that such criticism was chiefly constructive, that Christianity ended up both purer and stronger, and that one's faith was firmer than before. As the devout Joseph LeConte explained to his science students, Christianity, unlike other religions, emerges from every intellectual contest the victor, for Christianity "loves the light, seeks the light, lives in the light; it loves the truth, seeks the truth, lives in the truth; its Divine founder was both light and truth."[6] What then had liberal Protestantism to fear from biblical critics who first removed Tradition in order to find Scripture, then removed Scripture in order to find Truth?

Finally, the early decades of the twentieth century saw the discipline of history move from the desks of the amateur—if skilled—storytellers to the swollen ranks of the professional, even "scientific," historians. Everything had a history, even dogma, as the German Protestant Adolph Harnack had shown. Very little, if anything, was "the same yesterday, today, and forever." Very little, if anything, had been believed "by all men, always, everywhere." Very little, if anything, escaped the captivity of its own culture, the relativity of its own terminology, the perceptual limitations of its own advocates. Thus historians wrote of the *Evolution of Religion* (1893), of the *Origin and Growth of the Moral Instinct* (1898), of *A Sketch of Semitic Origins* (1902), of *Christian Origins* (1906), of the *Origin and Development of Moral Ideas* (1908), of the *Origin and Evolution of Religion* (1923), of *The Birth and Growth of Religion* (1923), and many, many more such topics.

To liberal Protestants in the first quarter of the twentieth century, history nonetheless seemed more ally than enemy. For if all that "growth" and "development" can be found in the past, one has every reason to expect—and work for—even more development and fulfillment in the future. The Kingdom of God was just around the corner, not a cosmic concept of vague and distant attraction, but a call to men and women to labor as they pray, to look with confidence to what the morrow may bring. "The modern age," Arthur Cusman McGiffert wrote in 1909, "is marked by a vast confidence in the powers of man." And history "has given us new insight into the origin and growth of Christianity." This insight is that the Kingdom of God was "not a kingdom made up of isolated human lives moving along their several and separate paths toward heaven, but of the society of all humankind banded together in common labour under the control of a common purpose." It was the right time to be alive, for we "are on the eve of great happenings. No one familiar with history . . . can for a moment doubt it."[7] What then was there to fear from history, as there had been nothing to fear from science or philosophy or the literary craft. No wonder, given that comforting alliance, that Harry Emerson Fosdick, in distinguishing the liberals from the fundamentalists, could conclude that his fellow liberals were "intellectually hospitable, open-minded, liberty-loving, fair, tolerant" with "always our major emphasis . . . upon the weightier matters of the law."[8]

II

The problem is that liberal Protestantism's comfortable cultural alliance ceased to be comfortable and ceased to be an alliance. The liberals may have chosen the wrong partners. Placing their faith in progress, reason, and the innate goodness of humankind,[9] a sensible choice in 1922, liberal Protestants suffered one disappointment after another. Not only did their allies fail to triumph in the cultural conflicts that followed a generation or two later, some of them seemed to forget where the lines of conflict were drawn and whose side they were on. The liberals had forged a firm alliance to prepare for McGiffert's "great happenings." On the way to the future, strange things happened.

Seven years after Fosdick's sermon, America's economic world had collapsed and much of its moral world as well. Two 1929 critiques of America's modernity sounded a tone strikingly different from that of Fosdick: Walter Lippmann's *Preface to Morals* and Joseph Wood Krutch's *The Modern Temper*. Both Lippmann and Krutch saw those natural allies of liberal Protestantism in a far less favorable light; both also viewed liberal Protestantism itself (or Christianity in any form, for that matter) in a quite unfavorable light. Old loyalties had snapped, old assumptions had gone down fighting, old values and institutions had crumbled. The Kingdom of God, moreover, was nowhere in sight. America's social fabric was being dissolved in the acids of modernity, declared

Lippmann. But just a few years before, modernity had seemed a good thing, an emancipator and purifier. And now not the fundamentalists but the humanists were taking dead aim at what the modern world had to offer. Religion had not gained authority and respect but had lost both; people, having "lost their belief in a heavenly king," now had to "find some other ground for their moral choices."[10] And the science that John Wesley Powell and others had held up so confidently a generation earlier as the one sure guide turned out to be no guide at all. Krutch noted: "We are disillusioned with the laboratory, not because we have lost faith in the truth of its findings, but because we have lost faith in the power of those findings to help us as generally as we had once hoped they might."[11]

So one turned to philosophy for succor. But the nation's dominant philosopher, John Dewey, gave to the religious seeker answers that were emotionally, intellectually, and spiritually unsatisfying. Though Dewey made the universe open-ended and therefore replete with possibility, that very openness and indefiniteness brought more dismay than direction. When Dewey in 1934 dealt directly with religion, he used the language of faith; it turned out, however, to be "faith in the possibilities of continued and rigorous inquiry . . . faith in intelligence."[12] What Dewey called for was a faith in reason. What reason, then, for faith? To be sure, the days of the historic religions were over, Dewey concluded, and "religion" as a noun was no longer useful. But "religious" as an adjective could still be functional, assisting us in constructing our "common faith" wherein we adopt a religious attitude "toward every object and every proposed end or ideal." "Free from all historic encumbrances" and "from matters that are continually becoming more dubious," religion survives as a faith in the power of the ideal.[13] Dewey's "reconstruction in philosophy," the last comprehensive philosophical vision for American society, found readier alliances with education, art, and politics than with religion. Liberal Protestantism (Dewey's own heritage), thinking back to the warming words of a James or a Royce, found only cold comfort in Dewey's instrumentalism. And after Dewey, the philosophers turned away from discussions of the problems of men—against Dewey's example—to return to a discussion of the problems only of philosophers.

Biblical critics in Fosdick's day and well before repeatedly explained how their criticism aided the churches and improved Christian life. Or, if on occasion it was not a positive benefit, it certainly did no real harm. Criticism never threatened those "weightier matters of the law" of which Fosdick had spoken. When Charles Augustus Briggs defended himself before the Presbytery of New York in 1892, he explained that any errors he discovered in the Bible had been minor, trivial, and nonessential to faith and order. It was therefore quite possible to "hold that Holy Scripture is 'the only rule of faith and practice' and yet hold that there are errors in Holy Scripture in matters that do not in any way impair its infallibility in matters of faith and practice."[14]

Critics showed themselves to be loyal church members, good parents, responsible citizens, sensitive teachers—demonstrating thereby that from literary analysis of even the Bible liberal Protestantism had nothing to fear. But the days of heresy trials ended, the church control of universities weakened, and the wariness or concern of denominational officialdom diminished. As a result, while the biblical critic might retain all of those virtues noted above, it was no longer necessary to demonstrate them constantly. Nor was it necessary to show, every step along the way, just how criticism strengthened the visible institutions of Protestantism and added richness to the lives of the members of those institutions. The further result was that biblical criticism became increasingly an academic matter, ingrown, jargon-laden, esoteric, and aloof. Only occasionally, as with the translation and publication of the Revised Standard Version in the 1940s and 1950s, were sustained efforts made to keep lines of communication fully open between the ecclesiastical and the scholarly communities. On many an earlier occasion church leaders had defended the right of scholars to pursue their linguistic and literary tasks. Now they found such scholars largely indifferent to the needs and crises within the church. Another alliance collapsed.

The problems in the discipline of history were simply those of too much stiff competition, in both the university and the seminary. In the university, the emphases of progressivism and Marxism turned attention away from religion to politics and economics. Later the role of ideas and institutions yielded to the microcosm of localities and private lists. In the seminary, church history had to justify itself against new disciplines and demands, against the well-known if imperfectly understood information explosion. Psychology, sociology, finance, and management crowded the curriculum. Beyond all that, however, history just didn't hold the same charm that it did when the church was triumphant. History no longer suggested that liberal Protestantism stood at the threshold of a great new day. It seemed to stand at the beginning of a long narrow passageway where the light grew dimmer and the outlets fewer as one walked along.

In the first generation after Fosdick's homiletic query, from 1922 to 1952, it was not yet clear who among America's Protestants might be "winning." The Depression and World War II made large demands and constituted all-absorbing distractions. Moreover, a case could be made that in this period everyone was winning: Churches were growing, members were giving, religious publishing and programming were thriving. The liberals, with the strong voices of the Niebuhr brothers and of Paul Tillich, still won notice in the national press and Protestant theology still seemed a relevant enterprise. True, some groups—notably Northern Presbyterians and Northern Baptists—continued to be trapped in internecine struggles and each, from time to time, was bled by further fundamentalist schism and separation. But Methodists managed in 1939 to reunite northern and southern branches divided for nearly a century. Congregationalists in 1931 merged with the smaller General Convention of the Christian Church, while Lutherans in this period began reversing their long-standing pattern of ethnic and national separation. Episcopalians, momentarily diverted in the first decade of this century by the heresy trial of Algernon S. Crapsey, returned to a flexible and mediating stance. So it was not until the second generation after the Fosdick sermon, from 1952 to 1982, that evidence of fundamentalist victory began to accumulate.

III

What is the case for liberal "slippage" in the last thirty years? A minor point is the use of the word *liberal* itself. Only Unitarians and Universalists grant it official status, but few others would embrace it as boldly, as proudly, as defiantly as Fosdick did. And *modernist* now has a quaintly dated, curiously unmodern sound. The preferred language of the inheritors of the Fosdick mantle is *mainline, mainstream, established,* or even (as turn-of-the-century liberals groan in their graves) *traditional.* In addition to not being fundamentalist, mainstream churches are neither "fringe" nor "marginal," neither "new" nor "sect-like," and tend to have in their name neither "orthodox" nor "Bible." They may, of course, be "evangelical," which is only to say that all Protestants do not divide neatly into "liberal" and "fundamentalist" halves. Yet when liberal Protestantism declines, fundamentalism rises, as one hears and reads more of virgin birth and bodily resurrection, more of vicarious atonement and visible Second Coming, and much more of biblical inerrancy and scriptural infallibility.[15]

How does liberal Protestantism fare in these latter years? The answer, coming from many sides, is "not well."[16] In 1920 one could speak of unfailing progress, of refined theology, of building programs, and of glorious destiny. Hymns now being lined out are set in a different key.

Progress has not smiled lately upon many areas: economic development, international relations, political integrity, moral responsibility, and more. But for liberal Protestants the frown on the face of progress is more personal than that: mainline churches have themselves ceased to make progress, and several have suffered steady decline. Apart from the inescapable statistical data is the widespread perception that their influence and impact have also dropped. Whose voices are heard in national affairs? Where are the Beechers, Abbotts, Coffins, and Fosdicks of yesteryear, or the Niebuhrs and Tillichs of yesterday? (Billy Graham's voice is heard, but it would not seem fair to claim him for liberal Protestantism.) It might be argued that one no longer hears those voices because this is no longer a Protestant nation. Yet a vocal and visible Protestant Right suggests that it is not mere pluralism that has softened or silenced the pulpits of the Fosdick tradition.

Liberal Protestantism emerged from World War II in good shape, as did American religion generally. The war had been a national effort with—one says from the perspective of the 1980s—a remarkable degree of unity of effort and will. Pacifism aside, few theological lines could be drawn to distinguish between Protestant efforts during the war or the many repairs to body and spirit undertaken after the war. In the cold war, however, lines were drawn. Liberals of all kinds found themselves accused of being sympathetic to communism, duped by communism, or even converted to communism. Liberal churches and liberal church leaders made convenient targets in the McCarthy era, sometimes even welcome targets. Socially and politically active, compulsive joiners and signers, frequent speakers and writers, liberal ministers were suddenly called upon to prove their orthodoxy; this time, however, the orthodoxy was political, not theological. The National Council of Churches, bastion of mainline Protestantism, was thrown on the defensive as governmental agencies and bureaucracies looked with jaundiced eye—for the first time in the nation's history—upon the Protestant establishment.

Surviving that ego-bruising period, liberal Protestantism, already in some disarray, plunged into the sixties. Then everything seemed to happen: authority questioned or defied, establishment religion treated with coolness or disdain, society shaken, and churches wracked. Theology in this decade took either a back seat or a wrong turn. The back seat was taken with respect to civil rights, Vatican II, and Vietnam. The civil rights movement absorbed the energies and attention of great numbers of the clergy, even as it disturbed or alienated great numbers of the laity. Interested Protestant observers took their seats at that greatest church council since Trent, noting that Roman Catholicism was making its peace with modernity even though many in the Curia cared for it no more in the 1960s than had their predecessors in the 1860s. Vietnam aggravated every social division while it raised questions of patriotism and loyalty once more in the liberal ranks.

The theological wrong turn concerned the death of God. To many already on their way to thorough disillusionment with modernity, this announcement seemed the ultimate capitulation. One could imagine the solid ranks of fundamentalism drawn up, preparing to accept liberalism's sword of surrender. Could it be that Dewey was right after all? In this new age, Dewey had written in 1934, "whenever a particular outpost is surrendered it is usually met by the remark from a liberal theologian that the particular doctrine or supposed historic or literary tenet was never, after all, an intrinsic part of religious belief, and that without it the true nature of religion stands out more clearly than before." Dewey went on to speak of "the growing gulf between fundamentalists and liberals," with the former being much more consistent methodologically while the liberals tried to keep their faith and disbelieve it too. "The positive lesson is that religious qualities and values if they are real at all are not bound up with any single item of intellectual assent, not even that of the existence of the God of theism."[17] The death of God, however explained or explained away, was a "positive lesson" for which few in the pews were ready.

In the 1970s the accumulation of guilt grew too heavy to bear. Much was wrong with American society; much was unlovely in the American past. Had Protestantism been so closely identified with the nation's culture, so involved in its major moral decisions, that all ills and hypocrisies could properly be charged to its account? The treatment of the Indian, the development of slavery, the exploitation of the environment, the inequities of class, race, and gender, the nativism and the anti-Semitism, the moralism and "social control," the imperialism and colonialism—were all these integral parts of that Protestant empire once envisioned? WASP had become a four-letter word, and liberal Protestant leaders were obliged to admit that they were indeed mostly white, mostly Anglo-Saxon (or Teutonic, if that helped at all), and indubitably Protestant. They were also mostly male and middle class. Even in the midst of civil rights efforts on behalf of the blacks, "White Christian Churches . . . and All Other Racist Institutions" were assaulted in 1969 by a black manifesto that demanded repentance and reparation. The WASP-ness of liberal Protestantism had somehow become akin to the racial and religious attitudes of the Ku Klux Klan. Traditional Protestant morality was dismissed as bourgeois, patronizing, and obsolete. Protestantism's habitual involvement in social and political affairs was characterized as elitist and patriarchal. Its maleness was chauvinistic and exploitative. All that guilt eroded self-confidence and left leadership flaccid.

If and when a liberal Protestant did lift his or her voice in the early 1980s, it was with little assurance that anyone was listening. Such Protestants did not appear to be determining destinies in this world or the next. What in American society would be left undone, what vacuum in private life left unfilled, if liberal Protestantism were suddenly to disappear? Any unfinished business could be quickly polished off by a presidential commission or the community chest.

One asks how this sorry state may be amended. What is really needed is a new cultural alliance. Such old allies as philosophy, science, history, and literary criticism must tilt not in the direction of liberal Protestantism alone, to be sure, but in the direction of any and all religion that is morally sensitive and intellectually responsible, that enhances and enriches life, neither degrading nor impoverishing it.

Meanwhile, in these last thirty years, fundamentalism has scored many successes and may stand on the verge of many more. The airwaves are filled, and the coffers too, with radio and television versions of fundamentalism. Publishing houses, bookstores, and best-seller lists testify to its power. Apocalyptic millennialism is in; patient labor for the Kingdom of God is out. Bible colleges are now matched by Bible schools, both assuring that all humanism (and by definition all humanism is "secular humanism") is avoided, all cultural heterodoxy denied. What is left of public education, moreover, must again and again face the demands (presidential and otherwise) for the intrusion of religion into the curriculum ("creationism") and into the school day ("voluntary group prayer"). Theological fundamentalism is buttressed by political fundamentalism in these demands, as in other stances taken by Moral Majorities, Christian Voices, and the like. Mainline denominations, such as Missouri Synod Lutherans and Southern Baptists, suffer new stresses and schisms. The ordination of women, the adoption of a new prayer book, the revision of an old creed—each became an apt moment for the flexing of fundamentalist muscle. "Back to Basics" is a book title, campaign slogan, and battle cry; it makes little difference whether the topic is education, economics, family life, or religion. In 1925, three years after the Fosdick sermon, it all looked so different in Dayton, Tennessee. Then Henry Mencken and Clarence Darrow were heroes to nearly everyone, and John Scopes a young martyr, except for that easy-to-ridicule, disappearing rural fringe that clung to William Jennings Bryan as the dying Moses of a shrinking remnant. In the 1980s, however, Dayton is the new Jerusalem.

So who won? What did Harry Emerson Fosdick mean by "winning"? At a minimum, he no doubt hoped that denominational boards, journals, colleges, and seminaries would not be handed over to the fundamentalist side by default, that liberals would not roll over and play dead or concede until they had no turf left to defend. But he was also concerned, more broadly and deeply, with the nature of Christianity itself: that his religion not be robbed of all poetry and subtlety, that it not be reduced to the prosaic and propositional. Fosdick knew that "dogmatism in theology, whether 'liberal' or 'orthodox' is ridiculous." Theological formulations are always partial and cloudy. "To take the best insights of them all, to see the incompleteness and falsity in them all, to trust none of them as a whole, to see always that the Reality to be explained is infinitely greater than our tentative, conditioned explanations—that seems to me wisdom."[18]

Over one hundred years ago, another Protestant theologian, Horace Bushnell, declared "Our Gospel a Gift to the Imagination" and Christ the metaphor of God. The truths of religion, he wrote, are "lively, full, fresh, free," but we insist on making out of them procrustean propositions and "scientific" definitions. "Before they were plants alive and in flower; now the flavors are gone, the juices dried, and the skeleton parts packed away in the dry herbarium called theology."[19] Fosdick, like Bushnell, had little use for herbariums.

Did the fundamentalists win? If one is still not quite ready to answer that question, then a somewhat easier one may be put: Did liberal Protestantism lose? So phrased, this query permits us to array alongside fundamentalism all the Protestant catechizers and positive thinkers, all the semi-Protestant New Thought-ers and prosperity promisers, all the personality cultists and conservative majorities, together with the turned off, dropped out, disenchanted, and otherwise engaged. Now we're ready: Did liberal Protestantism lose? Yes. This round.

REFERENCES
[1]Harry Emerson Fosdick, *The Living of These Days* (New York: Harper & Brothers, 1956), pp. 145-46.
[2]*Monist*, VIII (1898), p. 203.
[3]Lyman Beecher, *Reminiscences* (Boston: Houghton, Mifflin & Co., 1915), p. 458.
[4]Elwood Worcester et al., *Religion and Medicine* (New York: Moffat Yard and Co., 1908), p. 5.
[5]Harry Emerson Fosdick, *The Modern Use of the Bible* (New York: Association Press, 1924), p. 6.
[6]Joseph LeConte, *Religion and Science* (New York: D. Appleton & Co., 1874), p. 229.
[7]Quoted in H. Shelton Smith et al., *American Christianity: Interpretation and Documents*, II (New York: Charles Scribner's Sons, 1963), pp. 286, 287, 290.
[8]Ibid., p. 301.
[9]For the best full discussion of modernism, see William R. Hutchison, *The Modernist Impulse in American Protestantism* (Cambridge: Harvard University Press, 1976). Hutchison prevents the term *modernism* from being hopelessly slippery by identifying three persisting elements: a conscious adaptation of religious ideas to modern culture, a belief in the immanence of God in human nature and cultural development, and an optimistic assumption that society is headed for a Kingdom of God on earth.
[10]Walter Lippmann, *Preface to Morals* (New York: Macmillan & Co., 1929), p. 137.
[11]Joseph Wood Krutch, *The Modern Temper* (New York: Harcourt, Brace & Co., 1929), p. 58.
[12]John Dewey, *A Common Faith* (New Haven: Yale University Press, 1934), p. 26.
[13]Ibid., pp. 6, 10, 44.
[14]Charles A. Briggs, *The Defence of Professor Briggs before the Presbytery of New York* (New York: Charles Scribner's Sons, 1893), p. 91.
[15]No attempt is made here to describe the wide variety within fundamentalism in America; see the excellent treatments by Ernest Sandeen, *The Roots of Fundamentalism* (Chicago: University of Chicago Press, 1970), and George Marsden, *Fundamentalism and American Culture* (New York: Oxford University Press, 1980).
[16]See, for example, Dean Kelly, *Why Conservative Churches Are Growing* (New York: Harper & Row, 1972, 1977); Dean R. Hoge and David A. Roozen, eds., *Understanding Church Growth and Decline 1950–1978* (New York: Pilgrim Press, 1979); and recent *Yearbooks of the American Churches*.
[17]Dewey, *Common Faith*, p. 32.
[18]Fosdick, *Living*, pp. 231, 232.
[19]Horace Bushnell, "Our Gospel a Gift to the Imagination," *Hours at Home*, 10 (December, 1869), 168.

RICHARD P. MCBRIEN

Roman Catholicism: *E Pluribus Unum*

THIS IS NOT AN ORDINARY HISTORICAL MOMENT for Roman Catholicism. For the first time since the Middle Ages the Church has a non-Italian pope; for the first time since the Middle Ages there has been a direct attempt on a pope's life. Not since 1605 had the papacy changed hands twice in a single year. But it happened again in 1978.

There are other, more serious (if less dramatic) symptoms of crisis in contemporary Roman Catholicism: the sharp decline in attendance at mass and in vocations to the priesthood and the religious life; the higher incidence among Catholics of divorce and remarriage; the widening of theological dissent (the Hans Küng and Edward Schillebeeckx cases, for example); diversity and pluralism to the point of confusion and doubt in theology, catechetics, and religious education generally; the rejection of papal authority in the matter of birth control, and resistance to that authority on other issues such as the ordination of women and priestly celibacy; the ecumenical movement's indirect challenge to Catholic identity and distinctiveness; the alienation of young people from the Church; the abiding social and cultural dominance of science and technology, with its correlative impact upon traditional spiritual values and motivation; the continuing and inevitable involvement of the Church on both sides of the historic struggle between rich and poor, oppressor and oppressed; the raised consciousness and increased activism of women in the Church.[1]

These developments, taken singly, wholly, or in cluster, have prompted many observers inside and outside the Catholic Church to conclude that Catholicism as a distinctive form and expression of Christianity is in process of such radical transformation, that little of its original core will survive. This essay takes direct issue with that kind of judgment. Roman Catholicism has simply entered the modern world (in the sense in which Peter Berger defines and describes modernity in *The Heretical Imperative*[2]), and that world is an inherently pluralistic one. As the Second Vatican Council insisted in its Pastoral Constitution on the Church in the Modern World *(Gaudium et spes)*, the Church is itself a part of this pluralistic world, and not something over against the world. The very title of the conciliar document defines this relationship. It is deliberately called "Pastoral Constitution on the Church *in* the Modern World," not "*and* the Modern World." And just as the world is pluralistic in character, so too is the Catholic Church. There is a significant difference between the papal style and policies of Pius IX and John XXIII; between the organizational models adopted by the Catholic Church in Australia and the Catholic Church in the Netherlands; between the theological approaches of Edward Schillebeeckx and Jean Galot (one of Schillebeeckx's inquisitors in Rome); between the liturgical practices in many English parishes and those of many American congregations; between the devotional life of African Catholics and those of Irish Catholics, and so forth.

Those who take seriously the American motto, *E Pluribus Unum*, know that pluralism and unity are not incompatible values. Pluralism does not imply the mere coexistence of antagonistic world views, movements, and groups. To be sure, what we have here is the classical philosophical problem of "the one and the many." And Christians have always answered that problem with an equally classical principle enunciated by St. Paul: "For just as the body is one and has many members, and all the members of the body, though many, are one body, so it is with Christ. For by one Spirit we were all baptized into one body—Jews or Greeks, slaves or free—and all were made to drink of one Spirit" (1 Corinthians 12:12-13).

The purpose of this essay is not to describe the contemporary crisis in Roman Catholicism more fully than I have already done, much less to explain it. This is a theological, not sociological, analysis. I intend, rather, to identify its theological core to assist the reader in understanding what Roman Catholicism is, in light of, and perhaps also in spite of, the diversity one perceives within it, within the larger community of Christian churches, and within the wider network of religions and movements worldwide.

Catholicism is not a reality that stands in solitary splendor. The word "Catholic" is not only a noun but an adjective. As an adjective, it modifies the noun "Christian." The word Christian, too, is both a noun and an adjective. As an adjective, it modifies "religious." The word religious also functions as an adjective and a noun. As an adjective, it modifies the word "human." Thus the Catholic Church is a community of persons (the fundamentally *human* foundation of Catholic identity) that believes in, and is committed to, the reality of God, and shapes its life according to that belief and in fidelity to that commitment (the *religious* component of Catholicism). The Church's belief in, and commitment to, the reality of God is focused in its fundamental attitude toward Jesus Christ (the *Christian* core). For the Catholic, as for every Christian, the old order has passed away, and we are a "new creation" in Christ, for God has "reconciled us to Himself through Christ" (2 Corinthians 5:17, 19). Catholic, therefore, is a qualification of Christian, of religious, and of the human. To be Catholic is to be a kind of human being, a kind of religious person, and a kind of Christian.

To be Catholic is, before all else, to be human. Catholicism is an understanding and affirmation of human existence before it is a corporate conviction about the pope, or the seven sacraments, or even about Jesus Christ. But Catholicism is also more than a corporate understanding and affirmation of what it means to be human. Catholicism answers the question of meaning in terms of ultimacy. With Dietrich Bonhoeffer, Catholicism affirms that there is more to life than meets the eye, that there is "a beyond in our midst." With Paul Tillich, Catholicism affirms that there is a ground of all being which is Being itself. With Thomas Aquinas, Catholicism affirms that all reality is rooted in the creative, loving power of that which is most real *(ens realissimum)*. Catholicism answers the question of meaning in terms of the reality of God. In brief, Catholicism is a religious perspective, and not simply a philosophical or an anthropological one.

But Catholicism is not some undifferentiated religious view. Catholicism's view of, and commitment to, God is radically shaped by its view of, and commitment to, Jesus Christ. For the Christian, the ultimate dimension of human experience is a triune God: a God who creates and sustains us, a God who draws near to us and identifies with our historical condition, and a God who empowers us to live according to the vocation to which we have been called. More specifically, the God of Christians is the God of Jesus Christ.

But just as Jesus Christ gives access to God, so, for the Catholic, the Church gives access to Jesus Christ. But the Church itself is composed of many churches. The Church universal is the communion of local churches, and the Body of Christ is composed of denominations (for want of a better term). Thus the noun church is always modified: the Catholic Church, the Methodist Church, the Orthodox Church, the Lutheran Church, and so forth. Moreover, even these modifiers can themselves be modified: the Lutheran Church, Missouri Synod; the Lutheran Church of America; the American Lutheran Church; and so forth.

There are many churches, but one Body of Christ. Within the community of churches, however, there is one Church that alone embodies and manifests all the institutional elements that are necessary for the integrity of the whole Body. In Catholic doctrine and theology, that one Church is the Catholic Church. As ecumenical as the Second Vatican Council certainly was, it did not retreat from the fundamental Catholic conviction:

> They are fully incorporated into the society of the Church who, possessing the Spirit of Christ, accept her entire system and all the means of salvation given to her, and through union with her visible structure are joined to Christ, who rules her through the Supreme Pontiff and the Bishops. This joining is effected by the bonds of professed faith, of the sacraments, of ecclesiastical government, and of communion.[3]

But much has happened since that council to suggest that the traditional lines of distinction have been blurred. Is it really so easy to tell the difference between a Roman Catholic and an Anglican, for example? Is it not becoming increasingly evident that there are sometimes sharper divisions *within* the Roman Catholic Church than there are between certain Catholics and certain Protestants? Anyone who reads the Catholic press in the United States might legitimately wonder if the editors and readers of *The Wanderer* and the *National Catholic Reporter* belong to the same Church.

Not so many years ago Catholics of both liberal and conservative orientations would have fundamentally agreed on where that line should be drawn. In the most influential book written just prior to the Second Vatican Council, the now-celebrated Swiss theologian Hans Küng wrote that

> the chief difficulty in the way of reunion lies in the two different concepts of the Church, and especially of the concrete organizational structure of the Church. . . . Ultimately all questions about the concrete organizational structure of the Church

are crystallized in the question of *ecclesiastical office.* . . . But the heart of the matter of ecclesiastical office, the great stone of stumbling, is the Petrine office. The question "Do we need a Pope?" is the key question for reunion.[4]

I shared Küng's view in a piece written in 1975:

> What finally differentiates Roman Catholics from all other Christians is in the realm of ecclesiastical order. Roman Catholics alone are committed to the papacy as a necessary and indispensible office within the Church. The Pope, by the will of Christ, exercises the Petrine ministry of supervision for the whole Church. . . . The papacy may not be the most important element in the Church . . . , but Roman Catholics are committed to the view that the Church cannot fully be the Church without the Pope. . . . *The* ecumenical question which still divides Roman Catholics from all other Christians is the question of ecclesiastical office. Authority, infallibility, apostolic succession, and the like, are but component parts of that issue.[5]

I am persuaded that, in spite of the distinctiveness of the Catholic claims for the papal office, Catholic identity is rooted in much broader and richer theological values. Indeed, it is not beyond the range of possibility that Roman Catholics and other Christians may soon reach basic agreement on this most controversial of issues. The Lutheran-Roman Catholic Consultation in the United States, for example, has achieved a remarkable measure of consensus already on the question of papal primacy.[6] Therefore, a more fruitful, and more theologically and historically nuanced, approach to the question of Catholic distinctiveness would seem to lie in the direction of identifying and describing various characteristics of Catholicism, each of which Catholicism shares with one or another Christian church or tradition. But no other tradition possesses these characteristics in the same way as Catholicism. In other words, there is a configuration of characteristics within Catholicism that is not duplicated anywhere else in the community of Christian churches. This configuration of characteristics is expressed in Catholicism's systematic theology; its body of doctrines; its liturgical life, especially its Eucharist; its variety of spiritualities; its religious congregations and lay apostolates; its official teachings on justice, peace, and human rights; its exercise of collegiality; and, to be sure, its Petrine ministry.

Roman Catholicism is distinguished from other Christian traditions and churches in its understanding of, commitment to, and exercise of, the principles of sacramentality, mediation, and communion. Differences between Catholic and non-Catholic (especially Protestant) approaches become clearer when measured according to these three principles.[7]

Sacramentality—In its classical (Augustinian) meaning, a sacrament is a visible sign of an invisible grace. The late Pope Paul VI provided a more contemporary definition: "a reality imbued with the hidden presence of God." A sacramental perspective is one that "sees" the divine in the human, the infinite in the finite, the spiritual in the material, the transcendent in the immanent, the eternal in the historical.

Over against this sacramental vision is the view, strengthened by memories of past excesses in the sacramental vision, that God is so "totally other," that the divine reality can never be identified with the human, the transcendent with the immanent, the eternal with the historical, and so forth. The abiding Protestant fear is that Catholics take the sacramental principle to the point where we are just short of, if not fully immersed in, idolatry.

The Catholic sacramental vision "sees" God in and through all things: other people, communities, movements, events, places, objects, the world at large, the whole cosmos. The visible, the tangible, the finite, the historical—all these are actual or potential carriers of the divine presence. Indeed, for the Catholic, it is only in and through these material realities that we can even encounter the invisible God. The great sacrament of our encounter with God, and of God's encounter with us, is Jesus Christ. The Church, in turn, is the key sacrament of our encounter with Christ, and of Christ with us; and the sacraments, in turn, are the signs and instruments by which that ecclesial encounter with Christ is expressed, celebrated, and made effective for the glory of God and the salvation of men and women.

The Catholic, therefore, insists that grace (the divine presence) actually enters into and transforms nature (human life in its fullest context). The dichotomy between nature and grace is eliminated. Human existence is already graced existence. There is no merely natural end of human existence, with a supernatural end imposed from above. Human existence in its natural, historical condition is radically oriented toward God. The history of the world is, at the same time, the history of salvation.

This means, for the Catholic, that authentic human progress and the struggle for justice, peace, freedom, human rights, and so forth, is part of the movement of and toward the Kingdom of God (Vatican II, Pastoral Constitution on the Church in the Modern World, n. 39). The Catholic, unlike Luther, espouses no doctrine of the Two Kingdoms. The vast body of Catholic social doctrine, from Pope Leo XIII in 1891 to Pope John Paul II today, is as characteristic of Catholic Christianity as any element can be. In virtue of the sacramental principle, Catholics affirm that God is indeed present to all human life and to history. To be involved in the transformation of the world is to be collaboratively involved in God's own revolutionary and transforming activity.

For the Catholic, the world is essentially good, though fallen, because it comes from the creative hand of God. And for the Catholic, the world, although fallen, is redeemable because of the redemptive work of God in Jesus Christ. And for the Catholic, the world, although fractured and fragmented, is capable of ultimate unity because of the abiding presence of the Holy Spirit, who is the "first fruits" of the final Kingdom of God.

Mediation—A kind of corollary of the principle of sacramentality is the principle of mediation. A sacrament not only signifies; it also causes what it signifies. Indeed, as the Council of Trent officially taught, sacraments cause grace precisely insofar as they signify it. If the Church, therefore, is not a credible sign of God's and Christ's presence in the world, if the Church is not obviously the "temple of the Holy Spirit," it cannot achieve its missionary purposes. It "causes" grace (i.e., effectively moves the world toward its final destiny in the Kingdom of God) to the extent that it signifies the reality toward which it presumes to direct the world.

On the other hand, sacraments are not only signs of faith, as Protestants affirmed at the time of the Reformation. For the Catholic, God is not only present in the sacramental action; God actually achieves something in and through that action. Thus created realities not only contain, reflect, or embody the presence of God, they make that presence effective for those who avail themselves of these realities. Encounter with God does not occur solely in the inwardness of conscience or in the inner recesses of consciousness. Catholicism holds, on the contrary, that the encounter with God is a mediated experience, rooted in the historical, and affirmed as real by the critical judgment that God is truly present and active here or there, in this event or that, in this person or that, in this object or that.

Again, the Protestant raises a word of caution. Just as the principle of sacramentality edges close to the brink of idolatry, so the principle of mediation moves one along the path toward magic. Just as there has been evidence of idolatry in some Roman Catholic piety, so there has been evidence of a magical view of the divine-human encounter in certain forms of Catholic devotional life. Some Catholics have assumed that if a certain practice were performed a given number of times in an unbroken sequence, their salvation would be guaranteed. A magical world view, of course, is not a solely Catholic problem, but it is an inherent risk in Catholicism's constant stress on the principle of mediation.

Catholicism's commitment to the principle of mediation is evident, for example, in the importance it has always placed on the ordained ministry of the priest. God's dealings with us are not arbitrary or haphazard. God is present to all and works on behalf of all, but there are also moments and actions wherein God's presence is specially focused. The function of the priest, as mediator, is not to limit the encounter between God and the human person, but to focus it more clearly for the sake of the person, and ultimately for the community at large.

The principle of mediation also explains Catholicism's historic emphasis on the place of Mary, the mother of Jesus Christ. The Catholic accepts the role of Mary in salvation on the same ground that the Catholic accepts the role of Jesus Christ. God is present in, and redemptively works through, the humanity of Jesus. This is the principle of mediation in its classic expression. The Catholic understands that the invisible, spiritual God is present and available to us through the visible and the material, and that these are made holy by reason of that divine presence. The Catholic, therefore, readily engages in the veneration (not worship) of Mary, not because Catholicism perceives Mary as some kind of goddess or supercreature or rival of the Lord himself, but because she is a symbol or image of God. It is the God who is present in her and who fills her whole being that the Catholic grasps in the act of venerating yet another "sacrament" of the divine.[8]

Communion—Finally, Catholicism affirms the principle of communion: our way to God, and God's way to us, is not only a mediated, but a communal way. Even when the divine-human encounter is most personal and individual, it is still communal, in that the encounter is made possible by the mediation of a community of faith. Thus there is not simply an individual personal relationship with God or Jesus Christ that is established and sustained by meditative reflection on sacred scripture, for the Bible itself is the Church's book and the testimony of the Church's original faith. There is no relationship with God, however intense, profound, or unique, that dispenses entirely with the communal context of every relationship with God.

And this is why, for Catholicism, the mystery of the Church has always had so significant a place in its theology, doctrine, pastoral practice, moral vision, and devotion. Catholics have always emphasized the place of the Church as the sacrament of Christ, which mediates salvation through sacraments, ministries, and other institutional elements and forms, and as the Communion of Saints and the People of God. It is here, at the point of Catholicism's understanding of itself as Church, that we come to the heart of the distinctively Catholic understanding and practice of Christian faith. For here, in Catholic ecclesiology, we find the convergence of those three principles that have always been so characteristic of Catholicism: sacramentality, mediation, and communion.

The Protestant again raises a word of caution. If we emphasize too much the principle of communion, do we not endanger the freedom of individuals? If sacramentality can lead to idolatry, and mediation to magic, the principle of communion can lead to a collectivism that suppresses individuality, and an authoritarianism that suppresses freedom of thought. One can find many instances in history where the Protestant concern has been justified. Church members have been burned at the stake, literally and figuratively, for articulating opinions at variance with those of the Church's ruling class.

But stress on the individual also has its inherent weakness, just as there are inherent weaknesses in the historic Protestant insistences on the otherness of God (over against the Catholic sacramental principle) and on the immediacy of the divine-human encounter (over against the Catholic principle of mediation). In recent years, in fact, some important Protestant theologians have come to acknowledge these inherent problems in Protestantism and the corresponding truth of the Catholic sacramental vision. Paul Tillich's *The Protestant Era*[9] and Langdon Gilkey's *Catholicism Confronts Modernity: A Protestant View*[10] are two cases in point. For Gilkey, Catholicism manifests "a remarkable sense of humanity and grace in the communal life of Catholics. . . . Consequently the love of life, the appreciation of the body in the senses, of joy and celebration, the tolerance of the sinner, these natural, worldly and 'human' virtues are far more clearly and universally embodied in Catholics and Catholic life than in Protestants and Protestantism." The Catholic principle of symbol or sacramentality, according to Gilkey, "may provide the best entrance into a new synthesis of the Christian tradition with the vitalities as well as the relativities of contemporary existence."[11]

It is the correlative thesis of this essay that contemporary Catholicism is marked by vitality, growth, and positive excitement at those points where it reaffirms its abiding commitment to these three principles, and to the sacramental principle in particular.

Catholicism has, since the Second Vatican Council, increasingly affirmed that the Church is first and foremost the People of God and, as such, the sacrament of the Lord's presence among us.[12] The Church is, before all else, a mystery—that is, "a reality imbued with the hidden presence of God" (Pope Paul VI). But, therefore, it must begin to appear to be what it is. Because the Catholic Church perceives itself now primarily as a people rather than as a hierarchical organization, the mode of coresponsibility is becoming fully operative at every level of ecclesiastical life and government. The liturgical renewal, in process since the earliest decades of this century, continues to advance at a remarkable pace, so much so that Catholics take for granted that worship (the Eucharist, the new rites of Baptism and of Reconciliation, and so on) must be intelligible, meaningful, joyous, and spiritually enriching—and at the same time should engage the active participation of all for whom and by whom it is celebrated.

The principles of sacramentality, mediation, and communion are also at work in the widened and widening scope accorded to ministry in the Catholic Church. Ministry is seen less and less as a clerical preserve and increasingly as a service open in principle to every qualified member of the Church, without regard to sex, marital status, or ordination. The emergence of pastoral ministry degree programs in Catholic colleges and universities and the presence of lay persons, including lay women, in Catholic seminary programs are indicative of this new trend. So too is the prominence of lay persons in the religious education field, often as parish, or even diocesan, directors.

These three principles, in their distinctively Catholic configuration, are operative as well in the Church's abiding commitment to social justice. However conservative Pope John Paul II may appear on matters like birth control, divorce and remarriage, obligatory celibacy for priests, ordination of women, and so forth, he stands in the mainstream of the Church's social doctrine tradition with his forceful statements on behalf of social justice and human rights, delivered in places as disparate as Brazil, the Philippines, Poland, Mexico, and here in the United States. His more formal pronouncements—his first encyclical, *Redemptor Hominis*, published in March 1979, and his address at the United Nations in October of the same year—have given an even more systematic and coherent shape to these occasional public statements.

Correlative with the Church's renewed involvement in the sociopolitical order is its deepened sensitivity to the public impact of its corporate, institutional "life-style" and that of its leaders. A bishop's purchase of an expensive residence evokes strong protest nowadays. Congregations of religious women commit themselves to live simply, as a way of identifying themselves with the poor. Catholic missionaries and even bishops are harrassed and sometimes murdered for their commitment to the poor, as in El Salvador.

Catholicism's persistent effort to exploit its own best tradition is reflected also in its current theological renewal. Scholars like Avery Dulles, David Tracy, Richard McCormick, Raymond Brown, Charles Curran, Joseph Fitzmyer, and others continue to stand out in the United States, as do Karl Rahner, Edward Schillebeeckx, Yves Congar, and Hans Küng on the European front. Important theologians have also recently emerged in the Third World— Gustavo Gutierrez, Leonardo Boff, Jon Sobrino, and others. The sacramentality of Jesus Christ is underscored in recent efforts to construct a Christology "from below," focusing on the humanity of Christ ("man for others") as the mediating principle of divine grace. Revelation is understood no longer as simply a "deposit" of truths given once and for all and then handed over to the proprietary care of the hierarchical magisterium, but as a continuing process of divine self-disclosure and self-communication through "the signs of the times."

Why this sudden renaissance of Catholic intellectual activity? The superficial answer is that the Second Vatican Council gave birth to a whole new body of Catholic scholars. But the council itself would have been unthinkable had it not been able to draw on important currents of theological, biblical, and philosophical thought already flowing inside the Catholic Church. Well before the Second Vatican Council convened in September 1962, Catholic biblical scholarship had been making extraordinary progress under the leadership of such pioneers as Marie-Joseph LaGrange. Biblical scholars, long operating under a cloud of suspicion, received a major endorsement in the 1943 encyclical of Pope Pius XII, *Divino Afflante Spiritu*. Yves Congar, the most important ecclesiologist of this century, perhaps did more than any other theologian to prepare the way for the council. Its major themes were already anticipated in Congar's pre-Vatican II books. He wrote of the Church as the People of God.[13] The laity are called to full participation in the mission of the Church.[14] The Church is more than the Roman Catholic Church alone.[15] The mission of the Church is not to grow and multiply but to be a minority in the service of the majority. Like the French Underground of the Second World War, the Church is a small community that prepares the way for the salvation of all in the coming Kingdom of God. The Church exists in itself but not for itself.[16] This Church, ecumenically conceived, is always in need of reform, even institutional and structural reform, in head as well as in members.[17]

Other major theologians were also already at work, influencing the Church and preparing the way for the council. Among the most prominent were Karl Rahner, Edward Schillebeeckx, Hans Küng, John Courtney Murray, and Henri de Lubac.[18] The renaissance of Catholic theological scholarship, then, is not easily explained by the phenomenon of the Second Vatican Council alone. On the contrary, the council still can only be explained largely in terms of that renaissance. As the Catholic Church, including its scholarly community, moved progressively into the modern world—a world characterized by ease of communication and of movement—the Church and its intellectual leaders were progressively influenced by work being done and events transpiring beyond its ecclesiastical borders. Thus the biblical scholars were increasingly influenced by the published research of their Protestant colleagues, and Catholic ecclesiologists like Congar were increasingly affected by their contacts, both personal and academic, with their non-Catholic brethren.

It is practically impossible to sustain a caricature or a stereotype of "the other" when one comes into immediate contact with that "other." And as the Catholic Church widened its contacts, beyond even the Christian community, it came less and less to speak of itself as the axis on which the entire world turns. As Congar noted in one of his provocative pre-Vatican II essays, we are a "small church in a large world."[19] The Second Vatican Council itself acknowledged this in its extraordinary "Pastoral Constitution on the Church in the Modern World" (nn. 4-11). Significantly, the council noted a whole array of changes in the modern world (what it called "the signs of the times") without condemning them as Pope Pius IX had done in his *Syllabus of Errors* the previous century.

But any report on contemporary Roman Catholicism is necessarily mixed.[20] For every impulse toward growth, consistent with Catholicism's adherence to the principles of sacramentality, mediation, and communion, there seems to be a corresponding pull in the opposite direction. Where parish councils exist, for example, they are often without decision-making authority, are bogged down by relatively trivial issues, and do not attract the most gifted members of a local congregation. Few dioceses have a pastoral council, and almost none of those work at or near their full potential as representative, decision-making bodies.

Vatican bureaucracies, in the meantime, try to play by the "old rules." They try to repeal major elements of the Second Vatican Council through a revision of the Code of Canon Law, to correct "abuses" in American Catholic pastoral practice regarding marriage, and to exercise greater supervision over theological inquiry, by conducting secret investigations of even moderate scholars. Autocratic styles of leadership still obtain in many dioceses, parishes, and religious communities, and bishops are still selected by a process that is at once secret and restricted. Those who are appointed to the large, prestigious archdioceses are for the most part theologically "safe" and pastorally "prudent," which means that they are often either firmly conservative or personally colorless.

Ministry, newly broadened to appeal to lay as well as clerical and religious candidates, frequently attracts the hurt, the alienated, the naive, and the intellectually weak. And in the case of the ordained ministry of priesthood, one senses a disturbing frequency of rigidity, fascination with clerical prerogatives, and social and political indifference or naiveté, or both. Women, meanwhile, are still excluded from ordination, and so too are the married and those who would like the option to marry. The new pope gives little promise of change on these issues.

At the same time, conservative opposition to Catholic social doctrine is as strong as ever. Catholicism, particularly in the United States, finds itself torn between a commitment to a whole spectrum of social justice and human rights issues and a concern for unborn human life.

Ecumenism, if the truth be told, is almost dead in the water, at least at the officially approved levels. Bishops in the United States regularly receive reports on the progress of the bilateral consultations (between Catholics and other Christian groups), and just as regularly ignore them in practice. We are no closer to intercommunion, even under canonically controlled circumstances, nor to the mutual recognition of ordained ministries, recommended by the most sophisticated of the dialogues, the Roman Catholic-Lutheran Consultation.

It would be a serious mistake to try to plot the future course of Roman Catholicism on the basis of the policies and personality of the incumbent pope alone. The recent attempt on Pope John Paul II's life only dramatizes the fact that individuals occupy the Chair of Peter for relatively brief periods of time. It is not the person of the pope that counts, but the nature of papal authority. And how we understand papal authority is a reflection of how we understand the nature and purpose of the Church; and our understanding of the Church, in turn, is a reflection of our understanding of the person and mission of Jesus Christ; and that, in turn, is a reflection of our understanding of God and, correlatively, of the meaning and direction of human existence.

Roman Catholicism confronts these questions in light of its fundamental conviction that the God who gives ultimate meaning to our lives is present in human experience (the principle of sacramentality); that the God who is present and available to us in human experience and in the world at large is a God who works through secondary causes (the principal of mediation); and that the God who works through secondary causes is a God who wills to bring us "many" into a final unity (the principle of communion), without destroying the individuality of any of the created: *E Pluribus Unum*. In political life, that is always as much a goal as an achievement. And so too is it for Roman Catholicism.

REFERENCES

[1]For a fuller statement on the crisis in Roman Catholicism, see my *Catholicism* (Minneapolis: Winston Press, 1980), vol. 1, pp. 3-20 and passim. For a Protestant analysis, see Langdon Gilkey, *Catholicism Confronts Modernity: A Protestant View* (New York: Seabury Press, 1975), pp. 1-60.

[2]New York: Anchor Press/Doubleday, 1979, pp. 1-31.

[3]Dogmatic Constitution on the Church *(Lumen gentium)*, n. 14, in *The Documents of Vatican II*, Walter Abbott and Joseph Gallagher (eds.) (New York: America Press, 1966), p. 33. The best resource for understanding the council documents is the five-volume *Commentary on the Documents of Vatican II*, Herbert Vorgrimler (ed.) (New York: Herder & Herder, 1967-69). An abbreviated commentary is available in my *Catholicism*, vol. 2, chapter 19, pp. 657-90.

[4]*The Council and Reunion* (London: Sheed & Ward, 1961), pp. 188-89, 193.

[5]*Roman Catholicism* (Royal Oak, Michigan: Cathedral Publishers, 1975), pp. 9, 11; reprinted in *Our Faiths*, Martin Marty (ed.) (Royal Oak, Michigan: Cathedral Publishers, 1975), pp. 11-43.

[6]See *Papal Primacy and the Universal Church: Lutherans and Catholics in Dialogue V*, Paul Empie and T. Austin Murphy (eds.) (Minneapolis: Augsburg Publishing House, 1974).

[7]What follows is a highly compressed statement of a thesis developed in my two-volume *Catholicism*.

[8]McBrien, *Catholicism*, vol. 2, chapter 24, pp. 865-96.

[9]Chicago: University of Chicago Press, 1948.

[10]Gilkey, *Catholicism Confronts Modernity*, pp. 1-60.

[11]Ibid., pp. 17-18, 20-22.

[12]Dogmatic Constitution on the Church, pp. 15, 24-37, 56.

[13]*Le mystère du temple* (Paris: Editions du Cerf, 1958); English translation, *The Mystery of the Temple* (Westminster, Maryland: Newman Press, 1962). For a general overview and assessment of Congar's work, see Jean-Pierre Jossua, *Yves Congar: Theology in the Service of God's People* (Chicago: Priory Press, 1968).

[14]*Jalons pour une théologie du laicat* (Paris: Editions du Cerf, 1953); English translation, *Lay People in the Church* (Westminster, Maryland: Newman Press, 1957; 2d ed., 1965).

[15]*Chrétiens désunis* (Paris: Editions du Cerf, 1937); English translation, *Divided Christendom* (London: Burns Oates, 1939).

[16]*Vaste monde, ma paroisse* (Paris: Témoignage chrétien, 1959); English translation, *The Wide World, My Parish* (Baltimore: Helicon, 1961), pp. 1-26.

[17]*Vraie et fausse réforme dans l'Église* (Paris: Editions du Cerf, 1950). Translated only into Spanish.

[18]For a useful survey of pre-Vatican II Catholic theology, see Mark Shoof, *A Survey of Catholic Theology 1800-1970* (New York: Newman Press, 1970).

[19]Congar, *The Wide World, My Parish*, pp. 8-16.

[20]See also my article, "The Roman Catholic Church: Can It Transcend the Crisis?" *The Christian Century* 96(2) (January 17, 1979): pp. 42-45.

PETER HEBBLETHWAITE

The Popes and Politics: Shifting Patterns in "Catholic Social Doctrine"

POPE JOHN PAUL II, on September 14, 1981, published his third encyclical letter, *Laborem exercens*. This title was translated as *In the Exercise of Work*, which is about as uneuphonious and unilluminating as the Latin. The purpose of the encyclical, according to its author, was "to highlight—perhaps more than has been done before—the fact that human work is *a key*, probably *the essential key*, to the whole social question, if we really try to see that question from the point of view of man's good" (3).[1] The "social question": it is a long time since anyone had used this nineteenth century expression. "Human work": it is a long time since anyone had dared to address the Church and "all men of good will" on a topic of such vast generality. Many Anglo-Saxons are skeptical about the philosophical or theological discussion on work, and are more sympathetic to the down-to-earth approach of Bertrand Russell: "Work is of two kinds: first, altering the position of matter on or near the earth's surface relatively to other such matter; second, telling other people to do so."[2]

John Paul's encyclical, however, is not just a lofty philosophical disquisition; it also contains some practical proposals. It weaves a path between capitalism and communism in suggesting that the way ahead lies in joint ownership of the means of work; sharing by the workers in the management or profits of businesses, or so-called shareholding by labor; and so on (14). There are also sharp condemnations of transnational and multinational companies that alleged-ly "fix the highest price for their products, while trying at the same time to fix the lowest possible price for raw materials" (17). John Paul declares that unemployment "is in all cases an evil and, when it reaches a certain level, can become a real social disaster" (18). These are presented as moral rather than political judgments. But unless they are meaningless statements, designed merely to soothe the conscience of the utterer without changing the situation, they are political through and through. If I come to believe, for example, that unemployment in the United States or Britain has reached the level at which it is "a real social disaster," especially for the young who have never known what it is to work, I am in duty bound to oppose the monetarist policies that have contributed to it.

But my purpose is not to discuss this most recent encyclical in any detail. My interest in the encyclical is that it puts itself forward as an instance of "the Church's social teaching" (3), which has more usually been called "Catholic social doctrine" (henceforth CSD). Moreover, it is explicitly presented as in continuity with the "great social encyclicals" of the past, starting with Leo XIII's

Rerum Novarum of May 15, 1891, which it commemorates. Seen against that background, the originality—or lack of originality—of John Paul's latest encyclical will appear more clearly.

For some years there has been an animated debate on CSD. The English-speaking world has paid little attention to it because most of the discussion has taken place in France, with an occasional contribution from Latin America. The argument was about whether CSD was dead or alive, and if dead, what should replace it. But what may seem like a futile academic quarrel in fact raised some far-reaching questions about how Christians should relate to the world, and the world of politics in particular. Some account of this debate will also enable us to see that John Paul, in trying to breathe new life into CSD, is taking a very firm stand against some recent trends in the Church. He is taking sides.

As representative of the "CSD-is-finished" school, we can take the veteran French Dominican, Marie-Dominique Chenu, who in 1979 published a short book called, significantly, *La "Doctrine Sociale" de l'Eglise comme Idéologie.*[3] By placing *doctrine sociale* in quotes, Chenu is suggesting that it is a figment; by calling it an ideology, he is saying why it is unacceptable. Chenu's position has been utterly rejected by Fr. Roger Heckel, S.J., who at the time was Secretary of the International Justice and Peace Commission in Rome,[4] the pontifical body responsible for issues of social justice and international relations. In a series of pamphlets published by the Commission, Heckel notes the frequency of the term "social doctrine" in the speeches of John Paul, and defends its use.

In practice, CSD starts with Leo XIII's *Rerum Novarum* in 1891. I say in practice, because (as we shall see) John Paul and Heckel are extremely reluctant to speak in this way, since it would involve the admission that the Church had *no* social doctrine until 1891. Thus the attempt is made to put together a tradition based on the book of Genesis ("Subdue the earth"), the fact that Jesus was a carpenter and worked with his hands, and the remarks of some ancient Church Fathers to the effect that the poor are the real treasure of the Church. This attempt to found a tradition leaves large tracts of time uncovered; it is difficult to imagine what sort of CSD could come from the Borgia popes or indeed any pope who was saddled with ruling the Papal States. In any case, one can perfectly well admit that some kind of social *thinking* has gone on in the Church, but that it was scattered and sporadic; it would become social *doctrine* only if it were more systematic and complete. This point relates to the main discussion in the following way: If there has always been a CSD, it is less likely to have died in the 1960s. If, on the other hand, it actually came into existence in 1891, it will be time-bound, bear the marks of its age, and perhaps be doomed.

Thus—more cautiously this time—it may be said that CSD in the modern sense, as a more systematic pontifical exercise, began in 1891. What is not in dispute is that it caused a sensation at the time, for *Rerum Novarum* was the first pontifical document to pay any attention to the consequences of the industrial revolution. "Gradually," Leo noted, "the workers, isolated and defenseless, are handed over to the mercy of inhuman masses and made the victims of frenzied competition." Nearly fifty years after the *Communist Manifesto*, the Church was trying to recover lost ground.

Leo's justification for tackling what was known at that time as "the social question" (the very language used ninety years later by Pope John Paul) was that "no effective solution to it could be found without recourse to religion and the Church" (8). The Church was not interfering in politics when it made pronouncements on these matters, because politics itself was a moral activity, directed towards the realization of the common good. Not to speak would be a dereliction of duty.

On this one may make three comments. Leo could only come to the defense of the workers because his predecessor, Pius IX, had lost the Papal States in 1870. Though Leo felt resentful about this loss, and still hoped that something would be restored, he also realized that it was a liberation for the papacy that could become the "conscience of the world" or (to use a much later expression) the voice of those who have no voice. Second, to make use of the term "common good" was a splendid move. Not only did it carry a reminiscence of Aquinas (whose study Leo also revived), but it provided as well a middle terrain in which the difficult question could be eluded: Which, when the crunch comes, has primacy—the papacy, now reduced to a spiritual power, or the Italian state, now the acting temporal power? Third, the kind of CSD put forward by Leo had a condescending and paternalistic note that would prove difficult to get rid of. The poor are the object of the discourse; they are not seen as agents in their own transformation. Most dangerous of all, CSD comes actually to mean, "what *popes* have to say on social questions."[5]

Forty years later, Pius XI published *Quadragesimo Anno*, the title indicating continuity. He agreed that the world had changed in the intervening period. The financial crash of the late twenties had alarmed everyone, and was seen by Marxists as presaging the final end of capitalism. The Bolshevik Revolution had introduced a new and menacing factor into international affairs. But while noting these changes, Pius continued the line of Leo XIII. CSD is envisaged as a set of principles, enunciated by the Church (actually the pope), that if acted upon, could transform the world. Unfortunately, these principles had not been heeded, and consequently the world was in a mess. The approach to problems was moralistic and individualistic. There was no examination of the structuralist, built-in causes of modern problems. There was no attempt to interpret contemporary movements in the light of their Christian potential. Socialism was rejected out of hand.

The result was that Catholics had to hive off into movements of their own. Catholic Action, which organized groups by categories, was seen as the best way to implement CSD. This meant forming separate Catholic labor unions wherever this was possible. On this, Chenu comments: "To divide the labor movement in order to evangelize it was to make an error about the Gospel. For the real task was not to create a separate Catholic workers' group but to bring the Church to birth within the workers' movement as it actually existed."[6]

CSD as conceived in the 1930s lectured the world from the outside. It stated abstract, intemporal principles that ignored the diversity of situations. It was nostalgic for a vanishing rural and peasant world. It ignored the fact of class conflict, which it tried to gloss over with the concept of *interclassismo*—the harmonious collaboration of all social classes—which brought comfort only to dictators like Franco in Spain and Salazar in Portugal, both of whom claimed to be implementing CSD.

The difficulty of CSD was this: it could fly so high in the stratosphere of principles that, from above, the whole landscape was flattened out and no details could be perceived; or—more rarely—it could hew so close to the ground that its particular statement was too localized to be applicable elsewhere. The problem, to put it another way, was how to relate Christian faith to ongoing history.

The change began with Pope John XXIII, who succeeded Pius XII in October 1958. Despite his seventy-six years, there was freshness and vigor in the way he set about his pontificate. He had a keener sense of history than any other pope of this century. "History will be our guide," he told the Second Vatican Council, which will always be associated with his name. He inaugurated a new approach (it was of course a rediscovery) to social problems that depended on a new methodology. He began to speak of the need to discern "the signs of the times." In Luke's Gospel, Jesus says to the Pharisees and Saducees, after quoting proverbs about weather-forecasting, "You know how to read the face of the sky, but you cannot read the signs of the times" (Luke 12:54-56). The parallels to this text (cf. Matthew 11:3-5; 12:28; and 16:3) suggest that "the times" refers to the new messianic age, and that "the signs" are the miracles worked by Jesus. Pope John used this text and gave it an accommodated meaning, not always to the satisfaction of the exegetes. In *Humanae Salutis*, the apostolic constitution by which he convoked the Second Vatican Council, he writes of the immense new tasks facing the Church, the tragic period of history the world had just come through, and the need to bring the Church and the world together, so that "the vivifying and perennial energies of the Gospel" should be brought to bear on the temporal ordering of the world.

But how was this to be achieved? Pope John went on: "Indeed we make ours the recommendation of Jesus that one should know how to discern 'the signs of the times,' and we seem to see now, in the midst of so much darkness, a *few indications which augur well* for the fate of the Church and humanity."[7] *(italics added)*

The indications that augur well remain rather vague. One gets a better idea of what was in his mind from *Pacem in Terris*, his final encyclical, which was, in effect, his last will and testament. (It also has the distinction of being the only papal encyclical that has been set to music: by Olivier Messaien.) Each of the four sections into which it is divided concludes with a review of contemporary developments. For example, the section headed *Order between Persons* notes that "workers refuse to be treated as if they were irrational objects," that "women will not tolerate being treated as mere material instruments," and that the nations emerging from colonialism have found a new sense of dignity. So far, so banal, it might be thought.

But if these trends, or tendencies, however difficult to pin down, are not merely regarded as a Good Thing but can actually be related to the Gospel, an important shift has occurred. No longer does CSD simply parachute down principles from a great height. Instead, it takes the hopes and aspirations that people really have and reads in them a message from the Holy Spirit. The Spirit is at work in the men and women and movements of our age. This is not a matter of blessing every contemporary fad or fashion. But it does mean starting from what is happening (the "world will provide the agenda for the churches" was the way the World Council of Churches would say the same thing later). It means a new humility before the data. It means listening carefully to what is being said, and then discerning (i.e., seeing in difficult circumstances) the hand of the Lord. The consequences of this shift of emphasis were considerable. They affected the work of the Second Vatican Council and the subsequent postconciliar history of the Church. The main consequences as they relate to CSD are:

1. The first was the simple principle that one should look before pronouncing. A credible empirical starting-point is needed. If men of God are unconvincing in their account of this world, they are unlikely to carry conviction when they speak of the invisible world. The more accurate the preliminary description, and the more it leads people to say, "Yes, that's the way it is," the more its subsequent teaching will carry authority. But it will be the authority of competence, and not merely of hierarchy.

2. Who is charged with this task of discerning the Spirit? As *Gaudium et Spes*, the document of Vatican II closest to the aspiration of John, put it: "With the help of the Holy Spirit, it is the task of the entire people of God, especially pastors and theologians, to hear, distinguish and interpret the many voices of our age, and to judge them in the light of the divine word" (44).

3. It follows, further, that the Spirit, far from being held captive within the boundaries of the Church, can be found in the most surprising places. *Gaudium et Spes*, for example, speaking of the concern for human rights and where the impulse to defend them comes from, says, "God's Spirit, who with a marvellous providence directs the unfolding of time and renews the face of the earth, is present to this development. The ferment of the Gospel arouses in men's hearts a demand for dignity that cannot be stifled" (26).[8]

4. The "ferment of the Gospel": this phrase was not lightly chosen. It refers to the way the Gospel can shatter conventional and comfortable ways of thinking and acting. It further implies that this ferment, once released upon the world through the preaching of the Church, can perfectly well break loose from its ecclesiastical moorings and invade what we think of as secular society. Yet even when this happens, there will still be a real relationship between the aspiration toward human dignity and the Holy Spirit. The whole concept of "anonymous Christians" starts from this truth.[9] The Spirit "without" speaks to the Spirit "within."

5. Thus the whole relationship of Church and world changes. The Church is not "over against" the world: such a view leads to the reduction of the Church to a sect that fundamentally rejects the world and is content merely to snatch a few brands from the world's fire. Nor was the Church seen as a fortress besieged by a fundamentally hostile world. It was a

people, a people on the march toward the realization of the Kingdom of God, its eventual true home, but which meanwhile shared for good or ill in everyday human problems. This was why *Pacem in Terris* could be addressed, for the first time ever, to "all men of good will." It was not at that time a platitude; it was a breakthrough. For John's teaching was no longer based on the authority or the claims of the Church; it was based on the Church's *experience*, and appealed to the aspirations of ordinary people and the tissue of hopes and basic solidarities that make up human history.

6.   This was the deeper meaning—now largely forgotten—of the magnificent opening chord of *Gaudium et Spes:* "The joys and the hopes, the griefs and the anxieties of the men of this age, especially those who are poor or in any way afflicted, these too are the joys and the hopes, the griefs and anxieties of the followers of Christ" (1). The Kingdom, or better, the Reign of God, that horizon toward which Christians consciously move, was to be discovered in solidarity with others, not in separation from them. Normally it would be unnecessary to congratulate a human grouping on discovering that it belonged to the human race; but in the case of the Roman Catholic Church, which, especially with its CSD, had talked *at* people rather than *with* them, it was an important shift of attitude.

7.   Finally, this opening statement of *Gaudium et Spes* also contained a hint—not fully worked out in the rest of the document, but pregnant with the future—that the poor were to be privileged in the Church. This was a return to the evangelical source: "The Spirit of the Lord is upon me because he has anointed me; he has sent me to announce good news to the poor" (Luke 4:18)—Jesus quoting Isaiah.

The same evangelical spirit was reflected in Pope Paul VI's social encyclical, *Populorum Progressio* (1967). Its express aim was "to throw the light of *the Gospel* on the social questions of our age" (2). It avoided any use of the term "social doctrine." Its main theme was the interdependence of all the peoples of spaceship Earth. It was a prophetic document in that it was ahead of most conventional wisdom of the 1960s. It anticipated that the North-South conflict would turn out to be more important than that between East and West. No doubt that was why *The Wall Street Journal* dismissed it as "souped-up Marxism."

Meanwhile, local churches had begun to work out for themselves the implications of the stand taken by Pope John and the Council. The "signs of the times" could not be discerned universally: they had to be studied on the local level. The Latin American bishops (CELAM), meeting at Medellin, Colombia, in 1968, interpreted "salvation" for their peoples as liberation from social, political, and economic oppression. This was the starting point of "the theology of liberation" that proliferated during the next decade. It involved a more sympathetic, though not uncritical, approach to Marxism (with the emphasis on the young, humanistic Marx); sometimes the *anawim*, or poor, of the Gospels were identified with the oppressed proletariat; and there was a firm insistence that orthodoxy (thinking right) needed to be filled out by orthopraxy (living out what one thought, or being consistent). CSD as traditionally understood was abandoned, and frequently derided, as well.

Although Paul VI did not show any contempt for CSD, he abandoned it on the grounds that it was unworkable. In his letter to Cardinal Maurice Roy,[10] published in 1971 on the occasion of the eightieth anniversary of *Rerum Novarum*, he wrote, "In view of the varied situations in the world, it is difficult to give one teaching to cover them all or to offer a solution which has universal value" (4). But that had been precisely the claim of CSD. It was now abandoned, and Paul VI even added that the pretension to a universal message was neither his intention nor his mission.

But this did not mean that the Church had nothing to say on these social issues. The task that Paul VI felt incompetent to fulfill was entrusted to Christian communities throughout the world, who had the duty of scrutinizing "the signs of the times" in their own situation. No one else could do this on their behalf. This was not a feeble abdication on the part of Paul VI: it was, rather, a recognition of the change in the method sketched above. Solutions could not be handed down from on high: that was the illusion of CSD. Rather, they could only be discovered through patient work, in which the human sciences would play a part, in collaboration with others involved in the same field.

The Justice and Peace Commission, set up by Paul VI in 1967, was an organizational expression of the same principle. Though it had a central office in Rome, its strength lay in the national branches, who saw it as their task to "sensibilize" Catholics to local problems. It did this patchily, with more or less success, and with more or less support from the local hierarchy. "Justice and Peace" became, in effect, the Catholic euphemism for politics in the 1970s. No one ever indulged in "politics" (still regarded as a somewhat tainted occupation); they strove for justice and peace. One of the most significant pointers to the changed attitudes was a statement by the 1971 Synod of Bishops, which had on its agenda the admittedly vast topic of "justice in the world," that said, "The struggle for justice is a *constitutive* dimension of the preaching of the Gospel." *(italics added)* In other words, it is not an optional extra, not something you think about when you have preached the Gospel; it is, rather, the way to preach the Gospel in the world of today. The Society of Jesus made this text the basis for a rethinking of its entire work at its 32nd General Congregation in 1975.[11]

At this point one might be tempted to conclude that CSD was finished. All that remained was to write its epitaph, which Chenu did in his book. For him, it is a museum piece, the social equivalent of that "deism which neutralized the Gospel and which was the ideology of the bourgeoisie in the nineteenth century." He means that Leo XIII, while claiming to present some kind of intemporal Catholic social doctrine, was in fact merely reflecting the current bourgeois ideology toward the end of the nineteenth century, a charge difficult to deny. Leo's denunciation of socialism and assertion of the right to private property were just what the bourgeoisie wanted to hear in 1891. But, as Chenu concludes, "faith is not an ideology":[12] that is, it is not an unconscious way of legitimating my unexamined prejudices. There could be no more devastating way of undermining CSD.

CSD is dead, apparently, but it will not lie down. John Paul II has deliberately set about the task of rehabilitating it. He has done so knowing perfectly well that the term "social doctrine" has its critics. But that stimulates him even more. He is not someone who ducks a challenge. He told the Latin American bishops, assembled at Puebla in 1979 for a follow-up meeting to Medellin, that the social doctrine of the Church must be studied and applied, "even though some people seek to sow doubts and lack of confidence in it" (III, 7). Quite clearly, he does not accept these criticisms.

On the other hand, he is not doing battle for a mere word. This can be seen in the way he sometimes puts social doctrine in quotation marks and uses, more commonly, a whole arsenal of semiequivalent expressions: social morality; social thought of the Church; social and humanitarian teaching; doctrine, or directives, of the encyclicals; doctrinal inheritance; social teaching of the apostolic see, or social doctrine of the popes.[13]

This multiplication of semiequivalent terms can be seen as an attempt to assert that the Church, the popes, and the Gospel—the three terms are not in fact interchangeable—have always had something to say on social questions. The tradition did not begin with Leo XIII. The most striking affirmation of this supposed continuity is to be found in the apostolic constitution[14] *Catechesi Tradendae*. After noting that catechesis must include "the search for a society with greater solidarity and fraternity, the fight for justice and the building of peace," John Paul goes on:

> Besides, it is not to be thought that this dimension of catechesis is altogether new. As early as the patristic age, St. Ambrose and St. John Chrysostom—to quote only them—gave prominence to the social consequences of the demands made by the Gospels. Close to our own time, the catechism of Saint Pius X explicitly listed oppressing the poor and depriving workmen of their just wages among the sins that cry out to God for vengeance. Since *Rerum Novarum*, especially, social concern has been actively present in the catechetical teaching of the Popes and the Bishops (29).

Potted history is always dangerous, and "disingenuous" would be a mild term to describe this summary of twenty centuries of history. The leap from Ambrose and John Chrysostom to Saint Pius X is enough to make one suspicious. And the latter's paternalistic concern for the workers should be set alongside the outrageous statement made in his 1906 encyclical *Vehementer*: "As for the multitude, it has no right other than to be led and, as a faithful flock, to follow its pastors."[15] The claim to a continuous tradition is extremely dubious.

This does not deter John Paul. *Catechesi Tradendae* is not presented as an original work, but as a synthetic response to the 1977 Synod that was devoted to catechetics. Thus his desire to revivify CSD appears as a request put at the Synod: "Many Synod Fathers rightly insisted that the rich heritage of the Church's social teaching should, in appropriate forms, find a place in the general catechetical education of the faithful" (29). One of them was Cardinal Karol Wojtyla. He was thus in perfect agreement as pope with what he had said as cardinal.

But in his interpretation of the 1977 Synod, a crucial position taken by an earlier Synod (1971) is implicitly abandoned. In 1971, when the Synod was allowed to write its own texts, it stated that "the struggle for justice is a constitutive dimension of the preaching of the Gospel." "Constitutive" was the key word, for it meant that not to struggle for justice was to be unfaithful to the Gospel. It was a blow aimed at separated spirituality or escapist mysticism. The 1977 Synod, as presented by John Paul, says, rather, that this struggle is *another* dimension of catechesis, necessary no doubt, but one that is tacked on at the end after other, more essential elements have been dealt with. It appears as an afterthought. It is certainly no longer seen as "constitutive" of the preaching of the Gospel.

John Paul clearly believes that CSD has a future. On the other hand, his use of the term is circumspect. Roger Heckel points out that "social doctrine" has been talked about in two principal contexts: Latin America and Poland. CSD was mentioned during the visits to Mexico and Brazil, and has recurred in many of the *ad limina* visits of Latin American bishops to the Vatican. As for Poland, the first visit home in June 1979 provided an opportunity to develop his thoughts on CSD for the benefit of Edward Gierek, still at that time Secretary of the Polish Communist party, and the Polish bishops, who were doubtless more familiar with these ideas.

It is legitimate to ask why Latin America and Poland provide the "right" context. The answer will not be quite the same in each case. "Social doctrine" was used in Latin America because CSD has been much criticized there for its abstractness. In fact, in the sixties and seventies it had been very largely abandoned and replaced by various versions of "the theology of liberation." The failure of the "decade of development" led to a radicalization of political oppositions, with the growth of military governments on the one hand and revolutionary or guerrilla movements on the other. The middle way between capitalism and communism, which CSD was commonly supposed to represent, had chalked up no successes in Latin America, and was now squeezed out altogether.

But John Paul *needed* CSD in Latin America; it provided the ground on which he could stand to criticize the theology of liberation. It would be hard to criticize it without either offering something to put in its place or retreating from political commitment altogether. There can be no doubt that John Paul was highly critical of liberation theology. A whole section of his Puebla speech to the assembled bishops of Latin America is devoted to "a correct Christian idea of liberation" (III, 6)—the implication being that there are incorrect ideas in the air. John Paul's concept of liberation, however, rejects the primacy of politics that has so often been asserted in Latin America, and replaces it with "the primacy of the spiritual." He speaks of a liberation "that in the framework of the Church's proper mission is not reduced to the simple and narrow economic, political, social or cultural dimension, and is not sacrificed to the demands of any strategy, practice or short-term solutions." There was a populist appeal in his suggestion that "the humble and simple faithful, as by an evangelical instinct, spontaneously sense when the Gospel is served in the Church and when it is emptied of its content and is stifled with other interests" (III, 6).

But the assertion of the primacy of the spiritual does not mean an abstention from the world of politics. CSD fills the vacuum. At this point, something very odd happens. John Paul seeks to answer the objection that social doctrine had confined itself to the abstract and therefore irrelevant statement of principles. "This social doctrine," he explains, "involves . . . both principles for action and also norms for judgment and guidelines for action." Social doctrine, in other words, is "cashed" in "praxis." The oddity is that this observation is backed up by a reference to *Octagesima Adveniens* (4), which says nothing of the kind, and is precisely the passage in which Paul VI abandoned the ambition of propounding a social doctrine for the whole Church, and entrusted the task of "discerning" particular situations to the local Christian communities.

John Paul's use of social doctrine in the context of Poland is more easily understood, and provides a key to his attitudes more generally. In the Belevedere Palace on June 2, 1979, beneath the chandeliers and the television lights, John Paul was in a unique situation. He had just listened to Edward Gierek extol the splendors of "thirty-five years of socialism." John Paul pointedly ignored this, spoke instead of the tradition of more than a thousand years of Christianity, congratulated Gierek on rebuilding the Royal Castle in Warsaw "as a symbol of Polish sovereignty," and multiplied quotations from his predecessor Paul VI on the theme of disarmament and better relations between nations. "In these words," he added, "the doctrine of the Church is expressed, which always supports authentic progress and the peaceful development of humanity." He then denounced "all forms of political, economic or cultural colonialism which are in contradiction with the basic demands of international order." Few Poles watching this on television did not think of the Soviet Union at this point. The ground for Solidarity was being prepared. And once again the social doctrine of the Church provided the base from which to attack, deftly, but nonetheless clearly, the reigning Marxist doctrines. It was criticized in the name of the common good.

Political activity, John Paul told the Polish bishops at Czestochowa on June 5, 1979, is defined by its concern for the good of man, and therefore is of its very nature an ethical activity. Then he spoke of the "so-called social doctrine of the Church":

> It is here that the deepest roots are to be found of the so-called social doctrine of the Church which, particularly in our period, beginning at the end of the nineteenth century, has been enormously enriched by all contemporary problems. This does not mean that it emerged suddenly in the last two centuries: it existed in fact from the beginning as a consequence of the Gospel and of the Christian vision of man in his relations with other men, especially in community and social life.

Like the passage in *Catechesi Tradendae* quoted above, this attempt to broaden the basis of CSD delivers the concept from too narrow an interpretation. At the same time, however, the use of "so-called" indicates a certain hesitation. In using the term, John Paul does not mean, or does not simply mean, a return to the teaching found in the social encyclicals of Leo XIII and Pius XI. By admitting that "new problems have arisen," he is conceding that new solutions have to be sought.

Despite his philosophical background, John Paul is not a systematic thinker. He strikes out in one direction after another as occasions present themselves, journeys suggest, or his speech-writers propose. The result is that despite the immense number of words already uttered during his pontificate, and the enforced leisure imposed by the bullets of Mehemet Ali Agca, it is still difficult to perceive the precise direction in which he is moving. The revival of CSD does not mean a return to Pius XI. But there are signs that it involves a critique of some aspects of the approach of Pope John and the Council. Here are three examples of the difficulties that remain, even after one has used the quasi-magical term CSD.

The first symptom of change is that the phrase "signs of the times," whose importance we have seen, has almost completely disappeared from the papal vocabulary. Thus the preliminary empirical grip on social and political realities is bypassed. Yet the term has been used, but in contexts that distort its meaning. Addressing sisters in Washington on October 7, 1979, John Paul said: "As daughters of the Church . . . you are called to a generous and loving adherence to the authentic *magisterium* [teaching authority] of the Church, which is a solid guarantee of the fruitfulness of all your apostolates and an indispensable condition for the proper interpretation of 'the signs of the times.' " A similar warning was issued in his address to Indonesian bishops on June 7, 1980.[16] But the relevant text of *Gaudium et Spes* makes no mention of the *magisterium* of the Church. It simply says: "To carry out its task, the Church has always had the duty of scrutinizing the signs of the times and interpreting them in the light of the Gospel" (4). That is a task for the *whole* Church. To reduce it to a function of the central authority is to bowdlerize the text and domesticate the doctrine. It makes the local churches once more dependent on the center, it deprives them of initiative, and it suggests that the study of local situations can be replaced by judgments emanating effortlessly from the *magisterium*. This is the most "reactionary" statement uttered by John Paul. But since everyone knows it is unworkable, perhaps it does not matter.

More serious was a speech in Turin on April 13, 1980. It was his first real encounter with the world of work. Turin, headquarters of the Fiat car industry, now in recession, was also the city where the drive toward Italian unity began in the nineteenth century. But John Paul made no mention of the *Risorgimento* or of Camillo Cavour, its main architect. No Italian pope could have gone to Turin without reconciling himself to the democratic history of his country. But the Polish pope has another image of Italy, the land of countless shrines to the Madonna. In his map, Turin represented the Holy Shroud and St. John Bosco. And from this vantage point he denounced the two intellectual forces that have shaped the modern world—liberalism and Marxism:

> There is on the one hand the rationalist, scientist, enlightenment approach of the secular so-called "liberalism" of the Western nations, which carried with it the radical denial of Christianity; and on the other hand the ideology and praxis of atheistic Marxism whose materialistic consequences are taken to their most extreme consequences in various forms of contemporary terrorism.

As a matter of fact, the last phrase was toned down, at the last moment, to avert the suggestion—offensive and misplaced in Turin—of a link between Marxism and terrorism. The result was that the condemnation of "so-called 'liberalism' " seemed even harsher than the condemnation of Marxism. It seems that John Paul was not seeking dialogue or an overlap with secular systems. The evenhanded criticism of East and West may give the impression of independence from power blocs, but it can also suggest a plague-on-both-your-houses lack of serious commitment. Are there not some criteria for preferring one system rather than the other? Once the Church is placed outside the melee, as in the Turin speech, there is no longer any need to answer that question. Mother Church knows best—though she cannot in fact point to any instance of the realized Kingdom on earth. But she knows that the others are wrong.

No one could claim that the People's Republic of the Congo is a vivid realization of the Kingdom of God. It calls itself a Marxist state, but even so has diplomatic relations with the Holy See. Having gone to Kinshasha in Zaire, John Paul could not have omitted to cross the Zaire River and visit the People's Republic of the Congo. He duly did. On May 6, 1980, he addressed the President, Denis Sassou-Ngnesso, and developed the theory of Church and state as two not quite coincident societies:

> The Church is a spiritual institution, even if it also has a social expression; it lies beyond temporal "fatherlands" [patries] as the community of believers. The state is an expression of the sovereign self-determination of peoples and nations, and is its ordinary realization in the social sphere; from it derives its moral authority. To become aware of this difference of nature will permit one to avoid confusion and to go forward in clarity.

The two realms having been thus distinguished, the way was open for an appeal for religious liberty, which is, said the pope, "at the heart of the respect for all freedoms and all the inalienable rights of the person." In exchange for religious liberty, the Church would offer "loyal collaboration."

But, one might ask, are there no further questions to be asked of the president of Congo-Brazzaville other than that he should respect religious liberty (of Catholics)? It may be fundamental, but it is not the only human right that needed to be asserted. At the end of his long life, Pope John had concluded that "today, more than ever, we must be concerned to serve man as such and not just Catholics, and to defend the rights of everyone and not just of the Catholic Church."[17] That vision is lost sight of when "loyal collaboration" (with no further questions asked) is offered in exchange for religious liberty.

*   *   *

The reintroduction of social doctrine does not of itself indicate a return to the teachings of Leo XIII and Pius XI (though they are honored as pioneers). It contains a reference to the Gospel that they, in their concern for natural law, tended to omit. But it reveals a deep suspicion for the theology of liberation and for the new signs-of-the-times method that set it in motion, and involves also the conviction, or the presumption, that something of universal validity can actually be said. To test whether this is true, I want to take two examples from *Laborem Exercens*, the encyclical of John Paul with which we began. Though his approach is austerely philosophical (based on the axiom of "the primacy of labor over capital"), he does reach some extremely precise conclusions. Two in particular have aroused surprise.

The less emotional example had best be taken first. There is a section on labor unions that, come what may, will inevitably be read in the light of the experience of Solidarity in Poland. Like Leo XIII ninety years ago, John Paul defends the "right of free association." But that is the basis of Solidarity's *very existence* as an autonomous and free union in a country that previously had only unions that were the "conveyor belt" of party decisions. What are unions for? John Paul's answer is that "their task is to defend the existential interests of the workers in all sectors where their rights are concerned" (20). That positive implies a negative, and it duly comes. Unions should be concerned with "struggle" only insofar as it is motivated by a quest for justice. They are not a reflection of class divisions or an instrument of the class war. They are not out to eliminate their opponents. And they should not "play politics, in the sense this is usually understood."

John Paul's welfare concept of unions leads him to conclude that "unions do not have the character of political parties struggling for power; they should not be subjected to the decision of political parties or have too close links with them" (20). As a piece of pragmatic advice for Solidarity, this is eminently sensible. Given that the Polish government cannot renounce "the leading role of the communist party" without committing suicide, it is wise for Solidarity to "stay out of party politics." There is no room for party politics in Poland. This interpretation is confirmed by the fact that within two days of the encyclical, the Polish bishops published a statement quoting this passage and urging Solidarity "to return to the negotiating table." There can be no doubt that John Paul's view of the purpose and role of unions is relevant to the Polish situation.

The question is whether it is equally relevant anywhere else. Transfer this judgment to other countries, and it becomes immediately problematical. The British Labor Party, for example, is locked in with the unions constitutionally, and other Western socialist parties have the same system. This may be a bad thing, and a perfectly sensible case can be made for saying that unions should be independent of political parties and vice-versa. What is difficult to swallow is that this should be presented as a major tenet of Catholic social doctrine. This, unfortunately, is characteristic of the whole approach of CSD, even in its updated form. Where it is vague, it can be blamed for its vagueness; but where it is precise, it can be blamed for its precision.

My second example concerns women. Catholic feminists, already outraged by his use of the generic "man" for human being and his refusal even to consider the possibility of women entering the ministry, will be inclined to dismiss John Paul altogether when they read that

> it will redound to the credit of society to make it possible for a mother—without inhibiting her freedom, without psychological or practical discrimination, and without penalizing her as compared with other women—to devote herself to taking care of her children and educating them in accordance with their needs, which vary with age. Having to abandon these tasks in order to take up paid work outside the home is wrong from the point of view of the good of the family when it contradicts or hinders these primary goals of the mission of a mother (19).

If we try to understand this position—as contrasted with attacking or defending it—the first thing to notice is that he is not speaking of the role of the *woman* but of the role of a *mother*. That is an important distinction: a woman does not have to be a wife and a mother, but if she is, certain consequences follow. But perhaps the most important point about this passage is that what John Paul is objecting to is not that women should work outside the home, but that they should be *forced* to work outside the home, that they should have no option. And what he is objecting to is precisely what happens in Poland, where women are expected to work and merely add their work in the factory or wherever to their domestic work. Two recent Polish films by women directors, J. Kamienska's *Working Women* and K. Kwinta's *The White Women*, confirm this. According to David Robinson, they are both "terrible indictments of working conditions that seem to belong to the last century."[18] If in other countries it can be a liberation for a woman to go out to work, in Poland it is more likely to be an added burden. Therefore, to say that women should not be forced to work serves their cause.

Thus on two major points John Paul's contribution to CSD springs from his Polish experience and speaks eloquently to that experience. But it is difficult to apply elsewhere. His statements cannot be generalized—or only after so many modifications that they become valueless. I believe that Paul VI was right when he said, "In view of the varied situations in the world, it is difficult to give one teaching to cover them all or to offer a solution which has universal value" (*Octogesima Adveniens*, 4). But John Paul regards such an attitude as defeatist and fainthearted. That is why he needs a revived CSD as a form of universal teaching on social questions. He is unwilling to relinquish this task to the local churches. But unless the present revival of CSD becomes a stimulus to local discussion of social morality, and not regarded merely as a substitute for it, it will go the sad way of its predecessors.

REFERENCES

[1]Papal encyclicals and texts of Councils are usually set out in numbered sections. That is how they will be referred to here.

[2]*In Praise of Idleness* (London: Allen & Unwin, 1935).

[3]Editions du Cerf.

[4]Fr. Heckel has since been made Archbishop of Strasbourg, France.

[5]A course in "Catholic Social Doctrine" used to be given at Plater College in Oxford. It consisted exclusively of a commentary on papal social encyclicals.

[6]Chenu, La *"Doctrine Sociale" de l'Eglise comme Idéologie*, p. 22.

[7]Walter Abbott, *The Documents of Vatican II* (America Press, 1966), p. 703.

[8]I have modified the Abbott translation here because the Latin puts it positively: *Spiritus Dei . . . huic evolutioni adest*. Abbott has "was not absent," which is more grudging than "is present."

[9]For a treatment of this point, compare my *The Status of "Anonymous Christians"* in *The Heythrop Journal*, January 1977, pp. 47–55.

[10]Quite obviously, this text was designed as an encyclical: it has the sweep and the scope of an encyclical. But at the last minute it was turned into a letter to Cardinal Maurice Roy, Archbishop of Quebec, and President of the Pontifical Commission for Justice and Peace. Only a pedant would conclude that it therefore had less authority.

[11]The Jesuits are important not only because of their size—despite losses they still number above twenty-six thousand—but because of their influence on other religious congregations, especially the women's congregations, which treat Jesuit documents as though addressed to themselves. This is one of the reasons for the misunderstanding between Pope John Paul II and Fr. Pedro Arrupe, Superior General of the Jesuits.

[12]Chenu, La *"Doctrine Sociale,"* pp. 90, 96.

[13]Cf. Roger Heckel, *The Social Doctrine of John Paul II*, Justice and Peace Commission, p. 25.

[14]Though lower in status than an encyclical, an apostolic constitution is still an important document. This one is presented as the papal response to the Synod of 1977. But in 1977 Cardinal

Karol Wojtyla was a member of the Synod. Elected pope in October 1978, he thus became the recipient of his own advice.

[15]Chenu, *La "Doctrine Sociale,"* p. 30.

[16]Fearing that the expatriate missionaries were likely to be expelled at any time, the Indonesian Bishops had been advocating the ordination of married men.

[17]Diary for May 24, 1963, in *Giovanni XXIII, Profezia nella Fedeltà*, Angelina and Giuseppe Alberigo (eds.) (Brescia: 1978), p. 494.

[18]*The Times*, London, September 17, 1981.

III. The Ongoing Conversation

GEORGE ARMSTRONG KELLY

Faith, Freedom, and Disenchantment:
Politics and the American Religious Consciousness

I

THIS ESSAY IS CONCERNED with two incommensurable enterprises. First, I want to suggest hypothetically some sets of relationships between the understanding and practice called politics and the one called religion—at least as these terms apply in modern Western culture. In this complicated and uncharted area I shall not expect to clinch arguments so much as crystallize ways of stating a problem. Second, using this theoretical guidance, I shall make a highly compressed assessment of politics and religion in recent America, evoking history, but depending chiefly on the perspectives of two great sociologists, Alexis de Tocqueville and Max Weber, who were also political theorists of repute. We will not be troubled to find in Tocqueville a fully fleshed-out theory about American religion and its role in public life, while in Weber only intimations to extrapolate. For our question is not really how the United States has been interpreted by others; rather, it concerns the available conceptual resources for grasping our present situation.

When I speak of the United States, I am referring to what in my judgment is a Protestant or, to use Martin Marty's term, a "post-Protestant" culture (one might speak of the *Aufhebung* of Protestantism).[1] Although Roman Catholics are, by far, our largest single church and have an average per capita income slightly higher than that of the Protestants, few who have lived their lives in the United States would doubt that dissenting Protestantism is the wellspring of our ethos. Despite distinctive Catholic and Jewish contributions to our political, professional, and intellectual life, America is most plausibly to be examined as a land of the avatars and the pathology of Protestantism.[2] Both Catholicism and Judaism, by multiplying and prospering in America, have become partly Protestantized and are partly suffering from the same kind of culture shock. Pluralism has not been their invention, despite the ways in which they have expanded it.[3]

I shall attempt to develop briefly the theoretical points on which my subsequent argument rests. The first is that *there are many intriguing resemblances between religious and political evolution.* I do not intend evolution to mean progress or anything global or eschatological; indeed, it includes pathology. I also consider religion and politics as understandings and practices that are discrete, though comparable, for reasons to be given. For other reasons, which we will examine presently, a decline of politics has tended to follow a decline of religion—at least in the West—meaning that political analysis or therapy would ordinarily depend on an understanding of religious evolution. Some of these ideas were suggested to me by reading a remarkable passage written a number of years ago by Peter Berger with reference to a worldwide theological crisis characterized by secularization and pluralism. Berger wrote:

> Indeed, it makes sense to include in the same overall crisis the difficulties faced by the legitimators of non-religious *Weltanschauungen*, particularly that of dogmatic Marxism. In a very real way, however, the Protestant development is prototypical to the point where one can even say that quite possibly all other religious traditions in the modern situation may be predestined to go through variants of the Protestant experience.[4]

He implied that this might be true also of cosmopolitan nonreligious ideologies. This idea of course recalls that Marx and Engels, in some moods, saw themselves as completing the work of Luther by "destroying the priest within" as an emancipatory project.[5] What I shall call the "Protestant paradigm" is a doubly tempting point of departure for the analysis I am proposing. First, Protestantism, widely considered as an agent of modernization, harbors both a tendency to abolish intermediaries between the mundane and the transcendent and an impulsive urge toward the same kind of sectarian fission observable in the liberal and Marxist worlds. Second, the "Protestant paradigm" seems, a fortiori, to be a useful way of looking at political predicaments in a liberal, "post-Protestant" culture.

The second point is that *as categories of human experience and action, politics and religion are our chief modes of behavior in the spheres called society and culture.* I shall not tarry long over the concepts of society and culture, except to argue (together with most anthropologists) that they are highly interwoven and that politics and religion are indifferently anchored in both. Society and culture, sparingly useful as conceptual antagonists, are seamlessly connected by history—that is, by the collective memory. As opposed to politics and religion, which are active resources and closely related to will and conviction, they tend to be passive or given fields of enterprise. Of the many social theorists who set them apart, a recent example is Daniel Bell: he stipulates a distinction between a unilinear, progressive, and "secularizing" sphere of society (including politics) and a cyclical, existential sphere of culture (prominently including religion).[6] It seems to me quite arbitrary to deny that both politics and religion cut across these boundaries.

Third, *politics and religion, state and church, are both fundamentally species of control systems, of countervailing, but different, sorts.* "Control" is not meant to sound ominous: there may or may not be considerable latitude of freedom within the controls, and the competition of the controls itself may provide for freedom. I call these controls ultimate, meaning of first priority, and meaning also that neither politics nor religion appears to "wither away," although their transient forms may cease to inspire conviction or impose higher order. Using a familiar vocabulary with roots in St. Augustine as well as Durkheim, we might say that politics is the ultimate control system of the profane and that religion is the ultimate control system of the sacred. These substantives seem de rigueur when one considers the confusions that the corresponding nouns would produce. Furthermore, both these spheres are what I call "preservative"—

especially when a healthy balance between them and between each and its members is maintained, or when one must take up the slack of the other. Specifically, religion provides preservation as a consolation for mortality, as expiation, as a sign of dignity and meaning in a cosmos with which we have no direct dialogue, and as a primary instrument of social cohesiveness. It has also typically legitimated political structures and personnel. Politics is preservative, too, in the sense of a secular ongoingness, with the obligation of maintaining the profane world in being and causing it not to be despised. Though grave disputes have been fought over persons and ranks, goods and territories, forms and functions, self-images and values, it is their priority, not their existence, that is at stake, except in the maddest moments of political depravity. I would also add that politics, often requiring some variety of religious legitimation, has found it prudent to protect religion. Without going to the extreme of discovering a "civil religion" in America, one cannot doubt that the existence of a public religion, a blurry sort of "public theology," and periodic practices of public piety have been aspects of this legitimizing process.

The fourth point is that *neither religion nor politics can be properly understood—at least in our civilization—without cognizance of both their inner and outer features.* Both are internal and personal reservoirs of conviction (which we might distinguish, respectively, by the concepts faith and allegiance);[7] both are also structured, purposeful, external organizations (church and state). The balance of power between the internal and external aspects of religion and politics is a matter of critical interest in the history of the West, especially as regards the fortunes of the "Protestant paradigm." In Protestant and liberal culture it is a well-known fact that the internal (or autonomous) features of religion have been afforded supremacy over the external. To cite Immanuel Kant: "At the very outset, we must carefully distinguish the church from religion, which is an inner attitude of mind."[8] Or, carried a stage further in John Dewey: "The opposition between religious values as I conceive them and religion is not to be bridged. Just because the release of these values is so important, their identification with the creeds and cults of religion must be dissolved."[9] With greater nuance, the same may be stated for politics: that is what the stress on the conditions of individual obligation, conscientious objection, passive disobedience, and ultimately, the right of rebellion is all about. Pluralization encourages both individuation and conflicting rules of allegiance. As Michael Walzer writes, "If the business of the 'lesser' groups is not trivial, then the 'universal affairs of state' will lose their distinction. And the authorities in turn will lose their distinction: they will be challenged by a multitude of 'lesser' authorities 'dutifully discharging their public functions.' " Thus "it is not so easy . . . to identify the traitor with the faithless citizen."[10] No doubt in America the tensions between the internal and external aspects of both politics and religion have been traditionally sustained at a very high pitch, for in no other land, it seems, is the "Protestant paradigm" so intimately related to the national consciousness.

My final point is that *there is, generally speaking, a lag in Western civilization between the trajectories of power and conviction in religion and politics.* It is because the age of religious faith in the West appears to have crested and declined before the age of political loyalty that there may be a possibility of reaching some understanding of current political pathology, in terms of a religious pathology that is already there to witness. Although the rise of Western politics was conditioned by a decline of external religious strength, the relation does not even approximate inverse proportionality. There is an intimate connection between politics and religion involving all sorts of empirical mixtures. Both are forms of organized power; both are forms of constellated conviction; both can—in given conditions—drive people toward anarchy or antinomianism. Each has impinged on the other, but there has been no fight to the death. The competition cannot be rendered graphically as a crossing of ascending and descending lines. The more likely image is that of parabolas, certainly not of the same shape, reproducing a similar effect at a considerable distance in time. According to this image, which underlies what I shall later have to say about "disenchantment," the descending arcs have tended to draw closer in our present age, especially in the United States, where, for reasons best left aside here, the religious decline was retarded.

Before proceeding to Tocqueville's thesis about the relationship between religion and civil freedom in a democratic society, I should like to mention three views of what I have called the sacred and profane control systems. The first of these is clearly Augustinian, but it is more easily expressed in the contemporary formulation of Karl Barth. According to Barth, the things of God and Caesar are distinct, but the morally compelling ordinances of the one temper the physically coercive immediacy of the other, while the legitimate compulsion of the second provides an armature for free spirituality in the first. "Political systems," Barth writes, "create and preserve a space for . . . the fulfillment of the purpose of world history, a space for faith, repentance, and knowledge"; at the same time, members of the religious community with the state "bring [the Kingdom of God] to man's attention . . . reminding the state of those things of which it is unlikely to remind itself."[11] I cite Barth, not because his ideas are prevalent in America today, but because, even better than Tocqueville, he expresses the religious-public continuum as it was more or less understood by our early settlers, the Puritans of New England, who found a positive value in community-oriented action because it spiritualized the span of human time in which the Kingdom of God might arrive.[12]

My second illustration is from Montesquieu's De l'esprit des lois. Montesquieu is of course not concerned in this work about the advent of the heavenly kingdom. Neither, in my judgment, is he insidiously attacking the Christian religion. As he puts it, he is writing not as a "théologien" but as an "écrivain politique"—his mission is a detached exploration of the political and social dimensions of religion.[13] His interesting hypothesis is the following: "Since both religion and the civil laws should principally contribute to making men good citizens, we can see that when one of the two strays from its goal, the other should be more firmly fastened on it: the less religion disciplines (sera réprimante), the more the civil laws ought to."[14] This is blunt enough: given that a state wants good citizens (elsewhere in the work Montesquieu implies that Protestants can make good citizens), the more it can rely on religious control, the milder its political constraints can afford to be. We should mark Montesquieu's aphorism carefully: if it is not axiomatic, although many believe it to be—especially "sociologists and anthropologists"—that "we cannot escape membership in some civic faith even if we wished to, for the alternative to organizing belief is chaos,"[15] then the other conceivable solution would be some alternance or balance of moral control by the sacred and profane institutions.

I turn finally to John Locke. In his *Letter Concerning Toleration* he exquisitely balances the realms of the sacred and the profane. In the first instance, Locke notes: "Every man has an immortal soul, capable of eternal happiness or misery; whose happiness depends [upon] his believing and doing those things in his life, which are necessary to the obtaining of God's favor, and are prescribed by God to that end." "There is nothing in the world," he continues, "that is of any consideration in comparison with eternity." But, in parallel, there is the profane sphere: "Besides their souls, which are immortal, men also have their temporal lives here upon earth; the state whereof being frail and fleeting, and the duration uncertain; they have need of several outward conveniencies to the support thereof." The preservation of these "conveniencies" and of a secure liberty "obliges men to enter into society with one another; that by mutual assistance and joint force, they may secure unto each other their proprieties, in the things that contribute to the comforts and happiness of this life." The profane system has no license to control the sacred, its proper business being only "to provide . . . for the safety and security of the commonwealth, and of every particular man's goods and person."[16] Locke did not believe that a citizen could be without religion—for otherwise his public oaths would be untrustworthy—but he asked only that religion not be expressly antipublic; he did not see it as public.

These texts prepare us for Tocqueville. Before considering his contribution, one last question needs to be raised. Was America a "new" country or was it only a "young" country? Once formed as a federal nation, Americans had little doubt about the answer. And Tocqueville decisively took the position that not only was America a new country, but that the world was inevitably to be made anew, with America almost surely as the vanguard model of these changes.[17] Tocqueville did not discover this philosophy of history in America or induce it from American experiences. But America seemed to him an overwhelming confirmation of his *idée-force*. This heavily colored his functional interpretation of the American religion.

II

Tocqueville, like Montesquieu, approaches the question of religion in terms of its public function and, specifically, of what effects it brings to bear publicly on a disestablished democratic (implying also "liberal," "republican") state.[18] Tocqueville has also imbibed Locke's creed of separation and toleration, for he adverts more than once to the travesties of state-manipulated religion and enforced conviction, which "risks that authority which is rightfully its own."[19] Yet it is far more Montesquieu's sociological path than Locke's philosophical path that Tocqueville treads: he is immediately impressed by the role of formally voluntary religion in shaping the civil experience. Thus we may say that Tocqueville inverts the Barthian-Augustinian formulation. Politics is not seen as providing sufficient time and testing for the spiritualization of man; rather, religion is seen as mediating between civic duty and limitless egoism in a regime unconstrained by self-conscious tradition, social hierarchy, or strongly centralized political force. Religion provides the matrix in which republican politics, shorn of antique virtue, can mellow without destructive excesses of individualism.[20] Religion shapes naked self-interest into "self-interest rightly understood."[21]

Tocqueville saw especially in the religion bequeathed by New England "the triumph of an idea"—an evolving belief system able to create buffering zones of freedom against the leveling passions of democracy—for, he argued, "Puritanism was not merely a religious doctrine, but corresponded in many points with the most absolute democratic and republican theories."[22] It is, of course, highly contestable that the "holy commonwealth" was a crucible of liberal freedom.[23] Still, if one looks at the Puritan culture in both its civic and evolutionary dimensions, Tocqueville's claim does make a certain sense. Bigotry aside, one can recognize in early Massachusetts and Connecticut the sprouting germs of republican civic cooperation. Citizenship and mutual help were strict duties in these communities. Though the vested power of a harsh creed was pervasive, state and church were distinct, and the clergy had less control over politics than anywhere in Europe.[24] Moreover, learning and piety went hand in hand with the Puritans: schooling was next only to churching and survival on their value scale. The freedom and initiative of the citizen had their sources in the probity of the private man and his family life, which were rather mercilessly exposed to public view. Thus religion had early links with both public activity and with the pursuit of useful knowledge. As Tocqueville asserted, "In America religion is the road to knowledge, and the observance of the divine laws leads men to civil freedom."[25]

The astute and skeptical Tocqueville could scarcely have believed that Cotton Mather had sired Jefferson, or even Adams. I think that he was making a much more sophisticated argument based essentially on two points. He expressed the first of these as follows: "By the side of every religion is to be found a political opinion, which is connected with it by affinity. If the human mind be left to follow its own bent, it will regulate the temporal and spiritual institutions of society in a uniform manner, and man will endeavor, if I may so speak, to *harmonize* earth with heaven." Tocqueville referred here neither to the utopian fantasy of creating a heaven out of profane materials, nor to the Hebraizing tendency of many American spokesmen to regard their birthright as specially "chosen" or their land as one of "milk and honey." Rather, he meant that there could be a religious solution that engendered the wide exercise of civil freedom, one involving a common practice of self-control emanating from private conviction but organized by free churches. With the austere edges of early Calvinism rounded off, its inherited discipline—which was both intensely personal and communal at the same time—could compensate for a boundless Arminianism in politics. Tocqueville was of course also warning France and Europe, where the religious underpinnings most certainly did not favor a smooth glide toward democracy; for in France "it is not the people who [would] preponderate in this kind of government, but those who know what is good for the people." America, on the other hand, had become "the slow and quiet action of society upon itself."[26]

In the second place, Tocqueville, again echoing Montesquieu ("He who has no religion at all is that terrible animal who can feel his freedom only when he is destroying and devouring"[27]) and also Benjamin Constant ("Religious peoples can be slaves, but no irreligious people ever remained free"[28]), believed that man is unnatural, less than human, without religion: "Man alone, of all created beings, displays a natural contempt of existence, and yet a boundless desire to exist: he scorns life, but he dreads annihilation. . . . Religion, then, is simply another form of hope, and it is no less natural to the human heart than hope itself. . . . Unbelief is an accident, and faith is the only permanent state of mankind." If man does not live by hope, he lives in fear, and is, by that token, unfree. Or he becomes savage, and must be denied freedom. "For my own part," Tocqueville writes, "I doubt whether man can ever at the same time support complete religious independence and entire political freedom. And I am inclined to think that if faith be wanting in him, he must be subject; and if he be free, he must believe." Without religion, men will resolve their public fate in bursts of anarchy or servility. Moreover, they will be unfit for knowledge and clear vision: "When the religion of a people is destroyed, doubt gets hold of the higher powers of the intellect and half paralyses all the others." In counterpart, "religion perceives that civil liberty affords a noble exercise to the faculties of man and that the political world is a field prepared by the Creator for the efforts of mind."[29]

The Americans were fortunate in having a religion that inculcated the needed republican repressions so that they could proceed to develop a wide sphere of liberty in their civic affairs. Tocqueville was persuaded that religion played no direct role in government (he commented three times on the neutrality of the clergy[30]), but, he remarked, "it must be regarded as the first of [American] political institutions; for if it does not impart a taste for freedom, it facilitates the use of it." In other words, Tocqueville was never deluded that religion itself was "free" in some "every man his own church" sense. On the contrary, he saw the numerous sects everywhere, even the Catholics, teaching a common ethic, creating a culture of "self-interest rightly understood," a common strength which, if not very deep, was terribly inclusive.[31]

I do not wish to stray from the boundaries of this essay in the direction of that difficult subject, "civil religion"—either as applied to the founding of the republic, or to current predicaments, or to the general needs of nationhood.[32] Still, we might well ask here: Are we justified in calling Tocqueville's model an "American civil religion"? He certainly did describe it as "democratic and republican," and he had no illusions about its want of theological profundity.[33] It also served to condition a common response to profane issues. But it does not seem to have been "civil" in the strong sense. It enabled civil freedom; it did not create it. It proceeded not from national festivals à la Lloyd Warner[34] or from political preaching, but from the separate congregational pulpits and the inner convictions of persons and families. It was not a manipulation of oaths and profane symbols or some Polybian elitist intrigue to keep ordinary men in fear of the gods. Until a generation ago one might have called it "mainstream Protestantism," minus exotic differences of dogma. It was, to borrow Michael Oakeshott's illuminating typology, a mixture between a "morality of communal ties" (the *Gemeinschaft* of a largely rural society) and a "morality of individuality" (the guidance mechanism of the person alone with his choices).[35] Only through "slow and quiet action" did these eventuate in a "morality of the common good": the American religion did not sacralize the state for the citizen's worship and wonder. It was out of their separate accretions of experience that the Americans could "profess to think that a people ought to be moral, religious, and temperate in proportion as it is free."[36]

Of course, not all Americans observed a Tocquevillian *juste milieu* in these matters. In arguing that religion provided republicans with those inner controls of morality—domestic, municipal, and economic—that made a free public life possible, Tocqueville was neglectful of religion's own unleashed power. He expected religion "to purify, to regulate, and to restrain," not to release Dionysiac passions. He did not see that explosions of the sacred were creating much of the civil community that was to be had in the sparsely populated wildernesses of the West, nor did he sense the intimate connection of circuit riders and camp meetings with the spread of American democracy. He did not note the resemblances between the stump preacher and the stump politician and the implications of their common stock of salvationary rhetoric. When Tocqueville encountered a few frenzies of evangelism, he commented: "From time to time strange sects arise which endeavor to strike out extraordinary paths to eternal happiness. Religious insanity is very common in the United States."[37] Although his view of American religion surely went beyond what Sidney Mead has called a "religion of the republic,"[38] it certainly could not account for Millerites, Pentecostalists, or Mormons. He was misinformed both about the imagination of American sectarianism and about the iron grip of the major Protestant denominations over the developing social order. He did not estimate the lasting impact of all this religious fertility on our politics.

A second critical feature escaped Tocqueville, if I read him correctly. He seems to have believed that an essentially Calvinist rigor in religious belief and training (moderated, to be sure, by the civil doctrines of the Enlightenment) was a necessary moral complement to the emergence of a perfectly Arminian political and social person. These attributes checked each other in the citizen's behavior. Fortunately or not (and I must dispense with the laborious history), political Arminianism—a sovereignty of the people that is explicitly, definitively free in the profane sphere, and manifest in its works—called forth an Arminian liberation in the sacred sphere as well. Democratic man needed to be reassured of the worth of his visible works; he needed to feel that his repentant surge toward God's mercy was efficacious; above all, he needed the conviction that most persons, unless they flouted God's ways outrageously, would be saved.[39] It was not Catholic absolution but a sense of renewed innocence that Americans required to practice their politics. The Methodist Church, which grew swiftly in the early nineteenth century, provided the most exemplary vehicle for this outlet of emotion and riveting of conviction: amid our two or three hundred sects, it remains today (vastly liberalized, somewhat less democratized) the closest thing we have to a national church. Methodism and Calvinism, both highly congregationalized—which is the tendency of all American churches—drew together to forge the spiritual base of American politics, with many significant consequences up to our own time. In counterpoint, of course, there was a continuing proliferation of sects outside of the oligopoly of the ruling denominations, a tendency in itself no less American.[40]

We must take at face value—whatever may have been Tocqueville's private religious skepticism—the statement that if a man is to be free, he must believe. Tocqueville approved of the fact that unbelievers kept silence in America, and he nowhere imputed this tactic to the political elite. Whether or not we call his views a political theology is a matter of perspective. It is, however, surely mistaken to interpret Tocqueville's idea of an American "providential mission" as if the formation and destiny of the Americans had been in the mind of God. When Tocqueville wrote of continental expansion, he treated it as an imperative of nature, not as a divine oracle—a consequence of profane abundance. He cites "climate . . . inland seas . . . great rivers . . . exuberant soul . . . love of prosperity and spirit of enterprise" and "the knowledge that guides [the Americans] on their way."[41] No doubt these things are infused with religion, but it is a faith whose function is to temper what geopolitics has ordained.[42] Thus Tocqueville is not a source of the imperialistic hybris later so vocal in America, when motives of religion and politics united to encourage an evangelistic expansion of world power.[43]

Tocqueville felt that the democratic and irreligious impulses had formed an unwholesome alliance in France. He was thus reassured to discover religion and the new era of the common man in partnership in America. He did not ask religion to perform saintly wonders, nor did he demand Roman virtue from the politics of the coming age. His goal was a moderate "harmonization." It depended on the principle that the sects could and did transmit a common moral guidance for the conduct of citizens. Tocqueville was perhaps mistaken, even in his own time, in holding this proportionate behavior to be the fact of the case. Many things since his time, not least of them the "pursuit of individual life-styles" and what Robert Coles has described as a condition of "the self [as] our transcendence [where] politics becomes, along with everything else, a matter of impulse, whim, fancy, exuberant indulgence, bored indifference, outright angry rejection,"[44] have undermined the delicate politico-religious balancing of Tocquevillian democracy. He would have been disquieted by the results we have obtained and by the way we have gotten here.

III

In his lectures on the philosophy of history delivered in Berlin in 1830, the year before his death and the year before Tocqueville's arrival in the United States, Hegel discerned in America "an unbounded license in religious mat-ters." It was the sectarian imagination run wild, a complete exposure of the "Protestant paradigm." For Hegel, America was as yet only a rude "civil society," lacking a fully developed "state." Thus it was both religiously diffuse and politically inchoate, or—to return to an earlier point—a "young" nation, but certainly not a "new" nation in the sense that Tocqueville was about to claim. According to Hegel, "North America will be comparable with Europe [i.e., as a "state" and as a part of the "Germanic" or "Teutonic" phase of world history] only after the immeasurable space which that country presents to its inhabitants shall have been occupied, and the members of the political body shall have begun to be pressed back on each other." A real state in America can be formed "only after a distinction of classes has arisen, when wealth and poverty become extreme, and when such a condition of things presents itself that a large portion of the people can no longer satisfy its necessities as it has been accustomed so to do."[45]

In this view, America matures and becomes an object worthy of historical comprehension by reaching territorial saturation and acquiring a well-defined class structure and a class conflict over scarce goods. For it then, of necessity, must develop over, above, and against its institutions of civil society that superior structure of order and allegiance called a state. Without stretching the imagination too far, one could argue that a plausible version of the Hegelian scenario had been played out in the United States from the New Deal on, and especially since the experience of the Second World War. To be sure, there are certain anomalies in the application: for example, Hegel would doubtless have included in his forecast an abatement of the religious imagination and a passage from republicanism to constitutional monarchy (perhaps we have a functional one). But the major issue is that this "land of the future" would enter European history and world history, instead of shaping history in a novel fashion, as Tocqueville had believed. Connected with all this is a certain implication of limits and cosmic humility. Reinhold Niebuhr perceived these consequences more readily than most other Americans. "Escape from our ironic situation," he wrote a generation ago, "obviously demands that we moderate our conceptions of the ability of men and nations to discern the future; and of the power of even great nations to bring a tortuous historical process to, what seems to them, a logical and proper conclusion."[46] Since this involved not only an acceptance of responsibility, but an acknowledgment of "the idea that guilt accompanies responsibility,"[47] it was a notion that many Americans still find difficult.

Hegel and Niebuhr prepare us, in a way that Tocqueville does not, for the possibility of disenchantment in our religion and in our politics. Weber's now classic coinage "disenchantment" (*Entzauberung*) has stressful mood connections with *fin de siècle* and the holocaust of World War I. It was exploited in a public lecture where Weber counseled his audience stoically not to seek emotional adventure in science. There are also obvious affinities with the various portraits of alienation drawn by Rousseau, Schiller, Hegel, Marx, and their successors, with a particular link to Novalis, who had written in his *Christenheit oder Europa* (1799) with regard to the Enlightenment: "In Germany . . . attempts were made to give the old religion a more modern, rational, and universal sense by carefully divesting it of everything wonderful and mysterious."[48] For Novalis, disenchantment was reversible; for Weber, not. Disenchantment expresses more than a vanishing of the religious or supernatural justification of human purposes and existence; more than the surrender of public spirit and leaderly energy to bureaucratic routine: "It means that, in principle, there are no mysterious incalculable forces that come into play, but rather that one can, in principle, master all things by calculation." It is the philosophy of Hobbes finally realized in the spaces of society, and perhaps *in foro interno* besides: "the world's transformation into a causal mechanism."

Throughout Weber's complicated and sometimes ugly locutions a pervasive ostinato is always heard, a heavy tread of the depersonal stone guest upon the vanquished corpse of the personal. There is also tragic irony: prophetic Calvinism begets rationalistic progeny; religious election establishes a doom in which the new elect or elite "commit" themselves to callings in which all passion is dangerous and must be routinized by "methodology"; modern life must memorialize the capitalist entrepreneur as its last hero (a theme carried forward by Schumpeter). This tendency is not unrelieved by pathos and resistance, for, according to Weber, the more the external world is rationalized, the more some people will attempt to escape from that world into mystical and salvationary solutions. Science has the unavoidable capacity to stimulate sects. This has bearing on both the resurgence of fundamentalism and the rise of cultism, matters touched on only very lightly in this essay. The fundamentalism recalls the reaction of Novalis and Adam Müller earlier on. And it is not without significance, as J. Milton Yinger has suggested to me, that Weber goes so far as to reutilize Plato's famous image of shadows in the cave: new and comforting, but perhaps illusory, mystiques such as those practiced by the growing number of syncretistic or scientist cults in contemporary America may, as judged by circumstances, provide a kind of "enchanted" solace through shadow-play. Thus there ensues an increasing tension between mechanical and irrational extremisms, between matter-of-factness and despair. This process was doomed, in Weber's view, to "succumb in the end to the world dominion of unbrotherliness," mastered by "the technical and social conditions of rational culture." Yet disenchantment was not only a collective state of mind or an institutional fatality; it was also a history of Western man's spiritual closure. That history was long and inexorable: a process moving in cadence with an intellectualization that "has continued to exist in Occidental culture for millennia."[49] Seemingly, it had already canceled out what the theologian Paul Tillich would later call "matters of ultimate concern."[50] For, as Weber writes, "since death is meaningless, civilized life as such is meaningless."[51]

How do we locate America in this doom and gloom? Were the seedlings of disenchantment already planted in the psyche of our first ancestors who came to build a "holy commonwealth" or to flee from profaned ones? Had they sprouted in the undogmatic "reasonable" religion of our Founders, only to bud in Tocqueville's climate of "self-interest rightly understood," and burst into flower in an advancing industrial culture where preachers and politicians were continually confusing material progress with God's intentions? America, it is true, did develop attributes of shallow spirituality and a gift for technical smugness: we produced no Montaigne or Pascal, only an Emerson. Yet, until fairly recently, most Americans imagined transcendent, conceivably magical properties in their enterprise. Both religion and politics were charged with the symbols of an optimistic, even redemptive, national Providence in which God was a hearty collaborator. That Providence, it seemed, could embrace Weberian calculation and still remain free, open, and enchanted. Rationalization had become revelation itself: part of a continuing aura of romance, part of the field of faith. America had no need of Europe's fabricated positivistic religions. Was there not abundant evidence that Jehovah was doing the job?

This strikes me as something a little more substantial than "false consciousness." America scarcely seemed to harbor the crises that made Marx militant and Weber fretful. America proved to be, at the same time, a geographical reservoir of the mystery that inspires hope and faith, a mental image begotten in part by salvationary anticipations; and yet, paradoxically, a crucible for the unalloyed casting of crude technical behavior. If Weberian disenchantment proceeded more slowly here than in the old countries, it was partly because the geographical and prophetic impulses overweighed the rational-technical mentality. Our civil war gave these things mythical proportions, while our insulation from international strain sustained belief in the constancy of Providence. Finally, our characteristic resistance to higher flights of the intellect helped to make disenchantment a highly un-American enterprise, appropriate to solitude or exile. Indeed, pragmatism and technicism cottoned the American soul from some of the worst pains of an unmysterious world, although they would later be poor guardians against its encroachment. We did not need to confront Hobbes head on, so long as God could be found as easily in the Stock Exchange as in a sunset, or in a Model-T car as easily as in Lincoln's tomb.

Now, however, disenchantment has, by stages, visited America. Disenchantment is porous: its social connectedness or social location is extremely hard to pin down because of its unmediated play of oppositions. It owes as much to success as nemesis; it relates to trend-setting middle classes as well as to the despairing poor, to the ethic of indulgence as well as to the ethic of toil; and it has deviantly branching historical roots in America. Some writers in this volume agree that it receives a part of its dynamic from the ascendancy of a predominantly secularizing force—sometimes called the "knowledge class"— the values it imposes, and the antagonisms it elicits in the wider society. There seems also to be a more generalized conflict between imperatives of production and patterns of consumption that we are now experiencing. Notions of the "self" and of the "public" are in grave dispute. What especially strikes the political theorist is that under this new-class aegis there is a special disenchantment with *being represented*, which is both intellectual and cultish at the same time (we could look back to Swedenborgianism and its impact on the Emerson-James tradition). Although new-classers are not austere religious solitaries like Kierkegaard, many could subscribe to this passage from his *Journals:* "The new development for our time cannot be political, for politics is the relationship between the community and the representative individual. But in our time, the individual is becoming far too reflective to be satisfied with being merely represented."[52] This is one of the contexts of meaning in which our present forces collide. It is close enough to reality to be able to function *as reality.*

There is, however, a more detached perspective from which to view disenchantment. I think it can be stated as follows. With the dawning of disenchantment (despite peculiar American features), we have joined, or rejoined, the Western world; and, I think, great changes have been wrought in both our religious sensibility and our political perceptions that have not yet been fully registered, because the curse or wound of belonging to the ordinary world is not yet a familiar feeling. We achieved disenchantment much in the way that Hegel said we would enter speculative world history: we filled up our territory, we suffered painful economic and social troubles, we acquired the machinery and habits of a Leviathan state, and we began to look outward with less political theology and more *Realpolitik.* My contention is that politics and religion have been similarly affected by this process. Although it was once widely held that politics, by accepting the procedures of science, and religion, by appearing to shrink beneath its blows, were poles apart, this cannot now be unproblematically asserted. Essentially it is a question of symbolization and faith. As regards religion and science, A. J. Ayer has written:

> The scientific world-picture which was current in the nineteenth century was reasonably simple and coherent. . . . But by now the situation of science itself has changed. . . . Its basic concepts are further removed from those of common sense; they make no immediate appeal to the layman's imagination. Thus, to the uninitiated, its account of the world, though more precise, is hardly less fantastic than the religious account.[53]

And as regards politics and science, there is a twofold problem: (1) Although science is widely conceded to be a "self-correcting enterprise," if it is anything at all,[54] other authoritative procedures are required in politics, where one cannot lightly correct a social order the way one might correct a body of research. (2) Science spawns reductionism, and "the trouble with reductionism, as far as politics is concerned, is not that it gives *all* the answers to the important issues but that it gives hardly any."[55] Thus science cannot appropriately integrate or divide the world picture we have drawn. Science itself is not exempt from the kind of disenchantment it sponsors.

One can, I think, break down the Weberian concept of disenchantment into a number of categories, where we will discover some profound parallels in the destiny of our religion and of our politics. As earlier noted, these parallels can be conceived in two senses: first, as between the institutional predicaments of the churches and the agencies of the state; second, as between the more psychic disorders of religious and civic commitment, what I earlier called faith and allegiance. These separate perspectives are linked by my designation of religion as the ultimate control system of the sacred, and politics as the ultimate control system of the profane. The categories I arrive at for fundamental analysis are seven in number: immanentism, bureaucratization, dissociation, indifference, privatization, secularization, and nostalgia. Since there is not room in this essay to give an adequate account of the religious-political correspondences in each of these phenomena, parsimony counsels me to dwell on the last three.

Privatization means essentially the withdrawal of an understanding or a practice from the public space of consensual or negotiable choice to the microcosm of individual choice, passing perhaps by way of the restricted number of friends and kin with whom one has "private relations."[56] Choices tend to become valued precisely because they come from personal (or, as it is said, "authentic") conviction, rather than because they conform to authority or tradition. Often the movement of choice in this direction has been interpreted as an expansion of autonomy; however, today it is increasingly felt by some that convictions driven inward are, by that token, unfree.

Among the privatistic tendencies in religion is the phenomenon of shopping around, or "consumerism," in adopting a belief. Religion is most easily marketed if it can be shown to be very relevant to private life. Consumerism may lead the customer to a comfortable, undemanding faith, or it may plunge him into the bowels of Harvey Cox's "secular city."[57] In either case, it will reflect what Weber had already called "the technical and social conditions of rational culture." Thomas Luckmann connects privatization with the fragmentation of sacred coherence: "The 'autonomous' consumer selects . . . certain religious themes from the available assortment and builds them into a somewhat precarious private system of 'ultimate' significance. Individual religiosity is thus no longer a replica or approximation of an 'official model.' "[58] This might seem to be the felicity that John Dewey was contemplating when he wrote about the opposition between religious values and religion.[59] But, contrary to what Dewey thought, the weakening of the meaning and validity of corporate worship appears to have been accompanied by a loss of corporate identity in general.[60]

Privatization is also present in the devaluation of the religious element of public legitimation. That decline is, to be sure, often regarded as liberating, and it is swaddled in the language of rights—the secular or profane rights of a disestablished polity. But secularism has gone too far in removing the sacralization of the public power by the faith of groups and communities: this is as much a warrant of pessimism as of freedom.[61] Although it has been often enough said that "the American state is . . . emphatically *not* separated from religion in general,"[62] it seems unlikely—except at high moments—that "a vague and somewhat sentimental religious syncretism," further defined as "a sort of state Shinto,"[63] whose panpluralist capacities have surely waned in the twenty years since the phrases were composed, disputes privatism or fulfills a Tocquevillian design. We should notice, too, that secularism itself is largely privatized in America.

The notion of legitimation furnishes a key bridge between the privatization of religion and the privatization of politics. For a long time the first tendency had been perceived by sociologists as a kind of reaction to the disenchantment of public life. Karl Mannheim, for example, wrote of "the gradual recession into privacy of certain spheres previously public (the spheres of life in which personal and religious feelings prevail)" as being "in the nature of a compensation for the increasing rationalization of public life in general—in the workshop, in the market-place, in politics, etc."[64] But religious privatization is not necessarily a storehouse of magic that buffers people against an inhospitable and mechanical public world. For we now see evidence that public life is itself being "privatized" and that privatized politics is itself an aspect of the same disenchantment.

In our politics, privatization has proceeded both from the base and from the pinnacle. Citizenship, as Sheldon Wolin wrote a number of years ago, has been reduced to a "cheap commodity."[65] Indeed, we speak perfectly naturally of the "private citizen." Any public commodity that is both universalized and minimized—and to which no particular merit is attached—might be expected to suffer this fate. The multiplication of so-called social rights in the United States does not appear to have enriched the status of citizens with what T. H. Marshall once called, a little hyperbolically, a "great extension of common culture and common experience." Nor perhaps could it have done this in a situation where "social integration [has] spread from the sphere of sentiment and patriotism into that of material enjoyment."[66] Adam Ferguson warned, two hundred years ago, of peoples who "have, sooner or later, been diverted from their object, and fallen prey to misfortune, or to the neglects which prosperity itself had encouraged."[67] Such, perhaps, is the natural trauma of "modern liberty."

The state, too, has become privatized, not only in the horizons of the citizen, but also under the approving scrutiny of some of the recent political theory. Even as the state has grown bloated with new functions (beyond the most imaginative Hegelianism) and has penetrated new areas of people's lives, it has become less a state, less focal as a center of allegiance. It has become more thoroughly dominated by segmented interests and passions. To quote Wolin, who was remarkably visionary about all this, once again: "This is a world which Hobbes might have enjoyed: one created by human wit, where rational action has become a matter of routine, and magic has been banished."[68] One may wonder whether human wit does not conceal a certain amount of chaos. Habermas's observation that "civic privatism denotes . . . little participation in the legitimizing process" is also symptomatic of the breakdown of both voluntary access and moral conviction in the Tocquevillian sense.[69] Privatization, moreover, leads to a "political Donatism" that ignores the public rite or office for the private image of the pontifex. This is expedited by the otiose way in which information is received and digested. And, with the public made more private, a "political Protestantism" infects citizens with a pretension to bestow legitimacy privately via the individual conscience or "transcendent self."

Secularization is not just a progress of worldliness but a concerted application of worldly techniques to establish the value and directedness of all problematic change. It is a submission of value-oriented activity to an unmysterious obedience. It is also, of course, a process that has been going on for a very long time.

American disenchantment is very much conditioned by the way in which secularization was received, for here it was amalgamated with religion itself. As Luckmann writes: "Traditional church religion was pushed to the periphery of 'modern life' in Europe while it became more 'modern' in America by undergoing a process of internal secularization."[70] This seems to me correct. In the earlier Tocquevillian vision, religion was, among other things, socially useful, indeed indispensable. That, too, was the thrust of Durkheimian sociology. In today's more secularized times, the emphasis has shifted to the psychological: here science and superstition meet uncomfortably in the atmosphere of disenchantment. As Peter Berger observes: "Religion is highly beneficial, perhaps even essential to the psychological integration of the individual. . . . In general, religion is conducive to mental health."[71] This fits nicely with Robert Coles's comment that among us "the self [is] the only or main form of (existential) reality."[72] William James had drawn religion into the self almost a century ago; as his colleague Josiah Royce commented: "James no longer finds in the religious life of communities the novelty and independence of vision which he prizes."[73] Although neither the sociological nor the psychological position is false, religion is more than social utility, because it is also an impending judgment from beyond society, and it is more than life-adjustment, because it is also unceasing disquietude.

For a variety of reasons, secularization in American religion has oscillated wildly between the intimacies of the sick soul and militant nostrums of social action, as in the Social Gospel at the turn of the present century or, more recently, in Harvey Cox's "new breed" of clergy.[74] Another major tendency has been the vitiation of theology—"the science of the sacred," akin to "political theory"—in the Protestant churches, first through an appeal to discursive toleration, then, in Vahanian's words, as a movement from "theological liberty" to a condition that "more and more imperturbably signified freedom from theology."[75] Attempts have also been made to create a "layman's religion" that "does not consist of definite articles of faith such as might be embodied in a credo and expounded in a theology,"[76] or a "political theology" (influenced by the "liberation theologies" of Germany and Latin America) that would be radically mundane and activist.[77] Scholars optimistic about the use-value, if not the truth-value, of American religion have tended to substitute the concept "differentiation" for secularization, meaning that religion becomes a stronger social element as its range is narrowed;[78] while still other scholars have praised "secularization" as a healthy response to our times (indeed as a fulfillment of Scripture), and have set the concept against the pejorative "secularism."[79] Much of this is, I think, mere word-play. We need not argue that religion in America is in danger of vanishing to remain persuaded that it is in a remarkably confused state.

"Secularized politics" as well? It seems obvious that politics is secular to the core, for it is the "control system of the profane." However, politics was a well-delineated mode of theory and conduct long before the secularization process began. Classical politics, whose legacy we share, was rooted in the imagery of cycles and duration: the political art stood against time and corruption. In Judaism, Moses created a people and endowed them with a politics that found its adequate earthly expression in the covenant and the law. Although Christianity treated politics as corrupt and perishable, it also saw it as a vital buffering of the earthly city against chaos. It is therefore plausible to speak of a secularization of politics that implies not only its resolute separation from religion, but also its submission to parallel forfeitures of conviction, force, and esteem.

Secularization in politics refers especially to the will to master the recurrently fortuitous in the control system of the profane. After achieving the constitutional separation between office and person, caprice and regulation, political science took the giant step of proposing to substitute administration for government in the interest of rational predictability, and it submitted justice to the same yoke. The idea was also, in the words of Saint-Simon, to "return the destiny of the peoples to the hands of devotion and genius . . . [to] return lovingly to obedience."[80] What Judith Shklar once described as "the decline of political faith" has been closely linked to this trend.[81] The older values or supporting myths of politics—Providence, nature, and history—have been challenged and defeated. For example, the value of history, according to Hannah Arendt, "owes its existence to the transition period when religious confidence in immortal life had lost its influence upon the secular and the new indifference toward the question of immortality had not yet been born."[82] History was then cheapened by the arrogant concept of "modernization," or else absorbed by the primacy of the self. As Henry Kariel writes of his response to the writings of Nietzsche, Freud, and Mannheim: "The logic of their work has the effect of removing a good deal of traditional political philosophy from the public scene. . . . At the same time it summons man to establish himself. It summons him to form and re-form the infinite potentialities which are truly his.

. . . The individual person is expected to make his own truth, thereby satisfying his own diverse needs."[83] Though Kariel's *homo creator* may seem worlds apart from the pseudo-science of technical values, both are terms of the dialectic of disenchantment.

Finally I would close with some words on *nostalgia*. Nostalgic reactions can take essentially three forms: that something gone is deeply to be regretted or commemorated; that something gone can be resurrected; that something that never was can supply the image for what is gone. There was a nostalgia of all three kinds in the response of Novalis and other German Romantics to the Newtonian world of the eighteenth century. But the political conditions of Novalis's time lent nostalgia a remote realism that has never been characteristic of any reliable reading of the American situation. If nostalgia seems currently to have gripped America, it may be, as I have suggested, that our "young" country is no longer in the nursery. Or, as Harold Laski put it, ambiguously, "America as the 'young' nation is at once both a defensive and a prophetic concept."[84]

Nostalgia includes both privileged and anxious reactions to change within the movement of disenchantment. It has its militant and quiescent modes of expression. Sometimes it reveals an authentic and sturdy provincialism. In some senses, it is obviously a countercurrent to other agencies of disenchantment. Although I cannot go into the matter here, I regard many contemporary cults and sects, fascinating as they are to sociologists, as nostalgic epiphenomena, not heralds of some new dawning. The same obervation applies to our recent, absorbing "civil religion" debate (I include Sidney Mead's "religion of the republic" also under this general rubric), although here the thrust came from a concerned minority of the "knowledge class." Martin Marty had it dead right when he wrote of civil religion: "It somehow now 'exists.' . . . It functions chiefly as what Peter Berger and Thomas Luckmann call 'a social construction of reality.' So far it remains chiefly the product of the scholar's world; the man on the street would be surprised to learn of its existence."[85] In any case, we should recall that Weber's concept allowed not only for specific—and even heroic—resistances, but for their incorporation into the very fabric of disenchantment.

Nostalgia has touched America, not for the first time, in religion and politics—both in the uneasy common ground that they occupy and in the jeremiads of the one against the other, which often take the form of appeals to the founding virtues of the republic. There is no need to specify what these currents are or to take a partisan position toward them. There is clearly much pent-up frustration in this country; and there are opposing frustrations that are not reciprocally endured with very much civility. This is nothing new in our history, or in the relations of politics and religion. However, we no longer really believe in Arcadia any more than we believe in the New Atlantis. None of this restiveness carries us beyond our problem; it poses the question: How are we to be spiritual, organic, and free—all at the same time, and in American terms? There has surely been a breakdown of Tocqueville's "common morality" inspired by religion. Nostalgia dissipates both "faith" and "allegiance" with its consummate suspicion of the present and the present's real links with the past.

In religion, nostalgia appears to induce, in the first place, an attempt to repolish old beliefs in the hope of salvaging the symbolic supports they once gave to national pride and faith. Second, there has emerged a kind of moral Manichaeanism that is intended to give battle to relativism and sloppy pluralism, but probably leads to even worse fragmentation. As some are beginning to argue, we now run the unappetizing risk of substituting for a manageable religious pluralism (in the nineteenth century a Protestant denominational oligarchy) a condition of incompatible, scarcely negotiable moral ideologies—the Tocquevillian nightmare. Nostalgics and secularists have both fostered this conflict. Third, there is a reluctance to confront the moral map of society as it exists, either to validate it or to reject it: courage is not *au courant*. In politics we first of all discern the return to a kind of tepid anti-intellectualism that accepts unexamined expertise but is not inclined to ask for its credentials. Second, there is a rise of scattershot individualistic utopianism of various sorts, bred indifferently on Right or Left, in cramped cities or in the wide-open spaces. Utopianism is admittedly an excessive term for it, because in all its shapes it compromises incessantly with powers that be and is parasitic on a world that we know. Finally, there are a good many unfounded presumptions about how the sacred and the profane interact. There are exaggerated imputations or denials of evil that ignore the necessity of evil in the profane sphere, while misunderstanding the ways in which a reverence for the sacred might temper it. The nostalgic reaction tries to reintroduce not just faulty remembrances of the past, but also the ancient notions of guilt and sin, into a society that, in large part, has become morally ill-equipped to receive them. There is a confused straining for both freedom and moral absolutes, which, as James Agee wrote many years ago, is "hardly surprising among those who have witnessed, suffered or perpetrated enough pragmatism and moral relativism—above all in their customary degraded use in public and private life."[86] There is also much hypocrisy: moral absolutism is difficult to reconcile with "secular man's concern with the question 'Will it work?' "[87]

Where Tocqueville declared, "By the side of every religion is to be found a political opinion, which is connected with it by affinity," we might prefer, in our time of disenchantment, to say that politics appears to generate religion.[88] Hannah Arendt has written: "The important historical fact is that an overwhelming majority has ceased to believe in a Last Judgment at the end of time."[89] According to all survey data, this is not the view of a majority of Americans (although it is so in other "post-Protestant" countries). Yet I believe that most of us act as if it were certainly true. That is the main reason the Tocquevillian thesis of the moral control of public life no longer works. This would suggest, in Montesquieu's unflinching terms, that we can sustain cohesion only through greater political restraints on freedom. In pronouncing the death of credible transcendental religion (based on future rewards and punishments), Arendt, in an analysis owing something to the passage from Montesquieu, chose to fall back on *homo eloquens* and the active political life within a well-defined public space, instead of some brooding belief in the continued efficacy of religious sanctions. It is instead my best guess that in the outdating of Tocqueville's formula, a more glacial and less promiscuous politics will be likely to ensue. But I doubt that this will be a "recovery of politics" in the classical and republican spirit of Aristotle. We have no well-defined public space, or any distinctive and effective political speech-habits: only the obtrusion of aggregated private meanings and desires everywhere. And as I have tried to show, in America, at least, politics and religion both suffer from the same affliction. I cannot easily see how a morally effective transmission between religion and public life, or a morally commendable stability within either of these understandings and practices, will be rekindled, whoever is our pontiff or our president. Even if Tocqueville remains cherished in the heart, can we deny Weber's icy grip on our intelligence?

REFERENCES

[1]Martin E. Marty, *The New Shape of American Religion* (New York: Harper, 1959), p. 32.

[2]Sociologist Will Herberg argued in *Protestant, Catholic, Jew: An Essay in American Religious Sociology* (Garden City, N.Y.: Doubleday, 1955) that the American religions had produced an indistinct amalgam ("the American Way of Life") that was basically functional in the profane sphere, but shallow and unwholesome for religion itself. However, other writers (cf. Marty, above), including Catholics like Henry J. Browne ("Catholicism in the United States," in *The Shaping of American Religion*, J. W. Smith and A. Leland Jamison [eds.] [Princeton: Princeton University Press, 1961], pp. 72-121) and John Tracy Ellis ("American Catholics and the Intellectual Life," *Thought* 30 [Autumn 1955]: 351-388), would dispute the amalgam thesis. Milton Himmelfarb, in "Secular Society: A Jewish Perspective" (*Daedalus*, Winter 1967, p. 230), expresses Jewish fears about Christian hegemony.

[3]Our pluralism has some of its deepest roots in what Marty calls "the denominational game" (*Protestantism* [New York: Holt, Rinehart, and Winston, 1972], p. 137). One of the most frequently cited discussions of denominationalism can be found in the essay by Winthrop S. Hudson, "Denominationalism as a Basis for Ecumenicity: A Seventeenth Century Conception," *Church History* 24 (1955): 32-50.

[4]Peter Berger, *The Social Reality of Religion* (London: Faber, 1969), p. 155.

[5]Karl Marx, "Contribution to the Critique of Hegel's Philosophy of Right: Introduction," *Karl Marx: Early Writings*, T. B. Bottomore, (ed.) (New York: Oxford University Press, 1964), pp. 52-53.

[6]Daniel Bell, "The Return of the Sacred? The Argument on the Future of Religion," *British Journal of Sociology* 28(4) (December 1977): 419-49.

[7]The idea here, not fully precise in my own thoughts, is that "allegiance" or "loyalty" has a distinct rational grounding, including the "socially useful purpose of preventing deterioration from becoming cumulative" in profane matters, as expressed by Albert O. Hirschman in *Exit, Voice, and Loyalty* (Cambridge: Harvard University Press, 1970), p. 79; while "faith" is not similarly constrained. Josiah Royce suggests ways to mediate these concepts of conviction in his "philosophy of loyalty," in which loyalty means "the *practically devoted love of an individual for a community*," in *The Problem of Christianity* (Chicago: Chicago University Press, 1968), p. 41, and "exists in countless forms and gradations" (p. 134).

[8]Immanuel Kant, *The Metaphysical Elements of Justice*, translated by John Ladd (Indianapolis: Bobbs Merrill, 1964), p. 94 (slightly revised).

[9]John Dewey, *A Common Faith* (New Haven: Yale University Press, 1934), p. 28.

[10]Michael Walzer, *Obligations: Essays on Disobedience, War, and Citizenship* (New York: Simon and Schuster, 1971), pp. 221, 204.

[11]Karl Barth, *Community, State, and Church* (Garden City: Doubleday, 1960), pp. 31, 33, 80.

[12]See John Winthrop, *A Model of Christian Charity*: "The care of the public must oversway all private respects by which not only conscience but mere civil polity doth bind us: for it is a true rule that particular estates cannot subsist in the ruin of the public. The end is . . . that ourselves and posterity may be the better preserved from the common corruptions of this evil world, to serve the Lord and work out our salvation under the power and purity of His holy ordinances." In *The American Puritan*, Perry Miller (ed.) (New York: Doubleday Anchor, 1956), p. 82. Cf. H. Richard Niebuhr, *The Kingdom of God in America* (New York: Harper, 1955), p. 75; Werner Stark, *The Sociology of Religions: A Study of Christendom*, vol. I: *Established Religion* (New York: Fordham University Press, 1966), p. 162; Guy Swanson, *Religion and Regime* (Ann Arbor: University of Michigan Press, 1967), pp. 49ff.

[13]Charles-Louis de Secondat, Baron de Montesquieu, *De l'Esprit des lois*, G. Truc, (ed.) 2 volumes, (Paris: Garnier, 1961), i.

[14]Ibid., XXIV, xiv.

[15]Sanford Levinson, " 'The Constitution' in American Civil Religion," *The Supreme Court Review* 21 (1980), p. 131.

[16]All citations from John Locke, *A Letter Concerning Toleration*, in *Locke on Politics, Religion, and Education*, Maurice Cranston (ed.) (New York: Collier Books, 1965), pp. 134-35.

[17]Alexis de Tocqueville, *Democracy in America*, translated by Henry Reeve, 2 volumes, (New York: Doubleday Anchor, 1945), I. p. 15.

[18]Cushing Strout's *The New Heavens and the New Earth: Political Religion in America* (New York: Harper & Row, 1974) is a distinguished contribution to the evaluation of American history from Tocqueville's religious perspective. I am indebted to the work for clues in my somewhat different mission.

[19]Tocqueville, *Democracy in America*, I, p. 321.

[20]Ibid., II, p. 104, for Tocqueville's interesting analysis of individualism.

[21]Ibid., II, pp. 133-135.

[22]Ibid., I, p. 33.

[23]See the corruscating remarks on this made by a French Protestant visitor a century later: André Siegfried, *Les Etats-Unis d'aujourd'hui* (Paris: Colin, 1927), pp. 32, 52-55; and his *Tableau des Etats-Unis* (Paris: Colin, 1954), pp. 82-92.

[24]See *Platform of Church Discipline*: "Church government stands in no opposition to civil government, nor in any way intrencheth upon the authority of civil magistrates in their jurisdiction, nor any whit weakeneth their hands in governing." Quoted in Thomas J. Wertenbaker, *The Puritan Oligarchy* (New York: Scribners, 1970), p. 71. Also, Edmund S. Morgan, *The Puritan Dilemma: The Story of John Winthrop* (Boston: Little, Brown, 1958), p. 96; and Strout, *New Heavens*, pp. 15-16.

[25]Tocqueville, *Democracy in America*, I, 43.

[26]Ibid., I, pp. 310, 433.

[27]Montesquieu, *De l'Esprit des lois*, XXIV, ii.

[28]Benjamin Constant, *Du Polythéisme romain considéré dans ses rapports avec la philosophie grecque et al religion chrétienne*, 2 volumes (Paris: Bechet, 1833), II, pp. 91-92.

[29]Tocqueville, *Democracy in America*, I, p. 321; II, p. 23; II, p. 22; I, p. 46.

[30]Ibid., I, pp. 314-15, 320; II, pp. 28-29.

[31]Ibid., I, p. 316, I, pp. 311-312.

[32]The contemporary "civil religion" literature is vast. It all began with Robert N. Bellah's famous "The American Civil Religion," *Daedalus*, Winter 1967, pp. 1-21, and is reflected in a progeny of responses and approaches, some of which are collected in *American Civil Religion*, Russell E. Richey and Donald G. Jones (eds.) (New York: Harper & Row, 1974). Bellah continued his argument in that volume and in "Religion and the Legitimation of the American Republic," *Society* 15 (4) (May-June 1978): 16-23. Catherine L. Albanese has applied the concept to the foundation of the republic in *Sons of the Fathers: The Civil Religion of the American Revolution* (Philadelphia: Temple University Press, 1976).

[33]Tocqueville, *Democracy in America*, II, pp. 28-29.

[34]See W. Lloyd Warner's account of Memorial Day in Newburyport in *American Life: Dream and Reality* (Chicago: Chicago University Press, 1953).

[35]Michael Oakeshott, "The Moral Life in the Writings of Thomas Hobbes," in *Hobbes on Civil Association* (Oxford: Blackwell, 1975), pp. 76-77.

[36]Tocqueville, *Democracy in America*, I, 433.

[37]Ibid., II, p. 27; 143.

[38]See Sidney E. Mead, *The Old Religion in the Brave New World* (Berkeley: University of California Press, 1977), esp. pp. 68-72 and 106-08.

[39]See Timothy L. Smith, "The Millenial Vision in America," *American Quarterly* 31 (1) (Spring 1979): 29-30.

[40]American sectarianism, though of prime importance, would take this essay too far afield. On the subject of sects, see *Patterns of Sectarianism: Organization and Ideology in Social and Religious Movements*, Bryan R. Wilson (ed.) (London: Heinemann, 1967); also the many particular accounts in Sydney B. Ahlstrom, *A Religious History of the American People* (New Haven: Yale University Press, 1972), passim. Sects are dealt with in an interesting typology of J. Milton Yinger in his *Religion, Society, and the Individual* (New York: Macmillan, 1965). On cults, see Robert S. Ellwood, Jr., *Religious and Spiritual Groups of Modern America* (Englewood Cliffs, N.J.: Prentice-Hall, 1973).

[41]Tocqueville, *Democracy in America*, I, p. 450.

[42]This has been particularly well expressed by Peter Dennis Bathory, "Tocqueville on Citizenship and Faith: A Response to Cushing Strout," *Political Theory* 8 (1) (February 1980): 33.

[43]See, inter alia, Arthur A. Ekirch, Jr., *The Idea of Progress in America, 1815-1860* (New York: Columbia University Press, 1944); Ernest Tuveson, *Redeemer Nation* (Chicago: Chicago University Press, 1968); and Paul C. Nagel, *This Sacred Trust: American Nationality, 1798-1898* (New York: Oxford University Press, 1971).

[44]Robert Coles, "Civility and Psychology," *Daedalus*, Summer 1980, p. 140. Cf. Tocqueville, *Democracy in America*, II, p. 106.

[45]G. W. F. Hegel, introduction to *The Philosophy of History*, translated by J. Sibree (New York: Dover, 1956), pp. 85, 86.

[46]Reinhold Niebuhr, *The Irony of American History* (New York: Scribners, 1952), p. 140.

[47]Reinhold Niebuhr, *Faith and History* (New York: Scribners, 1949), p. 100.

[48]Novalis, "Christianity or Europe," in *Political Thought of the German Romantics*, H. S. Reiss (ed.) (Oxford: Blackwell, 1955), p. 139.

[49]*From Max Weber: Essays in Sociology*, H. H. Gerth and C. Wright Mills (eds.) (New York: Oxford University Press, 1967), pp. 139; 350; 357, 140-41; 357; 139.

[50]Paul Tillich, *Theology of Culture* (New York: Oxford University Press, 1959), p. 42.

[51]*From Max Weber*, p. 140.

[52]Søren Kierkegaard, *The Journals of Kierkegaard*, translated by Alexander Dru (Evanston, Ill.: Northwestern University Press, 1959), entry of 1846, p. 97.

[53]A. J. Ayer, in *Partisan Review*, 1950 (2): *Religion and the Intellectuals: A Symposium*, p. 218.

[54]Cf. Wilfred Sellars, *Science, Perception, and Reality* (London: Routledge & Kegan Paul, 1963), p. 170.

[55]Don K. Price, "Purists and Politicians," *Science* 163 (3) (January 1969): 25-31.

[56]It is of course very important in many cases (not necessarily here) to distinguish between kin-privacy and self-privacy. See Oakeshott, "The Moral Life in the Writings of Thomas Hobbes."

[57]Harvey Cox, *The Secular City* (New York: Macmillan, 1965), p. 2.

[58]Thomas Luckmann, *The Invisible Religion* (New York: Macmillan, 1967), p. 102.

[59]Barth, *Community, State and Church*.

[60]See B. R. Wilson, *Religion in Secular Society* (London: Watts, 1966), p. 34.

[61]This is one of the grievances of groups motivated by *nostalgia* (see below), but the charge is more than animus or bigotry. Still, some religious elements have felt repressed by a secularistic society; and as Montesquieu put it with usual crispness: "Every religion that is repressed itself becomes repressive." *De l'Esprit des lois*, XXV, ix.

[62]Peter Berger, *The Noise of Solemn Assemblies* (Garden City, N.Y.: Doubleday, 1961), p. 59.

[63]Marty, *New Shape*, pp. 86-87.

[64]Karl Mannheim, "Conservative Thought," in *From Karl Mannheim*, Kurt H. Wolff (ed.) (New York: Oxford University Press, 1971), p. 146.

[65]Sheldon Wolin, *Politics and Vision* (Boston: Little, Brown, 1960), p. 353.

[66]T. H. Marshall, "Citizenship and Social Class," in *Class, Citizenship, and Social Development* (New York: Harper Torchbooks, 1963), pp. 92; 106.

[67]Adam Ferguson, *Essay on the History of Civil Society* (London: 1768), p. 316.

[68]Wolin, *Politics and Vision*, pp. 354-55.

[69]Jürgen Habermas, *Legitimation Crisis* (London: Heinemann, 1976), p. 58.

[70]Luckmann, *Invisible Religion*, pp. 36-37.

[71]Berger, *Noise of Solemn Assemblies*, p. 90.

[72]Coles, "Civility and Psychology," p. 137.

[73]Josiah Royce, "Individual Experience and Social Experience," in *Basic Writings*, vol. 2, J. J. McDermott (ed.) (Chicago: Chicago University Press, 1969), p. 1029.

[74]Harvey Cox, "The 'New Breed' in American Churches: Sources of Social Activism in American Religion," in *Daedalus*, Winter 1967, pp. 135-50; also William R. Garrett, "Politicized Clergy: A Sociological Interpretation of the 'New Breed,' " *Journal for the Scientific Study of Religion* 12 (4) (December 1973): 383-400.

[75]Gabriel Vahanian, *The Death of God* (New York: Braziller, 1961), pp. 140-141.

[76]Franklin L. Baumer, *Religion and the Rise of Scepticism* (New York: Harcourt Brace, 1960), p. 291.

[77]For a sympathetic discussion of these trends, see Charles Davis, *Theology and Political Society* (Cambridge: Cambridge University Press, 1980), esp. pp. 28-74. Cf. Cox's "God the Politician," in *Secular City*, p. 255.

[78]See esp. Bellah, "Religious Evolution," *American Sociological Review* 29 (June 1964): 353-74; and the comments by Andrew M. Greeley, "An Exchange of Views," *The Secular City Debate*, Daniel J. Callahan (ed.) (New York: Macmillan, 1966), p. 101.

[79]An early source of this view is Friedrich Gogarten, *Werhängnis und Hoffnung der Neuzeit: Die Säkularisierung als theologisches Problem* (Stuttgart: Vorwerk, 1956).

[80]Henri de Saint-Simon, *The Doctrine of Saint-Simon: An Exposition, First Year, 1828-1829*, G. G. Iggers, (ed.) (New York: Schocken, 1972), pp. 199-200.

[81]Judith N. Shklar, *After Utopia: The Decline of Political Faith* (Princeton: Princeton University Press, 1957).

[82]Hannah Arendt, *Between Past and Future* (New York: Viking, 1968), p. 74.

[83]Henry Kariel, *In Search of Authority* (Glencoe, Ill.: Free Press, 1964), p. 5.

[84]Harold J. Laski, *The American Democracy* (New York: Viking, 1948), p. 399.

[85]Marty, "Two Kinds of Civil Religion," in *American Civil Religion*, p. 140.

[86]James Agee, in *Partisan Review: Religion and the Intellectuals.* p. 108.

[87]Cox, *Secular City*, p. 60.

[88]If that were strictly true, fragmented pluralism might be expected to produce an immanentist polytheism, for example, as prefigured in William James, *The Varieties of Religious Experience* (New York: Longmans, Green, 1929), p. 324.

[89]Arendt, in *Partisan Review: Religion and the Intellectuals*, p. 115.

DICK ANTHONY AND THOMAS ROBBINS

Spiritual Innovation and the Crisis of American Civil Religion

IN THE 1970s, IN THE WAKE of the countercultural turbulence of the sixties, America witnessed the surprising upsurge of cults and new religions. A number of perspectives have sought to explain this upsurge. The simplest attributes it to the process of secularization, or the diminishing societal significance of religion, which may have the paradoxical consequence of temporarily increasing the number of religious groups and their range of variation.[1] Daniel Bell believes that "when religions fail, . . . when the institutional framework of religions begins to break up, the search for direct experience which people can feel to be 'religious' facilitates the rise of cults."[2]

Another approach points to a crisis of community in American society. Traditional mediating structures—extended families, homogeneous neighborhoods, conventional churches, and personalistic work settings—that once provided contexts for sociability, and gave to the individual a sense of rootedness in, and control of, his social environment, have been undermined by structural changes and public policies. Thus many individuals who feel homeless in a mass society dominated by formal organizations have turned to cults, communes, encounter groups, and other social inventions for support.[3] And as young people leave the warmth and intimacy of the nuclear family for the increasingly impersonal and bureaucratic adult world, many seek to fill the emotional gap with quasi-familial relationships.

A third approach ascribes the rise of new religions to cultural confusion and the loss of value consensus. The Protestant ethic or its components—the "work ethic," competitive individualism, and the sense of control over one's fate—is said to be eroding, producing an ideological and spiritual void and a lack of legitimation for dominant institutional patterns.[4] New religions are thus viewed as successor movements to the ferment of the late sixties and the countercultural revolt against utilitarian individualism and the hegemony of technical reason.[5] The undermining of consensual civic values such as patriotism in the aftermath of Vietnam, Watergate, and détente has also proliferated competing visions. "The cult phenomenon has substituted a myriad of fragmented visions for the central messianism we called Americanism."[6]

In this essay we will attempt to analyze contemporary American spiritual ferment in terms of American civil religion, described by Robert Bellah as a complex of symbolic meanings that many Americans share and that unite them in a moral community.[7] In our view, the perspectives of secularization, the

229

erosion of community, and the loss of value consensus can be interrelated and integrated by an analysis in terms of civil religion.

American Civil Religion

Our institutional separation of church and state notwithstanding, religious and political symbols are closely intertwined in American history. Yet our civil religion is more than merely a form of national self-worship. It entails as well "the subordination of the nation to ethical principles that transcend it and in terms of which it should be judged."[8] Our civil religion thus imparts a religious dimension to the whole fabric of American life, especially the political realm.

Bellah's view of civil religion has shifted over time, but an essential element remains the notion of America as a redeemer nation and Americans as chosen people. Implicit in this notion is the belief in a messianic universal mission, a sort of sacred nationalism that connects manifest destiny with universal ideals. American civil religion interrelates theism, patriotism, competitive individualism, and boundless faith in the potentialities of economic growth and prosperity. For Bellah, our civil religion is inherently pluralistic: America's diverse ideological and interest groupings put forward variations of civil religion, or competing "public theologies," that of necessity embody different visions of America's destiny and its relationship to social ideals. Reform movements such as Abolitionism, for example, expressed their goals in terms of civil religion and articulated a public theology. There is thus continual conflict and interaction between different public theologies.[9]

In *The Broken Covenant*, Bellah talks about a once-dominant communal or "covenantal" ethos rooted in New England Puritanism and in Old Testament-oriented biblical morality. Early New England political thought was strongly collectivistic, derived partly from classical philosophy and the conception of a *polis*, partly "from the Old Testament notion of the covenant between God and a people held collectively responsible for its actions," and partly "from the New Testament notion of a community based on charity or love and expressed in brotherly affection and fellow membership in one common body." Even the Calvinist emphasis on individual action "only made sense within the collective context. Individual action outside the bounds of religious and moral norms was seen in Augustinian terms as the very archetype of sin."[10] Puritanism grounded communal solidarity in moral absolutism.

By mid-nineteenth century, according to Bellah, the biblical covenant ethos began to be seriously threatened by utilitarian individualism, a new ethos that assumed that the pursuit of private materialistic goals by individual citizens would somehow result in a "collective" public welfare and civic virtue. Utilitarian individualism became the legitimation for burgeoning American capitalism, since it relativized the ends, or goals, of human action and stressed the rationalization of means, or technical reason. This ethos continues its hold over American culture, despite periodic revolts against technical reason such as the counterculture of the sixties.

Bellah believes that "today the American civil religion is an empty and broken shell," and that the present spiritual ferment is an attempt to bring about a "birth of new American myths" as a response to the decay of civil religion.[11] The new religions that flourished in the seventies are survivors of the crisis of meaning that characterized the sixties. They articulate variations of countercultural values of spontaneity and "love," while sometimes evolving composite symbol systems that accommodate these values to resurgent utilitarian individualism.

In our view, Bellah poses too sharp an antithesis between Puritan biblical absolutism and utilitarian individualism. Rather, the legitimation of American capitalism has been tied to a synthesis of both. This synthesis emerged after the Civil War,[12] and was embodied in a culturally dominant ethos, *implicit legitimation*. It held that the pursuit of selfish goals in the material realm is conducive to public good so long as egoistic materialism takes place within a framework of asceticism and moral absolutism in the private expressive realm. Put simply, so long as everyone upholds a limited set of negative moral absolutes—for example, not to murder, steal, fornicate, or drink—each person may pursue selfish materialistic goals and confidently expect that public welfare and civil virtue will arise from such individual strivings. Within an overall framework of moral absolutism, the "invisible hand" will harmonize private egoism in the economic realm. Economic laissez-faire is thus a moral as well as an economic imperative. Given moral absolutism and asceticism in private mores, plus economic laissez-faire, virtue will become its own reward, and success will come to those who deserve it.

A key feature of the civil religion ethos was the assumption that proscribed acts such as "theft" were to be strictly and narrowly defined; only then could the prohibition of "immoral" acts be absolute. Thus theft, strictly, narrowly, and negatively defined in relation to "property acquisition," meant that other means of acquiring property, proper because they were "not theft," were *implicitly* legitimated. This dualistic moral absolutism, which ultimately derives from Puritanism and precapitalist American moral culture, could be used to implicitly legitimate laissez-faire economic entrepreneurial activity free from moral or governmental regulation. "The concept of 'equal opportunity' within the 'free enterprise' economy provided a secular counterpart of 'free will.' Within this moral system, so long as participants in entrepreneurial capitalism obeyed certain narrowly conceived negative injunctions, they received moral sanction for engaging in economic activities that resulted in social inequality."[13]

Essential to this synthesis of moral absolutism and utilitarian individualism was the premise of individual responsibility: individuals were presumed to have a capacity to choose whether or not to be virtuous, and on that basis were held responsible for their behavior. Thus virtuous individuals could anticipate success in material endeavors, while those who did not "succeed" were considered to be morally deficient. This ethos was hostile to collectivist regimentation of the broader society, because choice and free will were deemed essential to the creation of virtue: regimented virtue could not be true virtue. Competitive individualism was thus given a moral aura.

Finally, the moral dimension of this civil religion ethos entailed a sanctification of American society, its laissez-faire economic processes, its democratic political processes, and its military and international might. The United States was viewed as a country in which equal opportunity—hence free will and the possibility of virtue—were preserved by the nature of our social processes.

Moreover, since success was the reward of virtue, American might and power reflected the virtue of American institutions, and ultimately the intervention of Providence. Americans were God's chosen people contending with evil adversaries. In the past, European monarchies, whose governments protected hereditary privilege and thus inhibited the triumph of virtue through equal opportunity, served as contrast symbols vital to American civil religion. More recently, communism has succeeded to this role.

Since the 1930s two factors have operated to undermine the moral system of implicit legitimation. First, the development of a managed and planned economy and an increasingly bureaucratized society have made the ideas of individualism, free will, and personal autonomy less plausible. Their credibility has been further diminished by a growing acceptance of the notion that any individual's course of action depends to a great extent on his socioeconomic status. Second, the development of a hedonistic, leisure-oriented "permissive" culture has challenged moral absolutism in the private expressive realm. A mass consumption capitalist economy inevitably expands into taboo areas and makes commodities of more and more private behavior, including sex. And the erosion of moral constraints in the private realm ultimately undermines the moral system that legitimates arrangements in the economic realm.

In our view, and in the view of others, a serious legitimation problem has existed for American institutions since the Great Depression. A cultural crisis of legitimation was forestalled by World War II and the moral solidarity created by pitting democracy against dictatorship. This solidarity was buttressed in the years after the war by setting "godless communism" over against the idea of America as the "home of the free and the brave." In 1974 the sociologist Arthur Vidich commented, "It was only World War Two and the cold war that rescued capitalism from its ideological poverty. The ending of the cold war once again reopens this issue for the capitalist countries and their political systems."[14]

The moral system of implicit legitimation of American capitalism proved to be unstable. As entrepreneurial capitalism was transformed into managerial capitalism, corporate technocracy became increasingly difficult to legitimate in traditional individualist and voluntarist terms. The American economy became increasingly dependent upon a mass consumption ethic that promised happiness through limitless material acquisition. But this vision contravened Protestant ethic ascetic norms. Finally, the stalemate in Vietnam undercut the faith in American power that had complemented faith in American enterprise.

RESPONSE TO MORAL FLUX

According to Bellah, the decline of consensual civil religion and the consequent crisis in national identity impinge most heavily on local institutions that are responsible for conveying moral ideologies. The "soft structures" that deal with human motivation—the churches, the schools, the family—have been weakened more than other institutions in recent American upheavals, especially with respect to "their capability to transmit patterns of conscience and ethical values."[15]

These views are borne out by Wade Clark Roof in a recent study that summarizes survey data on religious defection in the early and middle 1970s. According to Roof, the figures for defection from established churches are staggering. They suggest that the recent upsurge of unconventional new religions is merely "a small part of a larger climate of unrest taking place in the religious realm," which involves vast numbers of Americans dropping out of conventional churches and synagogues and "breaking with many of their institutional commitments."[16]

Roof's findings indicate that defectors from established faiths tend to be young, well educated, and middle class. They are likely to lack confidence in dominant political, economic, and communications structures, and are much more likely than nondefectors to be committed to the permissive "new morality" and to have liberal attitudes on issues such as homosexuality and abortion. Roof believes that the large defections from established churches are clearly related to the diffusion of countercultural values. Protestant and Catholic faiths are "internally split over such issues as homosexuality, abortion, and women's ordination." The religious tinge of recent crusades against abortion and homosexuality "reveals the depths of conservative reaction and the close affinity to religious symbols and values." Nevertheless, values and styles originating with youth are "percolating up" through the undersociety.[17]

Extrapolating from Roof's analysis, it can be argued that the Catholic Church and the "liberal" Protestant denominations are caught between the spread of "permissive" countercultural morality on the one hand and the strident moralistic evangelical revival on the other. If the churches opt for evangelical absolutism, they will continue to lose members among the well educated and affluent; but if they embrace the "new morality," they are, in effect, embracing a modern "secular" ethos hostile to theism. In the latter case, they are, in a sense, repudiating their own *raison d'être*. The dilemma may be insoluble, and illustrates the degree to which the churches no longer uphold a moral consensus and embody a national covenant.

Consequences of a lack of consensual spiritual purpose are a discrediting of the "secular" ideal of segregating morality from government and the creation in many persons of a hunger for a more authoritarian and morally purified "virtuous republic" to enforce moral law.[18] The present resurgence of evangelicism and its politicization, which stress primarily moral or life-style issues such as ERA, abortion, homosexuality, and pornography, can be seen as a response to the erosion of moral consensus and disenchantment with secular liberal constitutionalism. Paradoxically, the decline of moral consensus increases the demand for government regulation of morality.

TRADITIONALIST RESURGENCE

The "Jesus Movement" in the late 1960s and very early 1970s was the beginning of a rebirth of interest in morally conservative religion. The recent growth of conservative Protestant denominations, evangelical movements within liberal denominations, and the Catholic charismatic movement, as well as the surge of neo-orthodoxy within American Judaism, are all evidence of a widespread repudiation of cultural modernism.

Conservative Christian congregations practice the "cure of souls" within a moral community that shares a transcendent world view. Yet, despite their rejection of many aspects of secular society, they basically accept the institutional structure of the everyday world. Traditional religionists are no less

immune than others to the distresses of work, and they too are subject to the
alienation that is bred out of the impersonal bureaucracies of managerial
capitalism. Partly for this reason, perhaps, conservative and Christian evangelical groups are becoming increasingly politicized, and feel a need to alter the
political and governmental *status-quo* as a complement to saving individual souls.

Tied to a model of society that bases virtuous life on laissez-faire economics
and limited government,[19] conservative Christianity, particularly evangelical
Protestantism, has sanctified individualism and rejected collectivism as unholy
and inimical to man's obligation to choose righteousness. In consequence, "the
cultural resources available to Americans have emphasized the autonomy of the
individual and the individualistic and voluntaristic character of social relations."[20] In the nineteenth century, when the economic life of the nation was
carried on primarily through small businesses and farms, such a traditionalist
laissez-faire form of civil religion seemed plausible to most people, and social
experiences were not too glaringly inconsistent with it. With the growth of both
corporations and government in the current era of managerial capitalism,
emphasis upon personal autonomy and civic virtue as the wellsprings of
vocational motivation may serve to intensify the frustration of contemporary
life. The new, more innovative religious groups attempt to transcend these
stresses by developing utopian communal enclaves as models for the coming
revolutionary transformation of the larger society.

Youth Movements in Modern Society

As the nuclear family becomes increasingly segregated from other social
processes, it encounters some difficulties in fulfilling all of its members' needs.
Young persons who have left their original families but have not yet formed
their own are especially vulnerable. They feel keenly the discrepancy between
the "loving" quality of familial relationships and the "impersonal" nature of
relationships at schools and in the workplace. This discontinuity impels the
continuing search for surrogate families. Youth movements frequently minister
to this need and provide legitimations for novel patterns of quasi-familial
relationships by linking youths to "adult" political or spiritual concerns.
Through youth movements, young persons work out roles and relationships
that combine aspects of both adult and childish milieus.[21] Religious movements
are particularly well suited to evolve such combinations, because their symbol
systems have traditionally linked explicit familial and communal mystiques to
universal ideals formulated in terms of universal brotherhood or a fellowship of
believers.

Although youth movements, in particular youth-oriented spiritual groups,
are potentially integrative or adaptive because they tend to ease the stress of the
familial-vocational transition, the wide range of contemporary religious movements will have differing consequences for both devotees and the larger society.
Today's movements can be differentiated in terms of the crisis of civil religion.

Civil Religion Sects

The resurgent evangelicals and other neo-orthodox tendencies in American
religion are part of the "new religions" phenomenon only in a rather equivocal

sense. Apart from such conservative developments, the new religions that emerged from the counterculture of the late 1960s can be placed in one of two categories, each of which embodies contrasting strategies for coping with the decline of civil religion. Groups such as the Unification Church of Reverend Sun Myung Moon promise a revitalized synthesis of political and religious themes as the basis for crystallizing personal identities. Such totalistic groups, which look toward the restoration of a national covenant, might be termed new "civil religion sects." Jim Jones's ill-fated People's Temple approximated this pattern, as does Synanon and, to a lesser degree, some conservative Protestant and youth culture Christian groups emerging from the Jesus Movement. But "privatistic" mystical religions (Yogi Bhajan, Meher Baba, Tibetan Buddhism) and quasi-mystical therapeutic movements (e.g., *est*) implicitly reject the insertion of nationalist or political themes in spiritual life. In part because they lack overt political or civic emphasis, such groups are frequently labeled "narcissistic."

Civil religion sects aim ultimately at reconstructing the culture and reordering the polity. This is a difficult, perhaps insuperable task. Because the absolutist ideologies of these movements pose unique problems for the indoctrination of converts, and elicit hostility from outsiders, such movements must often create alternative communities as models of future American society. These morally "pure" and homogeneously integrated minisocieties afford their members escape from daily involvement with a morally chaotic society. But this approach is not without its costs. Part of the exhilaration of membership in a religious movement that is serious about its utopianism may come from the converts' sense of betting their all on a worthy ideal. Surely it is a high-risk game. A great deal rides on the choice of an organization or leader intended to exemplify civil religious ideals. As Robert Lifton argues, the embodiment of exalted utopian ideals in a fallible leader creates a contradiction that bedevils authoritarian "cults," and results in a "deification of idiosyncracy" that glorifies the leader's eccentricities and suppresses all doubts.[22]

Civil religion sects such as the Unification Church, the People's Temple, or Synanon provisionally heal the split between private feelings and public purpose by influencing their members to withdraw from normal vocational involvements. Members of these movements are encouraged to expend all their energies in developing self-sufficient utopian communities to serve as models for the transformation of America. These movements create moral solidarity only by encouraging a uniformity of opinion and degree of obedience to authority among converts that, some observers contend, violate norms of personal autonomy that are integral to a pluralistic and secularized society.[23]

Finally, the civil religious character of these groups commits them to the attempted total metamorphosis of the nation as a whole. This commitment encourages confrontations with the larger society. But unfavorable outcomes for these encounters can appear to undermine the plausibility of these groups' missions and render them volatile.

A number of well-known authoritarian groups seem to have such features in common. Their differences from each other, however, may be as important as their similarities in predicting a specific movement's course of development and the effects upon members.[24] We have studied in depth one such controversial movement.

CALLING AMERICA TO "UNITY"

The Unification Church of Reverend Sun Myung Moon is nearly unique in the systematic quality of its extrapolation of public theology. American civil religion has traditionally sanctified the separation of church and state, and legitimated cultural and normative diversity. The erosion of both civil religion and moral consensus has set the stage for a sectarian assertion of the authoritarian ideal of the morally purified and homogeneous virtuous republic. The Unification Church has transformed this ideal into an overtly theocratic vision. The religio-political synthesis advocated by the Unification Church entails what Irving Horowitz identifies as "a categorical denial of the Lockean-Jeffersonian principle of the separation of church and state."[25] The Unification Church "searches for the unity rather than the separation of the theological and the political. Unification Church members regard their efforts to breach the wall of separation between church and state as not so much an attack on civil liberties as a search for new foundations for the social order."[26] In an attempt to heal the extreme separation of public and private realms, and the fragmentation of personal identity in modern society, the Moon movement articulates a provocative authoritarian response to the decline of civil religion. "Reverend Moon's movement can be interpreted as an attempt at a totalitarian response to the cultural fragmentation of mass society."[27]

Although Bellah sees American civil religion at its best functioning to temper chauvinism and to subject American values to moral scrutiny, the Moonist Manichaean variant of American civil religion identifies all evil with communist societies and all virtue with the United States. This tendency can be called exemplary dualism; it refers to the inclination to perceive contemporary sociopolitical forces and movements as exemplifying absolute moral contrast categories. Exemplary dualism has frequently characterized the meaning systems of Christian millenarian movements—for example, late medieval visions of the papacy as the "Whore of Babylon." Exemplary dualism was implicit in the cold war anticommunism of the 1950s, but it is vividly explicit in the Moon movement, which conceives of the United States as a New Rome, providentially ordained to succor and support the Chosen Land, or New Israel: anticommunist South Korea! The new civil religion of Reverend Moon's Divine Principle is intended to reconstitute the connection between anticommunism and theism, and thus mobilize Americans to accept their country's providential role in sacrificing its wealth and power to combat satanic communism and facilitate the coming of God's kingdom. Moon explains the origin of contemporary political categories in this way: When Jesus was crucified between two thieves, the thief on Jesus' left taunted him, but the thief on his right begged for his grace.

At this moment the seed was sown by the left-hand thief that the God-denying world would come into being—the communist world today. And the seed for the existence of a God-fearing world was sown by the thief on the right-hand side. The free world is in the position of the right-hand thief. And America is the center of those God-fearing nations. America has been chosen as the defender of God, whereas communism says to the world, "There is no God."[28]

America, however, may not rise to the challenge. It has been corrupted by moral relativism, egoism, and permissiveness, and the false hopes of détente. If America does not accept the new civil religion of Divine Principle, Satan and communism will triumph, and the opportunity will be lost to restore harmony between God and man, and to crystallize a universal moral community. A "Moonie" commented in an interview with one of the authors:

> If America doesn't fulfill its role, then it will make it much, much more hard for the whole world to . . . unite behind the Divine Principle. . . . If Rome didn't unite with Christianity, Christianity could never have . . . spread all over the world to the level that it's at now. You know, so that if America doesn't unite with the Divine Principle, then Divine Principle will find it very hard to spread all over the world and, therefore, if this is the one tool against communism, the world will be overcome, the world will turn communist, and God will not have a foothold in the world anymore, and the world will go through terrible suffering.[29]

Communism is thus perceived as a fundamental threat to social and moral existence in the noncommunist world. The Unification movement is seen as the divinely designated (and thus absolute) contrast category for godless communism. The Moonist system reconstructs the moral absolutism of traditional biblical morality in America, but also redefines it. The Moonist system stresses "absolute values," but does not equate absolute values with universal moral principles. Instead, moral absolutism is associated with a divinely inspired interpretation of history. Moral categories are viewed as inherent in the historical process, such that the moral choice individuals must make between exemplars of divine and satanic forces in history is absolute.

> It's very unusual to see that you have the truth, because no one has had anything as clear as Divine Principle throughout history, so that if you believe you have something that is universally true, which is universal cosmic truth, then it doesn't make sense to say, "Well, you know, maybe this is wrong."[30]

The Manichaean anticommunist ideology of the Moon movement is only slightly more extreme than the message purveyed by a number of right-wing fundamentalist preachers in contemporary America. What distinguishes Moonism is its capacity to embody its ideology in a communal movement, such that the Moonist synthesis of political and religious values becomes a total identity for the convert, whose commitment is reinforced by the rewards of participation in a "loving" community knit together by a civil religion. As communism epitomizes the materialism and corruption that poisons relationships in the contemporary world, Divine Principle is seen as embodying the God-centered values that hold the key to harmony and cooperation in social interaction.

The interaction of ideology and social process in the Moon sect is of vital significance. According to Moonists, a truly united and harmonious family consists of "vertical" (e.g., man-God, father-son) and "horizontal" (brother-sister, husband-wife, friend-friend) relations that must be mutually supportive. Harmonious "give-and-take" must prevail among family members, peers, social classes, and nations, and between God and man, for man to fulfill his true purpose of constituting God's perfect creation. This philosophy is embodied in a complex system of rules governing all dimensions of interpersonal behavior. These Unification principles govern even seemingly casual social interaction that normally would be structured only by social etiquette or left to the vagaries of individual impulse. As a result, the social behavior of Moon followers has a somewhat mechanical and stereotyped quality that may seem repellent to outsiders. Nevertheless, these guidelines produce reassuringly structured settings for social interaction that are attractive to Moon converts.

To the potential convert who perceives a lack of harmony and authenticity in interpersonal relationships, the close-knit community and the philosophy of the Unification Church may appear to be a plausible remedy. The ultimate cause of failed relationships is held to be man's fallen nature. The sin of Adam and Eve, conceived by Moon as an unconsecrated sex act, has produced a world peopled by fallen beings, separate from God and incapable of authentic relationships. Through Divine Principle, man's fallen nature can be overcome, and humanity can be reunited into God's harmonious family. The communal solidarity of the movement is a prototype for the loving familial kingdom that is to come. It is a "family." Reverend Moon is "Father," and he and his wife are referred to by devotees as "our True Parents." "The Unification Church constantly emphasizes the breakdown of the American family, corruption and immorality in American life (divorce, pornography, suicide, drugs and scandal) and, by contrast the work of the church toward the 'perfect family' in a 'perfect world.' "[31]

The Unification community thus becomes the surrogate family. But it is more than merely a "family." The Unification community is legitimated in terms of universal values. Thus, despite the childlike quality of some aspects of interaction within the community, the role of the Unification family member has an "adult" quality that inheres in its orientation toward broader civic and spiritual values. Particularly important here is the theme of *sacrifice*. A lecturer at a Unification workshop stated, "We in the USA have relative economic security and welfare, but God may abandon America in a few years unless we reform and create a spiritual revolution. If we can't give up our little things— our privacy, our apartments, cars, record players—all the big things will go."[32] Young converts see themselves as fighting selflessly for universal ideals of love and harmony and world unity in a world permeated by relativism, cynicism, and selfish egoism. The Unification community thus combines the rewards of familial warmth and solidarity with an adult concern with universal values and broad social issues. A critic of the Moon sect has conceded, "The Unification Church as surrogate family may still affect only a small portion of the population, but for that portion it does provide an effective therapeutic setting that offers linkage to the larger society without its turmoils."[33]

Interaction within the Unification community is fairly authoritarian and regimented. Embodied in this totalistic communal milieu is a singular insight: in contemporary American society, moral absolutism is viable only if divorced from individualism. As we have noted, American civil religion has been stridently individualistic and has rejected collectivistic regimentation as a denial of moral choice. But the American synthesis of Puritanism and utilitarian individualism has run its course. It was linked to entrepreneurial capitalism, and has been destroyed by the emergence of a bureaucratically regulated society and managed economy, and by the breakdown of moral consensus in a permissive culture. Any communally viable reconstitution of moral absolutism must necessarily be authoritarian and collectivist. In this connection, it is significant that Moon devotees do not object to the collectivist character of communism, but to its atheism. Satan is seen as attempting to steer mankind to a premature materialistic socialism. Eventually, however, "there will ultimately have to come a socialistic society centering on God."[34]

THE PEOPLE'S TEMPLE

The tragic People's Temple community at Jonestown can also be analyzed as a civil religion sect embodying a politico-religious synthesis and attempting the creation of a new covenant. In an important paper, John Hall attributes the special volatility of the Jonestown community to its unstable combination of political and religious elements.[35] The People's Temple, according to Hall, was poised on the boundary between a totally politicized warring sect, which defines itself as locked in an inescapable struggle with a hostile environment conceived as demonic, and an other-worldly millenarian sect. Such sects exist beyond time in that they believe that in a postapocalyptic world they will be a "saved" remnant. They therefore lack the urgency of being personally responsible for bringing about the new dispensation, which will be brought about by a purely spiritual agency. But the fervor of the Marxist and antiracist elements in the movement's ideology weakened the viability of the People's Temple as an other-worldly sect. Jones exploited politicized conspiratorial themes to reinforce solidarity within the community. But by emphasizing the persecution of his group by an omnipotent conspiracy, Jones undermined the feeling of autonomy and insulation vital to stabilizing its identity. Yet neither could the movement be an authentic warring sect, since they were powerless to prevail over an all-powerful capitalist-racist "conspiracy." Mass suicide became a means of realizing a form of immortality. "They could abandon apocalyptic hell by the act of mass suicide. . . . Mass suicide united the divergent public threads of meaningful existence at Jonestown—those of political revolution and religious salvation."[36]

Although seemingly antithetical, Jim Jones's quasi-Marxist ideology and right-wing Moonism conceal an underlying convergence in terms of exemplary dualism. The capitalist-racist conspiracy fulfills the same function for Jim Jones as does communism for Sun Myung Moon. Both communism and capitalist racism embody historically grounded absolute contrast symbols that establish the identity of each civil religion sect as an exemplary utopia and vanguard of a new and higher civilization. Reverend Moon and his followers tend to interpret opposition to their movement as demonically inspired, in a manner evocative of the "paranoia" of Jim Jones.

Yet there are key differences between the two groups. "Moonies" do not view the noncommunist world as totally evil. It is corrupt and in danger of repudiating God's grace, but it is capable of spiritual revitalization. The Unification Church conspicuously departs from other-worldly millenarian traditions that envision divine agency as taking sole responsibility for the

Apocalypse and for the salvation of a sacred remnant of believers. Within such traditions the role of believers is essentially passive: to purify themselves and wait. "Moonies," however, see *themselves* as undertaking the responsibility for bringing in the Kingdom, by persuading the public, by political lobbying and other acts. Developments such as the current intensification of American hostility to Russia have been cited as indications that Reverend Moon's message is getting across, that the movement is "winning." It is precisely this optimistic activism that distinguishes the Moon movement from Jim Jones and his followers, who could envision neither divine intervention in their behalf nor triumph through their own actions.

The Monistic Alternative

As we have seen, the Moon movement and the People's Temple exemplify civil religion sects that evolve a synthesis of religious and political themes—a revitalized civil religion—as a basis for both total personal identity and close-knit "loving" solidarity embodied in authoritarian communal structures. These movements can be vividly contrasted with the many yoga, meditation, and human potential groups. These groups are stigmatized as "narcissistic"— precisely because they reject the intermeshing of civic-political and spiritual themes, and relegate utopian visions to the vague anticipation of the "New Age" that will come after enough individuals have evolved a higher spiritual consciousness. Such movements are usually more adaptive to conventional social expectations, and their participants are less likely to eschew normal social roles.

A key aspect of these groups is their generally monistic meaning systems, which affirm the latent metaphysical unity, or "oneness," of all existence and the primacy of consciousness (i.e., the illusory quality of phenomenal reality). Monistic ideologies assert a social unity hidden in the depths of the self. They posit a universal self immanent in particular "selves," whereby individuals are ultimately harmoniously related to each other and to nature.[37] Such hidden interconnections between people are not dependent upon consciously shared religious or political values; hence, monistic ideologies are relatively indifferent to civil religion. Belief in an implicit universal order can provide a value framework that supports conventional participation in a society in which shared values are disintegrating.

For monistic ideologies, progress toward spiritual enlightenment is seen as involving glimpses of the universal self behind the apparent chaos of experience. A greater degree of cultural fragmentation makes the relative or arbitrary quality of particular social myths (such as American civil religion) more apparent, and thus provides a basis for individuals to glimpse the unity hidden in life. But the realization of existential "unity" among persons does not require sociopolitical "unity."

THE MEHER BABA MOVEMENT

The Meher Baba movement is a monistic movement that we have studied for a number of years.[38] Avatar Meher Baba is a recently deceased (1969) Indian spiritual master who claimed to be the most recent manifestation of the avataric

(Hindu messianic) tradition. Meher Baba is the present incarnation of the divine redeemer, who in his previous incarnations manifested himself as Zoroaster, Rama, Krishna, Buddha, Christ, and Mohammed. Meher Baba is thus perceived by his followers as a universal savior. He is a messiah who incarnates on earth at crucial periods, "when the earth is sunk in materialism and chaos as it is now," and who comes to inspire humanity and lead mankind to a higher level of consciousness. Meher Baba is also universal in a special sense that involves his immanence in all beings.

Unlike the Unification Church or the People's Temple, the Baba movement has no clear or unified authority structure. Local Baba groups are more or less autonomous. Most are fairly egalitarian and "antistructural." The membership usually displays hostile attitudes toward any kind of formal ritual or procedure, as well as any formal system of authority. Many Baba followers rarely go to meetings, for they view their relationship to Baba as something deeply personal that cannot be collectivized. On the other hand, most Baba followers associate primarily (but not necessarily exclusively) with other "Baba Lovers." Baba Lovers in a given area thus usually constitute a definite community and a context for close friendships.

The essence of Meher Baba's universal message is "love," which in its purest form "arises in the heart . . . in response to the descent of grace from the Master."[39] In Baba's case, the medium is the message, in the sense that he is viewed by his disciples as a quintessentially "loving" Master. One follower commented to a researcher: "You can look at Baba's picture and know that he loves you and that he'll never leave you." Baba is thus viewed as a personification of universal love. A devotee comments: "Baba is love. Baba is God. It's like each one of us—we've got it within us. It's just finding it, and finding it through Baba is the best way."[40]

Meher Baba's status as the personified embodiment of love manifests itself through his relationship with his followers. Movies of Baba shown regularly at meetings depict his loving relationships with people. One shows Baba tenderly washing lepers, whom Baba is said to have called "beautiful birds in ugly cages." Baba is thus perceived as responding to the inner person rather than in terms of one's apparent circumstances or attainments.

Although he is the universal savior, Baba's followers perceive their relationships with him as one-on-one, and as idiosyncratic, in the sense that he deliberately manipulates what happens to them to confront them with important experiences, challenges, or opportunities. Followers frequently declare that they obtained their jobs through Baba's intervention. Thus Baba is perceived as intervening in the unique and particular details of each follower's life history, ministering to each person's distinctive spiritual needs, and aiding in the development of his human potential.

The relationship of the Baba Lover to the "Divine Beloved" also has a basic ascriptive dimension that derives from the immanence of Meher Baba within each lover as his real, or higher, self. Meher Baba's universal love is thus grounded in his universal identity; he loves everyone, since he recognizes himself in everyone.

Meher Baba's universal identity converts his loving dispositions into universal and archetypal patterns. As such, they are seen to hold the key to overcoming the barriers to spontaneous warmth in relationships. Meher Baba's perceived relationship to his followers becomes the basis for interpersonal relationships involving Baba Lovers. The exchange below demonstrates that Baba Lovers believe that loving relationships between themselves derive from loving relationships to Baba.

INTERVIEWER.   Why was it you felt good when you were at the center?

RESPONDENT.   Just because of the feelings. Just because of what people were expressing. I could feel Baba coming through these people. I even felt myself expressing these things which I never thought I would.[41]

Thus loving relationships between Baba Lovers, and the loving attributes or "vibrations" of a Baba Lover, are seen as emanations of Baba, who is immanent within the lovers. The harmonizing of interpersonal relations through Baba's vibrations is viewed as a natural process that operates without reference to systematic rules.

A Baba Lover commented at a meeting: "Any love I've expressed toward people is just a very, very dim reflection of the love I've received from Baba."[42] Baba's love diffuses among Baba Lovers through loving relationships. Expressive and loving relationships among followers are thus universalized, and achieve a transcendental legitimation.

The logic of Meher Baba as the real, universal self of all persons compels a certain tolerance for those who are not followers of Baba or who are very different from Baba Lovers. Baba Lovers do not, therefore, retreat to segregated enclaves, but are active in the world, working side-by-side with nonbelievers. Relative to civil religion sects, the Baba movement seems conspicuously adaptive.

Given both the belief that Baba is immanent in all beings and his loving orientations, it is not surprising that the practical ethic of Baba Lovers is one of selfless service. This ethic discourages a drop-out life pattern. Kitty Davy, co-supervisor of the Meher Center in South Carolina, states, "Love means action. Baba says the material and the spiritual must go hand-in-hand. You cannot stay in a spiritual retreat for your whole life and find God. God must be found in the world, through service, through selfless action."[43] And it is through selfless service that Baba Lovers see themselves as acting lovingly in the world. In so doing, they demonstrate the social relevance and universality of their meaning system, and reinforce their spiritual commitment.

There is in Baba's writing an emphasis on the integration of detachment and action. In a discourse, "The Dynamics of Spiritual Advancement," Baba advises his followers to act in the world in such a way that their actions are dedicated to the Avatar and each is inwardly detached from the consequences of his actions.[44] "The object of spiritual advancement is not so much 'works' but quality of life free from ego consciousness." Nevertheless, one "may have to take to the life of action to wear out the ego one has already developed." This places the spiritual aspirant in a dilemma: action is necessary to wear out one's ego, but action can create new layers of ego, particularly if one is "attached" to the fruits of, and takes pride in, one's actions. Baba resolves this dilemma by advocating a kind of action in which the aspirant views his own actions as not his, but Baba's; the aspirant thereby becomes detached from the consequences of his actions, which are "in the Master's hands."

Such inner detachment makes the impersonality of "technocratic" vocational routines less oppressive. A detached resolution of the problem of alienation from work roles is congruent with the increasing tendency of middle-class employees to segregate their personal identity from their occupational roles, a phenomenon that has been noticed by a number of sociologists.[45]

It can be seen how Baba's ethic of inner detachment, in conjunction with the expressive context of the loving Baba community, enables alienated individuals to accept work roles that are not intrinsically gratifying or expressive. Moreover, the ethos of selfless service actually appears to provide a basis for qualified renewal of personal involvement in interesting and exacting work roles. Thus, selfless service can eventually become a basis for career orientation. A sort of mutual validation occurs between the emergent work roles of Baba Lovers and the cult's meaning system. Selfless service facilitates career involvements, which in turn act out the spiritual "love" orientation and make it appear socially relevant. Thus Baba Lovers continually strive to relate all their worldly activities to their religious involvement in such a way that the former is viewed as inspired by, and derived from, the latter. A process of mutual, or reciprocal, validation appears to take place whereby the religious meaning system legitimates loving worldly roles, which in turn reinforce the meaning system.

MONISTIC MOVEMENTS AND CIVIL RELIGION

Although monistic mystiques provide value frameworks that can motivate social participation, such mystiques, almost by definition, repudiate American civil religion. Traditional American civil religion is dualistic, and exalts the value of our political, economic, and religious institutions vis-à-vis those of other nations. Monism regards all particularistic theologies and ideologies as arbitrary, and attachment to them as something to be overcome by the spiritual quest.

Such a repudiation of America's traditional civil religion has some advantages. Dualistic civil religion defines the nation in terms of the majority's conscious acceptance of a particular rational ideology. It cannot, by definition, be a minority orientation without causing great psychic strain in its devotees. In a pluralistic society associated with managerial capitalism, a monistic religion that affirms a hidden social unity beneath the apparent diversity of competing value perspectives offers obvious attractions. And by emphasizing "detachment" as a vocational attitude, monistic movements can lessen the alienation that comes from involvement in bureaucratic institutions. It might also be argued that the doctrine of karmic determinism (the roots of one's present circumstances in one's actions in past lives) taught by many such groups is more compatible with participation in "impersonal" large organizations than is the emphasis on free will associated with traditional civil religion.

The Meher Baba movement exemplifies general points about monistic movements. Many followers of Meher Baba originally sought an alternative meaning system because of the radical disjunction between private and public realms in modern America. As part of their search, some Baba Lovers had been involved in bohemian countercultural milieus that emphasized untrammeled emotional expression. These would seem to encourage narcissism, because they emphasize the expression of impulses rather than the delay of gratification on behalf of long-term emotional commitments. Conversion to the Baba movement, however, typically involves repudiation of such a "hang-loose" ethic. Baba Lovers generally are sexually monogamous, and tend to restrain impulses that would interfere with the development of communal life. They do so, moreover, without becoming further alienated from the morally confusing public sector.[46]

Monism, Dualism, and Cultural Shifts

We have argued that the present climate of moral ambiguity and the consequent polarization of monistic and dualistic world views are related to the erosion of a dominant American politico-moral ideology, or civil religion, that we call implicit legitimation. This meaning system combined three key elements into a consistent world view: (1) stringent moral absolutism reflecting both the Puritan covenantal tradition and subsequent evangelical awakenings; (2) a fervent belief in laissez-faire and competitive individualism in the economic realm; and (3) messianic conceptions of America as an instrument of Divine Providence and an exemplary utopia. This ideology was synthesized from the Puritan tradition and utilitarian individualism. An absolutist, hence narrow, conception of "theft" justified entrepreneurial practices and processes that produced extreme socioeconomic inequality. The dominant civil religion thus combined theistic moral fervor with legitimation of entrepreneurial capitalism; it was America's modernizing ideology.

The moral system of implicit legitimation has been eroding for some time owing to: (1) the negation of laissez-faire in an emerging context of state regulation of the economy; (2) a general loss of a sense of personal autonomy in a society dominated by impersonal bureaucratic organizations; (3) the flowering of hedonism and moral "permissiveness" in a mass consumption economy; and (4) recent challenges to American chauvinism growing out of our defeat in Vietnam, Watergate, and détente. The results have been politico-moral ambiguity and an attempt to reconstruct the traditional civil religion. Innovative religious movements respond to this growing climate of moral ambiguity, but they also make specific responses to the dissolution of the once dominant civil religion, and either celebrate or repudiate salient elements of the traditional civil religion synthesis.

The politicized evangelical surge and its ally, conservative "Reaganism," can easily be seen as constituting a drive to reconstruct the system of implicit legitimation and to recreate the synthesis of theistic moral absolutism, economic laissez-faire, and messianic interpretation of the meaning and destiny of America. The Reverend Jerry Falwell and President Reagan appear to share certain basic values that entail a celebration of early entrepreneurial capitalism and its legitimating mix of competitive individualism and evangelical Christianity.

Unfortunately for the neo-traditionalists, the essential elements of the traditional synthesis now lack the viability and mutual consistency they once manifested. The impersonal processes of bureaucratic managerial capitalism destroy the sense of personal autonomy and free will essential to the plausibility of both moral stringency and economic individualism. The extension of laissez-faire principles to more areas of commercialized leisure conflicts with moral absolutism. Finally, the celebration of messianic Americanism, once compatible with isolationism, is now linked with militarism and internationalism, both of which ultimately contribute to political and economic centralization. Thus the recreation of a national moral community based on a harmonious synthesis of utilitarian individualism and moralistic theism is not a likely possibility. It is for this reason, perhaps, that contemporary American evangelicism appears to waver between an apocalyptic vision in which a hopelessly depraved culture will shortly be destroyed as the world was destroyed "in the days of Noah"—the standard "premillennial" view—and a contrary triumphalist vision, in which the "moral majority" and its allies will purify the republic through political activism.[47]

The ideologies of the less traditional and more innovative spiritual movements are a reflection of the diminished viability of the traditional synthesis. Both the Meher Baba movement and the Unification Church provide therapeutic communities for converts, in which loving relationships are crystallized and legitimated in terms of universal spiritual mystiques. The warmth and expressivity of childhood familial settings are thereby combined with adult seriousness and idealism. But the values of each movement are sharply divergent. The Meher Baba movement is a monistic system in which ultimate reality is assigned to a realm of consciousness latent within the self. Although this universal consciousness is personified by a spiritual master, it cannot be translated into any rigid doctrinal or normative system. Rules and standards may be more or less useful for achieving certain goals, but they are not metaphysical absolutes.[48] Right and wrong are ultimately relative. In contrast, Sun Myung Moon propounds a system of stringent moral absolutism and "exemplary dualism." As a "Moonie" told one of the authors, "In the Bible, Jesus said, 'I don't come to bring peace on earth, I come to bring a sword.' And what that means is that what he is trying to bring us is a sort of symbolic sword to divide good and evil."

In our view, monistic and dualistic perspectives represent systematized responses to the moral ambiguity that arose from the decline of traditional civil religion and the moral system of implicit legitimation. Moral attitudes seem to be polarizing along a continuum, with systematic monistic relativism at one end and stringent dualistic absolutism at the other.

Although fully elaborated monistic systems such as the Meher Baba movement may claim relatively few adherents, numerous religio-therapeutic and human potential groups can be said to embody watered-down quasi-monistic perspectives that stress the primacy of individual consciousness and the discovery of the inner self, and that evaluate moral rules by relativistic standards. As Daniel Yankelovich discovered recently, permissive values from the counterculture of the late sixties and early seventies are continuing to spread. An increasing number of Americans are becoming "seekers of self-fulfillment" who are "forever preoccupied with their inner psychological needs."[49] At the same time, there is a fundamental shift of values, whereby "mystical" orientations, which attribute the causality of social outcomes to the inner experiential consciousness of individuals, are spreading at the expense of traditional theistic and individualistic orientations toward social causality.[50]

The former, as well as experimentation with mystical and religio-therapeutic movements, tend to be most prevalent among the highly educated and culturally sophisticated intelligentsia.[51] Although relatively few of the seekers of self-fulfillment studied by Yankelovich and others adhere to fully elaborated monistic systems, we view such systems as representing the most comprehensive and consistent expression of these new trends in moral attitudes.

The continued growth of postcountercultural values is particularly surprising in the face of the conspicuous resurgence of moral traditionalism associated with the "moral majority," the growth of evangelical Christianity, and the triumph of Ronald Reagan and political conservatism. In our view, many of the growing spiritual movements, including born-again evangelical groups, pentecostal churches, the Catholic charismatic movement, and certain totalistic groups such as the Unification Church, appear to share a fundamentally dualistic moral outlook. In general, these movements sharply distinguish between good and evil, and trace the latter to the inspiration of Satan, whose influence can be seen in the growth of communism, pornography, homosexuality, false gurus, and secular humanism. The dualistic moral outlook also affirms the existence of an imminent, irrevocable, all-important choice for individuals and humanity, one that admits of no evasion or mediation. One must either be saved or damned, serve God or Mammon; either Christianity or communism will triumph in the near future.

Today's dualistic movements generally tend toward political conservatism and anticommunist American patriotism. They identify America as humanity's bulwark in the present age against the scourge of godless communism. They are socially conservative and vehemently traditionalist with respect to unsettling changes in sex-role typing and exotic variations in hedonism. In contrast, persons involved in mystical and human potential groups, as well as persons with "secular" outlooks, tend toward social and political liberalism.[52]

America is in the midst of a dualistic revival. The triumph of Ronald Reagan and the surge of evangelicism are aspects of this revival. Nevertheless, values antithetical to the predilections of President Reagan and the Reverend Falwell continue to gain adherents. Moral attitudes are polarizing as Americans increasingly fall into one of two camps: seekers of self-fulfillment versus moral traditionalists. Systematic monistic relativism, as in the Meher Baba movement, and extreme exemplary dualism, as embodied in the "absolute values" of the Unification Church, define the poles of the continuum. The center may not hold.

REFERENCES

[1]See Bryan Wilson, *Contemporary Transformations of Religion* (New York: Oxford University Press, 1976); and Richard Fenn, *A Theory of Secularization*, Society for the Scientific Study of Religion, monograph series, 1978.

[2]Daniel Bell, "The Return of the Sacred? The Argument on the Future of Religion." *British Journal of Sociology* 28(4): 419-44.

[3]See James Coleman, "Social Inventions," *Social Forces* 49 (1976): 163-73; and John Marx and David Ellison, "Sensitivity Training and Communes: Contemporary Quests for Community," *Pacific Sociological Review* 18 (1975): 442-60.

[4]See Charles Glock, "Consciousness among Contemporary Youth: An Interpretation," in *The New Religious Consciousness*, Charles Glock and Robert Bellah (eds.) (Berkeley: University of California Press, 1976).

[5]Robert Bellah, "The New Religious Consciousness and the Crisis of Modernity," pp. 333-52 in *The New Religious Consciousness*.

[6]Willa Appel, "Satanism in Politics," *The New York Times*, January 15, 1980.

[7]Robert Bellah, "Civil Religion in America" in *Beyond Belief* (New York: Harper & Row, 1970), p. 171.

[8]Ibid.

[9]Robert Bellah, "Religion and Legitimation of the American Republic," *Society* 15(4) (May/June 1978). Reprinted in *In Gods We Trust: New Patterns of Religious Pluralism in America*, Thomas Robbins and Dick Anthony (eds.) (New Brunswick, N.J.: Transaction Books, 1981), pp. 35-50.

[10]Robert Bellah, *The Broken Covenant* (New York: Seabury, 1975), pp. 17-18.

[11]Bellah, *The Broken Covenant*, pp. 139-63.

[12]We are developing a paper on the history of American civil religion. The present discussion is the most comprehensive development of this theory to date.

[13]Dick Anthony and Thomas Robbins, "The Effect of Detente on the Growth of New Religions: Rev. Moon and the Unification Church," in *Understanding New Religions*, Jacob Needleman and George Baker (eds.) (New York: Seabury, 1978), p. 81.

[14]Arthur Vidich, "Social Conflict in the Era of Detente," *Social Research* 42(1) 1975): 69-87.

[15]Robert Bellah, "Religion and the Legitimation of the American Republic," p. 48.

[16]W. Clark Roof, "Alienation and Apostasy," *Society* 15(4) (1978): 41-45. Reprinted in *In Gods We Trust*, pp. 87-100.

[17]Roof's findings are compatible with more recent findings by Daniel Yankelovich in *New Rules: Searching for Self-fulfillment in a World Turned Upsidedown* (New York: Random House, 1981).

[18]Bellah, "Religion and the Legitimation of the American Republic."

[19]The "sacred cosmos" of evangelical Christianity can be viewed as a projection into the sacred realm of competitive entrepreneurial capitalism. Salvation is competitive in the sense that "many are called and few are chosen." Spiritual success is possible for a few, but many failures will inevitably be cast into "outer darkness." This dualistic conception of salvation approaches a zero-sum game.

[20]Benton Johnson, "A Sociological Perspective on New Religions," in *In Gods We Trust*, pp. 51-57.

[21]See the classic analysis of youth movements in modern society by S. M. Eisenstadt, *From Generation to Generation* (Glencoe, Illinois: Free Press, 1956).

[22]Robert Lifton, "The Appeal of the Death Trip," *The New York Times Magazine*, January 7, 1979.

[23]James Beckford, "Politics and the Anticult Movement," *Annual Review of the Social Sciences of Religion* 3 (1979): 169-90.

[24]The differences between the Jonestown community and spatially decentralized, hierarchical organizations such as Hare Krishna and the Unification Church are emphasized by James Richardson, "The People's Temple and Jonestown: A Corrective, Comparison and Critique," *Journal for the Scientific Study of Religion* 19(2) (1980): 235-59.

[25]Irving Horowitz, "The Politics of New Cults," in *In Gods We Trust*, p. 162.

[26]Ibid., p. 163.

[27]Thomas Robbins et al., "The Last Civil Religion: Reverend Moon and the Unification Church," in *Science, Sin and Scholarship*, Irving Horowitz (ed.) (Cambridge, Mass.: MIT Press, 1978), p. 51.

[28]Sun Myung Moon, *Christianity in Crisis: New Hope* (Holy Spirit for the Unification of World Christianity, 1973), pp. 61-62.

[29]Quoted, p. 89, Dick Anthony and Thomas Robbins, "The Effect of Detente on the Growth of New Religions," pp. 80-100, in *Understanding New Religions*, J. Needleman and G. Baker (eds.) (New York: Seabury).

[30]From Anthony and Robbins, "The Effect of Detente on the Growth of New Religions," in *Understanding New Religions*, p. 92.

[31]Irwin Doress and Jack N. Porter, "Kids in Cults," in *In Gods We Trust*, p. 297.

[32]Quoted in Robbins et al., "The Last Civil Religion," p. 65.

[33]Horowitz, "Politics of New Cults," p. 165.

[34]Reverend Sun Myung Moon, *Divine Principle* (Holy Spirit Association for the Unification of World Christianity, 1974), p. 444.

[35]John Hall, "The Apocalypse at Jonestown," *Society* 16(6) (September/October, 1979). Reprinted in *In Gods We Trust*.

[36]Ibid., p. 59.

[37]For discussions of contemporary American monism, see Dick Anthony et al., "Patients and Pilgrims: Changing Attitudes toward Psychotherapy of Converts to Eastern Mysticism," *American Behavioral Scientist* 20(6) (July/August 1977); Thomas Robbins, Dick Anthony, and James Richardson, "Theory and Research on New Religions," *Sociological Analysis* 39(2) (1978); and Gini Scott, *Cult and Countercult* (Westport, Conn.: Greenwood, 1980).

[38]Thomas Robbins and Dick Anthony, "Getting Straight with Meher Baba," *Journal for the Scientific Study of Religion* 2(2) (June 1972), and Dick Anthony and Thomas Robbins, "The Meher Baba Movement," in *Religious Movements in Contemporary America*, Irving Zaretsky and Mark Leone (eds.) (Princeton, N.J.: Princeton University Press, 1974), pp. 479-511.

[39]Meher Baba, *Discourses* (3 vols.) (Ahmedegar, India: Adi K. Irani, 1967).

[40]Robbins and Anthony, "Getting Straight with Meher Baba," p. 133.

[41]Ibid., p. 134.

[42]Ibid., p. 135.

[43]Quoted in Robbins and Anthony, "Getting Straight with Meher Baba," p. 132.

[44]Meher Baba, *Discourses*, vol. 2.

[45]Daniel Yankelovich, "New Rules in American Life," *Psychology Today*, April 1981, pp. 76-78.

[46]A number of writers, including Christopher Lasch in *The Culture of Narcissism* (New York: Norton, 1979) and Harvey Cox in *Turning East: The Promise and the Peril of the New Orientalism* (New York: Simon and Schuster, 1977) state that Eastern mystical and human potential movements manifest a narcissistic tendency that exacerbates rather than mitigates a participant's alienation. These (impressionistic) findings are not compatible with our analysis; however, it is possible to reconcile these contrary perspectives through distinctions between subtypes of monistic movements. See our discussion of these issues in "Culture Crisis and Contemporary Religion," in *In Gods We Trust*, pp. 9-31.

[47]The classic recent text for premillennial apocalpytic fatalism is Hal Lindsay's best-selling book of "biblical prophecy," *The Late Great Planet Earth* (Grand Rapids, Mich.: Zondervan, 1970). Lindsay articulates a widespread prophecy, whereby "The Last Generation" began in 1948 with the founding of the state of Israel. The spread of communism, pornography, homosexuality, and false gurus and cults will accelerate, until war in the Mideast will usher in the reign of Antichrist. This vision of inevitable moral decline and satanic ascension is strongly fatalistic. It is not entirely compatible with the very recent tendencies toward the politicization of evangelicism and the "moral majority" vision of a society purified by Christian renewal. The new tendencies thus implicitly challenge the dominant apocalyptic fatalism of seventies evangelicism, and will exert pressure toward reformulation.

[48]See the masterly analysis of *est* by Steven Tipton in the present volume. "Rule-egoism" justifies conformity to rules as instrumental in attaining valued states of psychospiritual well-being. However, it is these states rather than rules and moral authority that are the ultimate values.

[49]Yankelovich, *New Rules*, and "New Rules in American Life."

[50]See Robert Wuthnow, *The Consciousness Reformation* (Berkeley: University of California Press, 1976); Robert Wuthnow *Experimentation in American Religion* (Berkeley: University of California Press, 1978); and Charles Glock and Thomas Piazza, "Exploring Reality Stuctures," *In Gods We Trust*, pp. 67-83.

[51]Ibid.: Wuthnow, and Glock and Piazza.

[52]Wuthnow, *Experimentation in American Religion*.

JEFFREY STOUT

The Voice of Theology in Contemporary Culture

I. Theology in the Conversation of Mankind[1]

THEOLOGY SEEMS TO HAVE LOST its voice, its ability to command attention as a distinctive contributor to the conversation of high culture. Can theology speak persuasively to this culture without sacrificing its own integrity as a recognizable mode of utterance? The dilemma is by now a familiar one, much remarked upon by theologians themselves. To gain a hearing in our culture, theology has often assumed a voice not its own and found itself merely repeating the culture's platitudes in transparently figurative speech. The theologian with something distinctive to say is apt to be talking to him or herself—or, at best, to a few other theologians of similar breeding. Can the theologian speak faithfully for a religious tradition without withdrawing from the broader conversation in which philosophy, secular morality, and science each has a voice?

The worry that this question imposes an exclusive choice between two foci of loyalty, that one must turn one's back on tradition to be heard by the culture at large (and vice versa), has turned many theologians into methodologists. But preoccupation with method is like clearing your throat: It can go on for only so long before you lose your audience. Theologians who dwell for too long on matters of method can easily suffer both kinds of alienation they fear. They become increasingly isolated from the churches as well as from such cultural forums as the academy and the leading nonsectarian journals of opinion. This isolation helps explain why the much-heralded religious resurgence in American culture lacks a theological (as opposed to a prophetic or evangelical) voice and also why theology has not been able to benefit from that resurgence as one might have expected. Resurgent piety tends not to be disciplined by thought, just as academic theology tends not to be nourished by piety.

How, then, might theology become a conversable voice under such circumstances? How can it initiate a dialogue not only with its own tradition but also with the several voices of secular culture? Surely, no theology can today afford to be "prone to *superbia*, that is, an exclusive concern with its own utterance, which may result in its identifying the conversation with itself and its speaking as if it were speaking only to itself."[2] A conversable voice must take its place among the other voices, as often to be corrected as to correct. The time is past when theology can reign as queen of the sciences, putting each other voice in its place and articulating, with a level of conviction approaching absolute certainty, the presuppositions all share. For it is not at all clear that all voices share the same presuppositions; and, in any event, they would not nowadays be theological.

II. Theology and the Voice of Philosophy

A conversable theology can dispense with the quest for a method. There is no method for conversation save *being conversant*—that is, being well versed in one's own tradition and on speaking terms with other voices. David Tracy, the contemporary theologian most taken by the metaphor of conversation, nonetheless proposes what he calls a *fundamental* theology, defined by "a reasoned insistence on employing the approach and methods of some established academic discipline to explicate and adjudicate the truth-claims of the interpreted religious tradition and the truth-claims of the contemporary situation."[3] Fundamental theology draws a method from "philosophy or the 'philosophical' dimension of some other discipline" in order to establish "strictly public grounds that are open to all rational persons."[4] If I am right, however, a fully conversable theology will be skeptical that any such grounds can be found and suspicious that such a method, once in place, would succeed only in reducing all utterance to a single mode and thus in ending the conversation. As Michael Oakeshott has written, "the view dies hard that Babel was the occasion of a curse being laid upon mankind from which it is the business of the philosopher to deliver us, and a disposition remains to impose a single character upon significant human speech." The quest for a method to correlate the various modes of discourse, warns Oakeshott, "while appearing to accommodate a variety of voices, in fact only recognizes one . . . and all others are acknowledged merely in respect of their aptitude to imitate this voice."[5] There is no more certain way for theology to lose its voice than to imitate that of another.[6]

Tracy also speaks of *systematic* theology, an explicitly hermeneutical endeavor involving normative interpretation and reappraisal of one's tradition and contemporary situation.[7] Systematic theology, according to Tracy, involves "a profound acceptance of finitude and historicity" and a kind of understanding that "can be understood on the model of authentic conversation."[8] He sees systematic theology as one of theology's three basic forms. His *magnum opus* is projected as a trilogy that begins with a fundamental theology (*Blessed Rage for Order*),[9] receives further development in a systematic theology (*The Analogical Imagination*), and will achieve completion with the publication of a practical theology designed to draw out implications for ethics. I am raising the possibility that theology might usefully abandon its devotion to fundamentals, that there may be a conflict or tension between the first two parts of Tracy's trilogy, and that a conversable theology had better be hermeneutical all the way down.[10]

There is a sense in which Tracy's theology is, at bottom, hermeneutical, though it is not the sense I have in mind. Tracy aims to provide a "hermeneutical phenomenology" of human experience in reference to which reinterpreted Christian theological principles can be viewed as an intellectual necessity.[11] Hermeneutics appears here in part as the name for a method that will set the basic criteria of all rational discourse, grounding it in the elemental structures of human experience. But there is another sense of the term *hermeneutics*—the sense suggested, for example, by Richard Rorty's contrast between hermeneutics and epistemology.[12] Hermeneutics in this sense is not the first science of the human sciences, or the quest for a method of interpretation, or a theory of the nature of textual meaning. Nor is it an expression of the *epistemological* assumption that "all contributions to a given discourse are commensurable," that is, "able to be brought under a set of rules which will tell us how rational agreement can be reached on what would settle the issue on every point where statements seem to conflict."[13] Hermeneutics is, rather, the art of enriching our language in conversation with others, including old texts, and (at times) a kind of reflection designed to raise this art to self-consciousness (though without reducing it to a set of rules). It expresses itself in part as a struggle, in the name of finitude and historicity, against the assumption that the rules of rational commensuration have been found—and, thus, against the tendency to reduce all conversation to inquiry according to established rules.

Hermeneutics, in this second (more interesting) sense, is never having to say you're certain. The doctrine is reflexive: the thoroughly hermeneutical thinker will not be *absolutely* certain that he shouldn't be epistemological. Hermeneutics involves openness to the possibility that rules can change, that any successful attempt at rational commensuration is apt to be temporary, vulnerable to the next season of philosophical fashion or the next scientific revolution. That is not to say that there is no such thing as inquiry. Inquiry can go on so long as the rules remain fixed—but no longer. As Oakeshott puts it, "a conversation may have passages of argument and a speaker is not forbidden to be demonstrative; but reasoning is neither sovereign nor alone, and the conversation itself does not compose an argument."[14] "For epistemology," writes Rorty, "conversation is implicit inquiry" and thus somehow deficient until all the rules are made explicit. "For hermeneutics," on the other hand, "inquiry is routine conversation" and no more.[15]

So when I say that a fully conversable theology would be hermeneutical all the way down I mean that it would not presuppose or seek an epistemological basis in Rorty's sense. Unlike fundamental theology, it would not turn to philosophy as it would to a symposiarch or arbiter,[16] in the hope of discovering ground rules for rational discourse. It would not abandon its own theological idiom in favor of one that is more strictly philosophical. Hence, it would not be faced with the difficulty of finding (or transforming) a philosophical system the principles of which are either benign with respect to religious claims or already implicitly religious. And, ironically, it may be more secure precisely because it lacks a philosophical foundation, for its commitments are thereby less vulnerable to shifts in the prevailing philosophical winds.

Nothing I have said implies that theology ought to withdraw from dialogue with philosophy. One need not recognize philosophy as a kind of cultural symposiarch or adopt a specific philosophical idiom as one's own to converse with philosophy. Nor is rejection of a given philosophy's pretensions to the role of symposiarch necessarily a way to break off conversation with it. How, then, might theology proceed, if not by adopting a method from philosophy, if not by submitting to the verdicts of an arbiter?

Self-conscious reflection always begins in some place at some time. It is situated in a tradition at a given point in its history and in proximity to other traditions. Its problems and the resources available for resolving them are equally bound to a setting. To ignore the situation of reflection, or to try to make it irrelevant by somehow rising above it, is either foolishness or delusion. Reflection that begins in a context, as all reflection does, had better begin by acknowledging what that context involves. But this acknowledgment will necessarily be an interpretation from a point of view. Like all understanding, it cannot be a matter merely of allowing reality to impress itself directly upon the mind. So acknowledgment of context is itself conditioned by context. It can always be deepened, and possibly significantly altered, by setting a preferred interpretation next to its competitors and by subjecting its presuppositions to critical scrutiny. But never is the point reached when all presuppositions have been examined or given independent support. The process could in principle go on forever.

A conversable theology will not, however, use the so-called circularity and relativity of all human thought as an apologetic ploy to keep criticism at bay. It will not pull tradition over its head like a blanket. A tradition, used in that way, simply suffocates thought and very quickly becomes useless for anything, including blocking out the voices of those whom Friedrich Schleiermacher called the cultured despisers of religion. The circularity intrinsic to all reflection becomes vicious in theology only when it ceases to describe a spiral that delves deeper into its own assumptions and history while also passing through a broader, potentially threatening, cultural landscape that encompasses the perspectives of other traditions. The dependence of thought upon tradition is not at odds with the possibility of criticism of tradition. No living tradition is so settled, uniform, or unproblematical that it can simply be handed on as it is. Were that possible, theologians would not be needed. Change is reasonable, of course, only when it promises real benefits. There is no point in change for the sake of change alone. Too much pointless change could easily reduce thought to chaos, just as too little change of the right kind would rapidly render thought impotent. Critical rationality is a matter of knowing how and when to change your mind, given the problems and resources at hand.[17] It is not a capacity we all exercise by drawing reasons from the same well.

If there is no reservoir of reasons that does not belong to a particular social and historical setting, and if the available reasons tend to vary somewhat from setting to setting, it would be naive to expect a single argument to be equally compelling to everybody, regardless of setting. The apologist who aims for universal consent is courting frustration, whether the topic is religion, art, politics, or science. Theology had better expect to persuade only some while conversing with the rest. The theologian's arguments should not be deemed deficient simply because they do not, in Stanley Cavell's phrase, "work on people at random, like a ray."[18] But this does not absolve theology from winning a hearing—from earning the respect, if not necessarily the consent, of other parties to the conversation. It is as a voice of integrity, faithful to its own heritage without ceasing to be rigorously honest in its self-criticism, that theology might entertain what Auden called the poet's hope:

> . . . to be
> Like some valley cheese,
> Local, but prized everywhere.

Prized, that is, as a distinctive but respectable voice.

III. Theology and the Voice of Ethics

Hermeneutical theology will resist the epistemological attitude in ethics for the same reasons that lead it to be suspicious of the epistemological attitude elsewhere. Moralists with epistemological ambitions, who set their sights on the perspective of eternity, cannot help but fail, and their failure may have a moral as well as an intellectual aspect—a failure to consent to finitude as well as to acknowledge it. They are especially liable to exhibit the hubris that tries to escape the human condition itself.

Ethical rationalists, as we may call them, seek the moral equivalent of Esperanto. They want to rid themselves of the essential markings of historically conditioned thought. But the "sad little joke" about universal languages, as Mary Midgley says, is that nobody speaks them.[19] The only thing harder to imagine than how to put together a universal language is why anybody would want to be confined to one. Esperanto would impoverish thought and conversation. The same holds, if less obviously, for its moral equivalent, the language of ethical rationalism, which aims to lay down the rules all practical discourse must follow. The triumph of Esperanto is the stuff of which dystopian novels are made, not something fervently to be sought.

One tendency in ethical rationalism that embodies the prejudices of its age is its glorification of human freedom—a tendency it shares with existentialism, Marxism, and much else in modern thought. But to the hermeneutical theologian, or anyone else with a fully developed sense of human dependence and finitude, the modern glorification of human freedom will seem one-sided and exaggerated. The point is not that we should deny freedom but only that the modern equation of freedom and absolute self-dependence makes nonsense of human activity. This equation, as Charles Taylor has put it, defines freedom

> in such a way that complete freedom would mean the abolition of all situation, that is, a predicament which sets us a certain task or calls for a certain response from us if we are to be free. The only kind of situation which this view can recognize is one defined by the obstacles to untrammelled action which have to be conquered or set aside. . . . On this view, there is no situation such that the response it calls for would *be* free action at its fullest extent as against just clearing the way to such action. Full freedom would be situationless.[20]

"Complete freedom," Taylor adds, "would be a void in which nothing would be worth doing, nothing would deserve to count for anything. The self which has arrived at freedom by setting aside all external obstacles and impingements is characterless."[21]

A hermeneutical theology, in contrast, would have to work out a conception of *situated freedom*. As Taylor says, "What is common to all the varied notions of situated freedom is that they see free activity as grounded in the acceptance of our defining situation."[22] To be human is to be situated in nature, history, culture, and society—to have a particular location. It is to be embodied as a member of a species endowed with certain traits and needs, to occupy a specific position in the cosmos, in one's own tradition, and in a personal history that stamps the self with whatever character it has. No one can simply think or wish all of this away. We must, in the first instance, *accept* these facts about ourselves as our lot. We are, in any event, wise not to ignore the many ways in which they limit us, shape us, and give us our identities. Concerning such matters, presumably, a theology not dedicated merely to repeating what the most common forms of secular morality have been saying should have much to teach us.

IV. Theology and the Voice of Science

Among contemporary theologians in America, James Gustafson, Tracy's colleague at the University of Chicago, may best exemplify what I have been calling the hermeneutical attitude. Unlike Tracy, Gustafson projects a *magnum opus* of only two parts: the first, a systematic theology in Tracy's sense; the second, a more explicitly practical theology.[23] What is entirely missing from Gustafson's project is anything analogous to Tracy's first volume—a fundamental theology. Gustafson gently mocks the desire for a "propaedeutic to one's propaedeutic" (p. 64), eschews the "philosophy of theology," and proceeds directly to his interpretation of the theological situation. Gustafson writes in the conviction that methods are better seen as instruments for accomplishing a purpose than as foundations on which to secure one's arguments (p. 68). He speaks eloquently on behalf of his tradition, especially that strand of Calvinist piety in which the sense of dependence on God figures most centrally, though he also forcibly denounces elements of the tradition that either conflict with the themes he deems most central or cannot be given sufficient experiential warrant. Moreover, he attempts to show in considerable detail what a conception of situated freedom might come to when set in the context of a theocentric ethics. Yet one of the most noteworthy features of Gustafson's project is the dialogue it initiates with science.

Most theologians standing, as Gustafson is, in the tradition of liberal theology fathered in the early nineteenth century by Schleiermacher have been more concerned to negotiate a truce with science than to initiate a dialogue with it. The truce was to be a pact of nonaggression—what Schleiermacher called an "eternal covenant"—the point of which was to give science and theology separate realms of human experience to govern and then to prohibit all trespassing across boundaries as the intellectual equivalent of imperialism. Science was to govern the realm of cognition: It alone would have the authority to tell us what we know. Theology was to reign in the realm of religious affectivity: It alone would have the authority to tell us what piety implies.

This strategy can work, however, only if two conditions obtain: Science must turn out to have no knowledge, strictly speaking, concerning God's existence and attributes, whereas theology must somehow make sense of itself without claiming such knowledge either. In other words, the eternal covenant could be effective only so long as both parties remained silent on the issue in which both were once thought to have an interest—namely, knowledge of God. Far from initiating a dialogue, then, Schleiermacher's eternal covenant was in fact an attempt to keep both parties eternally quiet at precisely the point where their interests have always seemed to overlap.

How could such silence be enforced? On the one hand, Schleiermacher endorsed Kantian arguments intended to show that science cannot, in principle, either prove or disprove anything about God. Theology was therefore supposed to be free to have its say about God without fearing contradiction from science. On the other hand, Schleiermacher used an apparently sharp distinction between knowing and feeling to mark out the sphere of religious experience. The doctrines of Christian theology he then described as "accounts of the Christian religious affections set forth in speech."[24] Theology is permitted to speak of "divine attributes and modes of action" and of "the constitution of the world," but only if it does not claim knowledge of such matters, least of all as they are *in themselves*. Theology must confine itself to saying how God and the world are *for piety*, which is a feeling and not a knowing. As Schleiermacher put it, "every formula for that feeling is a formula for a definite state of mind; and consequently all propositions of Dogmatics must be capable of being set up as such formulae."[25]

I have argued elsewhere that Schleiermacher's covenant breaks down if a sharp distinction between knowing and feeling cannot be maintained but also that the attempt to exclude cognitive claims from theology threatens to eliminate the reasons that made people care about defending theology from scientific criticism in the first place.[26] Schleiermacher, it seems, could not have it both ways. The scientific threat can be kept at bay only by making theology utterly vacuous, a matter of mere feeling.

If you have trouble understanding the dilemma I am posing, imagine a follower of Sartre who sets out to do for nausea what Schleiermacher did for piety. He proposes a discipline the goal of which is to offer accounts, analogous to theological doctrines, of the feeling of nausea set forth in speech. These accounts indicate how things are *for nausea* without entailing or presupposing knowledge of any kind. One doctrine might be that God is dead. The death of God will be proclaimed as the *Whence* of nausea.[27] Now, must we take our Sartrean seriously? If not, what gives his proposal less serious a claim on our attention then Schleiermacher's theology? If we must take him seriously, are we to take his doctrines as incompatible with the corresponding theological doctrines? It would seem not, for he and the theologian alike present themselves as refraining from making theoretical claims. Each is telling us how God and the world are *for* affectivity of a certain kind—existentialist *nausée* and Reformed *pietas*, respectively. But then how long can theology be taken seriously if it is not taken to be incompatible with what our antitheologian has to say? On what grounds might we explain the difference between these two expositions of doctrine or the depth of feeling they express if not by ascribing to them the very theoretical claims each makes a point of eschewing?

Gustafson echoes Schleiermacher's theology in many ways. For Gustafson, as for Schleiermacher, "thinking always starts in history, *in mediis rebus*," and proceeds "as we continually revise our initial idea in light of empirical data and subsequently test the revised idea against the new pattern of data that has become relevant in light of the revised idea."[28] For both men it is this dialectical process of revision that gives theology its purchase as a *critical* discipline and saves it from the vicious circularity to which vulgar relativism condemns all thought. Moreover, Gustafson and Schleiermacher agree in seeing theology as grounded in the *piety* of a historical community, in the prereflective experience of religious feeling. Theology is conditioned by religious affectivity; it consists largely of reflection on the religious affections, and the persuasiveness of its arguments is relative to the piety it presupposes. And while Gustafson does not follow Schleiermacher in identifying the essence of piety with the sense of absolute dependence, the latter does come first on his list of the religious affections, the "aspects of piety." But Gustafson does not maintain the sharp distinction between knowing and feeling essential to Schleiermacher's strategy for dealing with science,[29] and that is why he is able to initiate a dialogue with science whereas Schleiermacher could not. He thus avoids some of the characteristic difficulties of Schleiermacher's theology, though only by undertaking the risk Schleiermacher was himself trying to avoid. For admitting that cognitive and emotive strands are thoroughly intertwined in religious affectivity implies that theoretical questions about the *explanatory adequacy* of theological doctrines cannot be ruled out in advance as irrelevant. It is because such questions must be deemed relevant that dialogue with science is necessary as well as possible.

When Gustafson says that piety is affective or prereflective, his point is not that it is noncognitive. To the contrary, he repeatedly insists that we should not draw oversharp distinctions among the affective, cognitive, and volitional aspects of experience. Any distinctions of this kind should be treated as abstractions from experience, useful perhaps for some specific purpose in a particular context, but not to be reified (pp. 116-17, 287). In saying that piety is affective, Gustafson is resisting a rationalistic or voluntaristic *reduction* of piety to a mere exercise of the intellect or the will; he is not trying to promote an emotivist reduction of piety to sheer feeling. Similarly, the point of asserting that experience is prior to reflection is to portray theology as a second-order activity, not to deny the role of cognitive categories "in the ordering of even very primary experiences" (p. 116). Piety is immediate only in the sense that it is not mediated by self-consciously intellectual activity. It is, however, mediated by the cognitive categories implicit in what Gustafson calls the first-order language of piety. If I have interpreted him correctly, when Gustafson speaks of religious experience he is not appealing to a kind of prelinguistic or nonpropositional awareness of God. Experience may be prior to reflection, but it is not prior to "the context of a religious community, with its first-order religious language, its liturgies and symbols, and its procedures for transmitting a heritage" (p. 318).[30] It follows, therefore, that the appeal to religious experience and affectivity is not, in Gustafson's work, an attempt to place the implications of piety beyond the pale of criticism. Piety employs a language the categories and presuppositions of which are corrigible in the light of the rest of what we know and feel, including what we learn in dialogue with science.

What does its dialogue with science teach theology? Mainly, concludes Gustafson, that "we have a Ptolemaic religion in a Copernican universe" (p. 190). If theology is to be reasonable, it must cease to be Ptolemaic. If our universe is that described by Copernicus and his successors, if the prehistory of our species is that explained by Darwin and his heirs, then Herbert Butterfield was right in saying "that it is absurd to suppose that this colossal universe was created by God purely for the sake of men, purely to serve the purposes of the earth" (quoted on p. 98). Ernst Troeltsch was right to conclude that "As the beginning was without us, so will the end also be without us" (p. 98). Given the best science of our time, says Gustafson, it would be indefensibly Ptolemaic to hold that our happiness is the chief end of creation or that salvation awaits us at the end of time. Theology has not yet fully reoriented its vision to accommodate what the likes of Copernicus and Darwin have been saying.

Truly to listen to the voice of science is to risk having one's vision transformed. It is, as Oakeshott says, to hear in science "not (as we had first supposed) the didactic voice of an encyclopedia, but a conversable voice, one speaking in an idiom of its own but capable of participating in the conversation."[31] Gustafson does not imitate the voice of science any more than he imitates the voice of philosophy, but he does subject his own theology to the kind of questioning that a dialogue with science necessarily entails. He concludes that we must reject as excessive the idea "that God has intelligence, like but superior to our own, and that God has a will" (p. 270). He believes we can meaningfully speak of divine purposes for creation, but he finds insufficient warrant for talk of divine intentions (p. 271) or for postulating a clear *telos* in God's creative and sustaining powers (p. 240).[32] Similarly, Gustafson's doctrine of God as Redeemer does not depend upon the possibility of eternal life, just as his Christology has nothing to do with the resuscitation of a corpse. According to Gustafson, we lack sufficient experiential warrant of such ideas. We may acknowledge them as part of our heritage. We may even cherish their symbolic import in the first-order language of Christian piety. But concerning the literal truth of such ideas, theology should confess ignorance. We must, finally, even displace salvation "as the principal point of reference for religious piety and for the ordering of theological principles." We must do without "the assurance that regardless of how difficult and tragic human life is, God will make it right, at least for those who trust in him" (p. 112).

The problem with such traditional doctrines is not, however, simply paucity of evidence. Many of the doctrines for which Gustafson finds insufficient evidential warrant "even in piety" (p. 271) are also, in his judgment, incompatible with full affirmation of the sovereignty and majesty of God. To Gustafson, the traditional doctrines of eternal life, of God as He who redeems us from death, who loves us as a supremely intelligent agent would love His children, and of human happiness as the chief end of creation are all supremely attractive. They are all-too-attractive to us, for we are all-too-human, too eager to be consoled by wishful thinking, too willing to acquiesce in the narcissism that masquerades as worship of Another.[33] Gustafson is an iconoclast, out to smash the idols of Christian narcissism in the name of God's sovereignty.

To listen to science, Gustafson argues, is to have one's sense of dependence and finitude deepened. Take, for example, the voice of modern biology, which in Gustafson's pages is represented by the writings of Mary Midgley. Midgley has done as much as anyone since the early pragmatists to help us reckon with the consequences of the Darwinian revolution. She has more consequences to reckon with than the early pragmatists did, of course, and her major aim has been to draw out the moral significance of the most recent work in ethology. Her advantage over some of the more famous spokespersons of "sociobiology," aside from a philosopher's eye for conceptual muddle, is her lack of territorial ambition. She wants to break down the walls separating disciplines in the hope of encouraging much-needed conversation—the kind Aristotle carried on between ethics and the best biology of his day simply by thinking out loud. She does not plot the conquering of the humanities by biology. What she does, as Gustafson sees it, is help us situate our freedom realistically. We are situated in culture, to be sure, and human culture shows a remarkable variation with which we should make ourselves familiar. But the variation occurs within limits set by the structural characteristics of our species, our basic motivations and needs, which are thrown into relief by comparison with those of other social animals. The most important features of our nature are not always those that make us different. Thinking hard about what we have in common with other animals can alter our perception of ourselves and of our place in nature.

For Midgley, neither reason nor conscience is rightly understood as a power looking down on our animal nature from above; they are expressions of that nature, of our innate tendency to organize and integrate experience. Morality varies from culture to culture, but culture does not deal with human beings as a printer deals with blank paper. We are culture-producing animals—that is part of our nature—and the cultures we produce are rooted in our basic motivations and needs. This is the context in which morality becomes intelligible by virtue of having a point, a function, in the life of creatures with motivations and needs the satisfaction and organization of which are not wholly governed by instinct.

Midgley's is not a theocentric vision. She does not postulate divine purposes, let alone divine intentions, in order to explain the data she assembles or to explicate the sense of dependence she feels. But there is room in her vision for wonder, awe, and even gratitude—a kind of piety, in short, for the powers that bear down upon us, for the majestic setting of our planet and its cosmos, and for the often marvelous company we keep here. "Stunting this response," she says, "is stunting our highest faculties."[34] She tellingly diagnoses the existentialist angst of those who bewail their own alienation from the cosmos after the death of God: It is the reaction of emotional cripples. Antitheism has already lost its point. If God is dead, asks Midgley, "why dress up in his clothes?" "If we know the house is empty, why ring the bell and run away?" And why feel alienated from the only "sort of universe in which our nature is adapted to live"—one that surrounds us with a sublimity we have only begun to explore?[35]

That Gustafson resonates to much of what Midgley says should hardly come as a surprise. The resonance is entirely authentic. It is not achieved by one voice's imitation of another. Each speaks honestly and deliberately on behalf of a distinct historical tradition—traditions that have at times seemed locked in mortal combat. Yet the resonance they achieve here may finally be as troubling as it is pleasing. Can we any longer tell these voices apart? What, in the end, makes Gustafson worth listening to if we already have Midgley?

This may seem like an idle question. Gustafson's perspective is theocentric; Midgley's is not. Gustafson's piety is directed toward a single other; Midgley's is more diffuse. Gustafson speaks of divine purposes; Midgley disentangles the scientist's concept of purpose from belief in a deity. But this list of differences only heightens concern. Is not Gustafson distinctive only at the points where he is also most elusive, where we have the most difficulty figuring out what he is saying and why he is saying it, where we have the most trouble discerning what the difference comes to and why he wants to maintain it?

A careful reading of Gustafson would show, I think, that he never explains with any clarity why we ought to go beyond Midgley to speak of "the powers that bear down upon us" as divine or what this addition in fact adds. Nor does he explain why the powers, which he nearly always refers to as plural, should be construed *mono*theistically. And he leaves the sense in which his deity is supposed to have purposes shrouded in mystery, telling us only that divine purposes should not be understood as intentions. My concern is not that he has failed to offer compelling arguments—arguments so powerful that any reasonable intellect would be forced to lay down its objections and submit. (Do such arguments play a major role in any discipline?) Neither am I simply indicating that *I* have not yet been convinced. My deeper worry is that Gustafson has not shown why *he*, "even in piety," might have reason to be convinced.

Gustafson would be a much less interesting theologian and my questions would have much less point if his appeal to piety were designed to place his conclusions beyond the scope of critical scrutiny, if he held piety to involve a contact with the really Real unmediated by cognitive categories and corrigible assumptions. It is to his credit that he does not evade hard questions in that way. Furthermore, it is by pressing hard questions about the meaningfulness and evidential warrant of theological claims that Gustafson builds his case against the less austere theologies of his predecessors. We can see *why* he concludes that his theology had better do without the doctrine of eternal life, the ascription of intentions and intellect to God, and so on. What remains entirely unclear is how the scruples that would lead to these conclusions would allow Gustafson to retain what little theological content he is left with at the end.

Gustafson's message, if abstracted from its specifically theological context, is both clear and reasonable: to keep our confidence, loyalty, hope, and love proportioned to their objects; never to make the merely finite our ultimate concern. Midgley could agree to that. Why add, as Gustafson does, that there is an Ultimate Other who deserves our ultimate concern? What difference does it make for ethics to place a Mystery at the center once Man has been displaced? It is ironic that a theocentric ethics would conclude its exposition of theological doctrine without making its answers to such questions clear.

These questions bring us back to the theological dilemma with which this essay began. Can theology retain its distinctiveness as a mode of utterance without ceasing to speak persuasively to the culture on which it would like to have an impact? I have commented at some length on Gustafson's dialogue with science because I can think of no writer who has struggled more valiantly or more honestly with the demands of theology's dilemma. He is also refreshingly free of the fundamental theologian's "epistemological" ambitions. His voice is supremely conversable. His effort would not be exemplary—it would not teach us so much about the predicament of theology in contemporary culture—if these things could not truly be said of his accomplishment. Yet precisely because he presses his scrupulous questioning so much further than most theologians are willing to go, his theology becomes an especially clear illustration of the difficulty posed by theology's current predicament. I take it as symptomatic of this predicament that Gustafson reaches a point where he cannot finally make the distinctively *theological* content of his proposal clear without violating the critical scruples that could win him a serious hearing in the broader conversation.

Gustafson sometimes expresses annoyance at secular intellectuals who say they wish theologians would be more orthodox—at those who are tempted to announce, without undergoing any risk of their own, that what we have here (say, in the case of Hans Küng) is a failure of excommunication. But there may be more to such remarks than the cheap shot. There can be no serious conversation with theology beyond a certain point if the voice of theology is not recognizably theological. One wants one's conversation partners to remain distinctive enough to be identified, to be needed. That is not the same thing as wanting them to stand still. Nobody really expects theologians to repeat the tired slogans we heard in Sunday school. The question is whether theology can be both critical enough to be respected and distinctive enough to be needed. What Gustafson's work shows, I think, is that this question survives theology's transition from the "epistemological" to the "hermeneutical" mode.

I do not mean to imply that Gustafson, or any other theologian for that matter, does not belong in the conversation. He has risked a great deal in his most recent work and richly deserves our respect. He is also to be thanked for seeking critical distance from the culture's platitudes. Nor do I mean to question the authenticity of his debt to the Reformed tradition. But there is legitimate doubt, it seems to me, concerning whether the Reformed tradition ceases, in Gustafson's discourse, to be primarily a matter of *Christian theology* at all. And he seems to be wondering about this, too.

"At what point," he writes, "are there beliefs and concepts the cost of whose abandonment would be the loss of identity and integrity of Christian theology itself? What degree of reformulation runs the risk of tipping the balance from a presumption in favor of the Christian tradition to a presumption against it?" (p. 144). He refers to the "agonizing honesty" with which Troeltsch faced the possibility that pursuit of theological inquiry might "lead unnoticed away from Christianity." "Such," comments Gustafson soberly and poignantly, "are the risks" (pp. 230, 274).

REFERENCES

[1] I allude to Michael Oakeshott, "The Voice of Poetry in the Conversation of Mankind," in *Rationalism and Politics* (London and New York: Methuen, 1962), pp. 197-247. See also Richard Rorty, "Philosophy in the Conversation of Mankind," in *Philosophy and the Mirror of Nature* (Princeton: Princeton University Press, 1979), pp. 389-94; Hans-Georg Gadamer, *Truth and Method*, trans. William Glen-Doepel, 2nd ed. (London: Sheed and Ward, 1979), pp. 325-51; and David Tracy, *The Analogical Imagination: Christian Theology and the Culture of Pluralism* (New York: Crossroad, 1981), pp. 101-02, 178, n. 1, 363, 422, 446-55.

[2] Oakeshott, *Rationalism*, p. 201.

[3] Tracy, *Imagination*, p. 52.

[4] Ibid., pp. 62, 64.

[5] Oakeshott, *Rationalism*, p. 197.

[6] "[F]or a conversation to be appropriated by one or two voices is an insidious vice because in the passage of time it takes on the appearance of a virtue. All utterance should be relevant; but relevance in conversation is determined by the course of the conversation itself, it owes nothing to an external standard. Consequently an established monopoly will not only make it difficult for another voice to be heard, but it will also make it seem proper that it should not be heard: it is convicted in advance of irrelevance. And there is no easy escape from this *impasse*. An excluded voice may take wing against the wind . . . or it may gain a hearing by imitating the monopolists; but it will be a hearing for only a counterfeit utterance" (ibid., p. 202).

[7] Tracy, *Imagination*, esp. chap. 3.

[8] Ibid., pp. 100-01, and passim.

[9] New York: Seabury, 1975. For a powerful criticism of Tracy's fundamental theology, see Van A. Harvey, "The Pathos of Liberal Theology," *Journal of Religion*, 56 (1976), 382-91. Tracy dismisses Harvey's criticism without argument in *Imagination*, p. 185, n. 32.

[10]Clifford Geertz, *The Interpretation of Cultures* (New York: Basic Books, 1973): "There is an Indian story—at least I heard it as an Indian story—about an Englishman who, having been told that the world rested on a platform which rested on the back of an elephant which rested in turn on the back of a turtle, asked (perhaps he was an ethnographer; it is the way they behave), what did the turtle rest on? Another turtle. And that turtle? 'Ah, Sahib, after that it is turtles all the way down' " (pp. 28-29).

[11]See Harvey, "Pathos," pp. 386-89.

[12]Rorty, *Philosophy and Mirror*, chap. 7.

[13]Ibid., p. 316. Note that Rorty does not explicate *commensurable* in terms of "sameness of meaning" (see p. 316, n. 1). Note also that Rorty's opposition to epistemology as the quest for rules of commensuration does not entail antipathy toward "epistemology" in the perfectly innocuous sense of "reflection on the possibility, nature, and content of numerous kinds of knowledge," as discussed in Ian Hacking's review of Rorty, "Is the End in Sight for Epistemology?" *Journal of Philosophy*, 77 (1980), 579-88.

[14]Oakeshott, *Rationalism*, p. 198.

[15]Rorty, *Philosophy and Mirror*, p. 318.

[16]See Oakeshott, *Rationalism*, p. 198.

[17]See Stephen Toulmin, *Human Understanding*, I (Princeton: Princeton University Press, 1972), especially p. x.

[18]Stanley Cavell, *The Claim of Reason* (New York: Oxford University Press, 1979), p. 326.

[19]Mary Midgley, *Beast and Man: The Roots of Human Nature* (New York: Meridian, 1980), p. 306.

[20]Charles Taylor, *Hegel* (Cambridge: Cambridge University Press, 1975), p. 561 (Taylor's italics).

[21]Ibid.

[22]Ibid. (Taylor's italics).

[23]James M. Gustafson, *Ethics from a Theocentric Perspective*, I (Chicago: University of Chicago Press, 1981).

[24]Friedrich Schleiermacher, *The Christian Faith*, ed. H. R. Mackintosh and J. S. Stewart (Philadelphia: Fortress Press, 1928), p. 76 (italics deleted).

[25]Ibid., p. 125.

[26]Jeffrey Stout, *The Flight from Authority* (Notre Dame: University of Notre Dame Press, 1981), chap. 7.

[27]Compare Schleiermacher: "As regards the identification of absolute dependence with 'relation to God' in our proposition: this is to be understood in the sense that the *Whence* of our receptive and active existence, as implied in this self-consciousness, is to be designated by the word 'God,' and that this is for us the really original signification of that word" (*The Christian Faith*, p. 16).

[28]Richard R. Niebuhr, *Schleiermacher on Christ and Religion* (New York: Scribner's, 1964), pp. 46, 48.

[29]I say that maintaining a sharp distinction between knowing and feeling is essential to Schleiermacher's strategy, not that Schleiermacher himself always keeps the distinction sharp.

[30]For confirmation of my interpretation of Gustafson on "immediacy," see *Ethics from a Theocentric Perspective*, I, p. 130, n. 1; James M. Gustafson, *Can Ethics be Christian?* (Chicago: University of Chicago Press, 1975), pp. 68, 183, n. 14; and John E. Smith, *Experience and God* (New York: Oxford University Press, 1968), pp. 52-53. Smith, in the passage Gustafson cites as influential for his own thinking, favors a notion of interpreted experience over either appeals to immediate experience (experience not mediated by "concepts, language, symbols") or an austerely rationalistic approach to religion that bypasses experience altogether. As for Gustafson's relation to Schleiermacher on this issue, I have trouble saying anything definite, mainly because of the exceedingly imprecise explication of feeling as "immediate self-consciousness" offered in *The Christian Faith*, pp. 6-7. For an interpretation and criticism of Schleiermacher on immediacy, see Wayne Proudfoot's forthcoming book on religious experience. For another relevant passage from Gustafson, see his 1975 Pere Marquette Theology Lecture, *The Contributions of Theology to Medical Ethics* (Milwaukee: Marquette University Press, 1975), pp. 5-6, 97-98, n. 4.

[31]Oakeshott, *Rationalism*, p. 213.

[32]Gustafson says rather little to distinguish purposes from intentions, but he does illustrate what he has in mind as follows: "A distinction has frequently been made between purpose and intention. Animals have purposes but, so far as we can determine, they do not have intentions; they cannot think about their ends and the means of fulfilling them in the way that human beings can" (p. 270).

[33]Cf. H. Richard Niebuhr, *Radical Monotheism and Western Culture* (New York: Harper Torchbooks, 1970), p. 119.

[34]Midgley, *Beast and Man*, p. 361.

[35]Ibid., pp. 198-99, 388, 363.

ARTHUR A. COHEN

The Religious Center of the Jews:
An Essay in Historical Theology[1]

Introduction

WHAT IS THE SCOPE and possibility of Jewish theology? I say *Jewish theology* intending by such usage a critical distance from both interpretation of historical Jewish thought and (which is as common) a Jewish rhetoric bonded to high issues and commitments that fails to become theology because it is too eloquent in urging in place of thought a mode of presumed and consensual feeling.

The present essay is not completely satisfactory since it braids history and theological thinking. But I must ask: unsatisfactory to whom? Principally I should think to those for whom theology is a species of philosophical thinking that the late nineteenth and early twentieth centuries considered under the rubric of "philosophy of religion." Theology, however, is never general. It is always thinking out of a tradition, reflecting the urgencies and requirements already articulated by an historical faith, liturgy, practice. Since theology is always wedded to a specific tradition, it is critical that it be understood at the outset that Jewish theology is not a speculative consideration of propositions about the nature of God and his Being, but is rather always an address to God amidst the historical life of the people of Israel. There is abysmal room within this formulation for a view that regards the people of Israel (the Jewish people, not the national people) as frozen into the eternity of the divine life,[2] hence making of the Jews a people beyond history, essentially ahistorical. It also leaves room for a view that regards the Jewish destiny as a working out of the divine-human nexus, never completed until the end of days and surely ruptured, if not definitively then decisively, by the caesura of the holocaustal *tremendum*.[3]

I have come to think, however, that Jews, more so than Christians, need to be seduced into theological thinking by what passes as history. If they come to think that their problem is historical rather than ontological they may be more ready to accredit philosophical gravities of speech than otherwise. It has there-fore been my method to use history as the medium that smuggles thought.[4] History need not thereby misrepresent thought. Not that kind of smuggling is involved. Nor mislabeling; no lying nor deception is involved. Rather history seems to the uninstructed a truly empirical medium of transmission and preser-vation. But history, no differently than theology, is a grotesque abstraction. There is no history *as such* either. There is only the history of my complexity of relations to the world—name, family, nation, culture, language, civilization, belief. Out of this welter of interior and external relations it is possible to devise the history of the narrative voice, the only voice that tells for others what it is that my mind thinks about myself in its conjunctions with the world. History is then always a particularity—my history and the history of the other, my history among Jews and God's history among Jews. That history is very specific and as such historical theology in my usage here is the delineation of the backdrop and the proscenium curtain between which the drama of man's being with God, the Jew's being with the God of Israel is enacted. As a theologian, it is enactment that I address—a theater of being whose script is ancient, whose directional markings are always altered as the epic is replayed throughout the centuries, whose actors and their accents are contingently historical, as different communities of the earth learn their historical roles. Despite the historical medium, the drama is continuously rehearsed and reperformed from the classic text. This is the subject matter of constructive theology. It is an order of theatrical speculation, requiring intimate familiarity with the historical modes of presentation and rendering throughout the ages, as well as the intellectual imagination to recognize that the same God is once more in travail with the same gifted people.

The People of a Civilization

It is reported, perhaps apocryphally, that Solomon Schechter, great scholar and founder of the Jewish Theological Seminary of America, once remarked, "You have to love the Jews a great deal in order not to hate them." It is obviously risky to interpret an epigram whose occasion is unknown. One suspects, knowing something of the tribulations through which Schechter passed in the formation and definition of Historical Judaism (what is known to us now as Conservative Judaism), that he was referring to the acerbity of the debates and cunning of the opposition with which he was obliged to deal. However its historical context, it is a stunning epigram. It makes Jews wince and smile, and any epigram capable of eliciting such an ambiguous reponse is worthy of examination on its own terms.

Jews are surely the most beloved and most hated people that ever lived. It is one of our tasks to make some sense of this historical conundrum. What is it that forms from the beginning of biblical history until the present day the remarkable constellation of affection and loathing with which Jews are regarded? As one unattractive but forthright critic of the Jews once observed to me: "There must be something in your people and its history that justifies such hatred for it to begin so early and continue until our day." To which I replied, thinking of Schechter: "Indeed, and so much love as well. Do not forget that we are beloved no less than hated."

The Jews are loved and hated. It is not only a question of anti-Semitism and philo-Semitism. It is not as it has come to be in the present moment anti-Zionism construed with all the panoply of anti-Semitic canard or pro-Zionism with all the distortion that any narrowly defined definition of a civilization entails.

The Jews constitute the people of a civilization. I take it, not incorrectly, that one means by a civilization a consensus of historically transmitted values that shape essential viewpoints on the origin and destiny of humanity; the nature of human character, action, and hope; care and solicitude for those artifacts of culture that express and refine those viewpoints (literature, art, language). A civilization also means in the course of centuries the formation and invigoration of psychological strengths and defenses that ensure and assault the survival and endurance of a people thus convoked.

The beset and hated Jewish people have outlived all their enemies. They have never been a large and multitudinous people, but they have been endlessly efficacious. They have been known to flee and they have been known to stand ground. They have been driven into exile and for centuries they did not return to the land of their beginnings. In this century, the Jewish homeless and survivors of the European decimation took the only land they have known and remembered, and caused it to flourish. In doing so, saving themselves, they have caused anguish to the others who dwelt in that land. In reacquiring love, they have reproduced hatred. And so contemporary Jewish history marches on, no less a congeries of affection and loathing than before.

There is no explanation for either. There are secular devisings and socialist readings of Jewish history that leave the Jews as miscreant as racist fascism conceived them. There are Christian scrutinies—Evangelical and Catholic—that fix the Jews in theological molds that leave them *in statu nascendi*, no different from when the biblical covenant with God was confirmed and the land promised to them and to their descendants. The hatred reads their present moment in the crooked light of a deformed past; the love describes them with theological fixities that allow little for their growth and unfolding beyond biblical times.

My interest in this discussion is to speak of Jews and the elements that set them forth as a civilization. Since it is my persuasion (not alone persuasion *parti pris*, but one that can be historically annotated and justified) that Jewish civilization begins in the religious center of the Jews, my interest is principally in the description of Jewish religion. It is the religion that supplies the dominant cast and motif to all those particulars that come through the course of centuries to spell the secular and socialist longings of sectors of Jewry, the messianic atemporality of its extremists, the inbred Yiddishist affections of yet other segments of Judaism, and the high intellectual and creative enterprise of other Jews who spend considerable energy ensuring that their genius be taken as general, rather than Jewish, and lastly the embattled citizens of the first Jewish state in twenty centuries who live off the Diaspora but despise it.

Every civilization has its beginnings. The beginnings of the Jews are religious, although religion conceived less as a body of formed and revealed specifics of doctrine than as a constellation of sharp and subtle viewpoints that in the course of time acquire the elaborateness of teaching and theology, sancta and polity, sacrality and normativeness. All these elements, describable in themselves, would nonetheless be falsely described if isolated from the medium in which they are borne. History is the medium of the Jewish people. Whether history be a demi-God whose worship deflects as profoundly as it illuminates, it is nonetheless the fluid bearer of the people, books, and events whose interaction with the inner spirit of the people and the external forces of the nations of the world forms what is specifically Jewish in Jewish civilization.

It is not my interest, except marginally, to argue with those who insist upon the denial of the religious center of the Jewish people, contending that some other more easily identifiable natural component is essential. I do not argue with secular nationalists who believe that the struggle of the Jews is for a land and society of their own or with secular socialists who see the only valuable component in Judaism to be its messianic lust for justice or with Yiddishists who believe the only authentic natural life of the Jews was to be found in an indigenous infraculture sequestered among the nations. I find nothing Jewish alien to me. Anything that is clearly an autochthonous construction of the Jewish people—whether ostensibly delicious or detestable—must have its place in what the Jewish people thought themselves to be once and what they have become.

Since this inquiry has as its purpose the setting forth of the essentials of Jewish civilization as a religious civilization, it must define parameters that both deepen the center and rationalize the borders where Jews touch and intermingle with their neighbors, whether in Israel or the Diaspora. Jews are not alone in the universe. They are a most remarkable people, but still only *primus inter pares*. They are always among others and their natural and theological task is to abide and ferment the lands of their ingathering as well as their dispersion.

The Jews begin with a view of God. They endure with a view of God. They come up to the end, expecting consummation in their view of God. But God is the assumption out of which they grow and against which they rebel. They are a people vivified and driven by a notion of God that has not released them. Individual Jews may leave the Jewish people, denying that they keep company with such a folk, and it is their right to depart. Whether history recalls them to what they deny, forcing them into slavery and death despite their protestation, is a working of historical process that it is still their freedom to refuse. They die in ignorance of why they are murdered. But in a more sanguine world they will be empowered by the secular state that governs to the ends of tranquillity and evenhanded justice to depart if they choose. Those who remain Jews—whether they be single-mindedly religious or mixed in their vision, nonreligious or antireligious and resolved—will be obliged by the extent and quality of the seriousness of their lives to take some stand on the civilization of the Jewish people, which above all elements has been marked by its religious viewpoint and content.[5]

Theological courage means for a Jew to publish a book that will be read by Jews and both extolled and excoriated by them and that will also be read by non-Jews who will confront a Judaism that they cannot help but find mystifying, perhaps slightly forbidding and distasteful. Should it be otherwise? Moreover, I doubt that Judaism can be made both truthful and attractive at one and the same time. I should opt for truth rather than felicity. And in so opting for truth, my way of dealing with alternative viewpoints to my understanding of Jewish doctrinal and historical center will be to argue with them—not simply to set them forth and leave them as viable options of other persuasions, but to take them to task as thoroughly as possible.

And so this essay will be easy for those who will be satisfied with half-truths and difficult and unresolved for those willing and prepared to deal with the complexity of the objective estate of Jewish civilization as well as with the ambiguity and confusion of their own belief and practice. I wish to provide no one—least of all myself—with a way off the hook. The hook is the millennial enterprise of what Spinoza rightly and wrongly took to be the God-obsessed people of Israel. But the hook is in *our* throat. And God (permit the completion of the image) is the tireless and obstinate fisherman.

The Terra Incognita *and the Explorer's Method*

There are many ways of undertaking the exploration and mapping of an unknown land. It is not simply that the land is wholly unknown. If wholly unknown, it would be by accident that one penetrated its borders. It is surely known, but principally by report of occasional travelers and unsophisticated wayfarers. The unknown land, whose report is buried in diaries and travel records, is revealed to the careful explorer as having broad lineaments and undescribed tracts of mountain range and parched wilderness. The explorer gathers all the reports available. He or she interviews whoever remains among those who happened into the land and survived; and gradually he builds a dossier of observation and detail that may guide and forewarn his own expedition. But all explorations are not alike, because all explorers are not alike. Darwin in Patagonia left us far fewer observations of its Indians and their civilization than he did of the fossil deposits that the rocks retained. Darwin was not an anthropologist or an indologist or an ethnographer. His curiosity was differently angled. Nor would a physical geographer or mountaineer have given us what the anthropologist or student of comparative anatomy would immediately seize upon to conserve and transmit.

The raw material of an unknown land is selected and winnowed by disciplines whose structure and method is prior to their presentation. Good students will alter their presuppositions to account for the new data or at least bend their assumptions to enable the raw novelty of exploration to shine forth undiminished by the quibbles and cavils of inherited doctrine.

This flourish is by way of introducing the difficult problem of method. How does one proceed to explicate Jewish civilization and its grounding in Jewish religious perception and understanding without foreclosing the exposition, stifling it, so to say, with blinders and halters that prevent its fair clarification? Theology and theological argument make people uncomfortable, principally I suspect because most people desire practical conclusions and hortatory maxims that rationalize and justify who they already believe themselves to be. Thought is an extraction most people cannot abide, and if thought about most things is considered tedious, theological thinking must be regarded by the impatient as exertion about what is already acknowledged as impossible to prove.

And yet there is no way to avoid theology if one is to speak about Jewish civilization. I could, of course, offer a historical discourse on the Jews that would leave one divided by precisely the same ambivalence that abounds in history itself. Historical research surely clarifies, but only with a point of view. There is no such thing as decent historiography that has no point of view. There is no way to avoid the armature of a perspective. Nor is it desirable. What is desirable is that the point of view be open to discussion. A scientific specimen should be sealed if it would suffer from airborne bacteria, but intellectual discourse never suffers from disagreement.

My perspective has always been from the vantage of theology. I think it possible to speak about God, to speak well and clearly about God, without making pretense to certitude. Were I to speak with the pretense of certitude I would be speaking not *about* God but as if I were privy to his counsel, indeed, in some sense his spokesman. I make no such pretense. That is left to the poorly appreciated prophet, for prophecy was not about pretending to be God, but about the certitude of being human.

Theology, late child of the age in which prophecy ceased out of Israel, is a discourse directed to clarification. The clarity is always a clarity about who God is and who God is not; what man is and what man is not. When asked to make plain who God is, one is always compelled to clarify who God is, but one cannot ever for certain demonstrate *that* God is. Proof of the existence of God about which philosophical theology has broken itself for twenty-five centuries is unavailing and helpless. There is no proof for what the stubborn mind cannot see. It cannot be proved that the merest apple exists, that a sound is made in the deserted forest, that the chair on which I sit or the machine with which I write is demonstrably existent unless there is the predisposition to consider the discomfort and intellectual embarrassment that results from denying their reality out of hand. One must be disposed to the inquiry for the inquiry to have merit. It must be a matter of will to clarify existence for the theological question to be ignited and inflamed at all. And if the theological departure cannot be accredited, then we are obliged to regard the Hebrew Bible from which all discussion of Jewish civilization departs as little more than a repository of conflicting and uncorroborated reports from various hands and sources regarding a people drawn out of Ur of the Chaldees, sent down into Egypt, convoked in the desert, and led up into the land of Israel.

What gives the Hebrew Bible the patent of authority, regardless of whether its text is treated as history or literature, is that it was transmitted to the age of critical scrutiny as a revealed text. That it is a document of unparalleled subtlety of redaction, its texts fashioned with strategies of narrative concealment and disclosure that continue to baffle and reward attention, is undeniable. But its hold upon generations of readers would be diminished were it not also regarded with the uncertain consciousness that it may well be the Book of God. The secular reader delights in its exposition and narrative complexity but cannot be insensitive to the liminal contention that it is speaking high matters and declaring truths that are represented as being the outcome of God's conversation with ancient Israel.

The origins of the civilization of Judaism are in the Bible. They have little collateral confirmation other than in the biblical text. Shards and monuments from other civilizations now gone confirm elements of the history of the ancient peoples of Israel, but if all that remained of ancient Israel were confined to the spare records of cuneiform or hieroglyphic reminiscence, there would be nothing.

It all begins perforce with the ancient Hebrew Bible. It grows from there as both historical narrative and recension of classic Hebrew self-consciousness. The Bible confirms and transmits the course of the generations from the calling forth of Abram, father of Israel, until the return of the Jews from the first exile in Babylon (586 B.C.E.), but at the same time it gathers together texts that comment and solidify the self-understanding of the people through whom that history passed. The Bible is both narrative of event and commentary upon event. It is the record of the impress of God upon the people and the emergent understanding of that impress. If indeed, as it is argued in rabbinic exegesis of the Bible, God always speaks in human language, a mighty theological supposition is affirmed. The majestically complex and difficult wisdom of God is available only as humans understand it. Slowly at first, the grand emphases of the primary narratives of creation and reception unfold, interpreted by various hands, received with differing emphases and stress, until by the close of the biblical canon, a consensus is formed, a unanimous understanding is affirmed, and a way of interpretation and application described.

What is already one in God is gathered and unified by the tradition as unanimous consensus and the procedures of bequest and transmission established for the maintenance of the historical community.

To speak, then, of the theology of the Jews, or more accurately to address the formation and transmission of Jewish civilization, it is necessary to speak first of the historical origins of the tradition and the theological interpretation of those origins.

The first doctrine of the Jews—the doctrine I suspect on which all its doctrine depends—is that the origins of the Jews are *not only* natural, *not only* the consequence of historical fortuity or historical causality conventionally understood. The first doctrine of the Jews regarding their origins is that in some fashion the people were called forth out of the nations by their God. This supernatural penumbra of the Jewish people is the beginning of its abnormality, the root issue of its vulnerability to irrational philo-Judaism and the no less intractable occasion for its most vicious detestation.

The issue of origins and beginnings devolves with no less force to the question of tradition, its own origins and beginnings. It is one thing to be within the flood of one's own history, convoked and covenanted, but quite another when the generation of origins passes but leaves behind the record of its experience. The Hebrew Bible is *prima facie* the first record of the transmission of written speech about the origins and beginnings of the Jewish people. But as written record it is subject to viewpoints and emphases that undertake to apostrophize aspects of the unitary experience with a view to providing concise emblemata and mnemonics that continue after. Beyond the question of beginnings, then, the source for the etiolation and formation of tradition is the Bible itself. The Bible is historical record as well as the first sacred work of the tradition. It is both account and liturgy, exposition and prayer, historical document and theological document. Believing themselves to be the recipient of God's first word to humankind, the Jews believed themselves to possess in the record of the divine word a teaching that needed to be conserved.

The task of conservation is the first work of tradition. Tradition is always perilous. It conserves, but it may also deaden. Clearly if the tradition as it emerged beyond the time of Ezra were a deadly conservation, the Jews would have abandoned the arduous faith. But they did not; indeed, they gathered strength in the aftermath of the return from the first Exile and instituted conventions that effectively transformed the living history of Scripture into the polity of the Second Commonwealth. They made the faith alive as one that succored and nourished, while at the same time defining patterns of behavior, models of leadership, literatures of sanctity and holy power that enabled one generation to give birth to another. In that age the living word of God became the word of Torah, a holy text succeeding the holy word, the sage and saint succeeding the judge and the prophet. Of necessity, then, I must account for the emergence of Torah as the conservator of historical norms of sacrality and wisdom.

The defined parameters of the tradition entailed implicit argument and controversy. The tradition was not installed as a pristine product of theological council and consent. The tradition was the tradition of a living historical people, beset from without by enemies who coveted their land as the crossroads of the ancient Near East as well as coping with issues of polity and society, poverty and wealth, cruelty and injustice, impiety and corruption. The sacredness of origins and the transmission of text as teaching in Torah required that the domain of human society be brought under the dominion of the teaching.

The ancient Jews did not know the issue of secularity as such. What they knew were other cultures and civilizations who devised wisdoms but no less retained social arrangements they despised. The Jews of the ancient world pursued God, but they also pursued justice. They were ancients out of ancient cultures, but they had already limned the possibility of compassion and forbearance in the management of their ways. They did not abolish all slavery but they brought it under the regimen of a different divinity, who considered abasement, cruelty, poverty, and humiliation unjust. Inevitably, concomitant with the elaboration of the earliest traditions of Israel is the tandem of law as the way of Israel and moral instruction as its point of ultimate reference and justification.

With the decline of Hellenism, and the regency, the civilization of the ancient Jews effectively opened to the world. By then more than a millennium had passed since the civilization first defined its origins, and though its memory foreshortened time, telescoping its reach to the confines of its national life, the Hebrew Bible, already elaborated by other texts and the beginning of commentary and internal discourse, was ready to encounter the world outside. The Jewish civilization had always known that there were others in the universe whom God had favored with a history and a dimly fashioned knowledge of his dominion, but it was not until the period of the earliest teachers, the Tanaaim, that it was prepared to formulate its perspective before all, to receive and indoctrinate others, to open out to the ancient world.

It was in this period of encounter and recoil that it faced the consequence of its paradoxical historical situation. Small in number, mighty in teaching, defenseless against the covetousness of larger nations and yet protected by the mightiest of Gods, the Jews of the last century before the common era reached out but were deflected. In that period the first controversy of mighty proportion shook Jews in self-definition. The civilization had fought over a millennium to define the conditions of its self-perpetuation, instituting rites and customs, defining ceremonies and obeisances unique to its cult and liturgy, developing a legislation of social and economic scruple that effectively discriminated its membership from those of the surrounding nations. But having developed all this religious and social teaching to secure the longevity of its nation and civility, it found that it had overdefined, overparticularized, overstressed what was unique and untransmissible. It now wished to spread and to convert, but it could not do so effectively without relaxation and release of its own strenuous vows of obedience. The willingness of Rome to accommodate to Israel and the readiness of the early Christian faithful to bypass Judaism in its reach for the Gentiles outside its precincts set the terms for the most enduring and painful theological war of all time.

In the centuries that passed from the advent of Christianity to the present day, the Jewish people were obliged to transfer the task of tradition from one of consolidating the national patrimony and aegis into a traveling dispensary of refuge and consolation. The tradition maintained in the land of Israel could attract the loyalty and support of Jewish communities already dispersed into the Mediterranean lands. Those Jewish communities, loyal but also assimilated, Hebrew-reading but Greek-speaking, maintained the faith in their nascent Diaspora, but as the Jews throughout the ages after them discovered, unless the faith is maintained by knowledge, study, and community, the only instrument of Jewish convocation that could compel endurance is persecution. The function of anti-Semitism as the spur to Jewish survival—a brutal means of psychological consolidation—set forth new terms and visions of Jewish destiny that had not been described by the ancient agenda. From a people confederated as an exemplar nation, the Jews became a civilization destined to an unfulfilled future. Time present in the ancient world—doing works of Torah, living the Law and its commandments, making justice efficient as a way of serving God— became time future in the Diaspora. The issue was no longer the Jews' vision of justice and mercy as instrumentalities of living community, but God's justice and mercy toward his own people. The Jews no longer enacted the just society. They were until our day restricted to studying the terms for its advent. The Messiah was construed as the King of Israel *redivivus*, as well as the Holy King of a transformed universe. Mystic reading of Jewish history vied with texts of the Law as sources for the description of the futurity and hope of the Jews.

By the modern era the essentials of Jewish civilization had been defined and its ambit transcribed. A denationalized people segmented throughout the nations of the world, the Jews nonetheless conserved in the Diaspora all the indispensable elements of a civilization. This civilization retained the institutions of its faith, the legitimacy of its vehicles of transmission, the languages and literatures of its interior and communal discourse, artifacts and objects of sacred usage, habits and camaraderies of intimacy. It was a dismembered universality, parts and pieces of its existence strewn over the habitable globe, synagogues and conventicles everywhere. But in its dismemberment it had lost what it had continued to lose since the decline of the Gaonate in the tenth century. It lacked unity; it bearly sustained unanimity. Its leaders were leaders to some but not to all; its sages legislated for one community but could not address all. It had no univocality although it maintained a choral voice, rich with assonance and dissonance, speaking with an odd harmonics that sounded in one refrain as though it were intact and melodically coherent while in many, many others its choral assault was shrill and ragged. The modern age has not been kind to Jews or Judaism. Other faiths and feelings have been roughened and riled by the divisiveness of the competing mundane loyalties of modernity, but uniquely in the modern world have the Jews been the elected victim of a total ferocity. No other people has ever been chosen to be systematically annihilated.

And so the rehearsal of history runs like an antiphon to the definition of elements of Jewish civilization and its articulate practice as religion. Religion, broadly or narrowly defined, is the armature of the Jewish presence in the world. Rejected and denied, accepted and practiced, religion is either the heart or the enemy of Jewish civilization. To be defined and embraced, to be defined and renounced, no matter, a Jew must come to face the religion and its polity or be done with it. One cannot read the literature of the Jews and the history of their expectation and continue dropping out the lines that reflect either their sacrality or their atheism. Jews are always taking their stand for or against the ancient civilization, and the ancient civilization and its beginnings were religious.

My proposal as a Jewish theologian is, therefore, to construct a work that will set forth what I take to be the primary elements of Jewish religious civilization, to contrast with my preferred reading those that diverge from it and to take issue with them, and to set both my own and the opposition within a historical context that makes clear in brevity why I see the matter as I do.

A religious civilization must take account of God and humanity, devise instruments for conserving its interpretation of them, and develop moral structures and emphases that embrace as much of the human condition as possible without relaxing the ground of containment and moral discrimination. It must articulate a liturgy and observance that make possible accessibility to the divine and the expression of the will to sanctification in the world. It must also maintain and transmit a literature for study, reflection, and teaching. Finally, it must elaborate and reinforce the criteria of normative participation in the collective community, and effect and strengthen bonds of loyalty and fellowship among its members.

Judaism is the religious precipitate of Jewish civilization. It is the constellated belief, teaching, and practice of those who call themselves Jews. Those Jews may ignore Judaism. But if what makes them Jews is as little as familial loyalty or gustatory triviality, or affection for other Jews, or praise for the Jews of Israel and their courageous undertaking, they begin *ad limine* to define self-images that can be pressed either to combust and disappear or to expand into larger considerations of human destiny that effectively reopen the religious question and address the religious reality. Jews may despise Judaism but they cannot nominate themselves for that identity without coming to the juncture of denying that the religion has any meaning or relevance to their lives. It is only too true that there are many Jews for whom the religious contention is quite simply meaningless. They may well say, as one Jew said to me not long ago, her words rich with irony and self-criticism: "There is no God and I am unwittingly God's servant." Doctrines, practices, laws, commandments—the whole regimen and discipline of the Jewish religious life—were for her meaningless, destroyed by a history too brutal to admit a caring divinity. And yet her life as historian of Jewish ways tested her daily, requiring that the detail of Jewish secular history, ribboned as it is with the strains and muscle of religious faith, be regarded as innocence and naiveté. What remains great for her, what remains great for us, is that the Jewish people lives at all, that its civilization endures, and that in our dismal age it begins new experiments with polities and societies that augur a renewed future.

It was possible three decades ago to write of the basics of Judaism without addressing continuously the question of evil. It is no longer possible. There can be no renewal of Judaism or its practice without setting alongside ancient contention and received tradition the demands that our times have opened for clarification and truthfulness. The ancient God of Israel is no less the God of the modern age, but the categories of description and understanding that have marked out the terrain of divinity must be remapped and reexplored. God may not have changed, but the people of Israel is a narrowed people. It is a civilization that has passed through the abyss, leaving behind in the underworld of catastrophe one third of its people and the destruction of a whole continent of its history. Such experience cannot fail to mark us and our faith with a limitless grief. And yet, it is the same God to whom we speak, the God of the ancient civilization and our own. We are different. We are more amazed at our endurance and more troubled by our destiny. This, of needs, must affect the way we speak with God, construe our civilization, and define ourselves.

REFERENCES

[1] This essay forms, *mutatis mutandis*, the first chapter of what will become a theological volume to be published by the Crossroads Publishing Company.

[2] As Franz Rosenzweig stated in his *The Star of Redemption*, Boston, Beacon Press, 1972.

[3] To this topic I addressed *The Tremendum: A Theological Interpretation of the Holocaust*, New York, Crossroad, 1981.

[4] See my *The Natural and Supernatural Jew*, New York, Behrman, 1979, and subsequent works.

[5] When my teacher Milton Steinberg published *Basic Judaism* (New York, Harcourt, Brace) in 1947, he set it as his task to describe a Jewish civilization just beyond the borders of the Holocaust and just before the advent of the remnant's return to Zion. Although coming out of the naturalistic framework that had defined his functional Judaism, Steinberg's conception of basic Judaism was mortally stricken by the uncertainty that penetrated his definitions of many complex and difficult elements of Jewish belief that are nonetheless doctrinally central to historical Judaism. I understand his tergiversation, but I no less criticize his unwillingness to face up. He was, in *Basic Judaism* and surely until his premature death, a *conservative* Jew. My principal criticism of *Basic Judaism* then and now was that it waffled. It was lucid, generous, fair, but it was not courageous.

MARTIN E. MARTY

Religion in America since Mid-century

For a great many years until mid-twentieth century, religion in the United States gave every indication of becoming increasingly secular, institutionalized, and less influential in American life. Yet the years since then have brought unanticipated changes in the relationship between religion and culture, and as a result, academic theorists have sought—and developed—fresh theories to account for these surprising cultural shifts.

First, contrary to expectations, religion is very much in evidence, which means that the secular paradigm and prophecy that had dominated Western academic thought has come to be questioned.[1] Second, rather than being contained within formal institutions, religion has unmistakably and increasingly diffused throughout the culture, and has assumed highly particular forms in the private lives of citizens. Third, traditional religion has not fallen away, as expected, but has survived and staged an impressive comeback, establishing itself firmly and enduringly in large subcultures.

Before exploring these shifts, three important points must be made. The first is that continuity—especially with regard to religiosity and secularity, the social locations of religion, and the durability of traditional faiths in the face of change—has long been a fundamental feature of American religious culture. Though academic theorists have often overlooked it, it has not gone entirely unnoticed. The "consensus historians" of the 1950s, for example, took note of it, and by minimizing the stresses and strains of American life, accented the "givenness," the stable threads of American religion.[2] Half-way through the period, historically informed sociologists, while impressed with the changes taking place, were able to keep their balance in the face of such change. In 1963 Seymour Martin Lipset, for example, in *The First New Nation* used the observations of both foreign visitors and American chroniclers to show that all-pervasive religion had characterized American culture through the years. While trying to do justice to the persistent secularity born of American pluralism—a secularity that manifests itself in the practical American temper—and the moral, as opposed to the transcendental, motif in much American faith, Lipset saw that voluntarism was the source of religious strength. American citizens *chose* to be religious because they were free not to be; religious organizations survived because they had to compete for loyalty.[3]

Second, academics trained in the sociology of knowledge—theorists in theology, religious studies, and humanistic or social scientific disciplines—were

273

tuned in to certain of the more subtle shifts in American culture. They saw that most of those living *in* the culture have fewer options for their lives than is generally realized, fewer tools for analysis, and many motives for resisting change. John Murray Cuddihy recognized that some core-culture analysts were theorists writing "from within the eye of the hurricane of modernization, where all [was] calm and intelligible." He knew that "for the underclass below, as for the ethnic outside, modernization [was] a trauma."[4] In their humble dwellings, they had neither the peace nor the time to reflect on possible alternative courses: the wind [was] coming their way, and they had to put up the sandbags, move on, or be destroyed.

Another way to put this is to caricature American society in terms borrowed from the comics and playpen; such an exercise leads to interesting results:

> Society can be diagrammed in a shape more or less like Al Capp's cartoon creation the Shmoo. The Shmoo's motion is largely in its head. A broad middle and a leaden bottom keep it earthbound. The child's roly-poly toy, all beaming and motion-filled in the face, is ungraspably broad in the middle, and burdened by weights so that it lands right side up when buffeted, and quickly comes to rest.[5]

The academic specialist naturally notices exaggerated tilts of the head among elites; mass communicators consistently report on all signs of novelty and sensation. Thus, when late in the sixties, for example, the offspring of certain professors, mass media communicators, and middle-class suburbanites took up astrology and began to express a belief in omens, the media at once exploited this "occult explosion," while theologians and social thinkers felt called upon to come up with fresh theories about neo-religiosity or transcendence. In fact, the number of the new devotees did not significantly alter the proportion of the population that had always believed in such phenomena. The body of the societal shmoo—or the weighted portion of the cultural roly-poly—had barely moved. Both head and body merit observation; theories drawn from observing only one are inevitably vulnerable.

Proof of religious continuity in American life can be found in many ways, not least in the polling data. Thus, for example, in a poll taken in 1952 as compared with one in 1965, the data seemed to show a widespread, if shallow, *revival* of religion, followed immediately by a sort of *revolution* in religion. There were "startling indications of change and . . . more puzzling indications of nonchange."

> Some . . . recalling the drama of the last dozen years, may look for more in these polls than they will deliver. Often . . . readers may have "felt in their bones" that epochal change in the world of science and the mass media or education will have induced epochal change in one or another of the sectors of the churches' lives. They will consult the statistics of those sectors and find a relatively undramatic change in percentages from 1952 to 1965.[6]

Polls today show that continuity persisting. This is not to say that there have not also been certain quite sudden documentable and dramatic changes. Attendance at mass and other religious observances, for example, fell off significantly after Vatican II, when true voluntarism hit Roman Catholicism.

Mainline Protestant and Jewish organizations have shown a continuing decline in their relative place among denominations, though it must be noted that this follows a trend as old as the one that began with the Methodist and Baptist revivals around 1800, when Episcopalians, Congregationalists, and Presbyterians began to lose primacy. The fundamentalist, pentecostal, and evangelical churches have clearly gained in visibility, morale, and strength; their code-words have become a part of American culture. Recent Gallup polls, for example, have found Americans more ready than ever to identify themselves as "born again."[7] Yet such shifts tend to occur within the borders of an "all-pervasive religiousness" and a concurrent and "persistent secularity."

It is essential to think of these issues in a context that takes account also of generations—our third point. Two or more must always coexist. If there are two generations of Americans with different religious experiences, there are as well two generations of academic theorists with quite different outlooks. A generational shift appears to separate the period from roughly the end of World War II (or the beginning of the Eisenhower Era) through the mid-sixties, from the late sixties into the 1980s. Still, the concept "generation" cannot be taken too literally in the biological sense, or too narrowly in the cultural sense. Robert Wohl in *The Generation of 1914* shows how the generational approach to self-understanding may confine and mislead if it is the only norm used for measuring cultural possibility.[8] In trying to grasp something as elusive as culture, however, the generational handle can be quite valuable. José Ortega y Gasset saw this; he defined culture as

> only the interpretation which man gives to his life, the series of more or less satisfying solutions he finds in order to meet the problems and necessities of life, as well as those which belong to the material order as the so-called spiritual ones. . . . [Culture is] the conception of the world or the universe which serves as the plan, riskily elaborated by man, for orienting himself among things, for coping with his life, and finding a direction amid the chaos of his situation.[9]

These interpretations, these "more or less satisfying solutions," tend to appear along generational lines. Ortega was almost certainly too mechanical in his idea that cultural generations occurred fifteen years apart; he was more subtle when he recognized that several generations of coevals are alive at the same time. Those who have undergone a similar set of experiences at decisive stages in their life-careers tend to develop common outlooks. This is as true of those within the culture who endow with meaning both their fortune and their suffering—the religious—as it is of those who recognize and label the cultural change they perceive. The latter belong also to the *Zeitgeist*, perhaps more than many of them realize. If their particular task is to analyze and understand their culture, they sometimes extrapolate on the basis of what they see emerging, inevitably prophesying futures that do not always unfold as they predicted. This is most obvious in the paradigm shifts that they experience or initiate. I use the term "paradigm" here to mean both the "disciplinary matrix . . . the entire constellation of beliefs, values, techniques, and so on shared by the members of a given community" *and* the "exemplars," those "concrete puzzle-solutions that, employed as models or examples, can replace explicit rules as a basis for the solution of the remaining puzzles of normal science."[10]

The Secular Paradigm Questioned

In the years following mid-century, as theorists not only found more evidence of religion than they had foreseen, but had to account for it as well, they began to waver in their support for the secular paradigm. They were committed by their academic "upbringing" to the view that, over the long haul, industrial societies like America could not do otherwise than become increasingly secular, yet plausible explanations were needed to account for the postwar revival of religion. Why, going against all trends, was so much favor shown to religious institutions in the 1950s? Theorists like Lipset believed that the revival was no more than a continuation of the all-pervasive religiousness of American life. Charles Y. Glock believed that there was more *talk* about revival than revival itself.[11] And as Michael Argyle looked at America from England, he tried to make sense of the signs of revived religiousness in America, noting their absence in Europe.[12] He cited Thomas Luckmann, who argued that, while "traditional church religion in Europe kept its religious functions and was pushed to the periphery of modern life, . . . in the USA, church religion has undergone a process of internal secularization, which has kept it 'modern' and visible." Religiosity was merely a veneer covering a deeper secularity. Argyle found a psychosocial explanation for religiosity in work done by Marcus Lee Hansen and Will Herberg in 1952 and 1955: they saw American religiousness as a secular search for identity, a "third generation return." Americans, they said, feel "alienated and unidentified unless they belong to one of the major religious divisions." Argyle also cited earlier conventional explanations that tied religiosity to immigration, ethnicity, and urbanization, and found it plausible to assume that "religion in America . . . is mostly secularized."

Scholars who looked at the problem in these terms tended to see religious people as being, in Cuddihy's terms, "underclass" or "ethnic" and marginal. Yet in the core-culture, the majority were entering the mainstream of Western industrial, technological, and hence, secular culture. Avant-garde theologians, reared in the same "disciplinary matrix" as humanists and social scientists, began to use the paradigm—and even exaggerated it—in what came to be called "secular theology," a school that emerged precisely at the end of the first of the two generations. By now it is no longer rude, it is merely boring, to keep showing how wide of the mark their theories and extrapolations were. But it *is* important to ask why these theories seemed so plausible at the time, and to see whether we can learn, from the experience of that generation, something about cultural direction.

As Western, if not world, citizens, scholars in the eye of the hurricane could discern all the European and Canadian trends that were noted by S. S. Acquaviva in *The Decline of the Sacred in Industrial Society*.[13] Their vision of America was by no means invented out of whole cloth, however selective it was. There was much that made the religious revival superficial. The 1950s were a time when Western faith in general, or religion in particular, produced few profound ethical responses. Yet, although a religious veneer often covered some very secular uses of religious institutions, the secular theologians overlooked the symbiosis of religious all-pervasiveness and persistent secularity that was continuous in America.

Acquaviva ended his book on a somber note, for he believed that religion in the Western world was in a state of almost universal decline:

> From the religious point of view, humanity has entered a long night that will become darker and darker with the passing of the generations, and of which no end can yet be seen. It is a night in which there seems to be no place for a conception of God, or for a sense of the sacred, and ancient ways of giving a significance to our own existence, of confronting life and death, are becoming increasingly untenable.[14]

The views of Argyle and Acquaviva were shared by many secular American social thinkers. In 1967, for example, Herman Kahn and Anthony J. Wiener, in a "surprise-free . . . basic long-term multifold trend analysis" offered as "a framework for speculation on the next thirty-three years" a scenario that managed to be challenged during the following three. They looked forward to "increasingly Sensate (empirical, this-worldly, secular, humanistic, pragmatic, utilitarian, contractual, epicurean or hedonistic, and the like) cultures." Kahn and Wiener were right about only the secular side of the religio-secular polarity and interplay.[15]

American theologians, however, in wanting a theology to match the increasingly agnostic and godless trend, had a more complex agenda than did social scientists. How could they square what looked like a religious boom with what, at the same time, they theorized about long-term religionlessness in the West, and then the world? American piety was undoubtedly "bad faith." The development of "religionless Christianity" or even "Christian atheism" would act, they believed, as a liberating force. To their critics, these relevance-hungry theologians, in attempting to "square the circle," to make faith and reason congruent, had sold out the faith.[16]

Despite the criticism, the secular perception and paradigm prevailed through the mid-sixties. In 1967 Larry Shiner, sorting out the uses of the term "secular," found five basic meanings. It could mean the simple decline of religion; mere conformity with the world; demystification, or desacralization of the world; disengagement from society (an ancient definition that had survived); or, as in its derivative, "secularization," the transposition of belief and patterns of behavior from the religious to the secular sphere.[17] The theologians of secularization did not see these meanings as adding up to anything like Acquaviva's dark night. Instead, they were part of the daylight of human freedom, a movement beyond spiritual adolescence to adulthood. Drawing on Friedrich Gogarten's concept that desacralization was what the Bible had in mind all along, or Dietrich Bonhoeffer's that "religionless Christianity" squared with much of the biblical design, they developed native American visions.[18] Gibson Winter called his *The New Creation as Metropolis*, just before the cities burned—not to be replaced by phoenixes and utopias.[19] Harvey Cox had the bad luck to write a best seller, *The Secular City*, that in the public mind made him captive to the secular paradigm, even though he broke away shortly after.[20]

Sociologists, however, became increasingly wary of the secular paradigm's monopoly. In England in 1965, David Martin, in an essay called "Toward Eliminating the Concept of 'Secularization' from Sociology," cautioned that most uses of the term grew out of rationalist, Marxist, existentialist, or other ideological motivations.[21] In *Unsecular Man* (1972), a far more polemical work, Andrew Greeley set out to replace the secular paradigm with the mythosymbolic view of humanity, by drawing on earlier theorists to support the durability of nonsecular models.[22] Peter Berger, at the threshold between sociology and theology, in 1969 published *Rumors of Angels: Signals of Transcendence in the Modern World*—a signal that, among some sociologists, words like "transcendent" and "sacred" pointed to experiences that were available in the culture.[23] And among the theologians, Harvey Cox went back to the drawing board and came up with *The Feast of Fools*, also published in 1969, wherein he celebrated the very magic, myth, mystery, and mysticism of religiousness that only a few years earlier had seemed to be waning.[24] Clearly, a shift was occurring in communities of religious elites. The new generation that the Bergers and Coxes spoke to and about simply spurned the realities that the secularization paradigm pointed to.

At the very least, to make uncritical use of the secular perception and paradigm after the late 1960s was to deprive oneself of a range of instruments and theories needed to do justice to a variety of religious phenomena. What Clifton F. Brown saw in the black movement of 1968 and called "religiocification" was happening in many subcultures.[25] Religion was not disappearing, it was relocating.

The Diffusion of Religion

Humanists, social scientists, and theologians, it appears, are as susceptible to fads as other mortals. In the second of these generations, they saw religiousness everywhere, for by 1970, religion was "in." Scholars who at one time could account for its signs merely by saying that religiousness was an underclass phenomenon, or that it belonged on the ethnic margins of society, could no longer do so. Too many of their own children were caught up in cults and the occult. The Beautiful People were "into" an alphabet of phenomena, from astrology to Zen. Middle-class Catholics and Episcopalians were "speaking in tongues" in pentecostal enclaves.[26] Certainly, the fervent evangelical culture could not be classified as "marginal" when successive presidents—Ford, Carter, and Reagan—openly claimed membership in it. All this occurred, paradoxically, while a moderate, but still marked, decline in support of mainline religious institutions was so clearly taking place.

The cultural turn that was evident among elites, and the durable, but newly visible, "pervasive religiousness" in the broad culture, found theorists with explanations in hand. Some employed a neo-Marxist view that saw religion as the "opiate" for the failed "revolution" of the late sixties. Freudian observations about the need for new illusions, Sartrean suggestions of bad faith as evasions of reality, or Weberian notions about how authentic and deeply held religious views could alter the social and cultural environment were used by others. None need concern us here. Instead, our focus will be the fundamental shift in paradigms; here "modernity," which could include diffused religions, replaced—or at least challenged—"secularity," which had to explain religion away. This occurred, first, when scholars redefined religion and saw it diffused in culture; and second, when they amplified the model of what it is to be human in culture. For the redefinition of religion, the notion of modernity as differentiation was rescued from Talcott Parsons's macrotheory. Cuddihy summarized well the "differentiated modernity" motif:

> Differentiation is the cutting edge of the modernization process, sundering cruelly what tradition had joined. It . . . separates church from state (the Catholic trauma), ethnicity from religion (the Jewish trauma) . . . . Differentiation slices through ancient primordial ties and identities, leaving crisis and "wholeness-hunger" in its wake.[27]

To this, Robert N. Bellah added the idea of diffusion, a motif he retrieved from oft-discredited evolutionary models. Bellah defined evolution as

> a process of increasing differentiation and complexity of organization that endows the organism, social system, or whatever the unit in question may be with greater capacity to adapt to its environment, so that it is in some sense more autonomous relative to its environment than were its less complex ancestors.[28]

Bellah tracked this definition through five stages, toward "postmodern religion," where it was "precisely the characteristic of the new situation that the great problem of religion, . . . the symbolization of man's relation to the ultimate conditions of his existence, is no longer the monopoly of any groups explicitly labeled religious." Religion, it appears, is diffused throughout the culture, difficult to grasp or observe. It has become a private affair, its fate no longer tied to organizations and institutions. Thus it had only been *apparently* paradoxical to observe that in the earlier generation religious institutions prospered while they shrouded a deeper secularization, yet in the second generation they languished while religion itself thrived.

We can summarize the change in religious definition in the phrase "from Thwackum to Geertz." Sidney E. Mead, historian and polemicist, looked back on the cultural laggards who had confined religion to institutions, and called them sectarians, temple-ists, or Thwackumites, after Henry Fielding's Parson Thwackum:

> When I mention religion I mean the Christian religion; and not only the Christian religion, but the Protestant religion; and not only the Protestant religion, but the Church of England. And when I mean honor, I mean that mode of Divine grace which is not only consistent with, but dependent upon, this religion; and is consistent with and dependent upon no other.[29]

Although Mead, like Bellah, believed that religion extended beyond churches and synagogues into civil or republican faiths, Luckmann, and others, saw it as diffused to the point where it had become "invisible" in private life. "Religious institutions," he wrote, "are not universal," but the very "social processes that lead to the formation of Self [are] fundamentally religious." Thus a new note was introduced into cultural anthropology in the West: the means that people use to transcend their mere biological nature, and all the symbolization and socialization that are part of these means, are inherently religious. In that sense, religion is universal and inescapable; it is, furthermore, incapable of disappearing.[30]

Expansive new definitions of religion began to appear. The most widely accepted one, that of Clifford Geertz, defined religion as (1) a system of symbols that act to (2) establish powerful, pervasive, and long-lasting moods and motivations in men, by (3) formulating conceptions of a general order of existence, and (4) clothing these conceptions with such an aura of factuality, that (5) the moods and motivations seem uniquely realistic.[31]

Suddenly, the problem of definition became, "Where does religion *stop?*" If everything is religious, is then nothing religious? Obviously, superhuman beings or forces, as well as belief, dogma, and institutions, have no place in Geertz's definition. It points clearly, however, to the diffusion of "pervasive religiousness" in culture, even at those times when sacred institutions are enduring a crisis of legitimacy. This Protean religion is ubiquitously available; it can be found in self-help books on airport newsstands, on television, in therapy groups, in university classes that deal with religion, or in the private search of lonely metaphysical windowshoppers and spiritual shoplifters as they put together individual world views.

In Geertzian terms, scholars whom the Vatican Secretariat for Non-Believers gathered periodically to study "the culture of unbelief" found only "cultures of *other*-belief." But true unbelief or pure-form secularization was found only rarely, least of all in America.[32]

Yet broad definitions of religion often met with protest, as, for example, when the US Supreme Court called secular humanism a matter of "ultimate concern," and thus, in Paul Tillich's version, a religion. Theologian Julian N. Hartt, fully aware of Buddhism and Taoism, sounded provincially Western when he tried to provide limits: "We ought to say that a man is not really religious unless he feels that some power is bearing down on him, unless, that is, he believes he must do something about divine powers who have done something about him." James Gustafson wanted to reserve the word "religious" for that "dimension of experience (in which not all persons consciously share) that senses a relationship to an ultimate power that sustains and stands over against humans in the world."[33] Anthropologist Melford Spiro agreed; the symbol system required the inclusion of "superhuman" forces or powers. Yet even these confinements, moving religion, as they did, far beyond Thwackum-ism, allowed for its extremely wide diffusion in American culture.[34] American religion thus seeped into the cultural cracks and barnacled itself to nonreligious phenomena.

The shift from the secular paradigm to religion as all-pervasive forced theorists, perhaps *enabled* them, to look for dimensions they had at another time ignored. Certain social scientists were able to confirm trends in their earlier work. Daniel Bell began to speak up for the values of the sacred and the transcendent.[35] Philip Rieff awaited the recovery of the sacred after the triumph of the therapeutic.[36] Scholarly definitions of "the sacred" were perhaps not what ministers, priests, and rabbis had in mind when they spoke of God. Humanistic thinkers, however, have often been in advance of theological thinkers; in this case, certainly, for avant-garde theologians who had accepted the secular paradigm now had to account for the survival of the sacred. The counterculture, the Age of Aquarius, the Jesus People, all had come and gone, leaving as their marks new evidence that humans seemed to be durably religious.

The new danger now is that the persistent secularity of American culture will be forgotten. The nation is as pluralist as ever, and in the operative aspects of its national life—in the university, the marketplace, or the legislature—America remains secular, with no single transcendent symbol to live by. Unless theorists and theologians reckon with *both* all-pervasive religiousness *and* persistent secularity, they will again be left stranded with each cultural shift, in search of theories to match their perceptions. The double paradigm will no doubt diminish the audaciousness of certain prophecies and projections: bold predictions of the purely secular city or a thoroughly sacral culture are obviously highly dramatic. But these predictions are as likely to be wrong as right, as the human record in general, and the recent American generational shift in particular, show.

At the end of the first of our generations, I argued that "*a preferable alternative seems to be the religio-secular model of indeterminacy, open to infinite transformations and toward the development of new kinds of consciousness.*" Admittedly, then as now, "the coinage 'religio-secular' to characterize the past, the present, and the tendency of American society, is not very fortunate, but we have not heard more elegant alternatives." But it is a historically accurate model, one that is evident in very many cultures—from Greco-Roman through Enlightenment to recent American—and both more true to what Wilfred Sellers has called "the manifest image of man," and richer for projecting the probable path of culture.[37]

Resurgent Antimodern Religion

Through the two generations when secularism reigned, one large subculture resisted its sway. It included Hassidic and other mystical or orthodox movements in Judaism; numbers of American-born "sects" like the Latter-Day Saints, Jehovah's Witnesses, and Adventists; pentecostal and charismatic movements in conventional Christianity; traditionalist Catholicism, to a lesser extent; and to a greater one, evangelical and fundamentalist Protestantism. That subculture is now resurgent, and in 1980, it could claim the loyalty of all three major presidential candidates, along with entertainers and entrepreneurs, athletes and beauty queens. Obviously, such a subculture can hardly be described as marginal.

Its recent gains come in substantial measure from the selective use of secular techniques and modern technology; it is characterized by certain signs of secular "worldliness" and modern "diffusion." Yet these appear to be inadequate to account for the survival and strength of this steadfastly antimodern force. If religion elsewhere in the culture is so diffuse, why is it here so organized? If most religious institutions have become "refined" and civil, why are these so belligerent and aggressive? If a good deal of religiosity dissolves into the culture, why does this variety remain lumpish, unwilling to be filtered?

Cuddihy's concept of "dedifferentiating" and "demodernizing" cultural elements points to an embracing theory. Modernity meant differentiation and diffusion; if carried too far, they could leave a "wholeness-hunger" in their wake that only antimodernity could address. But Cuddihy was no determinist: modernity was not an inevitable culminating stage of evolution. One could choose to go behind it or beyond it.

Demodernization, from Marx to Mao, is dedifferentiation. . . . Inward assent to the disciplines of differentiation, the practice of its rites, may be viewed as the *paideia* of the West. "Ideology" is the name we give to the various resistance movements mounted to stem the onslaught of the differentiation process. Essentially these movements are demodernizing, dedifferentiating, rebarbative.[38]

This "old-time" religion never really disappeared; packaged in modern forms and transmitted through sophisticated media, it came back with a vengeance during the second of the two generations. In its Catholic form, it survived in various traditionalist movements or in its selective support for certain of the more conservative policies of Pope John Paul II. Among Jews, it became a charismatic movement, attracting those who had a predilection for Hassidic or mystical forms of Judaism, as well as those whose faith encompassed biblical claims to the land of Israel. Among the elites in mainline Protestant denominations, it took form in movements of "lay concern" against liberal theology, and in opposition to liturgical revision.

The most interesting and apparently most durable of these phenomena by far was the Protestant fundamentalist resurgence. Threatened with extinction around 1925 after the Scopes trial, fundamentalists went underground. There they endured, learned modern techniques, and worked their way back to cultural visibility. Calling themselves evangelicals, the moderates among them gathered power through the benign ministry of Billy Graham in the 1950s and after. Fundamentalism was eclipsed by the secular theology, liberal civil rights and antiwar movements, the civil religion of the New Frontier, and Vatican II, but only momentarily, for it came back to new vogue—and with new force— during the late sixties.

By the early seventies the evidence was in: conservative churches clearly were growing, and overly modernized mainline ones just as obviously declining. In an apparently secular and certainly diffusive religious America, the "strong" churches were paradoxically prospering, perhaps precisely because they were antimodern—absolutist, fanatic, conformist, highly committed to the group, rigidly disciplined, and zealous to proselytize. They were, in short, uncivil.[39]

But it was not long before much of the new conservatism had become civil and moved into the cultural mainstream. In 1974 then-conservative Congressman John B. Anderson pointed out signs of the times at a meeting of the National Association of Evangelicals in Boston, signs so obvious that one needed no opinion poll to confirm them:

It was [the liberals] who denied the supernatural acts of God, conforming the gospel to the canons of modern science. . . . It was *they* who found financial support for architectural monuments to their cause. It was *they* who were the friends of those in positions of political power. *They* were the "beautiful people," and *we*—you will recall—were the "kooks." We were regarded as rural, reactionary, illiterate fundamentalists who just didn't know better.

Well, things have changed. Now *they* are the "kooks"—and we are the "beautiful people." *Our* prayer breakfasts are so popular that only those with engraved invitations are allowed to attend. *Our* evangelists have the ready ear of those in positions of highest authority. *Our* churches are growing, and theirs are withering. . . . *They* are tired, worn-out nineteenth century liberals trying to repair the pieces of an optimism shattered by world wars, race riots, population explosion, and the spectre of worldwide famine. *We* always knew that things would get worse before the Lord came again.[40]

The media, in its extensive coverage of the Protestant New Christian Right and the pressure it can bring to bear so effectively on vulnerable "public" institutions—schools, legislatures, broadcasters, and others—has been accused of focusing disproportionately on a not fully representative front. Yet by doing so, they draw attention to the groups' more militant counterparts around the world, the tribalisms that Harold Isaacs spoke of:

> We are experiencing on a massively universal scale a convulsive ingathering of people in their numberless groupings of kinds—tribal, racial, linguistic, religious, national. It is a great clustering into separatenesses that will, it is thought, improve, assure, or extend each group's power or place, or keep it safe or safer from the power, threat, or hostility of others.[41]

Wary as Americans must be of analogies to social movements elsewhere, they are yet mindful of the acute versions of tribal fundamentalisms in Hindu-Muslim subcontinental conflicts in Asia, in Tribal Africa, in Jewish-Muslim rationales behind struggles in the Middle East, or Protestant-Catholic versions in Northern Ireland. These elements in world politics, vivid and startling as they obviously are, might reasonably be expected to lead social theorists and theologians to conclude that these fundamental tribalisms are the only portent in America's cultural future. But if the polity holds, Americans are not likely to jettison their traditions of pluralism and civility, and in doing so, yield entirely to one or another of the contenders. These forces by now have perhaps brought into the fold all those in the culture for whom the fundamentalist message rings clear and true—though without, of course, having exhausted all of the uses to which well-organized minorities can be put. Furthermore, they will undoubtedly stimulate backlashing and counterorganizing coalitions. Finally, by making too much of them, we may overlook the creative apathy of much of the public, which, by ignoring them, usually outlasts them.

There are, however, good reasons for taking the extreme Right seriously. Much of its power comes from Lipset's voluntarism. Just as voluntarism once helped assure the life of strong denominations, this American response to the separation of church and state has now proved to be an effective instrument for rallying the demodernizers. Mainline religions—Catholic, Jewish, and Protestant—have become so bureaucratized, so remote from the aspirations of their adherents, that they are ineffective. But because the Right depends upon constant voluntary financial support and response to direct mail, it keeps in constant touch with its constituents, has its finger, so to speak, on their pulse.

In many ways the new traditionalisms—or newly visible old traditionalisms with new glosses—illustrate the antimodern or demodernizing impulse. First, they are frankly nostalgic, longing for that simpler, ordered, homogeneous world that once satisfied the "wholeness-hunger" of individuals, subcultures, and the larger culture, that prepluralist world in which Catholics dominated Christendom, Jews were at home in shtetl or ghetto, and Protestants ran the American empire. Second, they attract those discontented with the chaos of pluralism, the hallmark of modernity. Just as Marx and Mao accomplished dedifferentiation by ideologies that coerced the masses, these new voluntarists look to both legal instruments and persuasion to overcome the Babel of voices that cancel one another out. Third, they are intolerant of the pluralist society's moral anomie, its apparent inability to generate positive values for common action.

These themes are grounded in others. One is a hunger for authority. A century ago, in a similarly erosive situation, absolutes could be found in Roman Catholic claims of papal infallibility and Protestant appeals to biblical truth. Now, in a similar and more intense crisis, infallibility and inerrancy have again become symbols of potent absolutisms.

The newly assertive forces are not, however, merely content to exact intellectual fidelity to absolute propositions. The craving for experience is part of a larger "wholeness-hunger." In its compromise with secular, dissected religion, modern religiosity ministered to this hunger only passively. Yet modernity creates great pressure for the individual in culture who is seeking meaning for all of life, including the experiential dimensions. That is why so many of the new movements include glossolalia, or tongue-speaking, fervent devotional movements, and the like.

Finally, in what may appear to be a paradox—since it cancels out the aims of these parties to shape more than their own subculture, to have their way, that is, in much of the society around them—the Protestant Right tends to be explicitly premillennial. In their reading of history, the world will worsen in anticipation of the end of history and the Second Coming of Christ, who will restore all order and beauty. Why, then, bother to reform America if it is soon to pass away?

Here one must point to an adaptation of the older millennialisms. Present-day propagators of the vision take care not to set the date for the Second Coming. There is time for enjoyment of the world God gave, even if he will soon cause it to burn. Authors of best-sellers on impending Armageddon regularly and unabashedly flaunt Rolls-Royces, or plow their royalties into long-term real estate investments. On evangelistic television we see a frankly hedonistic side to the new Christian Right. And America, though not here to stay, has, of course, been elected by God to train evangelists to rescue individuals before the end. Humanism and pluralism will only deflect it from its mission. In this regard, the new premillennialism matches Marxist and other eschatologies, since it gives its adherents a sense that they alone know exactly where history is going.

In all these respects, the movements show that neither simple diffusion nor any single style of rationality or experience is acceptable to everyone in a pluralist culture. These forces attract people wary of what Robert Lifton calls the "Protean" personality style, favoring, rather, the "constrictive" style. The Protean satisfies "wholeness-hunger" with nibbles from many cuisines; the constrictive type favors spiritual home-cooking, in great gulps.[42]

Here are Cuddihy's people in the path of the hurricane of modernization. They do not all reside in humble dwellings; many of them are moving into higher social classes. The outsider has the perspective to make relative judgments on the many versions of religious traditionalisms, but those inside either lack such a perspective, or if they do not, perhaps set aside the problem because of other satisfactions in sharing a particular vision.

It may be that the traditionalisms may soon be bought off by the danegeld that is abundant in American life. They may, in the process of enlarging their subculture and winning some points, find themselves joining the mainline, and in doing so, bartering away their own particularity. To William McLoughlin, a historian of the revivalism from which the movements draw strength, they represent a partly permanent feature of American life, but also—and here, drawing on Anthony F. C. Wallace's "revitalization" theory—a passing stage. After a "period of individual stress" when an old cultural synthesis breaks up, there is a second "period of cultural distortion" before a new orientation takes shape. These prospering groups are part of this second stage. In that phase, a "nativist or traditionalist movement" arises, wherein older generational leaders, decrying the ecclesiastical and civil systems, call for a return to the way of the fathers, the old-time religion.

In a very risky scenario for the early 1990s, McLoughlin expects a new consensus to emerge. It will thrust into leadership a US president committed to the kind of fundamental restructuring that followed previous American awakenings—in 1776, 1830, and 1932. The new vision "will not come from Marxism or the Orient but from our own cultural past." Revitalization and reorientation are by definition syncretic; this combination will thus fuse some "softer" elements with more formal inherited Judeo-Christian and civil covenants.[43] Some political analysts contend that in 1981 the restucturing that McLoughlin prophesied is beginning, though it appears to be doing so without the softness of the flower children blended in.

McLoughlin's scenario, like so many others, presumes that there will be some sort of national consensus. Robert Heilbroner, in a script that foresees the collapse of the present American polity and ethos, agrees, but thinks it would be an imposed one. Although this looks very much like demodernization—presaging as it does the rise of a coercive state religion, a deification of the state itself, and the minimizing of pluralism—Heilbroner remains sanguine, believing that some sort of congenial socialist pattern will emerge.[44] The record of the American past, however, suggests that if this kind of mild Maoism were to appear, something called "Christian republicanism" would more likely be the nominal ideology to cover the adjustment to a new approved social contract.

We are left now with a many-layered culture. Legally, at base, and in many parts of the ethos, America is a secular, nonreligious culture; in practice, a pluralistic one. But that culture houses an impressive number of religious institutions that attract the loyalties of three out of five citizens, and the weekly participation of two out of five—and are likely to continue to do so indefinitely. Over these is a layer of particled religion, whose institutions count for less and which may take the form of private support. Some would put the whole complex in a container called "civil" or "public" religion, the consensus that presumably holds America together. Meanwhile, as we await a *new* consensus, traditionalist religion thrives. Through it all, a paradigm that seems ambivalent and equivocal, combining as it does both religious and secular elements, does justice to the viscous aspects of American cultural life.

At the very least, informed Americans are learning that their university, communication, literary, governmental, and intellectual elites overlook the dynamism of religion at their peril. In the emerging generation, during what appears to be a major cultural restructuring that goes from the nation's capital to its most remote precincts, to misperceive the role of religion, in what Ortega called the effort "to meet the problems and necessities of life, as well as those which belong to the material order as the so-called spiritual ones," will be more foolish than ever before.

REFERENCES

[1]The discussion of secularization was strongly influenced by European inquiry, where religious institutions were not prospering as in America. The literature on the subject is vast, of which Gerhard Szczesny's *The Future of Unbelief* (New York: Braziller, 1961) was typical. His kind of comment was born of cultural pessimism, while much of the American debate had a utopian aspect. In *Varieties of Unbelief* (New York: Holt, Rinehart and Winston, 1964) I attempted to assess the potency and validity of various secularizing tendencies and movements from a Christian theological viewpoint. Meanwhile, David Martin, in "Towards Eliminating the Concept of Secularization" in *Penguin Survey of the Social Sciences*, Julius Gould (ed.) (1965), pp. 169-182, was beginning to question the secularization motif.

[2]See, for example, Daniel J. Boorstin, *The Genius of American Politics* (Chicago: University of Chicago Press, 1953), chapter 5, "The Mingling of Political and Religious Thought," pp. 133-60.

[3]Seymour Martin Lipset, *The First New Nation: The United States in Historical and Comparative Perspective* (New York: Basic Books, 1963), chapter 4, "Religion and American Values," pp. 140-69.

[4]John Murray Cuddihy, *The Ordeal of Civility: Freud, Marx, Levi-Strauss, and the Jewish Struggle with Modernity* (New York: Basic Books, 1974), pp. 3-14, especially p. 9.

[5]Martin E. Marty, *The Fire We Can Light: The Role of Religion in a Suddenly Different World* (Garden City, New York: Doubleday, 1973), pp. 19-20.

[6]Martin E. Marty, Stuart E. Rosenberg, and Andrew M. Greeley, *What Do We Believe? The Stance of Religion in America* (New York: Meredith, 1968), pp. 8-9.

[7]The Gallup Opinion Index, *Religion in America 1977-78*, report no. 145 (Princeton, New Jersey: The American Institute of Public Opinion, n.d.) p. 43.

[8]Robert Wohl, *The Generation of 1914* (Cambridge: Harvard University Press, 1979).

[9]Ortega is quoted by Karl J. Weintraub, *Visions of Culture* (Chicago: University of Chicago Press, 1966), pp. 266-67.

[10]David Hollinger, "T. S. Kuhn's Theory of Science and Its Implications for History," in *Paradigms and Revolutions: Appraisals and Applications of Thomas Kuhn's Philosophy of Science*, Gary Cutting (ed.) (Notre Dame: University of Notre Dame Press, 1980), p. 219.

[11]Charles Y. Glock, "The Religious Revival in America" in Charles Y. Glock and Rodney Stark, *Religion and Society in Tension* (Chicago: Rand McNally, 1965), pp. 68, 84-85.

[12]Michael Argyle and Benjamin Beit-Hallahmi, *The Social Psychology of Religion* (Boston: Routledge and Kegan Paul, 1975), pp. 25-29. This book also has the references to publication data of Luckmann, Marcus Lee Hansen, and Will Herberg, whom the co-authors discuss.

[13]S. S. Acquaviva, *The Decline of the Sacred in Industrial Society* (New York: Harper & Row, 1979).

[14]See Acquaviva, *The Decline of the Sacred*, pp. 7, 201-02.

[15]Herman Kahn and Anthony J. Wiener, *The Year 2000: A Framework for Speculation on the Next Thirty-Three Years* (New York: Macmillan, 1967), p. 7. The authors do report that "almost all of the nineteenth- and twentieth-century philosophers of history seem to believe it likely that some new kind of 'religious' stage will follow a termination of Sensate culture" (p. 48).

[16]Thus *New Yorker* writer Ved Mehta, after touring the world of avant-garde theologians concluded: "The New Theologian set himself the old task of equating faith and theology with reason and secularism, and doing so without any sacrifice on either side—a task, in its way, no less tantalizing than squaring the circle." *The New Theologian* (New York: Harper & Row, 1966), p. 209. Most of the scorn by Christian conservatives or "transcendence-minded" thinkers was heaped on William Hamilton and Thomas J. J. Altizer for their *Radical Theology and the Death of God* (New York: Bobbs-Merrill, 1966).

[17]Larry Shiner, "The Meanings of Secularization," in James F. Childress and David B. Harned, *Secularization and the Protestant Prospect* (Philadelphia: Westminster, 1970), pp. 30-42.

[18]For a contemporary summary of these debates about Gogarten and Bonhoeffer, and about Harvey Cox and Gibson Winter, see Martin E. Marty, "Does Secular Theology Have a Future?" in *The Great Ideas Today 1967*, Otto Bird (ed.) (Chicago: Encyclopedia Britannica, 1967), pp. 38-53.

[19]Gibson Winter, *The New Creation as Metropolis* (New York: Macmillan, 1966).

[20]Harvey Cox, *The Secular City* (New York: Macmillan, 1965), which quoted (p. 2) Dutch theologian C. A. Van Peursen: secularization was the deliverance of man "first from religious and

then from metaphysical control over his reason and his language." Cox defined it as "the loosing of the world from religious and quasi-religious understandings of itself, dispelling of all closed world-views, the breaking of all supernatural myths and sacred symbols."

[21]Martin, "Toward Eliminating the Concept of Secularization," in *Penguin Survey of the Social Sciences 1965*, Julius Gould (ed.) (Baltimore: Penguin Books, 1965), pp. 169-82.

[22]Andrew M. Greeley, *Unsecular Man: The Persistence of Religion* (New York: Schocken, 1972), which is a polemic against propagators of the "secular paradigm" in the interest of various theories of sacralization, and in the light of what Greeley presents as empirical evidence against the secularizers.

[23]Peter Berger, *A Rumor of Angels: Modern Society and the Rediscovery of the Supernatural* (Garden City: Doubleday, 1969).

[24]Harvey Cox, *The Feast of Fools* (Cambridge: Harvard University Press, 1969).

[25]Brown was referring to a new trend in the black movement in America, with reference to the work of the Reverend Albert Cleage. See Clifton Brown, "Black Religion—1968" in Hart M. Nelsen, Raytha L. Yokley, and Anne K. Nelsen, *The Black Church in America* (New York: Basic Books, 1971), p. 18.

[26]The literature on the new religiosity is extensive. For samples, see *Religious Movements in Contemporary America*, Irving I. Zaretsky and Mark P. Leone, (eds.) (Princeton: Princeton University Press, 1974); *The New Religious Consciousness*, Charles Y. Glock and Robert N. Bellah (eds.) (Berkeley: University of California Press, 1976); Robert Wuthnow, *Experimentation in American Religion* (Berkeley: University of California Press, 1978); and *Understanding the New Religions*, Jacob Needleman and George Baker (eds.) (New York: Seabury, 1978).

[27]John Murray Cuddihy, *The Ordeal of Civility*, p. 10.

[28]Robert N. Bellah, *Beyond Belief: Essays on Religion in a Post-Traditional World* (New York: Harper & Row, 1970), pp. 21, 39-45.

[29]Sidney E. Mead, *The Nation with the Soul of a Church* (New York: Harper & Row, 1975), pp. 7-8, 118.

[30]Thomas Luckmann, *The Invisible Religion* (New York: Macmillan, 1967), pp. 43, 49.

[31]Clifford Geertz, "Religion as a Cultural System," in *The Religious Situation: 1968*, Donald Cutler (ed.) (Boston: Beacon Press, 1968), p. 643.

[32]*The Culture of Unbelief*, Rocco Caporale and Antonio Grumelli (eds.) (Berkeley: University of California Press, 1971), a report on a symposium at Rome in 1969.

[33]Both Hartt and Gustafson quotations are from James M. Gustafson, *The Contributions of Theology to Medical Ethics* (Milwaukee: Marquette University, 1975), pp. 97, 5. Phillip E. Hammond discusses the Court cases of the 1960s in the larger context of civil religion in *Varieties of Civil Religion* by Robert N. Bellah and Phillip E. Hammond (New York: Harper & Row, 1980), pp. 157-58.

[34]Melford Spiro, in *Anthropological Approaches to the Study of Religion*, Michael Banton (ed.).

[35]Daniel Bell, "The Meaning of the Sacred" in *The Winding Passage: Essays in Sociological Journals 1960-1980* (Cambridge, Massachusetts: Abt Books, 1981).

[36]See the appended essay in the new edition of *The Triumph of the Therapeutic: Uses of Faith after Freud*.

[37]Martin E. Marty, *The Search for a Usable Future* (New York: Harper & Row, 1969), chapter 4, "The Present's Twofold Sign," pp. 57-72, especially pp. 68, 72. See also Wilfred Sellars, "Philosophy and the Scientific Image of Man," in *Science, Perception and Reality* (Boston: Routledge and Kegan Paul, 1963), pp. 1-40.

[38]Cuddihy, *The Ordeal of Civility*, p. 10.

[39]Dean M. Kelley, *Why Conservative Churches Are Growing: A Study in the Sociology of Religion* (New York: Harper & Row, 1972); see, especially, the grid on p. 84.

[40]Quoted in James C. Hefley and Edward E. Plowman, *Washington: Christians in the Corridors of Power* (Wheaton, Illinois: Tyndale House, 1975), p. 195.

[41]Harold R. Isaacs, *Idols of the Tribe: Group Identity and Political Change* (New York: Harper & Row, 1975), p. 1.

[42]Robert Jay Lifton, *Boundaries: Psychological Man in Revolution* (New York: Vintage, 1969), pp. 43-44, 51-52.

[43]William G. McLoughlin, "Is There a Third Force in Christendom?" in *Daedalus*, Winter, 1967, p. 61. See also William G. McLoughlin, *Revivals, Awakenings, and Reform* (Chicago: University of Chicago Press, 1978), pp. 9-24, for the Wallace theories; pp. 211-216 for the projections.

[44]Robert Heilbroner, *Business Civilization in Decline* (New York: Norton, 1976), pp. 112-124.

Notes on Contributors

DICK ANTHONY, born in 1939 in Flint, Michigan, is research director of the Center for the Study of New Religions at the Graduate Theological Union in Berkeley. He is co-editor, with Thomas Robbins, of *In Gods We Trust: New Patterns of American Religious Pluralisms* (1981) and, with Thomas Robbins and Jacob Needleman, *Coercion, Conversion, and Commitment in New Religious Movements* (forthcoming). He is also co-author, with Thomas Robbins and Robert Bellah, of *Between Religion and the Human Sciences* (forthcoming). He is currently focusing on developing a style of transpersonal body-oriented psychotherapy.

ROBERT N. BELLAH, born in Oklahoma in 1927, is Ford Professor of Sociology and Comparative Studies and Chairman of the Department of Sociology at the University of California, Berkeley. His published books included *Tokugawa Religion* (1957), *Beyond Belief* (1970), *The Broken Covenant* (1975), with Charles Y. Glock *The New Religious Consciousness*, and with Philip E. Hammond *Varieties of Civil Religion*. Professor Bellah is currently directing a research project on American mores, the results of which will be reported in a forthcoming book, *Habits of the Heart*, with Richard P. Madsen, William M. Sullivan, Ann Swidler, and Steven M. Tipton.

PETER BERGER, born in 1929 in Vienna, Austria, is University Professor at Boston University. His most recent book (with Hansfried Kellner) is *Sociology Reinterpreted: An Essay on Method and Vocation* (1981).

ARTHUR A. COHEN, born in New York City in 1928, is a rare book dealer. He has written *The Natural and the Supernatural Jew: An Historical and Theological Introduction* (1962), *The Myth of the Judeo-Christian Tradition* (1970), *In the Days of Simon Stern* (1973), *The Tremendum: A Theological Interpretation of the Holocaust* (1981). His novel *An Admirable Woman* will be published in 1983.

MARY DOUGLAS was born in 1921 in Italy. She is Avalon Professor of the Humanities, a dual professorship in the departments of anthropology and the history and literature of religions, at Northwestern University. She is the author of *Purity and Danger* (1966), *Natural Symbols: Explorations in Cosmology* (1970), and *Implicit Meanings* (1976).

LOUIS DUPRÉ was born in Belgium. He is T. Lawrason Riggs Professor in the Philosophy of Religion at Yale. His books include *Kierkegaard as Theologian* (1963), *Contraception and Catholics* (1964), *The Philosophical Foundations of Marxism* (1966), *The Other Dimension* (1972), *Transcendent Selfhood* (1976), *A Dubious Heritage* (1977), and *The Deeper Life* (1981). His numerous articles have been published in a variety of religious and philosophical journals.

EDWIN S. GAUSTAD was born in 1923 in Rowley, Iowa, and is professor of history at the University of California in Riverside. Professor Gaustad has written or edited a dozen books in American religious history, the most recent being the two-volume *Documentary History of Religion in America* (1982, 1983).

PETER HEBBLETHWAITE was born in Ashton-under-Lyne, England, in 1930. He is Vatican Affairs writer for the *National Catholic Reporter*. His books include *The Runaway Church* (1975), *The Year of Three Popes* (1978), *The New Inquisition?* (1980), and *The Papal Year* (1981). Dr. Hebblethwaite now lives in Oxford and is engaged in research for a biography of Angelo Guiseppe Roncalli, Pope John XXIII.

GEORGE ARMSTRONG KELLY, born in 1932 in Pittsburgh, is Visiting Professor of the Humanities at Johns Hopkins University. He is the author of *Lost Soldiers* (1965), *Idealism, Politics and History* (1969); *Hegel's Retreat from Eleusis* (1978), and *Victims, Authority, and Terror* (forthcoming). Professor Kelly is pursuing work in politics and religion, and in French eighteenth century studies.

FRANK E. MANUEL, born in 1910 in Boston, is Alfred and Viola Hart University Professor at Brandeis University. His works include *The Eighteenth Century Confronts the Gods* (1959), *The Religion of Isaac Newton* (1974), and *Utopian Thought in the Western World* (1979). Professor Manuel is engaged in a long-term historical study of the intellectual relations of Christianity with Judaism.

GEORGE MARSDEN was born in 1929 in Harrisburg, Pennsylvania. He is professor of history at Calvin College and the author of *Fundamentalism and American Culture: The Shaping of Twentieth-Century Evangelicalism* (1980), *The Evangelical Mind and the New School of Presbyterian Experience* (1970), and co-editor with Frank Roberts of *A Christian View of History?* (1975).

DAVID MARTIN, born in 1929 in London, is professor of sociology at the London School of Economics and Political Science of the University of London. He is the author of *A General Theory of Secularisation* (1978) and *The Breaking of the Image* (1980). Professor Martin is president of the International Conference of the Sociology of Religion.

MARTIN E. MARTY, born in 1928 in West Point, Nebraska, is Fairfax M. Cone Distinguished Service Professor at the University of Chicago. Among his many works are *Righteous Empire*, for which he won a National Book Award in 1972, *A Nation of Behavers* (1976), and *The Public Church* (1980). He is associate editor of *The Christian Century*, co-editor of *Church History*, and president of the American Catholic Historical Association.

RICHARD P. MCBRIEN was born in Hartford, Connecticut, in 1936. He is Crowley-O'Brien-Walter Professor of Theology at the University of Notre Dame, and chairman of the department of theology. He is the author of *Do We Need the Church?* (1969), *Church: The Continuing Quest* (1970), *The Remaking of the Church* (1973), and *Catholicism* (1980). He is past president of the Catholic Theological Society of America, and received its John Courtney Murray Award for distinguished achievement in theology in 1976.

THOMAS ROBBINS, born in 1943 in New York City, is Visiting Scholar at the Center for the Study of New Religions at the Graduate Theological Union in Berkeley. He is co-editor, with Dick Anthony, of *In Gods We Trust: New Patterns of American Religious Pluralisms* (1981) and, with Dick Anthony and Jacob Needleman, *Coercion, Conversion, and Commitment in New Religious Movements* (forthcoming). He is also co-author, with Dick Anthony and Robert Bellah, of *Between Religion and the Human Sciences* (forthcoming).

WADE CLARK ROOF, born in 1939 in Columbia, South Carolina, is professor of sociology at the University of Massachusetts, Amherst. He is the author of *Community and Commitment: Religious Plausibility in a Liberal Church* (1978), and has written numerous articles on the sociology of religion. He is at work on a book on the "social sources of denominationalism revisited," a new look at H. Richard Niebuhr's earlier thesis. Professor Roof is the executive secretary for the Society for the Scientific Study of Religion.

WOLFGANG SCHLUCHTER was born in Ludwigsburg, West Germany, in 1938. Professor of Sociology at Heidelberg University, Schluchter has written *Max Weber's Vision of History: Ethics and Methods*, with Guenther Roth (1979), and *The Rise of Western Rationalism: Max Weber's Developmental History*. He has also edited books on Talcott Parsons and Max Weber in German.

JEFFREY STOUT, born in 1950 in Trenton, New Jersey, is assistant professor of religion and John Witherspoon Preceptor at Princeton University. He is the author of *The Flight from Authority* (1981). Professor Stout is currently writing a series of essays on the themes of ethos and tradition.

STEVEN M. TIPTON, born in 1946 in San Francisco, is assistant professor at the Candler School of Theology, Emory University. He is the author of *Getting Saved from the Sixties* (1982).